A Guide to Teaching Mathematics in the Primary Grades

ARTHUR J. BAROODY

University of Illinois, Urbana-Champaign

ALLYN AND BACON
Boston   London   Sydney   Toronto

Copyright © 1989 by Allyn and Bacon
A Division of Simon & Schuster
160 Gould Street
Needham Heights, Massachusetts 02194

Library of Congress Cataloging-in-Publication Data

Baroody, Arthur J., 1947–
    A guide to teaching mathematics in the primary grades.

    Bibliography: p.
    Includes index.
    1. Arithmetic—Study and teaching (Primary)
I. Title.
QA135.5.B2848   1989   372.7'2044   88-24138
ISBN 0-205-11792-9

Printed in the United States of America
10 9 8 7 6 5 4 3 2 1   92 91 90 89 88

For my children
Alexis Arthur, Alison Elizabeth, and Arianne Marie

Contents

Preface

Over the last several decades, psychologists have become increasingly interested in examining and explaining the learning of school subjects, such as mathematics. Cognitive psychologists have learned much about how children learn school content and why they encounter difficulty. This growing body of theory and research has direct application to classroom teaching. It can provide teachers with guidance about how to teach specific mathematical skills and concepts.

The aim of this book is to help teachers make use of these recent developments in the cognitive psychology of mathematical learning. Chapter 1 discusses, from a cognitive view, why many children have problems learning mathematics and become turned off by it. Chapter 2 delineates the general instructional implications or guidelines that stem from a cognitive approach. The rest of the book describes how children's basic mathematical skills *and concepts* develop and how teachers can foster these *specific* basic mathematical competencies.

Chapters 3 to 6 focus on *informal* mathematics: children's natural, largely counting-based, methods and concepts, which serve as the basis for coping with and understanding the *formal* (symbol-based) mathematics taught in school. Chapters 7 to 13 focus on formal mathematics. This book details how formal instruction can—by building on children's informal mathematics—be taught in an interesting, meaningful, and thought-provoking manner. In particular, the book delineates games and activities involving manipulatives and concrete experiences so important for developing proficient skill and understanding among young children. Such methods help make mathematical instruction entertaining and enjoyable as well as more effective.

The book focuses on informal and formal knowledge typically present at the nursery and primary level (pre-K to grade 3). It is useful to all those concerned with instruction and remediation of basic mathematical competencies, including preschool personnel, classroom teachers, resource-room specialists, special education teachers, curriculum supervisors, principals, school psychologists, and parents. Chapters 3 to 7 will be of particular interest to preschool caregivers, kindergarten teachers, and educators who work with children classified as mentally handicapped. First-, second-, and third-grade teachers will want to focus on Chapters 6 to 13. Material throughout the book can be used in remedial work with children of any age who are having difficulty understanding and mastering primary-level mathematics. The activities, games, and exercises in Chapters 2 and 8 through 13 vary in the mathematical ability required. A small portion of this material, particularly that which is usually introduced in the upper elementary grades (for example, improper fractions), may be suitable for gifted children only. The appendices detail a suggested sequence of skills and concepts for each level, prekindergarten to grade 3.

A workbook (*Elementary Mathematics Activities: Teachers' Guidebook* by Arthur J. Baroody and Margaret Hank, Allyn and Bacon, 1989) supplements this book in three important ways. First, it draws across the chapters of this book to delineate a sequence of lesson ideas—a core curriculum. Next, it provides (1) some of the ready-made materials needed for the games and activities and (2) copy-ready masters of the written exercises. And third, it provides additional activities and exercises not cited in this book. These materials fill in gaps in the instructional sequence and allow for smoother transitions.

This book is essentially a reference manual for practitioners. The intent is that after the text is read through once for a sense of the material, the user will come back and examine specific sections of the book carefully as the need for that material arises. Moreover, because this text provides only a sample of what can be done, the reader is encouraged to explore other rich sources of lesson ideas, such as the *Arithmetic Teacher* and the National Council of Teachers of Mathematics yearbooks. Understanding children's mathematical thinking and developing psychologically appropriate mathematics instruction takes considerable time, effort, and patience. Its rewards, though, are well worth it—children who really enjoy, understand, and think about mathematics.

ACKNOWLEDGMENTS

This book is based, in part, on research supported by Public Health Service Grant HD16757 from the National Institute of Child Health and Human Development (National Institutes of Health) and work supported by National Science Foundation Grant MDR-8470191.

I am deeply grateful to my research assistant, Margaret Hank, who carefully read and commented on earlier drafts of the book. Thanks are due to the students of my elementary mathematics methods courses (fall semester 1988 and spring semester 1987 and 1988) for their feedback, ideas, and case reports. The suggestions of Dr. Karen C. Fuson and several anonymous reviewers were most helpful. I am also indebted to Leigh Little, Donna Auble, Lana Bates, Teresa Jarvis, June Chambliss, Selena Douglass, and Teri Frerichs whose word-processing work made this book possible.

Chapter 1

The Nature of Children's Mathematical Thinking

Alexi, just five years old and about to enter kindergarten, was excited by the news of a neighbor-child's birthday party the following week. Three days before the party, the lad—as he had for the last four days—asked, "How many days before the party, Mom?" His mother repeated the now daily ritual, "Today is Friday (as she put one finger up), Saturday (two fingers), Sunday (three fingers). So there are *three* days before the party on Monday." The next day, Alexi used his knowledge of the counting sequence to figure out for himself how many days were left before the special event: "*Two* days, because we take away *one* (from three). Right, Mom?" Cognitive research (e.g., Court, 1920; Gelman and Gallistel, 1978; Ginsburg, 1982) indicates that, like Alexi, preschoolers learn and apply a surprising amount of mathematics and enter school equipped and willing to learn more (e.g., Resnick, 1983).

Once in school, this keenness for learning and using mathematics evaporates for all too many children (Hiebert and Lefevre, 1986). As Figure 1–1 illustrates, many children are utterly baffled and frustrated by school mathematics. Most see it as an array of unconnected and incomprehensible facts and procedures—strange stuff they are supposed to memorize (e.g., Baroody and Ginsburg, 1986; Wertheimer, 1945). They spend countless hours on assignments that *seem* pointless and surmise that mathematics is a boring subject. Because they conclude that mathematics is not supposed to make sense to them, children do their arithmetic assignments without thinking. Too many children, including "successful" students, *dislike* and even *fear* mathematics. Some even come to believe that mathematics is beyond their ability to grasp and give up on learning it.

1

Figure 1-1   Sally's Reaction to the Formalisms of School Math

© 1965 United Feature Syndicate, Inc.

The premise of this book is that learning mathematics can be enjoyable, meaningful, and thought-provoking. This is possible only when instruction takes into account the psychology of the child. When instruction meshes with how they really learn, children not only master the basics more effectively but become better thinkers and problem solvers. As a result, children are excited about mathematics rather than fearful of it. They can be confident about their mathematical ability rather than insecure about it.

Fortunately, over the last twenty years, cognitive psychology has made important advances in understanding how children really learn mathematics. This model, which is outlined in the next section, provides clear direction on how instruction can be matched to children's thinking and thus foster excitement, comprehension, and problem-solving ability.

A COGNITIVE MODEL OF MATHEMATICAL LEARNING

Meaningful Learning and Thinking

Everyone agrees that it is important for primary students to master basic mathematical competencies. But what does mastery of the basics mean? In a cognitive view, it is essential to distinguish between meaningful learning and rote learning. Successful students routinely master the arithmetic facts and procedures prescribed by the instruction. However, when this is done by rote, children may soon forget part or all of the information. Even if they do remember the materials, they are usually unable to apply such knowledge to learning new material, solving problems, or everyday situations. In brief, the fact that a student can produce correct answers is not necessarily indicative of understanding or critical thinking.

In a cognitive view, the essence of mathematical learning is the development of understanding and thinking strategies. It is not enough merely to memorize information. A child needs to understand and know how to apply school-taught mathematics. Thus the acquisition of facts and skills should be done in a meaningful manner. That is, a child should see how facts *relate* to each other and how skills *connect* with concepts.

Meaningful Learning Requires Active Learning

In a cognitive view, meaningful learning is not achieved simply by absorbing information. It entails more than passively hearing, seeing, and then recording information. Children, especially, often do not make exact mental copies of what they hear and see. They must actively build or construct mathematical knowledge or meaning.

Systematic Errors

A key indication of this active-learning process is children's errors. For example, during one of her frequent and spontaneous efforts to practice counting, five-year-old Alison reeled off, ". . . 27, 28, 29, *twenty-ten.*" Twenty-ten? This is not an imitated term that she has heard from her parents, "Sesame Street," books, or her older friends. It is a term she has *constructed* based on the *patterns* she has discerned in the counting sequence. Alison had not yet learned that twenties end with 29. In her mind, the term after 29 must be another twenty term. What twenty term follows 29? Well, she knew that ten follows nine. To Alison, it was entirely sensible that the term after 29 must be twenty-ten.

Alison continued to use this invented term for several weeks, until she learned the 29–30 connection. Indeed, children often persist in using an invented but incorrect term or procedure—even after they are told (perhaps repeatedly) the correct version. Children rely (and may resist abandoning) on such an invention because it makes sense to them. *Systematic errors,* then, are evidence of a child's active attempts to comprehend the world and provide a window to the child's mind.

Assimilation

Learners filter new information in terms of what they already know. The process of interpreting new information in terms of existing knowledge is called *assimilation* (e.g., Piaget, 1964). Children (and adults) cannot assimilate new information that is completely unfamiliar. Quite naturally, they quickly lose interest in the incomprehensible information and tune it out. Somewhat unfamiliar information can be related to existing knowledge and assimilated. Children are naturally interested in what Piaget called "moderately novel" information.

Assimilation and interest, then, go hand in hand. Like adults, young school children often do not make the effort to assimilate new information unless it makes some sense and hence is important to them. When a task piques their curiosity, children will spend considerable time and effort working at and reflecting upon it.

The cognitive principle of assimilation implies that understanding cannot be imposed upon children. It evolves as they actively try to make sense of the world. Meaningful learning occurs when children are actively engaged intellectually and emotionally. It occurs when they encounter moderately novel situations that excite their natural curiosity.

Informal Mathematics: A Foundation for Formal Mathematics

In a cognitive view, the meaningful learning of school mathematics is a building process that requires a foundation. The foundation for basic school-taught (formal) mathematical knowledge is children's personal (informal) mathematical knowledge. *Informal mathematics serves as the basis for assimilating (understanding and learning) school-taught mathematics* (e.g., Ginsburg, 1982).

Informal Mathematics

As the case of Alexi illustrates, children engage in mathematical learning and thinking even before they receive any formal training in school. Such informal mathematics is based largely on *counting*. For example, Alexi apparently reasoned that three take away one was two based on his knowledge that the number two comes before the number three. Informal mathematics often entails *invention* rather than mere imitation. No one showed Alexi how to solve the problem in the manner he did.[1] From their everyday experiences in which counting and numbers are an important part, children spontaneously learn and invent their own informal mathematics.

_____

[1]This interpretation is supported by the fact that Alexi did not know the sequence of days and so could not have used the method shown by his mother. The lad could count backwards from five or so, and so may have mentally counted back from the number remembered from the day before: "Three (days until the party), take away one (day that just passed) is two (days left now)." Though there was no evidence of finger counting before he addressed his mother, it is possible that he used a concrete counting procedure to obtain his answer. This would entail putting up three fingers to indicate the starting point, folding one finger down to represent the passage of a day, and counting or recognizing the fingers remaining as two. Whether he used a mental or concrete procedure, the lad was not merely imitating his mother's strategy. Instead, he used his counting knowledge in a strategic manner to figure out an arithmetic problem.

Children learn and use informal mathematics because it is *personally meaningful and interesting* to them. It was important to Alexi to know how many days there were before a special event occurred. And so, he actively applied his intelligence to figure out this real problem. Informal mathematics, then, is learned, invented, and applied in context—in everyday situations that are personally meaningful.

Informal knowledge does have its limitations. Research (e.g., Gelman, 1972) indicates that young children can deal effectively with quantitative questions regarding small numbers but not large ones. For example, Alexi did not himself figure out the days left to the party until the numbers in the problem were very small. Though calculating sums by counting objects works well when sets to be combined are small, it becomes difficult and then impossible as the size of the sets grows. Moreover, because informal mathematics does not leave a written record, a problem solution may be forgotten. Furthermore, informal knowledge may not be entirely consistent or logical. For example, a child may know that five blocks and one more are six but have no idea of how much one block and five more are!

Formal Mathematics

The formal mathematics, which is taught in school and which uses written symbols, can greatly extend children's ability to deal with quantitative issues. Indeed, the mathematical skills and concepts taught in the primary grades are not only the foundation for learning more advanced mathematics later in school but are basic "survival skills" in our technology-oriented society. This formal mathematics is powerful in various ways. It is a highly precise and logical body of knowledge. Written procedures greatly increase calculation efficiency, especially with larger quantities, and provide a long-lasting record.

Though formal mathematics can greatly extend their capabilities, cognitive theory proposes children cannot immediately comprehend abstract instruction. The meaningful learning of formal mathematics involves the assimilation of information, not merely its absorption. For primary children, this means interpreting school-taught instruction in terms of their relatively concrete informal knowledge. Mathematical symbols, computational algorithms (step-by-step procedures), and so forth can make sense to children if they are moderately novel, that is, connected to their existing, personal, counting-based knowledge of mathematics.

Indeed, cognitive research indicates that regardless of age or the specific content area, learners progress developmentally from concrete to abstract thinking (e.g., see Lunkenbein, 1985). That is, for a first grader learning to do written addition or a college student learning calculus, knowledge begins with the apparent. Both learn best when formal instruction builds concretely on what they already know. Both only *gradually* assimilate the formal symbolism and become adept at manipulating and applying it.

LEARNING DIFFICULTIES

Gaps

A gap between formal instruction and a child's existing knowledge prevents assimilation or understanding. When formal instruction does not suit children's thinking, it will seem foreign and difficult to them. Too often, the consequences are rote learning, learning difficulties, and debilitating beliefs.

Abstract Instruction

A *gap* can occur when instruction is too abstract and does not connect with children's relatively concrete informal mathematics. Indeed, gaps between children's relatively concrete informal mathematics and their relatively abstract formal instruction preclude understanding and are a key reason for learning difficulties (Allardice and Ginsburg, 1983; Ginsburg, 1982; Hiebert, 1984). Frequently, a highly verbal approach to instruction is not meaningful to children—even when accompanied by pictures and demonstrations. Too often, the written symbols and the manipulations of these symbols introduced in school make little sense to children (e.g., Davis, 1984). Like Sally in Figure 1–1, many children feel frustrated and helpless when confronted with the torrent of meaningless words and written symbols.

Lockstep Instruction

A gap can occur when formal instruction overlooks individual readiness and moves too quickly. Even among children just beginning school, there is a *wide range of individual differences.* Kindergartners and first graders are far from uniform in their informal mathematical knowledge and readiness to master formal mathematics (e.g., Baroody, 1987b; Ginsburg and Russell, 1981; Lindvall and Ibarra, 1979). With each grade, individual differences become greater. Because children do not have the same readiness to learn a mathematical concept or skill, a lesson or exercise may not be appropriate for everyone in class. Thus new instruction that is introduced to a group of students will probably not be assimilated by all. The problem is compounded when new topics are introduced before a child has had a chance to assimilate more basic lessons. Because new topics often build upon previous lessons, the child gets caught in a downward spiral of failure.

Consequences

Mechanical Learning and Use

When training is conducted in an abstract and lockstep manner, children are forced to memorize mathematics by rote. Even when they successfully memorize school mathematics, further learning and use of mathematics may be hampered. For example, children who memorize a renaming (carrying) algorithm for two-digit subtraction often do not see how it applies to three-digit subtraction. As a result, they may be error prone with the larger problems and have to memorize the step-by-step procedures for this (new) set of problems.

If children learn mathematics in a mechanical manner, they may use it without thinking or may be unable to use it at all. Arithmetic assignments can become a mindless ritual. In time, children expect to be "spoon fed," rather than challenged to think. When assignments or real-life situations require thinking, they may be caught unprepared. Moreover, because they do not really understand school mathematics, they may fail to see how it applies to everyday problem solving.

Faulty Learning

Some children fail to memorize what seems to be meaningless information correctly or at all. As a result, children learn concepts or procedures in an incomplete or altogether incorrect fashion. Some simply ignore (fail to learn) or forget (fail to retain) what they perceive as meaningless information.

Systematic errors are a symptom of children's efforts to cope with assignments that have little or no meaning to them. For example, incorrect recall of facts or faulty counting may cause some calculational errors. However, quite often calculational errors keep appearing even when children can recall or compute specific facts correctly. Systematic calculational errors are due to using incorrect or partially correct procedures (e.g., Buswell and Judd, 1925; Brown and Burton, 1978; Ginsburg, 1982).

Figure 1–2 illustrates two systematic calculation errors ("bugs"). Deborah's subtraction errors were due to a systematic but incorrect procedure: She always subtracted the smaller term from the larger, even when the smaller term was the minuend (top number). Children often use this bug when they have failed to learn a meaningful borrowing algorithm. Jerry's subtraction bug was the result of not learning a procedure completely. For $40 - 12$, for example, the lad realized that he could not subtract 2 from 0. By changing 0 to 10, he was able to complete the subtraction of the ones-place digits correctly. Unfortunately, the child did not remember that borrowing from the tens place also involves reducing.

Debilitating Beliefs

The way in which mathematics is taught affects how children view mathematics and themselves as learners (Baroody, 1987a). When mathematics is taught in an abstract and lockstep manner, children "hear" such unspoken messages as:

Figure 1-2 Systematic Errors*

A. An Incorrect Procedure

Name: Deborah   Grade: 2

22 −5 23	40 −12 32	44 −36 12	52−27=35

B. A Partially Correct Procedure

Name: Jerry   Grade: 2

22 −5	40 −12 38	44 −36	52−27=35

*The data on Deborah and Jerry were collected with the help of Dr. Barbara S. Allardice, now the mathematics coordinator of the Learning Development Center at the Rochester Institute of Technology.

- Only geniuses can understand mathematics. It's not something I am supposed to understand or can understand. This is because I'm not very smart.

- Mathematics has nothing to do with me or my world. Mathematics is just a bunch of facts and procedures that you have to memorize. What I know or think doesn't matter.

- Arithmetic answers must be given quickly. I have to count. That's because I'm stupid.

- Math problems should be solved quickly. The problem doesn't tell me what to do. There's no point in my trying. I'm not smart enough to figure it out anyway.

- Facts and procedures must be learned quickly. I can't seem to do that. I must be really slow.

Beliefs can have a powerful impact on how children go about learning and using mathematics (Baroody, Ginsburg, and Waxman, 1983; Garofalo and Lester, 1985; Reyes, 1984; Schoenfeld, 1985). For example, because they do not understand their formal instruction, and their written assignments do not make sense to them, many children conclude that mathematics is not supposed to make sense. Because of such a belief, they may not bother to monitor their work thoughtfully. This helps to account for the fact that children are not the least bit troubled by answers that are clearly unreasonable. For instance, Deborah, referred to in Figure 1–2, was quite willing to overlook the fact that subtraction cannot yield a difference that is larger than the minuend (the starting amount):

$$\begin{array}{r} 22 \\ -5 \\ \hline 23 \end{array}$$

SUMMARY

Mathematics does not have to be something that children view as dull, difficult, or dreadful. To design effective mathematics instruction, it is essential to take into account how children think and learn. A cognitive model proposes that even the instruction of facts and procedures should and can be done in a meaningful manner. Meaningful instruction requires that children assimilate formal mathematics. This requires their active involvement. It also requires that formal instruction build upon children's informal mathematical knowledge.

A gap between formal instruction and children's informal knowledge precludes understanding and forces children to memorize mathematics. This occurs when instruction is introduced abstractly or taught in a lockstep manner. The results may be the mechanical learning and application of mathematics, faulty learning (e.g., systematic errors), and debilitating beliefs.

The next chapter outlines the general educational implications of a cognitive model. It describes how mathematics instruction can be designed to suit children's thinking so that it can be interesting, meaningful, and thought-provoking.

Chapter **2**

Designing Effective Mathematics Instruction

In Chapter 1, it was noted that to be effective, primary-level mathematics instruction must be compatible with the nature of children's thinking and learning. The rest of the book is devoted to describing how instruction can be tailored to promote excitement, meaningful learning, and critical thinking. The general guidelines that stem from a cognitive conception of learning are delineated below. Chapters 3 to 13 will detail how to teach specific concepts and skills.

GENERAL GUIDELINES

1. *Mathematics education should actively involve children.*

To encourage meaningful learning and critical thinking, a child's mind must be actively engaged by instruction. Instruction that actively involves children is more interesting and more likely to promote self-confidence. Some suggestions for encouraging active involvement follow:

● *Games are a natural medium for mathematics instruction and practice.* Games can provide a meaningful and enjoyable way to learn a range of mathematical ideas and practice a wide variety of basic skills (Noddings, 1985) (see Example 2–1). They build on children's informal mathematics, provide a reason for learning skills and concepts, supply repeated practice that is not tiresome, give children and teacher an opportunity to talk over strategies and ideas, and generate excitement (e.g., Ashlock and Humphrey, 1976; Bright, Harvey, and Wheeler, 1985; Ernest, 1986).

Example 2–1   Animal Spots

Animal Spots, described below, is one of the many interesting games in the Wynroth (1986) Math Program that is designed to teach specific mathematical skills and concepts.* Because the rules of a game embody a mathematical concept or skill, children implicitly master these competencies by learning how to play the game. In this curriculum, then, *games* are the *primary learning device* for learning basic mathematics.

Objectives: (1) Oral counting to 5; (2) object counting with sets up to 5 (one-to-one counting and cardinality concepts); and (3) creating or counting out sets of one to five items (same-number concept). (Practice can be extended to larger values by substituting a 0- to 10-dot die for a 0- to 5-dot die. The game can also be used to practice addition by using two dot dice or two numeral dice.)

Grade Level: PK or K.

Participants: Two to five players.

Materials: An animal board (wooden board cut in the shape of a giraffe or leopard with 43 holes drilled for pegs) for each player; a die with 0, 1, 2, 3, 4, and 5 dots on a side; a container of pegs.

Procedure: Each player takes an animal board. On each turn, a player rolls the die, counts the number of dots, and then takes that many pegs ("spots") for his or her animal board. The first player to fill up his or her animal board is the winner.

---

*The essence of the game is described here. For a full description of the game, see Wynroth (1986). The instructions and materials for the Wynroth games and the accompanying worksheets can be obtained by writing: Wynroth Math Programs, Box 578, Ithaca, NY 14850. The telephone number for information about the program is (617) 273-8759.

Moreover, games provide an opportunity for children to learn important social skills (e.g., following instructions, taking turns, respecting others' needs and rights). In particular, children need to learn how to deal with competitiveness in constructive manners. Games can also require and promote team work and cooperation. When used judiciously, games are an invaluable tool for primary-level instruction.

● *Use meaningful activities in which mathematics is one integral part.* Mathematics is more meaningful and interesting to children when taught in context (Steffe, 1987). There are an immense number of enjoyable activities that involve mathematics as well as other school-related topics (see Example 2–2). For example, cooking entails counting, measuring, and fractions, as well as reading and following instructions. Teaching mathematics within an interesting and meaningful context can help children see the utility of mathematics, increase their interest in learning it, and decrease their tendency to approach mathematics thoughtlessly. Even if this is not always achieved, children do not have to realize that they are using and practicing mathematics to learn it.

Example 2–2   Count Disorderly's Biography: An Integrated Activity

---

Aim: This reading-and-vocabulary exercise should help students reflect on how much mathematical ideas are intertwined with everyday life and language usage.

Objective: Identify terms that imply mathematical ideas and define their mathematical content.

Grade Level: 1–3.

Participants: Small group or whole class.

Materials: Story sheet and pencil.

Procedure: Explain that Count Disorderly wants his biography (a story about his life) written. He has the Royal Writers compose it. After the biography is written, however, Count Disorderly becomes so confused by counting and numbers that he orders the Royal Writers to cross out any and all words that could have anything to do with counting and numbers. The Royal Writers who do the best job editing (crossing) out all words that involve counting and numbers will be rewarded. They will be called the Chief Royal Writers and will each be given a gold piece.

Have the children work individually or as a team. The latter is especially useful in encouraging discussion and sharing of ideas. After each individual or group has finished, discuss what parts of the biography should be crossed out. With a group of children, an overhead projector and grease pencil can be used so that everyone sees. The level of the discussion will, of course, depend upon the grade level and sophistication of the children. Some suggestions are indicated below.

Story Sheet: Count Disorderly's Life Story

Once upon a time, her highness[a] the Queen had baby twin[b] boys.[c] One[d] baby boy did not cry at all.[e] The Queen named him Count Orderly. The other[f] cried all the time.[g] The Queen named him Count Disorderly.

Count Orderly was the first[h] boy to walk and the first to talk. Count Disorderly was last[i] in most[j] things. Count Disorderly was the first to make messes.

Count Orderly was always[k] neater than Count Disorderly. When the boys were two years old,[l] the Queen gave them each[m] a box of blocks.[n] Count Orderly counted his blocks carefully, "One, two, three, four."[o] After playing, Count Orderly picked up his blocks and put them away on the lowest[p] shelf. Count Disorderly counted his blocks, "Three, four, two, one." He took one block[q] to make mud pies and left the rest[r] on the floor. The Queen fell over the blocks. She yelled, "Never, never[s] leave blocks on the floor!"

---

[a]This title refers to a person of high rank. It implies there are different classes of people and that these classes can be ordered from low or unimportant to high or important. (Numbers are ordered classes. For example, we can say that ○ ○ ○ and ○ ○ (over ○ ○) and ○ ○ (over ○) belong to the same group or class that we call "three" or label 3. The number three follows one and two and comes before four, five, and so forth when the numbers are put in order. This order implies that three is more than—in a sense higher than—two but less than four.)

[b]The term *twin* means *a pair of (two)* children born at the same time.

[c]The plural term *boys* implies more than one.

[d]*One* is the first count term.

[e]The phrase *not at all* implies an event that occurs *zero* times.

[f]*The other* refers to a remaining subset (the twin not previously mentioned).

[g]The phrase *all of the time* implies a measure—the whole measure.

[h]*First* is an ordinal number—a number referring to an order.

[i]*Last* implies an order.

[j]*Most* implies majority (more than half or 50%) or the largest portion, which implies an ordering.

[k]*Always* is a description of (relative) frequency (a measure of how often an event occurs). It implies a probability of one (1.0).

[l]Age is a measure of time—in this case *two* years.

[m]In this context, *each* implies a one-to-one correspondence; giving them each a box implies a matching process to create this correspondence.

[n]A box of blocks could be considered a set.

[o]The number words in this count are an obvious candidate for editing.

[p]The term *lowest* indicates a relative measure of height—that is, in relationship to the other shelves, the boy put the box on the bottom shelf.

[q]The phrase *took one block* implies subtraction (take away).

[r]*The rest* implies the remainder of a take-away action (subtraction operation).

[s]*Never* is a measure of time indicating a frequency of zero. Grammatically, the second *never* is not needed; it is redundant. (Sometimes parents talk this way just for emphasis—to make a point.)

● *Small-group activities are important for sharing ideas, cultivating problem-solving skills, and developing social skills.* Team-study or co-operative-learning groups can provide invaluable learning experiences (e.g., Slavin, 1983). Children have an important body of (informal) mathematical knowledge, and small-group work gives them a chance to share questions, insights, and strategies (Cobb, 1985). It creates an opportunity to see that others use informal mathematics (e.g., that other first graders rely on counting to compute sums) and that they are not peculiar. Small-group exercises can give children experience in discussing mathe-matical problems with others (Easley, 1983): defining the question or unknown, gauging what information is relevant and what is not, considering alternative solutions, and evaluating the reasonableness of answers. Thus it can help them recognize that mathematics involves thinking (Cobb, 1985).

Such experiences can also foster social or communication skills. Piaget (1965b) argued that young children are egocentric in that they do not put themselves in the place of the listener. Piaget suggested that a key mechanism for overcoming this self-centeredness is peer interaction. In effect, dealing with other children forces a child to consider others' points of view. Furthermore, peer interaction helps a child develop specific com-munication skills (e.g., rephrasing or simplifying a comment, changing position so that speaker and listener share the same orientation to ensure that directions are not reversed, or checking for signs of understanding). In brief, though sharing ideas may be difficult for children younger than eight years of age or so, peer interaction is an important vehicle for learning to communicate mathematical (and nonmathematical) ideas more effectively (see Example 2–3).

Example 2–3 Clay Numerals*

Objectives: Use cooperative-learning groups to encourage dis-cussion about (1) the importance of socially agreed upon conven-tions (number symbols) in accurately communicating (mathemati-cal) ideas and (2) the advantages of a place-value numbering system. The activity also provides practice of object-counting skills.

Grade Level: K–2.

Participants: Groups of about 4 to 6 children.

Materials: Handful of clay, colored construction paper (or other signs), and sets of 1 to 19 animal figurines or other countable objects to represent animals. (Picture of animals could be used.)

Procedure: Set out one (or two) set(s) of animals for each child in the group. Use colored construction paper (or other signs) as "landmarks" to designate the sets.

Form small groups. Distribute the clay to each child. Have the children pound, mash, twist, and roll the clay for several minutes in order to make the clay more malleable.

Then ask the children to imagine that they are living a long, long time ago. Their group is a "clan" of early hunters. They need to find a new hunting ground where the game is plentiful. Each member of the clan needs to explore—by themselves—one (or two) new hunting location(s) and report back to the group how many animals they observed. Have the children decide among themselves who will explore what location.

Before the children set out to explore their assigned location, explain, "Because we are pretending this happened long, long ago, there are no numbers spoken or written as we know them. Therefore, when you report back to your clan, you may not say or write a number. You may use your clay to show how many animals you saw—as long as you do not use the clay to make a number."

After the children explore their assigned location, they should return to their group meeting place and use their clay to indicate how many animals they saw. (Monitor these proceedings to ensure that the children do not state a number or write a numeral.) The children may use the clay to make tallies (e.g., ⬮⬮ to show two), to create their own numerals (e.g., ⬠⬡ to show four), or to make a tablet to inscribe tallies or invented numerals on.

After the children have exchanged or attempted to exchange information, encourage a discussion about any problems they had in communicating their information. Underscore the following:

- What happens when each person invents his or her own number symbols (e.g., Joe uses a + to show four, but Marta uses a #)? [Help children to see that to be an effective tool for communicating ideas, symbols must have *shared* meaning—everyone in the group must understand their meaning.]

- What are the advantages of tallies? [Tallies rather directly represent the observed sets. That is, there is a one-to-one correspondence or match between tallies and animals. Moreover, tallies have shared meaning. In other words, everyone in the group would readily recognize the number such a representation stands for.]

- What are the disadvantages of tallies? [With larger and larger sets, tallies become increasingly cumbersome to use.]

- What can be done about the problem discussed above? [Groups of, say, 5 tallies could be represented by a special tally such as . Six could be represented as .]

- Why do we use numerals (written symbols such as 5 to show five things) instead of tallies? [To represent large collections, numerals are much easier to use. To represent nineteen animals with numerals, for example, we need only two symbols (1, 9): 19 (as opposed to 19 tallies). By using 10 symbols (0, 1, 2, 3, 4, 5, 6, 7, 8, 9) we can represent an infinite number of collections in a relatively compact manner. Another advantage of numerals is that they are recognized in many places around the world. That is, they are symbols in which many different people of the world share their meaning.]

---

*Based on a lesson idea by M. Cathrene Connery of Urbana-Champaign, IL.

Primary mathematics instruction should, then, include regular opportunities for communicating mathematical ideas to peers. Such activities should provide constructive feedback and advice for improving communications. Indeed, the communication exercises can be made objects of class or group discussions to help children understand the importance of taking the perspective of the listener and learn the specific skills for ensuring accurate communication.

- *Whole-class instruction, direct-instruction methods, and drill should be used judiciously.* Whole-class instruction can be useful with some lessons. Lectures, demonstrations, written explanations, diagrams, and so forth can play a key role in meaningful instruction. (A well-tailored talk, for instance, can capture the imagination of children and stimulate them to think.) Children certainly need to practice written algorithms. Too often, though, there is too much whole-class instruction, teacher talk, or drill. And too frequently, it is not geared to the child's level or needs. To be effective, these tools—like any tool—need to be used appropriately and carefully. For instance, children should not be given so much written work that they feel overwhelmed, stop thinking about what they are doing, and rush blindly through the exercise. Whole-class instruction can be used, for example, for lessons that tap common, informal knowledge or experience.

2. *Formal instruction should build upon children's informal mathematical knowledge.*

Explanations and demonstrations should relate the formal instruction to the familiar. When instruction builds upon their existing (informal) knowledge, children are more likely to understand it. By exploiting their informal knowledge, children will not have to resort to learning formal mathematics by rote. This will minimize confusion and a sense of helplessness (see Example 2–4).

Example 2–4 The Case of Ken: An Informal Introduction to Multiplication*

A remedial mathematics teacher explained that Ken, a third-grader, had no concept of multiplication and was unable to give the multiplication facts quickly or otherwise. The boy appeared to have a learning block. Indeed, when given 6 × 2 and 3 × 3, Ken did not answer. With resignation, he explained that he could not answer and that multiplication was too difficult for him. Ken was shown how to figure out products by counting. For example, because 4 × 3 can be thought of as a group of four repeated three times, the answer can be figured out by counting four fingers three times: "1, 2, 3, 4 [one time], 5, 6, 7, 8 [two times], 9, 10, 11, 12 [three times]."

Ken exclaimed, "Oh, so that's all that multiplication is." He then had no difficulty with new problems like 5 × 3 or even larger problems like 50 × 2 and 100 × 2. (He solved the latter by using known addition facts. For instance, for 50 × 2, he realized that 50 two times was the same as 50 + 50, which he knew was 100.) When introduced to multiplication in an informal way, the operation made sense to him and he quickly assimilated it.

---

*Based on a case study originally reported in *Arithmetic Teacher* (Baroody, 1986b).

This general guideline can be implemented in the following ways:

● *Introduce new instruction in terms of counting.* Counting is a natural and sensible way for children to extend their number knowledge to arithmetic. As Example 2–4 illustrates, the arithmetic operations should be introduced and practiced in terms of counting. The fear that calculating by counting is habit forming is groundless. Children will abandon counting strategies as soon as they are ready—as soon as they learn a more efficient procedure that they understand and can trust. As we will see, a counting-based approach also can be used effectively to introduce topics as diverse as number theory, multidigit arithmetic, and place value.

● *Use word problems to introduce new instruction.*   Word problems are a very useful way of introducing arithmetic to children. Research (e.g., Riley, Greeno, and Heller, 1983) shows that even primary-level children will—if allowed to use objects—model the actions in simple addition and subtraction problems and figure out sums and differences. Using (appropriate) word problems is an important way to make mathematics instruction more concrete, real, and meaningful to children (see Example 2–5).

Example 2–5   Introducing Multiplication with Word Problems

Even before multiplication is formally introduced, many children can solve multiplication problems (Kouba, 1986), such as the one below:

> Luis, Montreyal, and Orion each had a bag of marbles. Each bag had four marbles. How many marbles did the boys have altogether?

Quite often, children solve such a problem by using objects or drawings to model or represent the problem. A sample solution is shown below:

By relating the symbolism 4 × 3 = 12 to such word problems and to children's informal solutions, the operation of multiplication can be formally introduced in a meaningful fashion.

● *Use pictorial representations as an intermediate step.*   Pictorial (semi-concrete) representations may be a useful intermediate step between using objects (concrete models) and written symbols. It gives children *additional* exposure to relatively concrete representations. Moreover, it exposes children to a *variety* of representation. Both may help children to consolidate and deepen their understanding.

The hieroglyphics, used by ancient Egyptians, provide a pictorial medium that is easy for children to understand and use. Example 2–6 illustrates an exercise for using Egyptian hieroglyphics as an intermediate step for four-digit numeral writing.[1] Later chapters will illustrate how to use Egyptian hieroglyphics for a wide variety of instructional purposes, including single-digit or multidigit arithmetic and base-ten/place-value instruction, as well as one-, two-, and three-digit numeral writing.

Example 2–6 Using Egyptian Hieroglyphics as an Intermediate Step in Numeral-Writing Instruction

---

The ancient Egyptians used characters to represent numbers*:

Λ (tally mark)	= 1
∩ (horseshoe stanchion)	= 10
℮ (coiled measuring rope 100 units long)	= 100
(lotus blossom)	= 1,000
(finger)	= 10,000

This picture-based system is an ideal intermediate step (see Frame B) between concrete representations of number (Frame A) and actually writing numerals.

A. Concrete model of 1,203 using Dienes blocks.

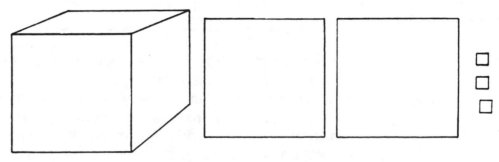

---

[1]Some authorities recommend an intermediate step that more directly models the introductory concrete representation. The gap between concrete and abstract representations can be more directly bridged by drawing pictures of the manipulatives used. For example, children can use • and | and ☐ to represent a Dienes blocks unit, long (10), and flat (100), respectively.

B. Pictorial representation of 1,203 using Egyptian hiero-glyphics.

$$\text{ЖℓℓΛΛΛ}$$

C. Numerals plus concrete representations.

$$\text{ЖℓℓΛΛΛ}$$

$$\textit{1, 203}$$

---

*Based on Bell, Fuson, and Lesh (1976) and Payne (1986).

● *Written work should follow concrete experience.*   School mathematics overwhelmingly consists of written assignments—work that is detached from any reality for the child. However, students (of all ages) usually learn best when mathematics instruction is introduced concretely, in terms that are real and intuitive. Written symbolism and procedures should be introduced *after* students have mastered concepts and skills informally. At this point, written symbolism and procedures can be learned meaningfully because children have a framework to assimilate the formal instruction (see Example 2–7).

Example 2–7   Wynroth (1986) Worksheets

In the Wynroth (1986) curriculum, written work is introduced only *after* a child has mastered a concept or skill informally (in the context of a game). In this way, the formal mathematics (written symbolism) can be introduced in a meaningful manner—assimilated in terms of a well-grounded informal knowledge. For example, Worksheet 6, regarding the equals, not-equals, greater-than, and less-than signs, is introduced after the children have mastered the concrete embodiment of these ideas by playing a variety of games, such as **Dominoes Same Number** (see Example 7.2 in Baroody, 1987a) and **Cards More Than** (discussed in Example 5–7 of this text).

Use: 0,1,2,3,4,5,6,7,8, or 9.

4 = 4	0 ≠ 1,2,...,9
4 ≠ 8	1 = 1
4 > 1	8 > 7,6,...,or 0
4 < 7	9 = 9
3 = 3	9 ≠ 8,7,...
3 ≠ [any no. to 9 but 3]	4 < 5,6,...,9
3 > 2,1, or 0	9,...,2,1 > 0
3 < [4,5,...,9]	0,...,5,6 < 7
6 > 5,4,...	5 = 5
4 < [5,6,...,9] Not 3 ≠ 3	

6

0,...,6,7 < 8	1 > 0
9,8,...,1 ≠ 0	9,8,...,2 > 1
9,8,7 > 6	Not 4 ≠ 4
0,1,or 2 < 3	2 < 3,4,...,9
4 = 4	7 = 7
3 > 2,1,0	9,8 > 7
0,1,...,3,4 < 5	0 = 0
5 = 5	0 ≠ 1,2,...,9
8 < 9	0 < 1,2,...,9
Not 8 ≠ 8	0 > No

(means "impossible")

I spoke with one special educator in a district using the Wynroth (1986) Program. The teacher noted that she did not allow her children to waste time playing the math *games* but did feel that the Wynroth worksheets were most worthwhile! Though this teacher was very dedicated and had the most noble intentions, she was a victim of the mistaken beliefs that learning mathematics basically involved written work and that it could not be fun. Once the central importance of the games was pointed out, she dusted off the games and put them to good use.

● *Point out how formal mathematics is linked to informal mathematics.* Even when a teacher does use manipulatives, children frequently fail to relate such concrete experience to formal (written) mathematics. Many do not spontaneously associate a concrete model for a mathematical concept with its written symbol. They often do not see the link between a concrete model for regrouping and written procedures that involve renaming (carrying and borrowing) (e.g., Resnick, 1982; Resnick and Omanson, 1987). A key to meaningful instruction is helping children to *connect explicitly* concrete models with written mathematics. For example, the numeral 0 is often interpreted by young children as the letter O. A teacher can quickly help most children to overcome this misinterpretation by pointing out that the formal symbol 0 (zero) is a way of representing existing informal mathematical ideas: It is the symbol that stands for no items or nothing added.

● *Help children to appreciate that formal symbols and procedures are a shorthand for existing (informal) concepts and strategies.* Like adults, children need to feel there is a reason to learn something. Holt (1964) noted that teachers should help children see that written arithmetic is just a shortcut for what they already know. For example, the informal fair-sharing model for division is intuitively appealing but cumbersome, especially as the amount to be divided gets larger. Written notation can be introduced as shorthand. Indeed, children can be led to discover the standard notation (see Example 2–8).

Example 2–8   Discovering a Shorthand Method for Informal Division*

Objective: Introducing formal representation of division in terms of an informal sharing model.

Grade Level: 3 (gifted) or 4.

Participants: A single child, small group of children, or possibly a whole class.

Materials: Division word problems presented orally, mechanically (tape recorder or computer), or graphically. Pencil and paper or other materials for recording work.

Procedure:

1. A teacher presents a word problem, such as the one below.

    Edgar has 18 stickers. If he divides up the stickers equally among his 6 race cars, how many stickers can he put on each?

2. Each student concretely represents the total (18) with stickers, blocks, pegs, etc.

3. Each student notes the number of the six groups the total will be divided into.

    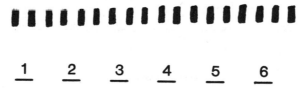

    <u>1</u>   <u>2</u>   <u>3</u>   <u>4</u>   <u>5</u>   <u>6</u>

4. The students then concretely model the dividing-up process.

    a. Process underway

    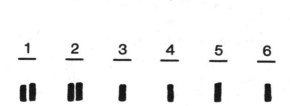

b. Completed processes

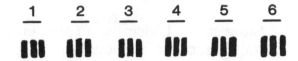

5. Encourage the children to summarize the process with symbols (numerals). Compare the various representations. Some illustrations are shown below.

6. Some children may discover for themselves that $18 \div 6 = 3$ is merely a shorthand for the more cumbersome notations advanced in Step 5.

7. Some children may recognize that using their knowledge of multiplication is a shortcut for the cumbersome concrete procedure (Steps 2 to 4). That is, they may realize that $18 \div 3 = 6$ could have been solved by recalling that $3 \times 6 = 18$.

*Based on an idea suggested by Lee S. Vanhille for teaching a multidigit multiplication algorithm.

3. Instruction should take into account children's individual learning needs.

Some suggestions for implementing this guideline are listed below:

● *Much mathematics instruction should be individualized at least to the point where children are grouped according to ability.* Conceptual instruction, particularly, can be better tailored to meet individual needs if children are grouped by similar strengths and weaknesses. Advanced children are less likely to lose interest in mathematics, and weak students are more likely to get the intensive attention needed to make progress. In playing competitive math games in which skill is a key factor, ability grouping minimizes the problems of more advanced children (1) becoming bored while they wait for their less advanced peers or (2) taking over the game and reducing their less advanced peers to the role of passive observers. Individual or small-group instruction is also important in diagnosing and correcting learning difficulties quickly—before they create further problems.

It is important to note that individualizing instruction is not incompatible with organizing a class into cooperative-learning groups consisting of children with a wide range of ability (Slavin, 1987). Indeed, a team-learning approach can help make efforts to individualize instruction practical. For example, while a teacher introduces new material to individuals of a particular developmental level, other children can use this time constructively to work on team projects or assignments. That is, team members can work on solving a problem or play a game to practice skills. A team member can help less advanced team members learn new skills or concepts, provide feedback or guidance on their assigned work, and/or serve as a referee or moderator for a game.

● *Instruction should be paced according to individual progress.* As with reading (or any other topic), different children are not equally ready to learn each aspect of formal mathematics. For example, some children readily benefit from concrete models of addition and quickly go on to mental addition. Others must use objects a long time before they are capable of more abstract addition. Indeed, the same child might be quite ready to learn one aspect of primary mathematics but be unready for another.

Meaningful learning of primary-level mathematics (of any kind) can take a long time. A teacher needs to take into account that real progress is often slow. For example, children may need a prolonged period of doing arithmetic with objects before they master mental arithmetic or understand written renaming procedures. It is unwise to push a child along into more advanced topics before he or she has had the opportunity to master more basic material (e.g., prerequisite informal skills and concepts).

Because children learn at different paces and because meaningful learning requires building carefully on more basic knowledge, a mastery-learning approach is important. In a mastery-learning approach, children do not proceed to the next, more advanced objective until they have mastered more fundamental material. In this way, the pace of instruction is determined by a child's readiness.

● *Start instruction with small numbers and introduce larger numbers as children are ready.* It is important to ensure that a child has mastered skills with small numbers before proceeding to assignments with large numbers. A major objective of primary-level mathematics should be helping children to adapt their existing strategies to meet the demands of dealing with larger and larger numbers.

● *Use a variety of instructional techniques.* Even good teaching ideas or suggestions will not work well with every child. What is engaging and educational for one child may be uninteresting and even confusing for another. Try various techniques or their modifications to find out what works best for a child. Using a variety of techniques also has the advantage of helping children to generalize their learning. By seeing different embodiments of an idea, children are more likely to develop a broader and deeper understanding of it.

4. *Instruction should cultivate the discovery of relationships, conceptual learning, and thinking skills as well as mastery of basic facts and procedures.*

Mastery of facts and procedures are a means to an end, not ends in themselves. Thus, though their mastery is important, the focus of instruction should be on meaningful learning and problem solving. Some suggestions for encouraging the discovery of relationships, conceptual learning, and thinking ability follow:

● *Instruction needs to focus on discovering patterns or regularities.* Children regularly should be given exercises in which they must search for and then define patterns or regularities (see Example 2–9). Instead of memorizing facts or skills in isolation, children should be encouraged to look for connections between seemingly different aspects of formal mathematics (e.g., the relationship between basic division and multiplication combinations as in Step 7 of Example 2–8). In Example 2–10, computational practice was designed as a means for discovering an important arithmetic relationship—the principle of commutativity (the sum of two terms is the same regardless of order). In a follow-up discussion, children can be encouraged to describe this principle in their own words and how they used (or could use) this knowledge to save effort when doing arithmetic. Such activities will help children develop a more accurate view of mathematics. It entails much more than arithmetic; its essence involves looking for, thinking about, and applying relationships. Such an approach is more likely to foster meaningful learning and mathematical thinking or problem-solving ability.

Example 2–9   In-Out Machines*

In-Out Machines are an analogy for the mathematical concept called *functions,* a very useful and widely used idea. An In-Out Machine takes what you put into it (input) and consistently produces a result (output) through some invisible internal process. In-Out Machine exercises encourage children to look for and define patterns (a process that is at the heart of mathematics). Moreover, such exercises provide practice of basic skills in a meaningful and interesting way.

By judiciously choosing the underlying function or relationship, exercises can be tailored to any grade level from kindergarten up. Note, for example, that Exercise A could be used with kindergarten children. In-Out Machine exercises also encourage realistic and constructive beliefs concerning mathematics and problem solving (e.g., some problems do not have solutions; solving problems takes time; mathematics involves a thoughtful analysis)—as opposed to the unrealistic and destructive beliefs that a drill approach too often encourages (e.g., all problems have solutions; problems should be answered quickly; mathematics is not supposed to make sense). Below are some examples of In-Out Machine exercises. Answers to selected questions appear on page 47.

- Exercise A can be used with kindergartners or first graders to introduce the idea of In-Out Machines and to practice the skill: When we count, what comes after this number?

- Exercise B can be used with first graders and up to introduce In-Out Machines as an analogy for functions and to practice simple addition.

- The aim of Exercise C is to help third-grade children learn the defining characteristics of an In-Out Machine (a function). Specifically, it addresses the question: What is a key characteristic of functions? Example C is included to clarify a common source of confusion concerning In-Out Machines: Can *different inputs* have the same output?

- Exercise D, which would be suitable for first to third graders, introduces inputs that consist of pairs. (Exercises that involve pairs of inputs and addition, subtraction, multiplication, or division can be used to help children discover important arithmetic relationships or principles. Such exercises will be illustrated later in Chapters 8 and 9.) Note that this exercise, like Exercise C, highlights the point that different inputs can have the same result.

- Exercise E illustrates a case in which a mathematical problem may have more than one solution. Such exercises are essential to counter the misconception that mathematical problems must be solved in one way and have one answer. This particular exercise would be suitable for third graders.

- Exercise F involves finding the missing inputs or outputs for various In-Out Machines. The exercise illustrates that under some circumstances, there may be the possibility of *no answer* or multiple answers. Because most of the questions involve multiplication, this particular exercise would be suitable for third graders. Exercises could be made up to illustrate the same points for younger children.

Exercise A

An In-Out Machine takes what you put into it (input) and consistently produces a result (output) through some invisible internal process.

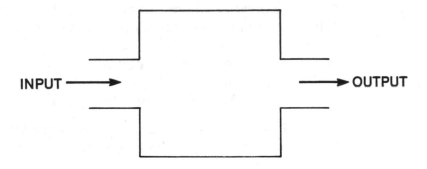

INPUT ⟶   ⟶ OUTPUT

Example: When 7 is put in the machine above, 8 comes out the other end. When 4 is put in, 5 comes out. When 2 is put in, 3 comes out. When 13 is put in, 14 comes out.

Summarize the information above in the table below. By listing each output next to its input, it may be easier to figure out what the In-Out Machine is doing—what the invisible internal process is.

Input	Output

Question 1:   What do you think will come out if 1 is put in?

Question 2:   What do you think will come out if 6 is put in?

Question 3:   What do you think will come out if 14 is put in?

Exercise B

An In-Out Machine takes what you put into it (input) and consistently produces a result (output) through some invisible internal process.

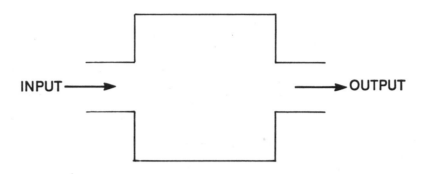

Example: When 7 is put in the machine above, 9 comes out the other end. When 4 is put in, 6 comes out. When 0 is put in, 2 comes out. When 13 is put in, 15 comes out.

Summarize the information above in the table below. By listing each output next to its input, it may be easier to figure out what the In-Out Machine is doing—what the invisible internal process is.

Input	*Output*

Question 1: Is there any pattern that you notice?

Question 2: What do you predict the output would be if the input were 3? 24?

Exercise C

Question 1: For each of the tables below, can you tell what the missing outputs would be? If so, fill in the missing output. If not, put a question mark (?) in the space.

A			B			C	
Input	Output		Input	Output		Input	Output
4	8		2	4		3	0
2	4		2	1		2	0
1	2		2	5		5	0
3	6		2	7		4	0
5	10		2			9	
4	8					7	
2						3	
						2	

Question 2: The data in Table B does not come from a real In-Out Machine—at least not one that is working properly. What makes an In-Out Machine different from something that is not an In-Out Machine? In other words, how does the data in Table B differ from the data in Table A or Table C?

Exercise D

In the In-Out Machine below, two inputs are fed into the machine at a time, the machine works on the inputs and a single output comes out.

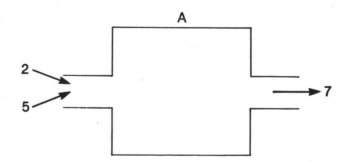

Table A below summarizes the input and output for this machine:

A

Input	Output
(2,5)	7
(6,3)	9
(1,1)	2
(4,4)	8
(5,1)	6

Question 1: What do you suppose the output would be if 3 and 2 were entered into Machine A?

Table B below shows the Inputs and outputs of Machine B.

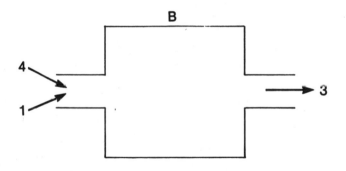

B

Input	Output
(4,1)	3
(3,1)	2
(6,2)	4
(3,2)	1

Question 2: What do you suppose the output would be if the numbers 5 and 5 (5,5) were entered?

Question 3: What do you suppose the output would be if the following pairs of numbers were put into Machine B?

(5,2)
(6,3)
(4,2)
(6,4)
(5,3)
(4,3)
(2,1)
(5,4)

Question 4: Can different inputs produce the same output?

Question 5: With Machine B, are there any inputs that will give the same output as (4,1)? That is, are there other pairs of numbers that will produce an output of 3? Below, try some number pairs to see.

Exercise E

Consider the inputs and outputs for In-Out Machine A.

A

Input	Output
cat	3
garbage	7
by	2

Question 1: Is there a rule or pattern that you can see?

Question 2: Are any other patterns or rules possible?

Consider the inputs and outputs for In-Out Machine B.

B

Input	Output
3	0
8	0
5	0
1	0

Question 3: Is there a rule or pattern that you can see?

Question 4: Are any other patterns or rules possible?

Question 5: Can problems sometimes be solved in more than one way?

Exercise F

Find the missing inputs and outputs for each of the following functions. Use only whole numbers that are more than 0. Be sure to give all possible answers. Write NP when it is not possible to give an answer.

1.

Input	Output
4	0
9	5
11	7
12	
19	15
	10
	8
0	
2	

2.

Input	Output
3	12
5	20
7	28
1	
10	
	16
	18
	7
	0

3.

Input	Output
3	7
2	5
5	11
10	21
20	41
6	
4	
0	
	15
	10
	27
	8
1	

4.

Input	Output
6,3	18
10,2	20
3,7	21
13,1	13
4,5	
7,1	
0,3	
	8
	26
	45
	29
	16
	12

*Based on Fendel (1987).

Example 2–10 Structuring Computational Practice to Foster the Discovery of an Arithmetic Relationship

Name: _____   Date: _____

Solve the following addition problems using any method you wish.

7	1	1	5	8	1
+1	+7	+5	+1	+1	+8

7	3	4	5	8	5
+3	+7	+5	+4	+5	+8

● *Help children find connections among aspects of formal mathematics.* A key to meaningful learning is finding connections to otherwise isolated and possibly meaningless information. Training needs to help children integrate the formal bits of information they learn.

For example, children are often taught the associative law of addition—

that multiple terms can be combined in different orders and still produce the same result. This principle is often illustrated in the following manner: $(4 + 3) + 2 = 4 + (3 + 2)$. Algebraically it can be illustrated as: $(a + b) + c = a + (b + c)$. Unfortunately, such examples may not help children appreciate the *importance* of this powerful principle. As a result, some children may learn the principle and its examples by rote; others may fail to do even this. The principle's importance and meaning can be made clearer if a teacher connects it to other aspects of formal mathematics in which the child is engaged. In particular, children should be encouraged to apply their knowledge of arithmetic principles to the task of calculation—for shortcutting their computational efforts (see Example 2–11). In a follow-up discussion, children can be encouraged to note what principle they used and how it was applied.

Example 2–11 Applying Arithmetic Principles to the Task of Calculation

Objective: Using the associative principle of addition to make calculating with more than two addends more manageable.

Grade Level: 1 or 2.

Participants: Can be done with a single child, small group of children, or a whole class.

Materials: Worksheet like that shown.

Procedure: Students can work on the written exercise individually or in small groups. In either case, follow up with a group discussion about the shortcuts you found. Note that the problems illustrated in the exercise can be worked out in several ways. A correct but relatively inefficient solution is to follow the standard left-to-right algorithm. For $9 + 5 + 5 = ?$, this would mean coming up with the sum of the relatively difficult combination $9 + 5$ and then adding another 5 to that. Some students will spontaneously use a more elegant solution: combining $5 + 5$ first ($5 + 5 = 10$ is relatively well known and an automatic combination) and then adding 9 to 10 (again a relatively easy combination). By "associating" the terms in a different manner the child reduces his or her computational effort. By using the "associative principle," a child can likewise transform Problems 3, 4, 6, 7, and 8 into relatively easy $10 + N$ combinations (e.g., in Problem 8, $9 + 6 + 1 = [9 + 1] + 6 = 10 + 6 = 16$). In Problems 2, 5, and 9, by starting with the larger term first, the computation can effectively be reduced to counting. For example, $1 + 1 + 1 + 1 + 8 + 1 + 1 + 1 + 1 = ?$ can be solved by beginning with 8 and then counting on from there as each one is noted: 8, 9, 10, 11, 12, 13, 14, 15, 16. Problem 9 has other solutions that are more elegant than the left-to-right algorithm. A child might see that $1 + 1 + 8$ is 10, plus the six remaining ones, sums to 16.

Name: _____   Date: _____

Figure out the sums of each of the following any way you wish. Are there any ways to shortcut your work?

    1. $9 + 5 + 5 = ?$

    2. $1 + 1 + 17 = ?$

    3. $7 + 8 + 2 = ?$

    4. $8 + 9 + 1 = ?$

    5. $1 + 1 + 1 + 1 + 1 + 1 + 1 + 19 = ?$

    6. $7 + 5 + 5 = ?$

    7. $8 + 5 + 2 = ?$

    8. $9 + 6 + 1 = ?$

    9. $1 + 1 + 1 + 1 + 8 + 1 + 1 + 1 + 1 = ?$

  10. $2 + 4 + 4 = ?$

● *Use negative instances or contrasting examples to help children master concepts.*   One example or one type of example is not enough to form well-defined concepts. To minimize overgeneralization and promote discrimination (correct definition and application), it is helpful to introduce negative instances or counterexamples of a concept (see Example 2–12). Indeed, children need to learn that negative instances are useful and informative. Moreover, they need to learn that their wrong answers can often act as a negative instance and can provide useful information and direction.

Example 2–12   What Does ½ Mean?

Objective: Use examples and nonexamples to explicitly define *one half* as one of two equal-sized parts.

Grade Level: 2 or 3.

Participants: Single child, small group of children, or whole class. Students can work on the activity as individuals or in small groups. The latter is recommended.

Materials: Each child or team should have an activity sheet (shown below) and something on which to record answers. Also, items such as pies or marbles to demonstrate the various examples and nonexamples of *one half* (optional).

Procedure: Explain to the students that they must figure out what a new symbol means. Pass out the activity sheet and read the following instructions: "Below are a series of clues to help you solve the mystery: What does this [write ½ on the board] mean? I'll show you some examples of what it is and some examples of what it is not. Let's see if you can figure out what this symbol means."

For each question, give the children an opportunity to think and record their responses before providing the answer indicated below. There are several advantages of having pupils work in small groups. One is that children may benefit from an exchange of ideas and more critically think about their answers. A second is that an incorrect response arrived at by group consensus is easier to accept than one derived on one's own. It may prove useful to discuss issues or questions raised by an item before proceeding to the next item. Some issues or questions raised by items are noted below.

Note that the nonexamples in 1b, 1d, 4, 7, 8, and 9 provide a contrast to the examples of ½ that highlight a key characteristic of the concept of one half: The two parts must have the same size. Unless the whole can be divided into *equal* parts, we cannot have ½ (or any other fraction).

Examples 3, 5, and 6 illustrate that more than one thing can comprise a half (as long as the other half has an equal number of things). Example 11 illustrates this idea at a more abstract level. The wrapped (light) portion of the candy bar could be divided into two equal pieces, which would have the same size as each dark piece. (A teacher may wish to postpone using Question 11.)

Key

2. Yes	7. No
3. Yes	8. No
4. No	9. No
5. Yes	10. Yes
6. Yes	11. Yes

What Does ½ Mean?

Name: _____   Date: _____

_____

1. a. The shaded area is ½ of the pie.

   b. The shaded area is *not* ½ of the cake.

   c. ½ of the marbles are dark.

   d. The dark marbles are not ½ of the marbles.

_____

2. Is the chocolate portion of the cake ½ of the cake?

_____

3. Is the chocolate portion of this cake ½ of the cake?

_____

4. Is the chocolate portion of the cake ½ of the cake?

_____

5. Are ½ of these coins dark?

_____

6. Are ½ of these coins dark?

_____

7. Are ½ of these coins dark?

_____

8. Is the unwrapped (dark) portion of the candy bar ½ of the candy bar?

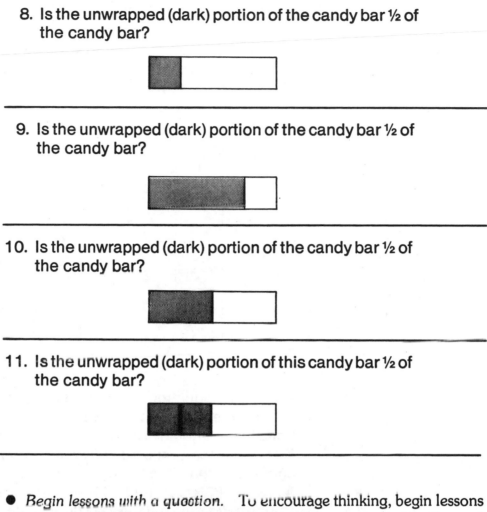

9. Is the unwrapped (dark) portion of the candy bar ½ of the candy bar?

10. Is the unwrapped (dark) portion of the candy bar ½ of the candy bar?

11. Is the unwrapped (dark) portion of this candy bar ½ of the candy bar?

● *Begin lessons with a question.* To encourage thinking, begin lessons with a question (Davis, 1984). This technique presents students with a real problem to consider and solve. It also makes mathematics challenging and interesting. For example, after third graders have learned to determine the area of a rectangle by counting the number of "squares" it contains (see Frame A of Figure 2–1), challenge them to find an easier way to figure out the area of a rectangle (see Frame B). Some children may suggest an informal strategy: skip counting (see Frame C) or adding on (e.g., $5 + 5 = 10$, $10 + 5 = 15$, and $15 + 5 = 20$). Provide additional problems and challenge them to continue their search. Some children may recognize the applicability of multiplication (Frame D). That is, they notice the general rule that the area of a rectangle can be determined by multiplying the length of a horizontal side and the length of an adjacent or vertical side (height). This method for learning $A = l \times h$ is more meaningful and interesting than directly teaching the formula.

Figure 2–1   Beginning a Lesson on Area by Posing a Question

A. Previous lesson: Counting square units to determine the area of a rectangle. The method is illustrated with a rectangle 5 units by 4 units:

1	2	3	4	5
6	7	8	9	10
11	12	13	14	15
16	17	18	19	20

B. Lesson introduction: "Yesterday we learned how to figure out the area of a rectangle by counting up all the square units that we could fit inside it." [Review the procedure units 5 × 4 unit rectangle as shown in Step A.] "On your worksheet (the chalkboard), you will find five rectangles (5 × 6, 5 × 9, 2 × 8, 10 × 6, and 10 × 9). *Is there a way we can make the job of figuring out the area of all of the rectangles easier?*"

C. Informal shortcut: Skip counting.

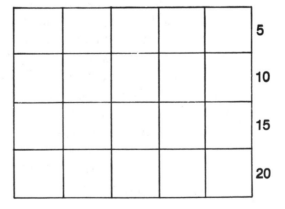

D. Using multiplication as a shortcut: "Five times four is 20."

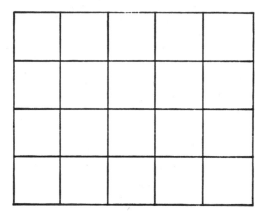

● *Routinely question children about their work.* Regularly ask children how they arrived at their answers and whether or not their answers are justified. For example, have them explain their reasoning by using objects to illustrate their solution method and answer (Peck, Jencks, and Connell, in press). A steady exchange encourages children to approach mathematics thoughtfully, to check the reasonableness of their answers, and to depend on themselves to evaluate their work (Lampert, 1986). It puts the emphasis on thinking and understanding rather than on producing answers (Peck, Jencks, and Connell, in press).

Challenge children to think by asking what-if questions about their work. For example, to help children discover an important property about addition, a teacher can ask: "When you started with five blocks and added three, you found out you had eight altogether. *What if* you started with three blocks and added five? Would you have the same number or a different number in the end?" What-if questions are especially useful in prompting children to justify their method and answer and to gauge whether they really understand what they are doing.

5. *Create an atmosphere where children are interested in learning mathematics rather than disinterested in or even afraid of it.*

A teacher sets the tone. If a teacher exhibits interest in teaching a topic, then there is a better chance that pupils will be drawn to learning it. If a teacher approaches mathematics instruction unenthusiastically, many children will approach learning it mechanically. Several suggestions for setting a positive tone are delineated below.

● *Discuss mathematics with children.* In addition to making connections explicit and encouraging thoughtful evaluation concerning the reasonableness of methods and answers, discussing mathematical problems sends a clear signal that this is a topic worth talking about, not something that is boring. In encouraging the discussion of problems, children are also more likely to pose questions and make a real attempt to understand mathematics. Discussing mathematics, then, fosters the belief that mathematics involves more than memorizing facts and procedures; it involves thinking.

Any number of occasions may present an opportunity to discuss mathematics (e.g., a child's question or error, a conflict of answers or opinion, something puzzling to a teacher). Indeed, mathematics touches our personal lives in many ways that are worth discussing (see Example 2–13).

Example 2–13   Discussing the Fairness of the Math Game: Necklace Chase*

Objectives: The game provides an opportunity for children to practice and reflect on what numbers can be used to make sums to 10. In playing the game, it should become clear that the rules give some children an unfair advantage. For sums to 10, some numbers can be used in more combinations than can others (e.g., 2 can be combined with 0 to 8 to make nine sums between 1 and 10, whereas 9 can be combined with only 0 and 1 to make two sums).

Grade Level: 2.

Participants: A portion of a class or the whole class.

Materials: Enough pin-on or tape-on number cards with a numeral 1 through 9 for each child, number deck (each a sum of single-digit addends ranging from 1 to 10 written on a 3″ × 5″ card), and numerous necklaces (ringlets made of construction paper and looped together) for prizes. (Other prizes can be substituted, such as play money.)

Procedure: One child is appointed "the guard"; all other children are players. The players blindly choose a pin-on number card. The guard is positioned midway between the players who line up on one side of the room and the prize is put at the other end. The guard draws a card from the number deck and announces the number.

The players whose pin-on card could be used in an addition combination that sums to the drawn number can make a run for the prize. For instance, if 6 is the sum (the number drawn), children with pin-on cards 1 to 6 could run. The players try to elude the guard and capture the prize. After a player has captured the prize or all the players making a run are captured, another prize is put out and the guard calls out another number. (The guard can capture a player by touching him or her with both hands simultaneously.) The game can continue until all the prizes are exhausted or the issue of fairness is brought up.

If no one raises the issue of fairness directly or indirectly (e.g., complaining to a friend or mumbling to themselves), then prompt with, "Was that a good game?" This invitation to evaluate the game may cause some children to address the fairness issue. If this does not work, ask bluntly, "Was the game fair to everyone?"

The discussion should bring out that children who drew 1 had an unfair advantage—they could make a run for the prize on virtually every turn. Those with 2 had an edge because they could go every time except for when 1 was called. Children with numbers 7, 8, and 9 should feel cheated because of the relatively few opportunities they had to contend for the prize. Some children may be interested in making a bar or line graph that summarizes the relative frequency in which the numbers 1 through 9 appear as addends for the sums 1 to 10. A genuine problem that can be the basis for further discussion is how to change the rules to make the game fair. One solution would be to change the format of the cards in the number deck. By using an expression in the form of $8 + ? = 10$, only specific players (those with a pin card of 2) could run on any given turn. By drawing up a deck in which 1 to 9 appeared as a missing addend an equal number of times, all players would have an equal chance. Incidentally, such a change would more effectively provide practice in finding a missing addend. (A player is forced to think of a specific combination that sums to a number.) Such a game would set the stage for learning subtraction facts.

The discussion can also focus on other nonmathematical issues. For example, the game can also be the basis for a social studies lesson. Sometimes rules are not fair and need to be changed to give everyone an equal chance. Sometimes laws are not fair to everyone (e.g., segregation laws that discriminate against blacks, or laws with a sex-bias that discriminate against women and, in some cases, men), and they need to be changed.

---

*Based on Factor First, described in Ashlock and Humphrey (1976).

● *Foster constructive beliefs about mathematics, mathematical thinking, and mathematical learning.*   Children need to see that mathematics is much more than just a body of arithmetic facts and written procedures. It also involves discovering and defining patterns or regularities, thinking through problems, and justifying intuitive answers logically. Children need to understand that mathematical thinking involves more than efficiently using a memorized procedure or quickly recalling *the* answer. It *can* involve thoughtfully defining the problem, carefully deliberating among possible solution procedures, and slowly working out a number of answers. Children need to appreciate that genuine understanding may not come quickly, that we all tend to use informal (concrete) methods when first learning a mathematical topic, and that we can learn from our mistakes.

Teachers can foster constructive beliefs directly by pointing out, for instance, that some problems can have more than one answer or that we can learn from mistakes. However, how mathematics is taught probably has a larger impact on children's beliefs. For instance, to develop a perspective about mathematics, children need to see exercises on a regular basis in which there is more than one possible answer. As Example 2–7 illustrates, Wynroth Program worksheets routinely include several problems in which a number of answers are acceptable. (Example 2–7 also shows that such exercises regularly include problems for which no answer is possible. This is done to counter the mistaken notion among children that mathematics always yields an answer.) Example 2–14 illustrates a problem-solving activity in which there is more than one way to solve the problem.

Example 2–14   A Problem-Solving Activity with Many Solution Methods: Number Target*

Objectives: This problem-solving activity illustrates that there can be numerous ways to solve a mathematical task. Sometimes, though, not all solution methods are equally efficient, and sometimes, a solution is not even possible. The exercise also provides a device for exploring the behavior of arithmetic combinations. (Subtraction by 10 is used in this particular case.)

Grade Level: 3.

Participants: A child or class can work on the exercise individually or small "think groups" can solve it in teams.

Materials: The problem can be verbally presented, but it might be helpful to present it in written form on the board or on an exercise sheet. Calculator optional.

Procedure: Explain that in Number Target, you start with a number and choose between arithmetic operations in order to get to a target number. In the exercise shown, the starting value is 48. The child's goal is to obtain 10 by adding 2 or subtracting 10. Illustrated is *one* solution: repeatedly choosing to subtract 10 until the total is reduced to 8 and then choosing to add 2.

Have the participants record each step in their solution method. Afterward, discuss the solution procedures used. Highlight that different solution methods were used. If necessary, ask, "Is there more than one way to get to the target?" Help the participants address the issue of efficiency. If necessary, ask, "Do all the solution methods require the same number of steps?" The most efficient solution for this particular exercise is five steps (see the filled-in worksheet below).

Either before or after the discussion of the exercise, you may wish to have participants explore other solution methods. You might prompt, "Are there other ways to get to the target number 10 from 48 by adding 2 or subtracting 10? Here are additional worksheets if you need them." (Another solution starts out in a counterintuitive manner by incrementing 48 by 2: $48 + 2 = 50$; $50 - 10 = 40$; $40 - 10 = 30$; $30 - 10 = 20$; $20 - 10 = 10$. Note that the solution is as efficient as that illustrated.) Actually working out various solutions for themselves might more deeply impress upon participants the fact that there is more than one solution.

Other exercises can help illustrate the point that not all solutions are equally efficient. For example, in starting with 28 subtracting 10 or 2, and a target of 4, efficient strategies would entail taking away 10 and 2 twice each ($28 - 10 = 18$; $18 - 10 = 8$; $8 - 2 = 6$; $6 - 2 = 4$ or $28 - 2 = 26$; $26 - 2 = 24$; $24 - 10 = 14$; $14 - 10 = 4$; and so forth). A relatively inefficient strategy would involve the repeated subtraction of 2, which would require 12 steps.

Other exercises can illustrate that solutions are not always possible. For example, with a starting number of 23, choices of -10 or $\times 2$, and any odd except 13 (e.g., 11), there is no solution. (As soon as the times two option is used, an even number is produced and there is no way to get another odd outcome.) Give the participants an opportunity to work on the exercise for a while and discover for themselves that a solution is not possible. A teacher will have to use his or her own judgment as to when to intervene if students do not discover this for themselves.

Worksheet: Target Number Exercise

Start: 48
Choices: + 2 or − 10
Target Number: 10

Step

1	48 − 10 = 38
2	38 − 10 = 28
3	28 − 10 = 18
4	18 − 10 = 8
5	8 + 2 = 10
6	
7	
8	
9	
10	
11	
12	
13	
14	
15	
16	
17	
18	
19	

*Based on a method originated by John E. Bernard (e.g., 1982).

SUMMARY

Mathematics instruction can be interesting, meaningful, and thought-provoking if properly designed to take into account how children learn and think. Instruction needs to involve children actively through games, meaningful activities, small-group discussion, and carefully tailored explanations and demonstrations. Instruction should be introduced concretely in terms of counting and meaningfully in terms of word problems. Work involving written symbolism should be introduced after and explicitly linked to this informal mathematics. Indeed, written notation can often be introduced as a shorthand for the mathematics already familiar to children. Instruction can be better tailored to meet individual needs by grouping according to ability, ensuring that a child has mastered previous content before continuing on, introducing work with smaller numbers, and using a variety of teaching methods. One focus of instruction should be relational learning such as discovering patterns or connections. Conceptual learning can also be aided by using negative instances, and thinking can be fostered by beginning lessons with a question. Finally, it is essential to create an atmosphere of inquiry and enthusiasm by discussing mathematics with children and by fostering constructive beliefs.

There is no one way to implement these general guidelines. The chapters that follow do provide numerous examples of how these cognitive principles can be applied to teach specific concepts and skills. Tables in Chapters 3 through 12 and the Appendices delineate a recommended instructional sequence for these competencies. The workbook (Baroody and Hank, 1988) that accompanies this text details a sequence of games, activities, and exercises for each of the content areas covered. However, even the specific examples and instructional sequences are intended as a guide rather than a definitive prescription. Most teachers will find that they will have to adapt the activities and the sequences to meet particular needs of their students and situations.

Answers for selected questions from Example 2–9:
Exercise C. *Question 1:* The missing output for A is 4; for B, ? (not determinable). The missing outputs for C are all 0. *Question 2:* The same input does not always give the same output.
Exercise E. *Question 1:* The output equals the number of letters in the word. *Question 2:* Yes. Cat begins with the third letter of the alphabet; garbage, the seventh; and by, the second. *Questions 3 & 4:* One rule is any input times zero is zero. A second rule is any input minus itself is zero.
Exercise F. *Question 1:* The missing inputs are 14 and 12; the missing outputs are 8, NP, and NP. *Question 3:* The missing inputs are 7, NP, 13, and NP. The missing outputs are 13, 9, 1, 8, and 3. (Double the number and add 1.) *Question 4:* The missing inputs are (1,8) or (2,4); (1,26) or (2,13); (1,45) or (5, 9); (1,29); (1,16), (2,8), or (4,4); and (1,12), (2,6), or (3,4). The missing outputs are 20, 7, and NP.

Chapter 3

Oral Counting

Counting is the basis of much of young children's mathematics. Counting can refer to either oral counting or object counting. The latter will be discussed in the next chapter. Children first learn to count orally by ones ("1, 2, 3 . . .") and then extend this skill to the task of object counting. Initially, oral counting may be little more than a meaningless chant (e.g., Ginsburg, 1982). Children only gradually see that oral counting can be used to count, number, and compare the magnitude of sets.

The count-by-ones sequence is the most basic of the *forward counts*: counts that go in order from small to large numbers. At first, a child may not realize that numbers follow a particular order. With development, though, children sense that counting involves generating numbers in a given order, and they set about mastering more and more of the standard *sequence of terms*. As they become familiar with the number sequence, children can acquire more sophisticated counting skills. For instance, they learn to recognize which numbers are neighbors (e.g., that the number next to 7 are 6 and 8). That is, without going through the whole sequence they can cite the *next term* before or after a particular number. At some point, the forward counts then serve as the basis for learning reverse or *backward counts*: counts that go in order from large to small.

LEARNING

Forward Counts

Sequence of Terms

The development of oral-counting ability begins very early (Baroody and Price, 1983; Fuson and Hall, 1983; Gelman and Gallistel, 1978). As early as eighteen months of age, children begin to learn to count by ones ("one, two, three . . ."). Through rote memorization, children learn to *count by ones 1 to 10* before they begin kindergarten. Indeed, by the time they enter kindergarten, most have learned to *count by ones 11 to 19* as well (e.g., Fuson, Richards, and Briars, 1982).

It is important to note that learning the number sequence beyond 13, or so, does not have to entail rote memorization. Children typically extend their oral-count sequence by discovering patterns or learning rules. For example, all but one of the teen terms past 13 can be produced by adding "teen" to a single-digit term (e.g., "six + teen, seven + teen"). Fifteen is an *irregular* variation of this pattern and hence is more frequently missed than other teen terms.

Children entering kindergarten can often count to 19 or 20 but then run into difficulty. Some children may not realize that 19 signals the need for a transition—a new series of terms (the twenties). Such children sometimes continue the teen pattern ("ten-teen, eleven-teen, twelve-teen"). Some children may recognize that 19 signals a transition point but have not learned the next (transition) term. Some children may have learned that 20 follows 19 but have not yet recognized the repetitious nature of the number sequence (i.e., that after twenty, the next terms are twenty plus the single-digit sequence). As a result, the child may not know that 21 follows 20. Once children master the fact that 20 follows 19 and recognize that the original one-to-nine sequence recurs at this level ("twenty + *one,* twenty + *two,*" . . .), a child can readily master the *count by ones 20 to 29.* It is evident that children are using rules to count larger numbers because they often make systematic (rule-governed) errors, such as counting "five-teen" for "fifteen," "ten-teen" for "twenty," or "twenty-ten" for "thirty." Because the teens do not follow a single, simple pattern, some children actually may master the highly regular twenties before mastering all the teens.

To count to 100, children have to learn the decades (10, 20, 30, 40 . . .) in their correct order. Like the count-by-one sequence, children probably learn the first portion of the decade sequence (10 to 50 or so) by rote memorization. The last portion of the decade sequence can be manufactured by adding "ty" to the corresponding single-digit terms (e.g., "six + ty, seven + ty" . . .). Once children master this pattern or rule, they can complete the *count by tens to 100.* At this point, to *count by ones 30 to 100,* a child need only recognize the patterns: (1) a series of terms can be formed by combining a decade term with the one-to-nine sequence (e.g., "seventy + one, seventy + two," and so forth); and (2) a nine term (e.g., "seventy-nine") is followed by the next decade in the count-by-tens sequence (e.g., "the decade after seventy is eighty; so after seventy-nine comes eighty").

As children proceed in school, they learn new count patterns, termed skip counts. In addition to counting by tens, they learn to *count by twos* ("2, 4, 6 . . .") and *count by fives* ("5, 10, 15 . . ."). Later, they learn to *count the odd numbers 1 to 19* ("1, 3, 5, . . . , 19"). When first learning a skip count, some children may count the intervening terms softly or subvocally. For example, in order to count by twos, a child may whisper one, announce two, whisper three, announce four, and so forth. As they master the skip count, the need for stating the intervening terms decreases and then ceases altogether.

Counting beyond 100 is also a rule-governed activity. In order to *count by ones 101 to 200,* a child need only notice that "one hundred" is followed by "one hundred one," that the rest of the hundreds can be manufactured by prefacing the count-by-ones sequence from 1 to 99 with "one hundred" (e.g., "one hundred + two, one hundred + three" . . .), and that 199 is followed by the transition term 200. A common stumbling block is 101; children stop at 100 because they do not know what comes next. Some do not get past 101 to 110 or so because they may not realize that the hundreds are simply a repetition of the count to 99 with the prefix one hundred added. Finally, many children may not realize that 200 follows 199.

Likewise, children can master the *count by tens 100 to 200* by prefacing the familiar count-by-tens sequence from 10 to 90 with "one hundred." Some children will be prone to miss 110, because they have not yet realized how their count-by-tens knowledge can be extended beyond 100. Others may miss 200 (e.g., say 191 or 199 after 190), because they do not realize that their count-by-tens knowledge can be connected with their count-by-hundreds knowledge (one hundreds are followed by two hundreds which in turn are followed by three hundreds, etc.).

Next Term

When asked what follows a given number (e.g., "What comes right after six?"), children initially count from one to determine an answer (e.g., "one, two, three, four, five, six, *seven*") (e.g., Fuson and Hall, 1983). After the sequence to 10 becomes highly familiar, children can immediately cite the *number after 1 to 9.* For example, when asked what number comes after 7, three-year-old Alison can say automatically that the next number is 8; she no longer needs to count from 1 to get the answer. Before they turn six years of age, most children can cite accurately the *number after 10 to 28* (Fuson, Richards, and Briars, 1982). As children extend their knowledge of the number sequence, they become capable of efficiently citing the *number after 29 to 99,* and eventually *100 to 199.* Likewise, as children become familiar with the decade sequence, they master citing the *decade after 10 to 90.* As implied above, this decade-after skill may play an important role in learning to count by ones to 100. Similarly, mastering the *decade after 100 to 190* is crucial to learning to count by ones from 100 to 200.

Backward Counts

Next Term

As familiarity with the number sequence grows, children can operate on it in the opposite direction. Specifically, they can cite the *number before 2 to 10*; later, the *number before 11 to 29*; and eventually, the *number before 30 to 100*. Some children have difficulty with such a task because they cannot work backwards on the number sequence efficiently or have not learned the meaning of the term "before." Moreover, as they become familiar with the decade sequence to 100, children can readily state the decade before a given term (*decade before 20 to 100*).

Sequence of Terms

Once children can cite the number before, the stage is set for counting backwards. Children may quickly learn to count backwards from 10 for several reasons. First, the sequence of numbers from 1 to 10 is highly familiar. Second, young children have wide exposure to backward counts from 10 (e.g., when they watch children's television programs like "Sesame Street" or televised space shots). *Counting backwards from 20,* or other numbers greater than 10, is more difficult because, in part, the teen portion of the sequence is less familiar to children.

The competencies discussed above are summarized in Table 3–1 by developmental order. For example, count by ones 11 to 19 appears below (after) count by ones 1 to 10 and above (before) count by ones 20 to 29 or number after. Also indicated in Table 3–1 are the approximate grade levels that children can be expected to master particular competencies. All competencies above the K are mastered by roughly 90 percent of the children before entering kindergarten. These skills and concepts are appropriate for preschool and Headstart programs. The competencies to the right and below the K and above the 1 are typically mastered during the kindergarten year. A child entering first grade, then, can be expected to have the competencies delineated in the first five lines of Table 3–1. By the end of first grade, the typical child should have mastered the competencies listed in lines 6 to 9 as well.

INSTRUCTION

Most children entering school should already have a good start on learning the count-by-ones sequence. Children's curiosity and natural interest in extending this knowledge can be exploited by focusing on patterns (rules for

Table 3–1 Sequence of Oral-Counting Competencies by Grade Level and Developmental Order

Level	Forward Counts		Backward Counts	
	Sequence of Terms	*Next Term*	*Next Term*	*Sequence of Terms*
PK	Count by ones 1 to 10	—	—	—
	—	Number after 1 to 9	—	—
	Count by ones 11 to 19	—	—	—
K	—	—	Number before 2 to 10	—
	Count by ones 20 to 29	Number after 10 to 28	—	—
	—	—	—	Count backwards from 10
1	Count by tens to 100	Decade after 10 to 90	—	—
	—	—	Number before 11 to 29	—
	Count by ones 30 to 100	Number after 29 to 99	—	—
	Count by fives to 100	—	—	—
	Count by twos to 20	—	—	—
2	Count odd numbers 1 to 19	—	—	Count backwards from 20
	Count by tens 100 to 200	Decade after 100 to 190	—	—
	—	—	Number before 30 to 100 & Decade before 20 to 100	—
	Count by ones 101 to 200	Number after 100 to 199	—	—

generating larger numbers) and relationships (e.g., how skip counts are a variation of the basic count-by-ones pattern).

For the most part, as they gain mastery over the number sequence, children pick up next-term skills with little or no direct teaching. As they master forward count skills, children generally begin to acquire backward count skills with no or minimal prompting. Backward counting skills that involve numbers greater than 10 are relatively difficult and may require special attention by a teacher.

Forward Counts: Sequence of Terms

Count by Ones 1 to 10

Children can be helped to master the rote count-by-one sequence to 10 by using a variety of activities. Regular exposure to and practice of the sequence is important for mastery. Counting objects is often more meaningful and interesting to children than oral counting (Fuson, Richards, and Briars, 1982). Most practice can and should be done in the context of counting objects, such as the **Spinner Game** (Example 3–6) and **Star Race** (Example 3–7) described later in this chapter, or the numbering games described in Chapter 4. Some suggestions for teaching and practicing oral counting are listed in Examples 3–1 to 3–5.

Example 3–1   Counting Stories

There are numerous children's stories that involve the counting sequence to 10. Regular reading of such stories can be an interesting way to expose children to the count sequence. Stories, like the one below, can also provide the basis for discussing important aspects of counting with children. To dramatize this and other counting stories, have the children act out the story. Alternatively, older children can be recruited to put on plays based on the counting stories.

The Importance of Counting Numbers in the Same Order

Count Disorderly invited some friends over for a game of hide-n-seek. Because no one in the kingdom had ever played this game, Count Disorderly had his brother Count Orderly explain the rules. Count Orderly said, "One person closes his eyes, and everyone else runs and hides. The person who closes his eyes then has to find the others who have hidden. To be fair, the person who hides his eyes must count by ones to 10. This gives everyone a chance to find a good hiding spot."

Count Disorderly was so excited that he cried out, "I want to hide my eyes first." Everyone thought this was a good idea. So Count Disorderly closed and covered his eyes and counted, "One, two, ten." Then he uncovered his eyes and said, "Aha, I can see everyone. I found everyone. I win. I win."

Count Disorderly's joy was short-lived. All of his friends grumbled, "You cheated. You opened your eyes too soon. You didn't count all the way to 10. We didn't have a fair chance to hide."

Count Disorderly complained bitterly, "You're just bad losers. I said 10."

Count Orderly then stepped in and explained, "But brother, you skipped some numbers between 1 and 10. Try again."

So Count Disorderly closed and covered his eyes again. This time he counted, "Eight, nine, ten." Count Disorderly uncovered his eyes and exclaimed, "Yes, yes, yes. I caught everybody! I win. I win!"

The other players were quite mad with Count Disorderly now. Altogether they shouted, "You cheated again. You still opened your eyes too soon. You didn't give us a fair chance to hide."

Count Orderly stepped between the angry crowd and his brother and said, "Now, now. Everyone calm down. I don't think Count Disorderly is *trying* to cheat; he just doesn't know what to do. Now brother, you have to count all the numbers between 1 and 10. That way we have a fair chance to hide."

So Count Disorderly closed and covered his eyes for a third time. He began counting numbers but in his own way, "One, two, five, three, seven, six, four, seven, five . . ." Count Disorderly kept counting and counting and counting. Even after he had counted for nearly an hour, Count Disorderly had not gotten to 10 because his counting was so confused. By this time, everyone who had been hiding had gotten tired of waiting and had gone home.

Count Orderly came out of his hiding place from behind a bush, walked up to his brother, and tapped him on the shoulder. Count Orderly asked, "Oh brother, what are you doing? Why are you not looking for the hiders? Why are you still counting?"

Count Disorderly replied wearily, "I tried to count to 10, but I cannot seem to get there from 1. Every time I try to count, different numbers come out and I never reach 10!"

Count Orderly now understood his brother's problem and said, "I think I can help you. Look brother, when we count by ones, we always say the numbers in the same order: One, then two, then three, then four, then five, then six, then seven, then eight, then nine, and then ten. See? That way we can get from 1 to 10 every time and rather quickly."

"Oh my!" exclaimed Count Disorderly, "I didn't realize that the numbers had to go in the *same order every time* we wanted to count by ones. That explains why I never got the same number when I counted my royal jewels." Count Disorderly took out three jewels from his pocket. "Sometimes I counted one, two, *five*. Sometimes eight, nine, *ten*. Sometimes three, seven, *four*. With my way of counting, you always come out with something different. Boy, was that confusing! With your way of counting, I would count, 'one, two, three.' And if I counted the jewels again, 'one, two, three,' it would come out the same."

Count Disorderly was ever so happy that he found out that the numbers always go in the same order every time he was supposed to count by ones. "Now," he said with a grin, "we can play hide-n-seek and *enjoy* ourselves."

Example 3–2 Good or Bad Counter

Objective: Identification of correct and incorrect oral counts (use of examples and nonexamples) to prompt a discussion of the characteristics of the number sequence.

Grade Level: PK.

Participants: One child, small group, or whole class.

Materials: Cookie Monster puppet, hand puppet, or stuffed animal.

Procedure: Many children greatly enjoy error-detection games, where they have to spot another's mistake. Point out that Cookie Monster (or substitute) is just learning how to count, sometimes makes mistakes, and needs help. Explain that a participant's job is to listen to Cookie Monster count and, when he is all done, to say whether he was a good or bad counter. If Cookie Monster does make a mistake, the participant can help by pointing out what he did wrong (and what he should say). While including an occasional correct count, try counts with errors such as the following:

1. Omitted term (e.g., "1, 2, 3, 4, 5, 6, 7, *9*, 10").

2. Incorrect order (e.g., "1, 2, 3, 4, 5, 6, *8, 7*, 9, 10").

3. Jumbled order (e.g., "*3, 1, 9, 6, 5, 8, 2, 10, 7, 4*").

4. Repeated term (e.g., "1, 2, 3, 4, 5, 6, 7, *7*, 8, 9, 10").

5. Incorrect substitution (e.g., "1, 2, 3, 4, 5, 6, *12*, 8, 9, 10"; "1, 2, 3, 4, 5, 6, 7, 8, 9, *tenny*"; "1, 2, 3, 4, 5, 6, *d*, 8, 9, 10").

This activity can provide the basis for a discussion about the count-by-one sequence. For example, key characteristics that children might note or that a teacher might want to highlight are:

1. There is a prescribed (or standard) order of terms; the same order is used every time we count by ones.

2. There are socially prescribed terms that are used (e.g., terms like *tenny* or letters like *d* are not allowable). Different cultures have different but parallel terms (e.g., in Spanish, *one is uno*, *two* is *dos*, *three* is *tres*, and so forth).

3. Each term is unique or different; we do not repeat terms. (This is very important when we use the number sequence to count objects. For example, if we repeated "four" "1, 2, 3, 4, 4" the following sets would be given the same label: OOOO OOOOO .)

In an alternative version (called **The Absent-Minded Counter**), a teacher can play-act an absent-minded counter and have the participants point out and correct the teacher's errors. Children may really enjoy the role reversal and the make-believe play.

Example 3–3 Snake Game

Objective: Count by ones to 10 in an interesting, object-counting context.

Grade Level: PK.

Participants: One to twelve children.

Materials: Ten countable objects, such as blocks.

Procedure: Say, "Let's make a snake with these blocks. To see how big our snake is getting, count the blocks as I add them to the snake."

Example 3–4 Taller Tower Game

Objective: Count by ones to 10 in an interesting, object-counting context.

Grade Level: PK.

Participants: One to six or a small team of children.

Materials: Ten interlocking blocks (and twelve-inch paper strips) for each child.

Procedure: The object of this game is to use interlocking blocks to build the tallest tower possible. Before a child (or team) can add a new "floor" (block), he or she (or they) must indicate the correct floor number. For example, to add a fifth block to a tower of four, the child must say the next floor is five or count from one to five. To encourage a child to compete against his or her own record, the height of the tower can be marked off on a paper strip bearing the child's name and taped to the wall behind the tower. The next time the child (team) plays the game, he or she (or they) can try to build past the mark. This may provide an incentive for some children to learn additional count terms. Note that the **Snake Game** (Example 3–3) can be used in a similar manner.

Example 3–5 Tape Recording

Some children may enjoy using or learning to operate a tape recorder. They may be naturally interested in hearing themselves on the tape recorder. Listening to the tape can provide an opportunity to note and correct errors.

Count by Ones 11 to 19 and
Count by Ones 20 to 29

Instruction on the teens and twenties should focus on helping children discover the patterns underlying these sequences. Specifically, help the children see how the single-digit sequence 1 to 9 recurs in these sequences.

Rule-governed errors, such as substituting "five-teen" for fifteen or "ten-teen" for twenty, should not be ridiculed. Indeed, such errors indicate that a child is attending to sequence patterns. A teacher can provide praise and correction for the child by saying, "Another name for ten-teen is twenty." Error-detection games (**Good or Bad Counter** or **The Absent-Minded Counter** in Example 3–2) can be used in a manner similar to that described for count by ones 1 to 10 or they can be used with abbreviated counts. For example, a teacher can have participants evaluate the correctness of a count segment (e.g., "13, 14, 14, 16, 17"; "13, 14, five-teen, 16, 17"; "18, 19, ten-teen"; "16, 18, 17, 19").

Practice counting up to 19 or 29 can be done using the **Snake Game**

(Example 3–3), **Tape Recording** (Example 3–5), the games described in Examples 3–6 and 3–7 or the **Train Game** described later for counting up to 100.

Example 3–6   Spinner Game

Objective: Count by ones up to 19 or 29.

Grade Level: K.

Participants: One to four children.

Materials: Spinner numbered 1 to 10; chalkboard and chalk or paper and pencil.

Procedure: Say, "We're going to play the Spinner Game. This spinner will tell us how many points we get when it's our turn." Say in turn to each player, "Let's see how many points you can get; go ahead and spin the spinner. Good, you got X points. Let's put a tally mark on this chalkboard for each point you got." Help the child make a tally mark for each point or, if necessary, record the marks yourself. Continue the procedure described above until the children have reached the desired counting level. Make sure the marks on the chalkboard form a straight line. If necessary curve the line. Do not begin a separate row. (There is a tendency for children to count from one again when they begin a separate row.) Conclude the activity by saying, "Let's see how many points you got." Point to the first mark and say, "I'll point to the marks, and you count them." Encourage the child to count all the marks.

Example 3–7   Star Race

Objective: Count by ones up to 19 or 29.

Grade Level: K.

Participants: One or two children.

Materials: Miniature spaceships and star track (a spiral race track with a star marking each of 19 or 29 spaces).

Procedure: Say, "We're going to play the Star Race Game. Which spaceship would you like? Okay, place it on the starting line. When I say, 'Go,' drive your spaceship down the star track. Be careful not to drive off the track. Let's see how many stars you can pass. Ready? Go." Allow the child to drive the car along the track. After the child reaches the finish line, say, "You got all the way to the finish line. Good. Let's see how many stars you passed." Point to the star at the starting place and say, "I'll point to the stars, and you can count them." Encourage the child to count all the stars.

Count by Tens to 100

Training should center on explicitly calling to the children's attention the parallel between the single-digit and decade sequences. Initially, this can be done by comparing the number lists for each sequence.

1	2	3	4	5	6	7	8	9
10	20	30	40	50	60	70	80	90

Encourage the children to describe the decade pattern and its similarities to the single-digit sequence themselves. Then summarize their discovery. If a child needs help figuring out the next term in the decade sequence, encourage the pupil to use his or her existing knowledge of the count sequence (e.g., "What comes after 60 when we count by tens? Well, what comes after 6 when we count by ones? 1, 2, 3, 4, 5, 6, and then comes? Yes, 7. So after six-ty comes seven-ty.") Later, the child should be encouraged to shortcut this process: "What comes after 60 when we count by tens? Think to yourself: What comes after 6 when I count by ones? Yes, 7. Now add -ty— Seventy." Error-detection exercises (**Good or Bad Counter** or **The Absent-Minded Counter** in Example 3–2) can be adapted to provide a stimulus for discussing decade patterns (e.g., "Why is *five-ty* incorrect? What is wrong with '70, 90, 80' and how do you know that it's wrong?").

Practice can then make the process automatic. It may help to begin practice with the aid of a number list, as in **Peek** (Example 3–8). With a running start (with the first portion of the count-by-ten sequence visible), it should be easier for a child to figure out the next decade in the sequence (e.g., "After 50, comes—10, 20, 30, 40, 50—oh, 60. Then 10, 20, 30, 40, 50, 60—oh, 70 . . ."). Practice can be made interesting by using **Count Teacher** (discussed later) or the **Strike Game** (Example 3–9). To provide maximum practice, the child can tally his or her score after every turn. **Count Race** (Example 3–10) can help illustrate that counting by tens is more efficient than counting by ones when enumerating large sets of objects.

Ideally, children will discover for themselves that counting by tens is much more efficient than counting by ones. If a child does not discover that counting by tens is applicable to the task—even after a number of repetitions of the activity—encourage the child to think about finding a shortcut. Have children discuss their shortcuts and the relative merits of different counting procedures. Even after the child discovers or learns the shortcut of counting by tens, the activity can be readministered to practice the skill of counting by tens. (Indeed, harder exercises, such as Exercise G, can be used to help practice counting by tens over 100.)

Example 3–8   Peek

Objective: Count by tens to 100 with the aid of a number list.

Grade Level: 1.

Participants: A single child or a small group.

Materials: Decade number list and sheath (shown below).*

Procedure: Say, "Let's play Peek. Here is a number list that we can use to count by tens. It starts with 10 and goes all the way to 100. Now I'll hide the numbers. This says 10." [Expose 10. "When we count by tens, what comes after 10?" If the child is correct, confirm the response, award a point, expose 20, and continue. If the child is incorrect, help him or her figure out what the next term should be, building on his or her knowledge of the one-to-nine sequence. After a child can cite the decades in order, play **Advanced Peek** by mixing the order in which the decades are quizzed.

---

*Using the number list shown, Peek could be used to practice decade after or decade before as well as counting by tens. By substituting a 1-to-10 number list, Peek could be used to practice number after 1 to 9. By inserting the 1-to-10 number list in the sheath in the opposite direction, Peek can be used to practice numbers before 2 to 10 and counting backwards from 10 (see instruction section under count backwards from 10).

Example 3–9 The Strike Game

> **Objective:** Mentally count by tens.
>
> **Grade Level:** 1.
>
> **Participants:** Two players or two small teams of children.
>
> **Materials:** Oblong block or other object that can serve as a bowling pin, (clay) ball, writing materials to keep score.
>
> **Procedure:** Explain that in the Strike Game, a player tries to knock down a bowling pin with a ball. Successfully knocking down the pin is called a "strike." A strike is scored as 10 points. (Record a 10 or a tally mark for each strike.)

Example 3–10 Count Race

> **Objectives:** Demonstrate the value of thinking in terms of groups of ten and practice counting by ones or tens.
>
> **Grade Level:** 1.
>
> **Participants:** A single child or a small group of children.
>
> **Materials:** Practice sheets such as those depicted below and a stopwatch or a watch with a second hand.

Exercise A	Exercise B	Exercise G
OOOOOOOOOO	OOOOOOOOOO	OOOOOOOOOO
OOOOOOOOOO	OOOOOOOOOO	OOOOOOOOOO
OOOOOOOOOO	OOOOOOOOOO	OOOOOOOOOO
	OOOOOOOOOO	OOOOOOOOOO
	OOOOOOOOOO	OOOOOOOOOO
	OOOOOOOOOO	OOOOOOOOOO
		OOOOOOOOOO
		OOOOOOOOOO
		OOOOOOOOOO
		OOOOOOOOOO
		OOOOOOOOOO
		OOOOOOOOOO
		OOOOOOOOOO
		OOOOOOOOOO

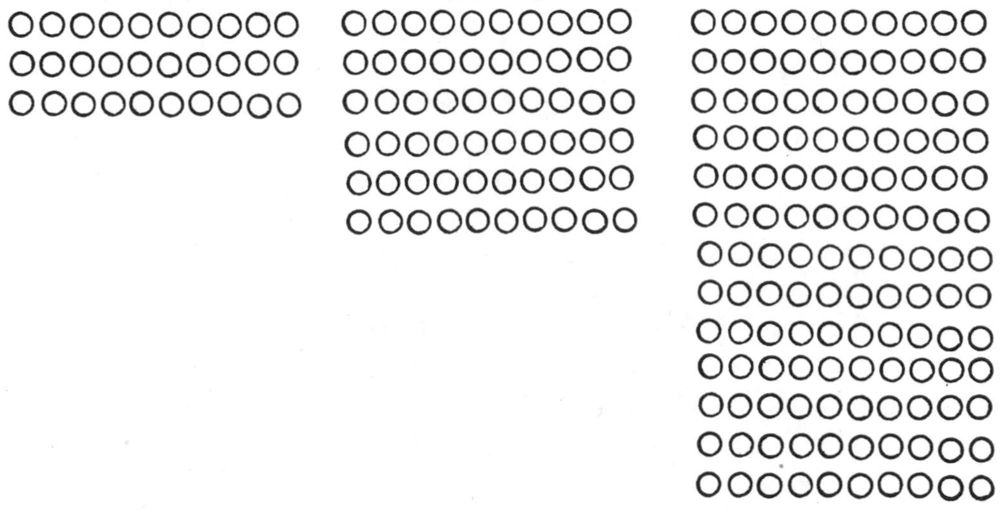

Procedure: Explain that in Count Race, the aim is to count the objects in a picture accurately, but as quickly as possible. At the signal, "Go," give the child the first exercise sheet and begin timing. If the child's count is accurate, record the time; otherwise, disqualify the trial. Give the child additional exercise sheets—repeating the procedure above. The number and difficulty (number of dots) of the exercise sheets should be geared to the child's capabilities. The activity can be repeated some time later—perhaps the next day or week. This is especially important to do if the child does not discover that counting by tens is applicable or discovers this part way through the activity. Encourage the child to break his or her own record for each exercise. On repetitions of the activity, the rule is that the child must count to give an answer. Guessing or recognition does not qualify.

Count by Ones 30 to 100

First ensure that a child can efficiently count from 1 to 10 and knows the count-by-ones sequences from 11 to 19 and 20 to 29 fairly well. Instruction should focus on helping children discover the patterns underlying the number sequences from 30 to 100.

1. If necessary, help children see that each decade-plus-nine term signals the need to call up the next term in the decade sequence.

2. Help them to see that the one-to-nine sequence recurs with *each* decade.

3. Help children solve the decade problem, that is, learn how to count by tens to 100 and how this knowledge can be used to count by ones to 100.

To help children explore the sequence patterns, play **What Patterns Do You See?** Have them examine a chart like the one shown in Table 3–2 and describe for themselves what patterns they see. Then summarize their descriptions, taking care to point out the repetitious patterns. Using abbreviated counts, error-detection activities can also provide a basis for discussing patterns, links, and common errors. For example, in playing **The Absent-Minded Counter** (Example 3–2), a teacher could say, "Yesterday I counted up the things on my shopping list, and I counted all the way up to '27, 28, 29, twenty-ten.'" The activity called **Count Teacher** (Example 3–11) can provide practice using rules to count to 100. The **Train Game** (Example 3–12) can provide practice in an object-counting context.

Table 3-2 Number Sequence to 100

0	1	2	3	4	5	6	7	8	9
10	11	12	13	14	15	16	17	18	19
20	21	22	23	24	25	26	27	28	29
30	31	32	33	34	35	36	37	38	39
40	41	42	43	44	45	46	47	48	49
50	51	52	53	54	55	56	57	58	59
60	61	62	63	64	65	66	67	68	69
70	71	72	73	74	75	76	77	78	79
80	81	82	83	84	85	86	87	88	89
90	91	92	93	94	95	96	97	98	99

Example 3-11 Count Teacher

Objective: Count by ones to 100.

Grade Level: 2.

Participants: One child, a small group of children, or a whole class.

Materials: Cookie Monster Muppet, hand puppet, or doll to serve as the pupil.

Procedure: Say, "Cookie Monster is learning how to count. He can count all the numbers to 29. Can you teach him to count even higher? We count 27, 28, 29, and then comes?" Continue with other questions, giving the participant(s) a running start (e.g., "We count 47, 48, 49, and then comes?" or "We count 50, 51, 52, and then comes?").

Example 3-12 Train Game

Objective: Count by ones to 100 in an interesting, object-counting context.

Grade Level: 1.

Participants: One child, a small group of children, or two to four teams of a few children each.

Materials: 100 interlocking blocks.

Procedure: Say, "We're going to play the Train Game. We'll pretend these blocks are train cars. Let's see how big we can make the train. Let's see how many cars we can put together. I'll give you one (or two) minute(s) to make your train. Ready? Go." Children can work individually (in which case 100 blocks are needed for each), as a group, or as a team. After a minute (or when the desired number of blocks have been put together), say, "Time's up. Let's see how many cars your train has." Point to the first cube and say, "I'll point to the cars, and you count them." Encourage the child (children) to count all the blocks. You may wish to record the number of blocks that the child or group was able to put together and count. Then, in successive practice efforts, you can encourage the child to compete against his or her own previous record. When the game is played with teams, count each team's train. The team with the most blocks in its train wins.

Count by Fives to 100

Remedy deficiencies in the count-by-ones sequence first. To introduce skip counting by five, play the **Prediction Game** (Example 3–13) with piles of five objects. The **Pattern-Chant Activity** can also be used as an introductory lesson. Instruct the children to whisper one, two, three, four, and announce five; whisper six, seven, eight, nine, and announce ten; and so forth. Children can take turns adding the next segment, or it can be done as a group. If a child can already count intervening terms to announce every fifth term, build on this skill.

The activities **Pattern Prediction** (Example 3–14) and the **Attack of the Fivers** (Example 3–15) can provide practice counting by fives. For additional practice, teach the children to mark off their points in other games in groups of five (e.g., **LHt LHt LHt**) and encourage counting by five as an efficient tallying method.

Example 3–13 Prediction Game (Piles of Five)

Objectives: Estimation and counting by fives with objects.

Grade Level: 1.

Participants: One child or a small group of children.

Materials: Interlocking blocks, pennies, other countable objects; slips of paper; and a pencil.

Procedure: Place on separate slips of paper, for example, three piles of five objects each and ask the participant(s) to find out how many objects there are altogether. After counting the first pile, have the participant(s) label its slips of paper with a 5. Then before counting the next pile, ask the child to predict the outcome of counting five more objects (see the case study cited in Example 6.2 in Baroody, 1987a). After counting the second pile, have the participant(s) label its slip with 10. Then repeat the procedure for the third pile. Try the same thing with four to nine piles of five.

Example 3–14 Pattern Prediction

Objectives: Mentally count by fives (preferably without intervening terms) and other skip counts.

Grade Level: 1.

Participants: One child or a small group of children.

Procedure: Say, "In this activity, you have to figure out a number pattern. I'll tell you some numbers, and you tell me what number you think should come next. Five, ten, fifteen, and then?"

Example 3–15 Attack of the Fivers

Objective: Count by fives.

Grade Level: 1.

Participants: Two to four children.

Materials: Target board (shown below),* chips, "spitballs" (moistened tissue paper) or other projectiles, and scoring materials.

Procedure: Explain that in this game, an alien force called the Fivers is about to attack earth. The aliens are called Fivers because

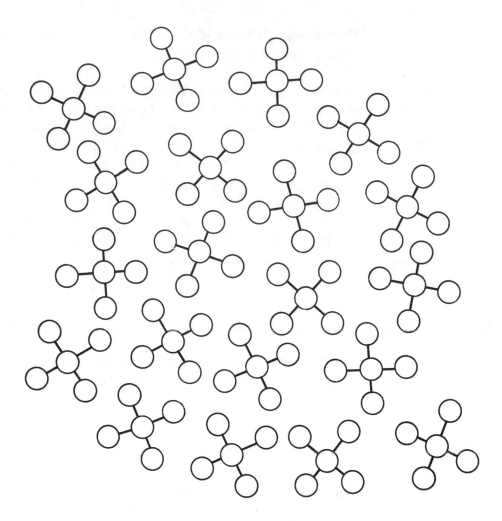

they always travel in groups of five and as a result, their spaceships have five compartments. The idea of the game is to knock out the alien attack force. To do this, each spaceship has to be hit. One hit will knock out all compartments of the spaceship. Hence, a single hit is scored and recorded as 5 points (~~IIII~~ or 5). After a player's turn, the child tallies the score on the card by counting by fives.

---

*The material of the target board depends upon projectile. If chips are used, then the fiver target can be drawn on a piece of cardboard or construction paper, which is then laid on the ground. The targets could also be drawn on the floor or a sidewalk. If spitballs are used the fiver targets can be painted on a metal surface or drawn in chalk on a chalkboard.

Count by Twos to 20

Remedy deficiencies in the count-by-ones sequence to 20 first. Introduce skip counting by twos with the **Prediction Game (Piles of Two)** (see Example 3–13) and the **Pattern-Chant Activity**. For the latter, instruct the children to whisper the intervening terms and announce the even terms loudly. Young children often enjoy repeating chants. Next, encourage the children to omit the intervening terms. **Pattern Prediction** (see Example 3–14) can provide some of the practice to make the skill automatic. **Basketball** (Example 3–16) can be used for instruction and extra practice by asking the players to tally their scores (by twos) after each shot.

Example 3–16 Basketball

Objective: Count by twos.

Grade Level: 1.

Participants: Two children or teams of a few children.

Materials: Miniature basketball net, sponge basketball, and materials to keep score.

Procedure: Point out that in basketball each basket is scored as two points. For each basket a player scores, record a checkmark or a 2. After a specified number of shots or amount of time, each child or team can tally their score sheet by counting by twos.

Count Odd Numbers 1 to 19

First ensure that the more basic skills (count by ones 1 to 10 and 11 to 19, and count by twos to 20) are rather automatic. Introduce the odd-number pattern in terms of the more familiar even-number pattern (count by twos) by pointing out the similarities and differences of the two sequences. Note that both involve skipping over one number in the count sequence. However, unlike starting with two to count the even numbers, counting the odd numbers entails *starting with one*. It may be helpful to use a number list to point out the similarities and differences of counting odd and even numbers. At first, use the **Pattern-Chant Activity** and allow or even encourage children to whisper the intervening terms ("one" with emphasis, "two" softly, "three" with emphasis, "four" softly, etc.). Later use **Pattern**

Prediction (see Example 3–14) to foster the automatic execution of the skill without the intervening terms. To extend knowledge of number patterns, ask the children to figure out other number patterns (e.g., skipping two terms, as in 1, 4, 7, 10, or counting terms with two in the ones place: 2, 12, 22, 32).

Count by Tens 100 to 200

First ensure that a child can count by tens to 100 fairly automatically. Help the child discover that the count-by-tens sequence recurs with each hundred term. Specifically, note that after 100, we simply use the prefix "one hundred" and recycle the original count-by-tens sequence (e.g., "one hundred + ten, one hundred + twenty," . . .). For some children, it may be necessary to point out that the *one* hundreds are followed by the *two* hundreds and that 190 indicates this transition. Therefore, 200 follows 190 when counting by tens. These count patterns or rules can be explored in the entertaining format of **Good-or-Bad** or **The Absent-Minded Counter by Tens to 200**. The **Strike-and-Spare Game** (Example 3–17) can provide practice counting by tens to 200.

Example 3–17   The Strike-and-Spare Game

Objective: Count by tens to 200.

Grade Level: 2.

Participants: Two children or two teams of a few children each.

Materials: Three oblong blocks or other objects that can serve as bowling pins, a (rubber, clay, or plastic) ball, and writing materials to keep score.

Procedure: Explain that in the Strike-and-Spare Game, a player has two tries to knock down all the bowling pins with a ball. If a player does so on a first try, then a "strike" is scored as 10 points plus a 10-point bonus. If a player topples all three pins after two tries, a spare is scored (10 points). Otherwise, 0 points are scored. Record a checkmark for each 10-point score (i.e., two for a strike and one for a spare).

Count by Ones 101 to 200

First remedy the prerequisite skills: Count by ones 1 to 10, 11 to 29, 30 to 100, and decade after 100 to 190. Instruction then should focus on establishing the links 100–101 and 199–200 and on pointing out the parallels between the hundreds sequence and the 1 to 100 sequence. Error-detection activities (e.g., **The Absent-Minded Counter** with abbreviated counts) can provide a focus for discussing patterns, links, and common errors. For instance, a teacher might ask, "What is wrong with counting '98, 99, 100, 1000'? What is wrong with counting '148, 149, 130, 131'?" Practice in using the rules to generate counts to 200 can be done using **Count Teacher** (e.g., "We count 127, 128, 129 and then comes?").

Forward Counts: Next Term

Number After 1 to 9

If necessary, introduce the number-after skill by giving the child a "running start." For example, ask, "When we count, we say, '1, 2, 3, 4, 5,' and then comes?" As the child catches on, shorten the running start to three terms (e.g., "3, 4, 5, and then comes?"), then to two (e.g., "4, 5, and then comes?"). Because it visually provides a number list, the game **Basic Number-After Dominoes** (Example 3–18) is useful during this stage of training. Other activities that provide support for a running start are described elsewhere: **Turn Over** (Baroody, 1987a) and **Walk On** and **Peek** (Bley and Thornton, 1981).

For children who already use a running start (count from one to respond), try a running start of three and then two terms. For children who can figure out the number after but do so slowly, training should focus on practice to make the skill automatic. The **Advanced Number-After Dominoes** (Example 3–18), **Rings for a King or Queen** (Example 3–19), **Number-After Race** (Example 3–20), and **Number-After Quiz Game** (Example 3–21) are useful for practicing this skill.

Example 3–18 Basic and Advanced Number-After Dominoes

Objective: Number after 1 to 9 with (or without) the aid of object counting, a number list, and a running start.

Grade Level: PK.

Participants: Two to five players.

Materials: Set of up to 20 domino-like pieces with the numerals 1 to 10 and a number list 1 to 10 (see Frame A below).

A. Basic Version

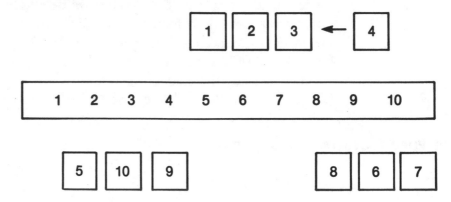

B. Advanced Version

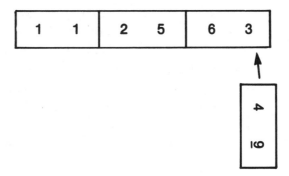

Procedure: Number-After Dominoes is based on a game from the Wynroth (1986) curriculum. It is played like Dominoes except that the added domino must be the number after the end item, rather than the same number (see figure). To begin with, limit the number of players to two and use five dominoes marked 1 to 5 only. Put out the "1" domino and turn the other four over so that the numerals do not show. Mix the latter and have each child pick two dominoes. Turn the dominoes over so that the numerals are visible to the child. Ask, "What comes just after one when we count?" If needed, add, "When we count, we say one and then?" If necessary, have the children count on a number list to determine the answer. Then ask, "Who has the 'two'?" The player with the "2" domino places his or her piece to the right of the "1" domino. Continue this procedure until everyone's dominoes are used up. The player who uses his or her dominoes first is the "first winner"; the next child is the "second winner" (and so forth).

Note that a regular set of dominoes (with regular number patterns of dots) can be used instead of dominoes with numerals. Wynroth (1986) suggests using dominoes with irregular patterns of dots. I would recommend that a teacher alternate between using dominoes with regular dot patterns and those with irregular patterns. For some children, the dot dominoes may afford a concrete representation that makes the task somewhat more meaningful. Moreover, by using dominoes with dots, this game can serve as a basis for practicing enumeration or fostering pattern recognition. For children who do not need such practice, I recommend numeral dominoes because the need to count sets of dots may distract children from the main objective of the game.

In time, the number list can be withdrawn. A child can then be encouraged to take a running start (count from one) to determine the number after. Once children have mastered the number-after skill for the numbers 1 to 4, the game can be expanded to number after 1 to 9 by including dominoes 6 to 10. For two players, have the children each select five dominoes. The player who draws the "1" domino goes first. For three players, set out the "1" domino and have each child draw three dominoes. A more sophisticated version of the game entails using 20 dominoes (two of each number 1 to 10). Have each of the two to five players draw three dominoes. After each turn, the players are given the option of keeping the dominoes they have or trading one in and picking another domino from the discard pile.

Advanced Number-After Dominoes, illustrated in Frame B, removes the visual prompts for a running start (i.e., the played dominoes are not in sequential order). The player with "double 1" begins play.

Example 3–19   Rings for a Queen or King*

Objective: Mentally determine the number after 1 to 9.

Grade Level: PK.

Participants: One or a few children.

Materials: Numeral dominoes 1 to 9 and unifex cubes ("rings").

Procedure: The game is played like Number-After Dominoes except that the child puts a "ring" (unifex cube) on his or her finger for each number he or she produces correctly.

———————
*William Boaz of Rochester, New York, suggested this game to me.

Example 3–20   Number-After Race

Objective: Mentally determine the number after 1 to 9.

Grade Level: PK.

Participants: Two to five players.

Materials: Small match-box type cars; spiral race-track game board; and die, number cards, or spinner.

Procedure: Give each player a car. Tell the children they are going to race. Have a player throw a die, draw a number card, or spin a spinner. Then say, for example "You got a three. What comes just after three?" If the child is correct, say, "You can move four spaces."

Example 3–21   Number-After Quiz Game

Objective: Mentally determine the number after 1 to 9.

Grade Level: PK.

Participants: One to five children or two teams of any size.

Materials: Deck of cards with a numeral 1 to 9 printed on each, prizes (optional), and stopwatch.

Procedure: Explain: "In the Next-Number Quiz I'll give you a number like 'one,' and you tell me what comes just after 'one' when we count. One and then comes? Each correct answer is worth a point." A stopwatch can be used to encourage automatic answering when players (or teams) take turns. (Players can be required to respond within a time limit such as three seconds.) Keeping time is unnecessary if players (or teams) compete to see who responds correctly first. Players win if they get a predetermined number of points. If played competitively, the first player or team to get a predetermined number wins.

Number After 10 to 28

First remedy any difficulties with the more basic number-after 1-to-9 and count-by-ones 1-to-10 skills. Because of the rule-governed nature of the number sequence, instruction on this skill can then proceed in conjunction with that for counting-by-ones 11 to 29. More specifically, error-detection activities, such as **Good or Bad Counter** (with an abbreviated count), can provide a basis for discussing patterns. For example, "Cookie Monster thinks that right after 25, 26, 27 comes 23. Do you think he's right or wrong?" When difficulties are encountered, help the child to exploit the rule-governed nature of the teens and twenties. For example, if a child has difficulty figuring out what comes after 27, say, "What comes right after seven when we count? [Allow the child to respond.] Eight, right. So what comes right after twenty-*seven* when we count?" Practice of both counting to 29 and answering number-after questions can thus help make the latter skill automatic. As with the error-detection activities, **Count Teacher** can be used to provide practice stating the number after *with a running start.* To provide practice without a running start, use adaptations of the various games used for number after 1 to 9: **Advanced Number-After Dominoes** (see Example 3–18), **Number-After Race** (see Example 3–20) and **Number-After Quiz Game: 11 to 28** (see Example 3–21).

Decade After 10 to 90

First remedy the prerequisite skills (e.g., number after 1 to 9). Instruction on the skill should be done in tandem with counting-by-tens to 100. At first, allow children to respond to decade-after questions by using a running start (starting with 10, counting by tens up to the given number, and then giving the next decade in the sequence). As soon as possible, though, help children to exploit recurring patterns in the number sequence. That is, help them connect the decade-after task with their existing number-after 1-to-9 knowledge. For example, point out: "To answer 'What comes after 60 when we count by tens?' think: 'What comes after six when I count by ones?' Six, *seven.* So when counting by tens, it is sixty, *seventy.*" Once a child has made this connection, practice the skill until it is automatic.

Number After 29 to 99

First remedy any difficulties with the more basic number-after 1-to-9 and 10-to-28 skills. Instruction on the skill should be done in conjunction with counting-by-ones 30 to 100. Help the child exploit the rule-governed nature of the number sequence. For example, if a child has difficulty figuring out what comes after 47, say, "What comes right after seven when we count? [Allow the child to respond.] Eight, right. So what comes right after forty-*seven* when we count?" Practice counting to 100 can help make the number-after skill automatic. Most of the games described for number-after 1 to 9 and 10 to 29 can be easily adapted for practice at this level.

Decade After 100 to 190

First remedy any difficulties with the prerequisite skills (e.g., decade after 10 to 90). Instruction on the skill should be done with that for count-by-tens 100 to 200. To help children enter the decade sequence at a given point rather than count out the sequence each time, exploit the rule-governed nature of the decade sequence. For example, say, "To figure out what comes after 130 when we count by tens, think: 'What comes after 30 when we count by tens? Thirty, forty. So after one hundred thirty comes one hundred forty when we count by tens.' " If need be, relate this skill to the even more familiar number-after 1-to-9 skill. Adapt the various suggested games for other number-after skills to practice this skill until it becomes automatic.

Number After 100 to 199

First remedy any difficulties with the more basic number-after 1-to-9, 10-to-28, and 29-to-99 skills first. Instruction on this skill should be along with that for count by ones 101 to 200. Help the child exploit the rule-governed nature of the number sequence. For example, if a child has difficulty figuring out what comes after 147, say, "What comes right after forty-seven (seven) when we count? [Allow the child to respond.] Forty-eight (eight), right. So what comes right after one hundred forty *seven* when we count?" Most of the games described for other number-after skills can be easily adapted for practice at this level.

Backward Counts: Next Term

Number Before 2 to 10

First ensure that the more basic skills (counting by ones 1 to 10 and number after 1 to 9) are quite automatic. To help a child understand the term before and that the number sequence can proceed in two directions, use a number list. Point out that a number (e.g., 5) has two neighbors or two numbers next to it: one that comes after (6) and one that comes before (4). Once children can figure out number-before responses, work on making the skill automatic. The various activities described for teaching and practicing number-after 1 to 9 can be adapted for number before. For example, Basic (Advanced) Number-After Dominoes (Example 3–18) can, by a simple change of the rules, become **Basic (Advanced) Number-Before Dominoes**.

Number Before 11 to 29

First ensure that the prerequisite skills (count by ones 11 to 19 and 20 to 29, number after 10 to 28, and number before 2 to 10) are quite automatic. If need be, begin practice of number before 11 to 29 with a number list available. The games used for number before 2 to 10 can be adapted for teaching and practicing this skill.

Number Before 30 to 100 and
Decade Before 20 to 100

First ensure that the prerequisite skills (count by ones 30 to 100, number after 29 to 99, number before 2 to 10 and 11 to 29, count by tens to 100, and decade after 10 to 90) are mastered. If needed, begin practice of these skills with a number list available. The games used for the other related skills can be adapted to teach and practice these skills.

Backward Counts: Sequence of Terms

Count Backwards from 10

First remedy any difficulties with the more basic skills of counting by ones 1 to 10 and citing the number before 2 to 10. Initially, have the child count backwards with a number list present. Once the child has an idea of what the count-backwards task entails, use only a partially visible number list as a cue. This can be done with the activity **Peek** (see Example 3–8). Insert a 1-to-10 number list into a sheath, left-end first, so that only the 10 on the number list shows. Before uncovering the next number, ask the child to predict what comes next when you count backwards. If he or she is correct, uncover the 9 and congratulate the child. If the child is incorrect, give him or her a second chance and then have the child uncover the preceding number. Proceed in this manner until you reach 1.

As soon as the child is ready, remove prompts like the number list and require the child to count backwards verbally. For some children, it may take some time and practice before verbally counting backwards becomes efficient.

Count Backwards from 20

First remedy any difficulties with the more basic skills of counting by ones 1 to 20, counting backwards from 10, and number before up to 20. Use the instructional guidelines outlined for counting backwards from 10 to teach and practice counting backwards from 20.

SUMMARY

Though the first portion of the count-by-ones or the decade sequence requires rote memorization, thereafter the counts are rule-governed. Instruction should help kindergartners and first graders find and learn these patterns. The most difficult terms to learn are the exceptions to patterns (e.g., 15) and transition terms (e.g., 40). Once children can automatically produce these forward sequences, they are ready to learn more sophisticated "skip counts," such as counting by twos or fives. Familiarity with forward sequences also permits the development of next-term skills. That is, when given a term, they specify the next term in the count-by-one (or decade) sequence without counting up from one (ten). Because of the rule-governed nature of the number sequence, instruction on counting-by-ones and number-after skills can proceed together for numbers greater than 13 or so. Once these skills are learned, children can begin to operate in the opposite direction and master the number-before (or decade-before) skill. After children can "take one step backwards," they should be able to count backwards in sequence. Though counting backwards from 10 will not present a problem to many primary-age children, counting backwards from larger numbers may.

Chapter 4

Numbering

Numbers are used in a wide variety of ways (see Example 4–1). Indeed, numbering skills are used so often and so automatically by adults that they typically take such skills for granted. For preschool, primary-level, and special education children, however, learning numbering skills and how to use numbers is a real challenge. Oral counting is an important first step but does not itself indicate a mastery of numbering skills or their uses (Ginsburg, 1982).

Numbering skills include *labeling an existing set* (e.g., given five pennies, a child identifies how many pennies there are) and *creating a set* (e.g., asked to get five pennies, a child counts out a set of five from a pile of pennies). Labeling a collection involves assigning a number name to a set. For the most part, children first rely on object counting (*enumeration*) to label collections. In time, children learn other means for defining *cardinality* (the number of items in a set). For example, shown a plate of three cookies ($\underset{O\ \ \ O}{\overset{O}{}}$), kindergarten-age children can, without counting, identify the number of items in the collection. *Recognition of sets* is the result of familiarity with number patterns.

To create a set, children again first rely on counting. Counting out a specific number of objects from a larger pool of objects is called *production of sets*. In time, children can become quite skilled in creating sets. For example, without counting out each finger, they can readily create a *finger pattern* (e.g., represent "3" by immediately and simultaneously putting up three fingers).

Example 4–1 The Importance of Numbers*

Count Disorderly was so confused by numbers that one day he decided not to try to learn them any more. He would just banish all numbers from the country and never allow them to come back. So he wrote out notices and put them up everywhere. When he woke up the next day he found that everyone he knew was packing to leave. His cook was going because she couldn't use numbers to count the amount of ingredients to use in the food she made. The gardener couldn't count the seeds he planted to grow vegetables and flowers. Nobody could tell time because the clocks had to go; they all had numbers. The storekeeper closed his store because no one could figure out how much money to give him without counting. And no one could call anyone or even go visit because there were no more phone numbers to call or house numbers for addresses. Poor Count Disorderly felt very lonely with everyone leaving him. He hadn't even noticed how much people used numbers. He decided to let numbers be used again. Then he gathered all the people together to ask for their help so he could learn how to do all kinds of things with numbers.

---

*This story was written with the assistance of Cathleen A. Mason.

LEARNING

Labeling an Existing Set

Enumeration

Very young children may engage in counting-like activities with sets of objects. However, they may do so without any intention of labeling the set with a number (Baroody, 1987a). Moreover, they may lack the know-how necessary for object counting (enumeration). Indeed, initially, a child may simply pass or wave a finger over a set while spewing out numbers (Fuson and Hall, 1983). If an effort is made to point at objects in a set, the child may just count the objects in any order—recounting some several times and perhaps missing others altogether.

In time, children learn that enumeration involves a one-to-one principle: assigning one and only one counting-sequence number to each

object in a set. In effect, enumeration requires that the child match one-for-
one the items of a collection (e.g., four cookies) and the tags of the number
sequence words (e.g., "one, two, three, four . . ."):

    "one"   "two"   "three"   "four"

Though preschoolers may appreciate the one-to-one principle, they
often have trouble executing it accurately (Beckwith and Restle, 1966;
Gelman and Gallistel, 1978). There are three different kinds of enumeration
errors. First, if children do not know the correct number sequence, they will
make *sequence errors* when counting objects. For example, a child may tag
three blocks: "1, 2, 10."

Second, some children have difficulty coordinating, in a one-to-one
fashion, the processes of saying the number sequence (oral counting) and
pointing to the objects in a set. *Coordination errors,* then, entail not properly
tagging an item (i.e., assigning too many tags to an item or pointing at an
object but not designating it with a tag). Children just learning to enumerate
sets and mentally handicapped children, in particular, may have difficulty
starting or stopping the oral-counting and pointing processes at the same
time (Baroody, 1986a). As a result, a child may point to the first item and
say, "one, two" and thereafter honor the one-to-one principle. Likewise, a
child may get to the last item of, say, a five-object set and let several tags slip
out before stopping the oral count (e.g., "five, six"). Children are especially
prone to this type of coordination error when they rush their counting.

Third, children may fail to keep track of which objects have been
counted and which need to be numbered. As a result, they may skip an
object or count an object more than once. Such *keeping-track errors* are the
most common type of enumeration error and are especially likely if a child
rushes (Fuson, 1988).

Enumeration difficulty is greatly influenced by the arrangement of the
set (e.g., objects in a line are easier to enumerate than those in a
disorganized array) and set size (small sets are easier to enumerate than
larger ones). By the time they enter kindergarten, children can accurately
enumerate sets of 1 to 5 even with disorganized arrays. With larger sets, they
may be able to enumerate those in a linear array but may have difficulty with
those in a disorganized array. Some children entering kindergarten have
not learned efficient keeping-track strategies (e.g., creating a separate pile
for counted items), which would allow them to deal effectively with relatively
complex enumeration tasks (Fuson, 1988). By the end of kindergarten,
though, most children can proficiently *enumerate sets of 6 to 11* or *sets of
11 to 20.*

Cardinality

Children learn early on that enumeration tells how many objects are in a collection (the cardinal designation of the collection). Typically, children learn how to respond to "how-many" questions very quickly. To indicate how many they have counted, preschoolers soon learn that they do not have to repeat the whole count (e.g., "1, 2, 3, 4, 5" for a set of five pennies) but need only repeat the last term of the enumeration process (e.g., "5"). This shortcut is called the *cardinality rule* (Schaeffer, Eggleston, and Scott, 1974).

An understanding of cardinality does not stop with mastering the cardinality rule. A deeper sense of cardinality requires understanding the *identity-conservation principle*—that the number of a set remains the same even though its appearance changes. For example, a set designated as "five" continues to have the same number even though it is lengthened and looks "bigger."

With counting experience, children discover another important aspect of cardinality: It does not matter on which end of a row they start, the outcome is the same (e.g., see Frames A and B of Figure 4–1). Indeed, as long as the one-to-one principle is observed, a set can be enumerated in any order and the cardinal designation of the set will not change (see Frame C of Figure 4–1). This property of the numbering process is called the *order-irrelevance principle*. Though a relatively sophisticated concept (Baroody, 1984c), it is typically acquired before children enter kindergarten (Gelman and Gallistel, 1978; Gelman and Meck, 1987).

Recognition of Sets

Young children learn to recognize immediately various number configurations (e.g., ⚬⚬⚬ is "three" or ⚬⚬⚬⚬ is "four"). *The recognition of sets 1 to 3* develops quite early, because such small sets are so easily distinguished from one another and other sets. (Indeed, children may recognize and label sets of one or two before they learn how to enumerate sets.) Later, children become familiar with the patterns of somewhat larger sets (e.g., ⚬⚬⚬⚬⚬ = "five" or ⚬⚬⚬⚬⚬⚬ = "six"). *Recognition of sets 4 to 6* primarily depends on the amount of exposure to such number patterns (e.g., experience playing dice games). Automatic recognition of number patterns provides children with important concrete models of number (von Glasersfeld, 1982) and later can facilitate the development of informal arithmetic (e.g., see Figure 6–1).

Figure 4-1 Some Different Ways to Count a Row of Five Items

A. A left-to-right count

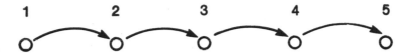

B. A right-to-left count

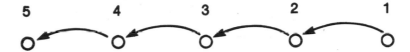

C. A count beginning with the mid-item

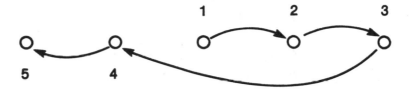

Creating a Set

Production of Sets

Preschool children also learn to count out (produce) a specified number of objects from a group of objects. Production of a given number is more difficult than labeling an existing set (enumeration), because it requires the child to remember how many objects have been requested and to stop counting objects when that many objects have been reached (Resnick and Ford, 1981).

A common error, especially among very young and mentally handicapped children, is continuing to count out pennies even after the specified amount has been reached (Baroody, 1986a). Children make a "no-stop" error (e.g., count all 10 pennies available) because they do not (1) understand the task (that they are supposed to stop at the requested amount); (2) forget the requested amount; or (3) forget to stop at the requested number. Another error that occurs with some regularity among young and mentally handicapped children is counting out an incorrect number of items but tagging the last item with the requested number (Baroody, 1986a). An example of this end-with-requested-number error is—in response for five pennies—counting out three pennies but tagging the pennies "1, 2, 5." Children make an end-with-the-requested-number error because they do not (1) understand the task or (2) care to make the effort to complete the production process. The latter can be checked by asking the child to take a specified number of highly desired items to keep.

Less serious errors include minor errors in counting out pennies in a one-to-one fashion or in keeping track of counted pennies and those still available. If a child does not have an efficient keeping-track strategy, he or she may come up with one or two too few (if counted items are recounted) or too many (if uncounted items are included in the counted pile).

Typically, accurate *production of sets 1 to 5* is achieved earlier than accurate *production of sets 6 to 20.* With small sets, it is relatively easy to keep track of the object-counting process and when to stop.

Finger Patterns

Children may often be more successful in creating cardinal sets with their fingers than with other objects (Steffe, von Glasersfeld, Richards, and Cobb, 1983). Initially, children have to count their fingers to put up, say, five fingers. In time, they learn automatic finger patterns (e.g., simultaneously extending all the fingers on one hand to represent five). Children master the *finger patterns 1 to 5* before the *finger patterns 6 to 10.*

The sequence of numbering competencies by grade level and developmental order is summarized in Table 4–1.

INSTRUCTION

Preschoolers need interesting opportunities to use numbering skills more than they need direct training. By the time they enter kindergarten, children typically have a good start on numbering skills at least with sets of up to five items. For those kindergartners who have not mastered these basic numbering skills, intensive remedial efforts are needed. They should be given interesting and extended practice with enumerating and producing sets of 1 to 5. Feedback and guidance are particularly important for such children.

If simply given the opportunity to practice numbering skills with larger sets, many children will master such competencies quickly. Some, though, will need guidance. For example, a portion of any kindergarten class would

Table 4–1 Sequence of Numbering Competencies by Grade Level and Developmental Order

Level	Labeling an Existing Set	Creating a Set
PK	Enumeration of sets 1 to 5	—
	Cardinality rule	—
	Identity-conservation principle	—
	Recognition of sets 1 to 3	—
	Order-irrelevance principle	—
	—	Finger patterns 1 to 5
	—	Production of sets 1 to 5
K	Enumeration of sets 6 to 10	—
	Recognition of sets 4 to 6	—
	—	Production of sets 6 to 10
	Enumeration of sets 11 to 20	Production of sets 11 to 20
1	—	Finger patterns 6 to 10

benefit from a teacher's tip or a discussion on how to organize their enumeration and production efforts in order to keep track efficiently. An ideal opportunity to provide needed feedback is when children are engaged in games or activities in which numbering skills are a natural and integral part.

Labeling an Existing Set

Enumeration of Sets 1 to 5

First ensure that a child can count by ones to at least five and do so automatically. If this skill is not automatic, it will be difficult for the child to coordinate oral counting with pointing to objects in a one-to-one fashion.

The nature of enumeration training depends on a child's specific difficulty. If a child does not appear to make any effort at one-to-one counting, it is essential to help the child appreciate the one-to-one principle (e.g., see the story in Example 4–2). Begin with a **Pointing Exercise**, using a relatively easy set of objects (e.g., three blocks in a row). Have the child point once and only once to each object in the set. After the child has mastered this skill, introduce enumeration. If necessary, first say the numbers for the child while he or she points to each block. Then have the child count out the number sequence as he or she points to the blocks. Gradually work toward more difficult (larger and less orderly) sets.

Example 4–2   The Importance of Counting One-to-One

Count Disorderly was planning a gala party that he hoped would be the social event of the year. He wanted to have such a wonderful party that everyone in the kingdom would say, "Oh, that marvelous Count Disorderly puts on such a nice party." Count Disorderly eagerly began planning his party, all the time thinking how wonderful it would be and how much people would thank him for putting on such a marvelous party.

The first thing that Count Disorderly did was to go down to the mailroom to find out how many invitations had been returned so that he would know how many guests were coming to his party. In the mailroom he found a big pack of invitations that had been returned. He poured the invitations out of the bag, and they scattered out all over the floor. Count Disorderly was so excited that he did not bother to arrange the invitations as he sang, "One, two— I'm so cool—three, four—I'm no bore—five, six—I'm the pick— seven, eight—I'm really great—nine, ten—I'm a gem." Count Disorderly was now so excited, he rushed to the kitchen and told the cook to prepare food and cake for ten guests for his party.

The day of the big party, everyone in the kingdom who sent in their invitations came to Count Disorderly's castle. A lot of people showed up—a lot more than the ten Count Disorderly had counted and was expecting. Because there was food and cake for only ten people, most guests had nothing to eat.

Everywhere people whispered, "I'm really hungry. Is there any food anywhere? This is a terrible party. What a mean trick Count Disorderly played on us, inviting all these people to a party but not giving them any food or cake. Count Disorderly is despicable!"

Count Disorderly was very sad. His big party was a big flop. He was now the most hated man in the country. Then Count Disorderly had an idea: "I'll give another, bigger party." So Count Disorderly sent out invitations to everyone in the kingdom, inviting them to his second party.

Unfortunately, nearly everyone in the kingdom thought that Count Disorderly was just trying to play another mean trick on them. All across the kingdom people said, "I'm not going to be tricked into going to a party without food and cake by Count Disorderly again." So just about everyone threw away their invitations.

A week later, Count Disorderly went down to the mailroom to see how many invitations had been returned. He opened up the mail bag; out fell two invitations. Count Disorderly started counting the invitations: "One, two." Dismayed, he said, "No, no, that can't be.

There has to be more." So Count Disorderly pointed at each of the invitations and said, "Three, four." He counted them again: "Five, six," and again: "Seven, eight," and again: "Nine, ten." Indeed, he kept recounting those two invitations into the night. When he stopped counting, Count Disorderly had reached 100. "One hundred guests," Count Disorderly exclaimed, "That's more like it. This is going to be the best party ever." So Count Disorderly told the cook to prepare food and cake for 100 guests.

On the day of the party, only two guests showed up at Count Disorderly's castle. Count Disorderly was very sad, because he was expecting 100 people. Not only was his party a flop, but Count Disorderly had spent all his candy-and-toy money for the year buying food and cake that would now not be eaten. Poor Count Disorderly.

Count Disorderly turned to his brother, Count Orderly, who was one of the two guests, and complained bitterly, "For my first party, I counted the invitations but I did not have enough food and cake. For this party, I counted the invitations and now I have too much food and cake. Why don't things come out right?"

Count Orderly felt badly for his brother, Count Disorderly, and offered to help: "Show me the invitations to your parties." Count Disorderly took Count Orderly to the mailroom. There, he showed Count Orderly the huge bag of invitations for the first party and how he had counted them: "One, two—I'm so cool—three, four—I'm no bore—five, six—I'm the pick—seven, eight—I'm really great—nine, ten—I'm a gem." Then Count Disorderly showed his brother the bag with two invitations for this party and how he counted, and re-counted, and counted them again until he got to 100.

Count Orderly just shook his head. "My dear Count Disorderly," he said, "you can't say and do anything you want when you count. You have to be careful. For this big pile of invitations, you can't just point at the pile and say some numbers. You have to point to *each* invitation in the pile as you say *a* number. And for this small pile, you can't keep pointing to the same two invitations as you say numbers. You have to point to *each* invitation as you say *a* number. See: 'one, two.'"

Count Disorderly was very happy that his brother Count Orderly had taught him to count carefully. He sent a letter to everyone in the kingdom explaining his mistake. He also sent everyone an invitation for another party, with the promise that he would count each invitation very carefully so that everyone would have food and cake.

If a child seems to understand the one-to-one principle but still frequently misenumerates sets, the child may need to learn keeping-track strategies. That is, the child must learn how to separate already-counted objects from yet-to-be-counted objects (see the story in Example 4–3). Point out that counted objects can be put in their own pile far enough away so that they are not confused with uncounted objects. For sets of objects that are fixed, start in a well-defined place, such as a corner or an end, and count in a particular direction.

Example 4–3   Orderly Count Story*

It was the day of the big baseball game. Count Disorderly was busy getting his players excited to win. The umpire came over and said, "We're ready to start, but we need to know if you have enough players. You need at least nine." So Count Disorderly began counting his players. While he counted, the players wandered around. Some of the players walked off to talk to players on the other team. Several of the others walked off to throw a baseball around, and a couple of players walked off to get drinks of water. Poor Count Disorderly kept getting confused. He did not know which players he had already counted and which needed to be counted. He finally ended up with a count of three players. He knew that was wrong because he had to have more than three players so he tried again. Because the players kept moving around, Count Disorderly got confused again and counted all the way to ninety-nine. Now Count Disorderly knew he did not have that many players.

Meanwhile, the other team was getting restless, and the umpire was getting angry because of the long wait. Count Orderly arrived on the scene to watch the game. His brother, Count Disorderly, rushed over and said, "You have to help me! I can't figure out if I have enough players. The umpire is going to cancel the game if I don't hurry." Count Orderly came over and saw all the players running around. "Well, we can't count everyone if they don't stay put." He had all the players sit on the bench. Count Orderly then told Count Disorderly to start on one end of the bench, walk down the row, and tap each one on the shoulder as he counted. Count Disorderly started on one end and counted each player on the bench until he got to the end of the row. He counted nine players. "Aha," said Count Disorderly, "we have exactly nine players."

"Play ball!" yelled the umpire and the game started.

*This story was written with the assistance of Cathleen A. Mason.

If the child has difficulty starting (or stopping) the oral counting and pointing processes simultaneously, have the child slow down. Indeed, with children who make any type of errors, it is important to emphasize that it is more important to count objects slowly and carefully rather than quickly and inaccurately.

Error-detection activities, such as **Good and Bad Counter** or **The Absent-Minded Counter** (Example 3–2), can readily be adopted for enumeration training and are great fun for children. Model correct enumeration and various enumeration errors (examples and nonexamples of the one-to-one principle). Then have a child, group of children, or class evaluate the correctness of the count and, if incorrect, indicate what was wrong. For example, count the fingers on a child's hand but make sequence errors (e.g., point to each finger while saying, "1, 2, 3, 9, 10"), coordination errors (e.g., point to the first finger and say, "1, 2," and then complete the count with, "3, 4, 5, 6"), or keeping-track errors (e.g., skip a finger or go back and count a finger a second time). Such exercises make an excellent vehicle for pointing out and discussing the one-to-one principle underlying enumeration and how to implement this principle correctly.

Enumeration practice can be accomplished with numerous games (e.g., **Animal Spots** described in Example 2–1; **Number-After Dominoes** as described in Example 3–18 but with a regular set of dominoes and **Number-After Race** described in Example 3–20; **Hidden Stars** described in Example 4–5 of this chapter; and **Lotto Same Number, Clue, Cards More Than**, and **Dice More Than** described in Chapter 5). Any board game that uses a die to determine the number of spaces a player can move (like the **Soccer** game described in Example 4–4) can provide enumeration practice as well.

The complexity of the dot arrangement can be varied according to children's readiness. For very young children just beginning to master the skill, use a linear array of dots. This minimizes the demands of keeping track of the starting point and what items have already been counted (as long as a child starts at one end and counts in one direction). With somewhat more experienced counters, arrange the signal dots in patterns such as:

$$\begin{smallmatrix} \circ \\ \circ\ \circ \end{smallmatrix}\ ,\quad \begin{smallmatrix} \circ \\ \circ\circ\circ \end{smallmatrix}\ ,\quad \begin{smallmatrix} \circ\ \circ \\ \circ\ \ \circ \end{smallmatrix}\ ,\quad \begin{smallmatrix} \circ\ \circ \\ \circ\circ\circ \end{smallmatrix}\ ,\quad \text{and}\quad \begin{smallmatrix} \circ\ \circ \\ \circ \\ \circ\ \circ \end{smallmatrix}\ .$$

These arrangements require some keeping-track effort. For relatively advanced children, use dice with irregular arrays that require careful keeping-track strategies.

It may be helpful to use enlarged dice made of balsa wood, and large signal dots covered with clear contact paper. Alternatively, a deck of 5″ × 8″ cards with 1 to 5 half-inch dots attached can be substituted for a die.

Example 4–4 Soccer

Objective: Enumeration of sets 1 to 5 (in either orderly or disorderly arrays).

Grade Level: PK.

Participants: Two players.

Materials: Soccer-field board (see below), ball marker, and cards or a die with 0 to 5 dots.

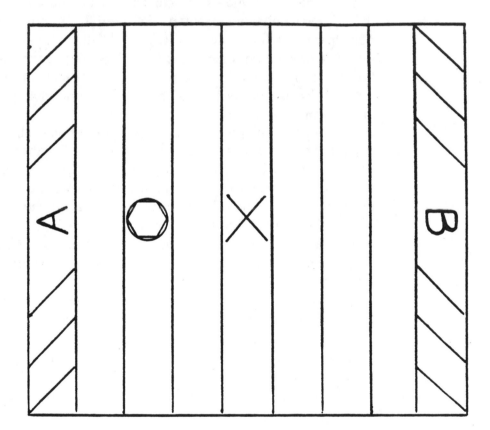

Procedure: Place the ball marker at midfield (on the space marked X). The players alternate turns. On their turn, the players draw a card or throw a die to determine how many spaces they can advance the ball. For practice in counting sets 1 to 5, start with the ball at midfield. A player scores by advancing the ball into an opponent's goal (hatched-marked space). Then replace the ball at the starting point and continue play until a predetermined number of points (or rolls) is reached, or time runs out.

Cardinality Rule

First ensure that a child can count orally to at least five and has some appreciation of the one-to-one principle governing enumeration before introducing the cardinality rule. Examples and nonexamples (correct and incorrect applications) of the cardinality rule can be demonstrated and discussed by using the error-detection exercise **Good or Bad Counter** (Example 3–2). The **Hidden-Stars Game** (Example 4–5) is another interesting and useful teaching device. Model the cardinality rule by counting a small set of, say, two objects ("One, two.") and then announce, "So there are *two* stars." Next, turn the card over and ask, "How many stars am I hiding?" Afterward, have the child count a different small set and ask, "How many stars did you count?" Then cover this set and ask, "How many stars am I hiding?" If necessary, ask, "How many stars did you count?" This exercise will be sufficient for most children to master the cardinality rule.

If the child does not learn the rule quickly, continue the modeling-and-practice procedure described above in conjunction with pattern recognition of sets 1 to 3. If the child picks up on the cardinality rule, play Hidden Stars with both small- and large-number sets. If a child cannot enumerate accurately sets of 6 to 20 items, enumerate the sets for the child. Then continue the game as usual: Turn the card over and ask the child how many stars there are. It is a good idea to practice with various objects. For example, **Animal-Spots** (described in Example 2–1) provides an opportunity to practice the rule with dots and pegs.

Example 4–5 Hidden-Stars Game

Objective: Cardinality rule with sets of 2 to 5.

Grade Level: PK.

Participants: One, two, or three children.

Materials: A number of "star cards" (3″ × 5″ cards on which two to five stars are pasted in a row about ½ inch apart).

Procedure: Explain, "In the Hidden-Stars game, the hider [the teacher or a child] shows the player(s) some stars. The player counts them. Then the hider covers them up and the player tries to tell how many stars the hider is hiding." If a player does not spontaneously count a star card, the hider can say, "Count this row of stars." After the player counts the set, the hider covers the card and says, "How many stars am I hiding?"

Identity-Conservation Principle

First ensure that the child masters the prerequisite competencies: counting by ones to 10, enumeration 1 to 5, and the cardinality rule. The **Hidden-Penny Game** (Example 4–6) can be used to help children induce the identity-conservation principle. Using small sets of two, three, or four items will facilitate discovery of the principle, because young children can see that the number of items in a set remains the same despite changes in appearance. Once children grasp this principle with small sets, try the exercise with larger sets. Moreover, use a variety of initial appearances (e.g., rows, circles, triangles, rectangles, random arrangements) and changed appearances (e.g., lengthening, shortening, creating a [new] geometric shape, mixing up the internal arrangement).

Example 4–6   Hidden-Penny Game

Objective: Understanding that changes in physical appearance do not change the number of items in a set.

Grade Level: PK.

Participants: A single child or a small group of children.

Materials: Six pennies, chips, or other small countable objects and a cover (8½″ × 11″ piece of thin cardboard).

Procedure: Explain, "In the Hidden-Penny game, you count the pennies, I cover them up, and you try to tell me how many I'm hiding." Set out a number of pennies in a row about one inch apart. Either have a child count the set or count the set together. Then say, "Watch what I do with these *n* pennies before I hide them." Change the appearance of the row by lengthening or shortening the row or creating a new pattern (circle, triangle, cross, etc.). Cover the set and say, "How many pennies am I hiding?" If the child is incorrect, count the set again and ask if it is the same number counted before.

Recognition of Sets 1 to 3

Typically, special training is not required for this skill. Any game that uses a die or requires children to count small sets of dots or other forms can be used (e.g., **Animal Spots**, described in Example 2–1; **Number-After Dominoes** with a regular set of dominoes and **Number-After Race**, described in Examples 3–18 and 3–20; **Hidden Stars**, described in Example 4–5; and **Lotto Same Number**, **Clue**, **Cards More Than**, and **Dice More Than**, described in Chapter 5). With repeated exposure, children will learn spontaneously to recognize immediately the various small-set arrangements. Children may learn to recognize sets of one and two and possibly three even before they can effectively enumerate very small sets. Thus, practice on this skill (e.g., use of the **Quick-Look Game** described in Example 4–7) need not await mastery of enumeration of sets 1 to 5 or even 1 to 3—*if* someone identifies the patterns by number for the child. On the other hand, learning to recognize patterns involving three or more objects is facilitated by accurate enumeration. It is important, after all, for a child to count a pattern repeatedly and arrive at the same cardinal designation each time. Imagine a child's confusion even if he or she recognized ⊙⊙⊙ as "three" but counted it several times and got "two" and "four."

Example 4–7   Quick-Look Game: 1–3

Objective: Automatic recognition of sets 1 to 3.

Grade Level: PK.

Participants: Two children or two small teams of players.

Materials: Cards with one, two, or three 2-cm dots, respectively. The dots should be pasted on the cards in random fashion.

Procedure: Explain, "I'm going to show you some cards with dots on them. I'll show you the cards very fast. So look carefully at the card and quickly try to see how many dots there are. Ready?" Show the child each card in turn for two seconds and say, "How many dots did you see?" If correct, the child gets to keep the card (scores one point) for his or her team.

Order-Irrelevance Principle

First remedy any deficiencies in the prerequisite skills: enumeration 1 to 5 or 6 to 10 and the cardinality rule. Provide the child with plenty of opportunities to enumerate sets—particularly small sets. It may be helpful to ask probing questions, such as, "Do you think you will get the same number if you count the other way?" The error-detection activity **Good or Bad Counter** (Example 3–2) can provide an opportunity to illustrate and discuss valid and invalid applications of the order-irrelevance principle. Another activity that may help direct children's attention to this issue is the **Count-Prediction Activity** (Example 4–8).

Example 4–8   Count-Prediction Activity

Objective: Understanding that as long as the one-to-one principle is observed, the items of a set can be enumerated in any order and the cardinal designation of the set will not change.

Grade Level: PK.

Participants: One child or a small group of children.

Materials: Five blocks and a Cookie-Monster Muppet (or other hand puppet, stuffed animal, or doll).

Procedure: Explain to a child that Cookie Monster is just learning to count objects and needs help. Request that the child serve as Cookie Monster's teacher. After a participant has enumerated a set, have Cookie Monster (or some other pretend pupil) ask what counting the set in another way produces (see Examples A and B below).

Example A.   Put out a set of four blocks and say, "Show Cookie Monster how to count these blocks." After the child finishes, ask, "How many are there?" If the child accurately enumerates the set and correctly uses the cardinality rule, proceed with the order-irrelevance questions. Point to the last item counted by the child and say, "Could Cookie Monster make this number one and count the other way?" If the child says "yes," ask, "Cookie Monster does not know what he would get if he counted that way. Can you tell Cookie Monster how many he would count?" If he or she begins to count, cover the set and say "Before you finish counting, what do you think you will get when you finish counting?"

Example B.   Put out a set of five blocks. Use the same procedure described above with the following exception: After the child counts the set and identifies its cardinal value, point to the *middle* item and say, "Could Cookie Monster make this number one and count the blocks? What would he get if he started here [point to the middle item] and counted all the blocks?"

Recognition of Sets 4 to 6

First remedy any deficiencies in more basic skills (recognition of sets 1 to 3 and enumeration of sets 1 to 5 and 6 to 10). Discussing the fact that sets of three or more objects form patterns may facilitate children's mastery. Encourage children to describe and illustrate as many different easily recognizable patterns a number can make (e.g., six can look like: ○○○ ○○○ ○○○ ○○○). The lesson does have to be restricted to numbers up to six.

Frequent exposure to games that use a die or require counting small sets of dots or other forms is often sufficient for pattern-recognition learning (see games described for pattern recognition 1 to 3). Kindergartners can practice this skill directly by playing **Quick-Look Game: 1–6.** Simply add cards with four, five, and six dots to the deck used for the basic version described in Example 4–7. (The teacher or an assigned judge can keep time by using a stopwatch or counting, "One-and-a-two.")

Enumeration of Sets 6 to 10

First remedy any deficiencies in prerequisite skills: counting by ones 1 to 10 and enumeration of sets 1 to 5. Because keeping track of counted and uncounted items with larger sets requires attention, it is essential that a child count by ones efficiently. Indeed, it is crucial that the one-for-one coordination of oral counting *and* pointing be automatic—that the tagging process require little conscious effort.

If counting by ones and one-to-one counting are automatic, then attention can be focused on keeping track of counted and uncounted items. If the child has not already mastered keeping-track strategies with smaller sets, encourage the child to consider how this can be done. If the child continues to have difficulty, point out specific keeping-track strategies (e.g., checking off objects in a picture or list, putting counted items in a separate pile or container). In this regard, note the suggestion by Count Orderly to Count Disorderly in the story of Example 4–3. For some children, it may be important to encourage them to count objects slowly and carefully.

Enumeration practice can be achieved by adapting the games recommended for enumeration of sets 1 to 5. A large-number die (balsa wood cube with five to ten dots) or large-number cards (5″ × 8″ index cards with six to ten dots) can be substituted for a small-number die or cards. For **Soccer**, for instance, change the rules so that the ball starts in a player's own goal zone (instead of midfield, where a score would occur on virtually every turn with a five- to ten-dot die).

Enumeration of Sets 11 to 20

First remedy any deficiencies in prerequisite skills: counting by ones 1 to 20 and enumeration of sets 1 to 5 and 6 to 10. Because keeping track of counted and uncounted items with larger sets requires considerable attention, it is important that more basic skills (counting by ones to 20 and one-to-one counting) be automatic to the point that they do not require conscious effort. For children who are having keeping-track difficulties, see the instructional guidelines outlined above for enumeration 6 to 10.

Enumeration practice can be achieved by adapting the games recommended for enumeration of sets 1 to 5. Large-number cards (5″ × 8″ index cards with eleven to twenty dots) can be substituted for small-number cards. For **Soccer**, for instance, use a field with fifteen instead of seven spaces between the goals and start play with the ball on a player's own goal zone (instead of midfield).

Creating a Set

Production of Sets 1 to 5

First ensure that the component skills (counting by ones and enumeration of sets 1 to 5) are accurate and automatic. If the child can read numerals, it may help initially in production instruction to put out a sign indicating the requested number. Explain, "We want to count out just three pennies from this pile of pennies. Count out pennies until you get to three. This number [point to the sign with the numeral 3] will remind you when you need to stop counting." If necessary, ask the child after each counted object if he or she should stop (e.g., "One. Is that the number you need to stop at? [point to the card with the numeral 3] Two. Is that . . . ?"). Then proceed to producing sets without prompt cards. This instruction can take place while playing a game with the child such as the **Modified Hidden-Penny Game** (Example 4–9).

If a child continues to make, say, no-stop errors, ask the child what the requested number is. If it appears that the child is having difficulty remembering the requested amount, point out the importance of re-membering the requested number and how the child can remember the number (e.g., rehearse the number by saying it several times before getting involved in a counting-out process). If the child makes end-with-the-requested-number errors, efforts need to focus on getting the child to use a one-to-one process until the requested number is reached (rather than helping the child to remember the requested amount).

With all types of errors, help the child acquire efficient keeping-track strategies. For example, when practicing production of sets, have the child put already-counted items in a jar lid or plate to separate them from the uncounted pile of items. Again, error-detection activities, such as **Good or Bad Counter** and **The Absent-Minded Counter** (Example 3–2) can be useful in modeling and discussing correct and incorrect production procedures.

Production of sets can be practiced with a game like **Animal Spots** (Example 2–1). After a child has counted the dots on the die, retrieving the corresponding number of pegs ("spots") from the dish of pegs is a production task. Games where a child has to move a specified number of spaces (e.g., **Number-After Race**, described in Example 3–18 and **Soccer**, described in Example 4–4) also serve to practice the production skill. (The set of "things" produced are, in these cases, the number of spaces moved.) **Star Collector** (Example 4–10) entails both counting out objects and spaces.

Example 4–9   Modified Hidden-Penny Game

Objective: Counting out one to five objects (as requested) from a pile of objects.

Grade Level: PK.

Participants: One child or two small teams of players.

Materials: Ten pennies, chips, or other small countable objects.

Procedure: Teach the participant(s) the Hidden-Penny game (used to teach the cardinality rule). If playing with a single child, say, "Let's play the Hidden-Penny game, but this time you hide the pennies. Here are the pennies." Then ask the child to put out two to five pennies for you to count. Have the child hide the pennies so that you can make a guess (correctly and incorrectly). If two teams of children play, have one side roll a (numeral) die to determine how many pennies they will put out. Then, a player from the other team has to count the set and judge how many are hidden.

Example 4–10   Star Collector

Objectives: Enumeration or pattern recognition of sets 1 to 5 and the cardinality rule as well as production of sets 1 to 5.

Grade Level: PK.

Participants: Two to four children.

Materials: Star-Collector Board (see below), dot die with 0 to 5 dots, and star forms or other countable objects to represent stars.

Procedure: On their turn, players role the die to determine how many spaces they can move. If a player lands on a square with stars, he or she can collect the number of stars depicted on the square. The player(s) with the largest number of stars at the end of the game wins.

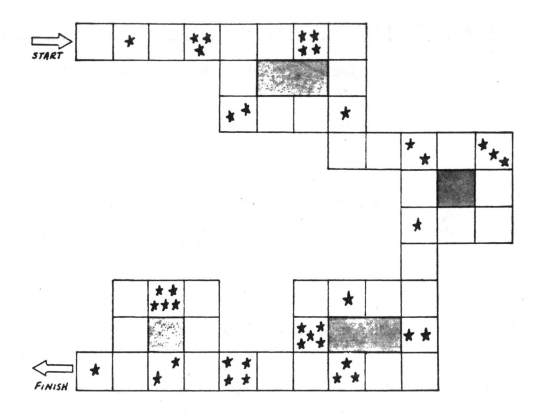

Finger Patterns 1 to 5

For some children, it may be productive to teach finger patterns 1 to 5 directly. Indicate the number and model its associated finger pattern. Then ask the child to imitate the finger pattern for that number. Some children may have to learn the finger patterns in a more roundabout but perhaps more meaningful way. For these children, it may be helpful to have them practice counting out a specified number of fingers. Many children will, in time, naturally adopt finger patterns because they require less effort. Several activities (**Hand Shapes** and **Finger Puppets**) for practicing finger patterns are described in Chapter 4 of Baroody, 1987. Another activity is **Long-Distance Number Communications**. A team of two (or more) children stationed across the room from each other have to communicate messages to each other composed of numbers. Because verbal and written communications are not allowed, the children have to use fingers to relay their number messages. In more elaborate forms of the activity, teams could compete against each other to see which was the quickest and most accurate. Alternatively, a team can compete against its own accuracy and speed record.

Production of Sets 6 to 10 and Production of Sets 11 to 20

First ensure that the prerequisite skills (production of sets 1 to 5 or 6 to 10 and counting by ones 1 to 10 or 1 to 20) are automatic. Then have the child practice the skill in a wide variety of settings:

- The games described for production of sets 1 to 5 can be adapted for this purpose.

- A child can serve as the teacher's helper and retrieve a specified number of straws, pencils, and so on.

- The child can be assigned the duty of scorekeeper and record with marks a specified number of points for players.

In each setting, it might be helpful to encourage the child to consider how to best separate counted and uncounted items to keep track of the count.

Finger Patterns 6 to 10

First ensure that the more basic skill (finger patterns 1 to 5) is automatic. For six, eight, and ten, at least, it may help to model the "doubles pattern": three, four, and five fingers up on each hand. Indeed, the finger pattern for ten should be relatively easy for children to pick up. Some children may find it easier to think in terms of five and so many more (e.g., six is five fingers up on one hand and one more on the other). The activities used to practice finger patterns 1 to 5 can be used to practice this skill as well.

SUMMARY

Even before they enter school, children typically master numbering skills—at least with small sets. Enumeration, which entails assigning *a* number-sequence term to each item in a set, is one mechanism for labeling an existing set. Only a few children entering kindergarten will need help coordinating the oral counting and pointing processes to produce a tag for each point. Many may need help learning keeping-track strategies, particularly with larger sets in disorderly arrangements.

Nearly all children naturally learn to recognize that the last tag in the enumeration process stands for the whole set (the cardinality rule) and that this number label is still applicable even after (1) the physical appearance of the set has been changed (identity-conservation principle) or (2) the set is recounted in a different fashion (order-irrelevance principle). With experience, children can simply recognize how many items are in a set, without enumerating it. As with enumeration, children acquire this set-labeling skill with very small sets (1 to 3) first and then somewhat larger ones. Creating sets with objects (production of sets) or with fingers (finger patterns) builds on and develops somewhat later than enumeration. Usually kindergartners will master these skills with numbers up to 5 on their own but may need help representing larger sets.

Chapter 5

Numerical Relationships

The numbering skills discussed in Chapter 4, such as enumeration and production, involve a single collection. Numerical relationships involve two (or more) collections. Two collections are equivalent if they contain the same number of items; they are inequivalent if they contain a different number of items. A concept of *equivalence* and *inequivalence* is a fundamental ingredient for understanding number and operations with numbers (arithmetic). Counting experience plays an integral role in learning about numerical relationships.

Two inequivalent collections can be compared or ordered in terms of which set is "more" and which is "less." A *gross comparison* refers to two collections or numbers that differ by many (e.g., Which is more: 1 or 10? Which is less: 4 or 7?). A *fine comparison* refers to collections or numbers that differ by one (e.g., Which is more: 2 or 3? Which is less: 3 or 4?).

LEARNING

Equivalence

A primitive ability to judge the equivalence or inequivalence of two collections is based on direct perception and may be present before children can enumerate accurately. The *perception of same* entails readily recognizing the equivalence of two very small sets of one, two, or three items. Even two-year-old children can see that OO and O O have the "same number" but are different from O or OOO (Wagner and Walters, 1982).

The perception of same can also involve an equivalence judgment based on perceptual cues. For instance, the two rows below have the same length. Thus, without counting, it is clear that there are the same number of white dots as black dots. A child who has difficulty with such a task may not understand the phrase "same number."

● ● ● ● ● ● ●

○ ○ ○ ○ ○ ○ ○

Direct perception is not always useful in judging same number. The accuracy of such judgments drops off dramatically as set size increases. Moreover, sometimes appearances can be deceiving. For instance, though two lines at check-out counters have the same length, it does not guarantee that there are exactly the same number of people in each.

In time, children learn that numbers can be used to compare quantities and that counting is more reliable than depending on direct perception: If two collections have the same number label, then the collections are equivalent (have the same number of objects)—*despite* differences or changes in appearance (e.g., Gelman, 1972). For example, in spite of different appearances, the following sets are equivalent because both have

"seven":

Because they can recognize small number patterns relatively early and count small sets more efficiently, children can determine *same number for sets of 1 to 5* before they can gauge *same number for sets 6 to 10* (Klahr and Wallace, 1973; Schaeffer, Eggleston, and Scott, 1974). Particularly with larger sets, a child may fail to establish the equivalence of two sets because he or she (1) inaccurately enumerates one set (or both), (2) does not think to count the sets, or (3) does not want to expend the effort needed to enumerate the sets.

Children eventually learn a noncounting method for gauging same or different (e.g., Elkind, 1964; Gelman and Gallistel, 1978; Lawson, Baron, and Siegel, 1974; Zimiles, 1963). *Matching sets* involves putting two sets in one-to-one correspondence: matching an item in one set to one in the other set. If two collections match up, then the collections are equivalent in spite of superficial differences in appearance or changes in the appearance of one of the sets. Children have little difficulty in learning to put out one item for each item of an existing set, and they readily recognize that the two equally long rows are equivalent in number. However, young children fail to realize that the equivalence relationship established by matching is unaffected by, say, lengthening one of the rows. Now a young child says the longer row has more. In time, the child will count each row and conclude that initial match still holds despite the fact that one row looks like more. Eventually, the child does not even have to count; it is obvious that nothing has been added or taken away and so the initial match is "conserved" despite changes in appearance. A "mature" concept of matching sets (number conservation) implies this last stage of logical certainty (Piaget, 1965a).

Inequivalence

Gross Comparisons

Like the perception of same, the ability to identify the larger of two grossly different sets as more does not depend on counting and develops very early. The *perception of more* is based on direct perception: Which of two sets is bigger, longer, or more crowded? For example, a set of pennies that covers a larger area than another frequently has more coins. Children naturally have the ability to see the differences in set size. What they must learn is the meaning of the term "more" so that they can label the larger set correctly and consistently.

At first, children do not realize that numbers are associated with magnitude. For instance, they do not realize that "three" stands for a quantity that is more than "two." When asked to compare two numbers, such children may simply guess or use a response bias of, say, always choosing the last number heard.

In time, children recognize that the number sequence represents increasingly larger quantities and can be useful in making comparisons. At first, they may be able to make gross but not fine comparisons of number. For example, they may know that nine is more than two but may be confused about whether nine is more than eight. They find the first comparison easier than the second because nine is much further along in the counting sequence than is two. Because of their familiarity with the number sequence to 10, children typically learn to make *gross comparisons involving 1 to 10* before they enter kindergarten (Schaeffer, Eggleston, and Scott, 1974). As they learn more of the number sequence, this ability is readily extended. By the end of first grade, children can make *gross comparisons involving 11 to 100* with facility. Obviously, if a child does not know or is not familiar with a portion of the number sequence, accurate gross comparisons are not possible.

Judging "more" is easier than "less," in part because the word more is used more frequently and more readily understood by children. A child who does not understand the term less may, for example, respond by giving the larger of two terms—the term that is more. As a result, the ability to make *gross comparisons of less involving 1 to 10* may develop some time after similar comparisons of more.

Fine Comparisons

With very small collections, even very young children usually distinguish between and choose the larger of two sets that differ by only one item (e.g., O O versus O O O). The *perception of fine differences with 1 to 4* objects, in fact, may be a concrete and important basis for realizing that numbers are connected with magnitude. Because children can *see* that "three" objects is more than "two," they learn that the term three is associated with a larger quantity than is the term two.

In time, children use their knowledge of the number sequence to make precise numerical judgments of more. Children learn to make such *fine comparisons with 1 to 5* first. At about four years of age, many children discover a general fine-comparison rule: A number that comes after another in the number sequence is (one) more than its predecessor (Schaeffer, Eggleston, and Scott, 1974). As children master the number-after relationships for more and more of the number sequence, they can apply the fine-comparison rule to larger and larger numbers. For example, once the knowledge that nine follows eight becomes automatic, children can quickly determine that nine is more than eight.

Knowledge of number-after relationships and the fine-comparison rule enables the majority of children entering kindergarten to make *fine comparisons with 6 to 10*. By the end of first grade, children have mastered the count sequence (number-after relationships) to 100 and so can make even *fine comparisons from 11 to 100*. However, a child who does not have command over the number-after skill will encounter difficulty in making fine comparisons.

Similarly, automatic knowledge of number-before relationships permits children mentally to make fine comparisons of less. For example, children learn that four is (one) less than five because four comes just before five when they count. Determining *fine comparisons of less with 1 to 10* may develop somewhat later than gauging fine comparisons of more than 1 to 10, and specifying *fine comparisons of less 11 to 100* develops even later.

The developmental order of numerical-comparison competencies discussed above are summarized in Table 5–1.

INSTRUCTION

Equivalence

To foster an understanding of equivalence, encourage a child to play with very small sets that he or she can readily recognize as the same (intuitively match) and can easily enumerate. By attaching number labels to sets that

Table 5–1 Numerical-Comparison Competencies by Developmental Order

Level	Equivalence	Gross Comparisons	Fine Comparisons
PK	Perception of "same"	Perception of "more"	—
	—	—	Perception of fine differences with 1 to 4
	Same number 1 to 5	—	—
	—	Gross comparisons 1 to 10	—
	—	—	Fine comparisons 1 to 5
K	Same number 6 to 10	—	—
	—	—	Fine comparisons 6 to 10
	—	Gross comparisons of less 1 to 10	—
1	Matching sets	—	—
	—	Gross comparisons 11 to 100	—
	—	—	Fine comparisons of less 1 to 10
	—	—	Fine comparisons 11 to 100
	—	—	Fine comparisons of less 11 to 100

children can see match up, children learn that "same number" does not refer to some physical property or appearance but rather to quantity.

To compare larger sets, which are difficult visually to judge as equivalent, encourage the use of counting (e.g., This row of white chips has six, and this row of red chips has six. The rows have the same number.). Use of a matching process to evaluate equivalence can be introduced later.

Perception of Same

Make a game (**Same-Number or Different?**) of estimating the equivalence or inequivalence of collections. At first, it may be instructive to compare sets of *objects* that are obviously the same in number (1 vs. 1, 2 vs. 2, and 3 vs. 3) or obviously different in number (1 vs. 6, 2 vs. 8, 3 vs. 9). Then training can proceed with pictures of sets (as in the case of the **Fair Cookie Portions** described in Example 5–1) and then with less obvious cases of equivalence (e.g., 4 vs. 4 and 7 vs. 7) and inequivalence (2 vs. 5 and 4 vs. 6). To help children to define better the same-number concept, use the training methods for same number 1 to 5 described in the following section.

Example 5–1   Fair Cookie Portions

Objective: Perception of same and different with pictured sets.

Grade Level: PK.

Participants: One child or possibly a small group of children.

Materials: Cards such as A to E shown below.

Card A:	OO	OOO
Card B:	OOO	OOO
Card C:	OOOOOOOOO	OOOO
Card D:	OO OO	OOOOO OOOOO
Card E:	OO	O O

Procedure: Present a card and say, "Ernie has this many cookies [point to one side], and Bert has this many cookies [point to the other side]. Did Ernie and Bert get the same number of cookies? Did they share the cookies fairly?"

Same Number 1 to 5

First ensure that a child has proficient numbering skills (e.g., can efficiently enumerate at least small sets of 1 to 5 items). Instruction should then focus on teaching the same-number concept and how counting can play a role in determining equivalent sets. Games, such as **Clue** (described in Example 5–2) and **Lotto Same Number** (e.g., see Baroody, 1987a; Wynroth, 1986), are useful. Briefly, to begin lotto, children select a number of dominoes (say, three) from a pile of turned over dominoes. The remaining dominoes are then turned face up. From this pile, players in turn try to find a matching set for each of the sets drawn at the beginning of the game. Such games have been used to teach a same-number concept to mentally handicapped children (Carrison and Werner, 1943; Descoeudres, 1928). If necessary, explicitly point out that counting can be used to determine if two collections have the same number. Explain that if counting results in the same (last) number, two collections have the same amount *despite differences in appearance.* Note that Lotto Same Number and Clue can serve to practice enumeration skills as well as to reinforce the idea of using counting to determine equivalent collections.

Example 5-2   Clue

Objective: Using counting to determine which of a number of sets has the same number of items as a given set.

Grade Level: PK.

Participants: One child or two teams consisting of one to a few children.

Materials: "Clue Cards" such as Cards A to E shown below.

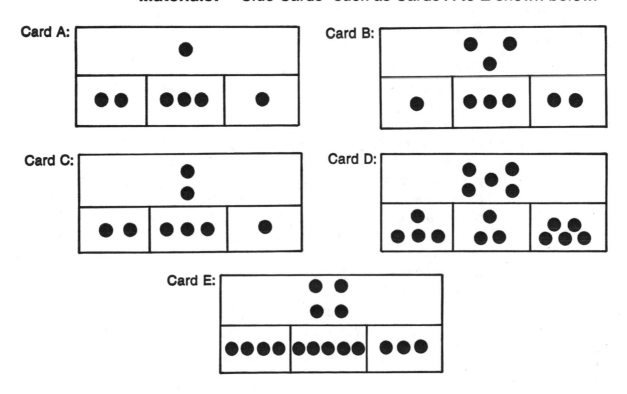

Procedure: Cover the bottom half of a card and show it to the child. Say, "This game is called Clue. You have to figure out how many dots I'm thinking about. Here's a clue to help you figure out just the right number of dots I'm thinking about [point to the set that is showing]. Now [uncover the bottom half of the card], am I thinking about this many dots [point to the first choice], this many [point to the second choice], or this many [point to third choice]?" If the child makes no attempt to respond, point to each choice in turn and say, "Does this have the same number of dots as the clue up here [point]?" If the child is wrong, encourage him or her to count the number of dots in the clue and each of the choices. If necessary, point to each choice and say, "Does this have the same number of dots as the clue on top [point]?"

Same Number 6 to 10

If a child fails the more basic same-number 1-to-5 item, begin work with this prerequisite skill first. If a child can establish equivalences with smaller sets but not larger sets, then explain how small-set-equivalence procedures also apply to larger sets. If the difficulty is due to inefficient larger-number enumeration, work on this basic skill before or during the training of equivalence 6 to 10. **Clue** can be used to teach and practice this skill by using a deck of cards such as those shown in Figure 5–1.

Matching Sets

First ensure that children can count to make same-number judgments with at least small sets. Mastery of this more concrete skill will enable children to learn more readily the more abstract matching skill (Gelman and Gallistel, 1978). Instruction can begin with asking a child to put out the same number of objects as that of a preexisting set. Start with sets that naturally go together and that highlight the one-to-one correspondence (e.g., sets of plastic tea cups and saucers). Then introduce sets with no functional match (blue and white sets of blocks) or with pictured sets of objects (e.g., drawings of girls and dresses).

Some children may need help in learning how to match sets one-to-one. As the example below illustrates, some children will simply put out a row of the same length but with too few:

Sample row: O O O O O

Child's row: O O O O

Figure 5–1 Clue: Same Number 6 to 10

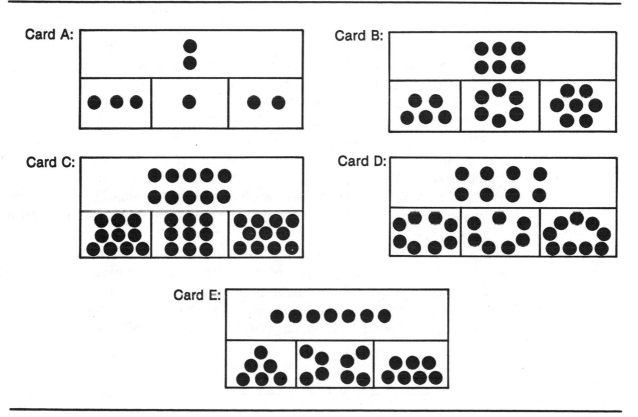

Card A: Card B: Card C: Card D: Card E:

As the example below shows, some put out a row of the same length, but with too many items:

Sample row: ○ ○ ○ ○ ○

Child's row: ○○○○ ○○○

If need be, help the child to line up the corresponding elements. Point out that to match up two collections, there must be one and only one item in one collection for each item in the other collection.

Next, give the child two sets in which the items are not arranged in any order and have the child match the two sets to see if rows can be put in one-to-one correspondence or if one set has items left over. During the initial phase of training, children should be encouraged to check their answers by counting.

Once children can make one-to-one matches, training efforts can focus on helping children see that changes in physical appearance do not affect equivalence relationships but that addition or subtraction transformations do. (See Baroody, 1987a, or Gelman and Gallistel, 1978, for a description of the **Magic Show** that can be used to demonstrate these ideas.) The number-conservation task can also be used as a training vehicle (see Figure 5–2). Initially, it may be helpful to have children count each set that is in one-to-one correspondence. After lengthening or shortening one row, have the child count again before indicating whether or not the rows have the same number. If the child indicates that one row now has more, point out that counting each row yields the same number—the same number that was obtained before the change in physical appearance. Another exercise is to have a child create matching sets. Then—while the child is watching—lengthen one row *and* add an item to the shorter row. Initially it can help children to count each row before asking if the rows have the same number or if one has more. If a child counts and still indicates that the longer row has more, check fine-comparison ability and remedy if necessary.

Work should begin with small sets for which pattern recognition can come into play. This reinforces the idea that differences in physical appearance are not relevant to judging equivalence or inequivalence. Frequently, children will spontaneously transfer this number-conservation learning with small sets to larger sets (Gelman, 1982). Indeed, direct

---

Figure 5–2 Number-Conservation Task

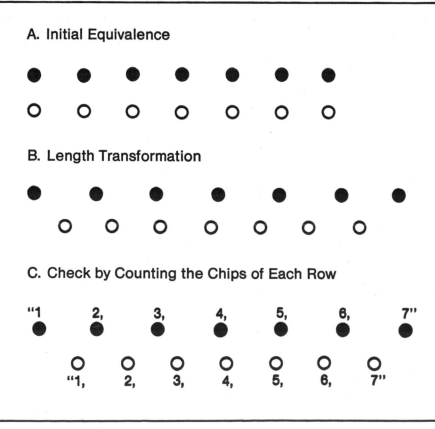

A. Initial Equivalence

B. Length Transformation

C. Check by Counting the Chips of Each Row

instruction on number conservation is not necessary for most children. If given ample experiences in counting and comparing sets, most discover matching procedures and the number-conservation concept on their own.

Inequivalence: Gross Comparisons

Learning about inequivalence can go hand in hand with learning about equivalence. Ordering sets (judging more and less) should follow naturally from children's informal experiences. As with equivalence, the child should be given ample opportunity to compare very small sets of objects. Later, the child can be given opportunities to compare small and then larger collections. A parent or teacher should encourage efforts to reason out the comparison by counting or thinking about the number sequence.

Perception of *More*

With the very few children who need training, teach a concept of more with small, easily recognized sets of objects that clearly differ in amount. For example, hold out one hand with four pieces of candy (or other highly desirable objects) and the other with one piece of candy and offer to give the child the set with "more"—"the bigger handful." If need be, compare very small numbered sets to sets with ten or more items. This instruction can be incorporated into a game that uses objects, such as **Snack Activity** (Example 5–3), or that uses pictures of sets, such as the **More-Cookie Game** (Example 5–4).

Example 5–3 Snack Activity

Objective: Perception of more with objects.

Grade Level: PK.

Participants: One to five children.

Materials: Chips or other objects to represent cookies; prizes (optional).

Procedure: Say, "Cookie Monster is getting very hungry. It is time for his snack, and he wants a big number of cookies. Can you tell me which pile of cookies is more so that Cookie Monster will get lots of cookies for his snack?" Present the child with various comparisons as suggested above.

Example 5–4 More-Cookie Game

Objective: Perception of more with pictured sets.

Grade Level: PK.

Participants: One child or a small group of children.

Materials: Cards such as those shown below.

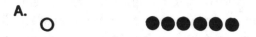

A.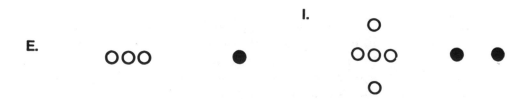

B.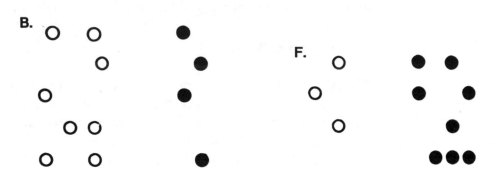

F.

C.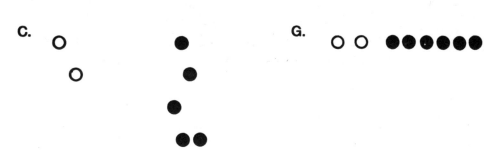

G.

D.

H.

I.

E.

Procedure: Show the child a card and say, "Let's try the More-Cookie game. On this side of the card there is a picture of a plate of cookies, and on this side of the card there is another plate of cookies. Look carefully and point to the plate that has more cookies." If the child is incorrect, say, "No. That plate has more. See it has a lot of cookies [make an exaggerated circular gesture over the side with more dots]. This other side has just a few—It is small [make a tiny circular gesture]."

Gross Comparisons 1 to 10

Deficiencies in counting to 10 or the perception of more should be remedied before training on gross comparisons of 1 to 10. Training on gross comparison should begin by helping a child realize that *the number sequence represents increasingly larger quantities.* The **Staircase Activity, Moon-Invaders Game**, and **Number-List Race Game** described in Baroody (1987a) and **Disappearing Numbers** (Example 5–5) can be used for this initial instruction. With early practice efforts, concrete representations of numbers should accompany verbal numerical comparisons. **High Die** (Example 5–6) is a good way to start such practice, because all comparisons involve small, easily counted or recognized sets. **Cards More Than** (with dot cards), described in Example 5–7, extends comparison practice to numbers up to 10.

Because the aim is to enable children to make numerical comparisons mentally, concrete supports should be withdrawn as soon as a child has mastered numerical comparisons with concrete models. To practice making comparisons mentally, play the *advanced* versions of **Disappearing Numbers** (described in Example 5–5) and **Cards More Than** (described in Example 5–7) with numeral cards. Other games for practicing this skill are the **Big-Number Game: 1–10** (Example 5–8) and the **Hit-the-Target Game** (Example 5–9).

Example 5–5 Disappearing Numbers

Objective: Gross comparisons of numbers 1 to 10 with a concrete representation of the number sequence (for beginners), with the aid of a number list (for somewhat more advanced children), or using a mental representation of the number sequence (advanced players).

Grade Level: PK to K.

Participants: One to three players.

Materials: Cards each with a numeral 1 to 10 and enough interlocking cubes to represent each number.

Procedure: Lay out the cards on a table face up and in numerical order. Have the child represent each number with interlocking blocks (see the figure below). After building a "staircase" with the blocks, give the player two numbers. Initially, as each number is stated, concretely identify its relative position in the sequence and relative size by pointing out its card and accompanying "step of cubes." If a player can say which is more, that child wins the card with the larger number of dots on it. Make sure to alternate the order of the smaller and larger term (e.g., "Which is more: eight or two? Which is more: three or seven?"). If incorrect, encourage the child to think about which number comes later when we count so that in the next turn he or she can win a card. The game continues until only one card is left.

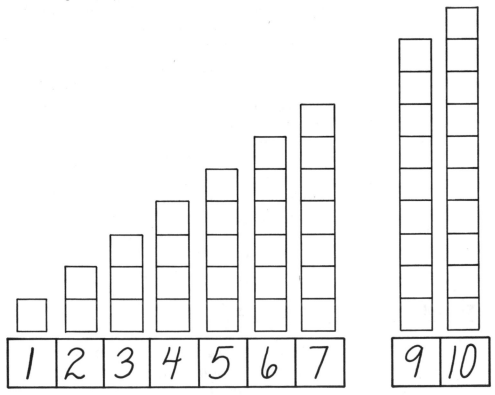

Previous question: "Which is more: 3 or 8?"
Previous response: "Eight." (Child takes the "8" card.)
Question: "Which is more: 9 or 2?"
Response: "Two."
Teacher: "Let's look at the blocks to see. Which is m-o-r-e?"
Response: "Nine."
Teacher: "Nine is more than two. Sure. When we count, we say two right at the start, and we say nine later: one, *two,* three, four, five, six, seven, eight, *nine.* See—nine comes after two when we count so we know that it is more."

For somewhat more advanced players, lay out the cards in numerical order without the staircase of interlocking blocks. Note that the cards serve as a number list. If a child has difficulty making a comparison, remind him or her that as we count (begin with Card 1 and point to the cards in order) each number represents a larger amount. If necessary, use interlocking blocks to represent the specific comparison. For even more advanced players, lay out the cards in *random* order. This requires the child to use his or her own mental representation of the number sequence.

Example 5–6   High Die

Objectives: Gross comparisons of numbers 0 to 5 using the concrete supports of counting, pattern recognition, or perception of more. The game also requires fine comparisons involving numbers 0 to 5 and same number (equivalence) 1 to 5.

Grade Level: PK.

Participants: Two to five players.

Materials: Large die with 0 to 5 dots for each player.

Procedure: Players roll their dice in turn. After the second child rolls his or her die and identifies the number (m) of dots, ask, "Is m [point to the player's die] more than n [point to the first player's die]?" (Note that this effectively randomizes whether the smaller or larger number is stated first.) Summarize or correct the player's response. With two players, the child with the "high die" is then awarded a point. (A block can be used as a point marker.) With three or more players, have the next child roll his or her die and compare it to the previous winner. Repeat this procedure with any remaining players. Keep rotating who goes first (e.g., on the next turn, the "second" player should go first.) This gives everyone an equal opportunity to make comparisons.

Note that during the course of the game, fine comparisons are inevitable (e.g., 4 vs. 3 or 3 vs. 4). Often players will have the same number of dots. A player should note that neither die has more—they have the same number. If necessary, point this out. After all the comparisons have been made, sometimes the high die will be shared by two or more players. All players tied with the high die are awarded a point (block).

Example 5–7   Cards More Than

Objective: Gross comparisons of numbers 1 to 10 using counting (for beginners) or a mental representation of the number sequence (for advanced players). The game also entails fine and same-number comparisons involving numbers 1 to 10.

Grade Level: PK.

Participants: Two to five players.

Materials: Dot cards with sets of dots from 1 to 10 (for beginners and children who cannot read numerals) *or* numeral cards 1 to 10 (for more advanced children).

Procedure: This game is played like the card game "War" and is based on the Wynroth (1986) game used to teach number after and before. Shuffle the cards and give one to each player, face up. Ask the children to count the dots (or read the numerals) on their card to determine what they have. Then, have the children compare their numbers (e.g., ask a player, "You have five and Sally has three. Which is more: five or three?"). *If* necessary, have the child compare the extent of each count. For example, "Do you have to count more numbers to get to five or to get to three? Let's count and see. One, two, *three*—that's Sally's number—four, five. When we count to five, we go past three, so five is more than three." Most children will quickly move on to using their mental representation of the number sequence. At this point numeral cards are easier to use.

It may be less confusing and more instructive to use a routine to make the comparisons. For example, have one child start and compare his or her number with the child to the left; the winner of that comparison then compares his or her number with that of the next child to the left; and so on. The game can be played, as in War, where the player with the bigger numbers keeps both cards. The player with the most cards at the end of the game wins. Use the dot cards as children begin working on this skill, then the numeral cards as they become more proficient.

Example 5–8 Big-Number Game: 1–10

Objective: Mental gross number comparisons 1 to 10.

Grade Level: PK.

Participants: Two to six players or several teams of players.

Materials: Deck of 3″ × 5″ cards indicating various comparisons (e.g., 9 or 1, 2 or 8, 3 or 7, 10 or 4, 3 or 9) and a chalkboard or other means to keep score.

Procedure: Explain, "In the Big-Number game, you have to pick the bigger number to win a point. For example, which is more: 10 marbles or 1 marble? Which is more: 10 or 1?" If necessary, point out that 10 is more than 1 and say, "Now remember to pick the bigger number so that you can win." On their turn, players draw a comparison card. If they choose the larger number, award the player (team) one point. If a child has difficulty, use a number list or interlocking blocks to illustrate the comparison concretely.

Example 5–9 Hit-the-Target Game

Objective: Application of gross number comparisons 1 to 10.

Grade Level: PK.

Participants: One to four players or two small teams.

Materials: Cardboard target about 8½ × 11 inches, ten chips, and paper and pencil or chalkboard and chalk to keep score. Prizes are optional.

Procedure: Explain, "In the Hit-the-Target game, a player tries to get these chips onto the target. After you have thrown the chips, we will count how many you get on the target. If you get more than two chips on the target, you score a point (win a prize)." After a player has thrown his or her chips, the teacher says, for instance, "You got five chips on the target. Is five more than two?" The criterion for scoring a point (winning a prize) can be varied to practice more than with a range of numbers from one to about six.

Alternative Procedure: Have children or teams compete against each other rather than a preestablished criterion. Record each child's (team's) score with tallies (or, for more sophisticated children, with numerals). The child (team) with the larger tally (number) wins the round. Keep score of each round, and determine the overall winner in the manner described above.

Gross Comparisons of Less than 1 to 10

Instruction should first remedy any deficiency in the prerequisite skill (gross comparisons 1 to 10). It then should focus on helping the child to understand the term "less." Techniques to teach the perception of more and gross comparisons of more 1-to-10 can be adapted for this purpose: **Snack Activity (Less Version), Less Cookie Game, Disappearing Numbers (Less Version),** and **Cards Less Than.** For example, in Cards Less, the player with the smallest dot card wins. **Finger Play** may also help teach the less concept. Have the child represent a number (e.g., five) with the fingers of one hand and another number (e.g., two) with the fingers of the other hand. Ask the child to raise the hand with the finger pattern that has *more.* Then have the child do the same with the hand with the finger pattern that has less. By contrasting the terms "more" and "less," a child can define the novel term "less" as the opposite of the familiar term "more." The **Number-Guess Game**, described in Example 5–10, can be used to practice using the terms "more" and "less" and reasoning about numerical relationships. The **Little-Number Game**, described in Example 5–11, can provide practice in mentally making gross comparisons of less.

Example 5–10   Number-Guess Game

Objectives: This relatively simple game can help achieve a number of important objectives. First, it can help familiarize children with the terms *more than* and *less than.* Second, it is typical of many real-life problem-solving situations where an *incorrect* solution can provide useful information about how to proceed. Third, the game can provide an opportunity to exercise deductive reasoning: reaching a conclusion by reasoning logically from a premise. Fourth, the game provides an opportunity to discover and discuss different solution strategies and their relative merits. More specifically, it illustrates that real problems can be figured out in different ways but that some strategies may be more efficient and desirable than others.

Grade Level: K to 3.

Participants: The game can be played by pairs of students or by two small teams.

Procedure: One side or a monitor picks a number between one and five. This can be done randomly by using a die or shuffled cards. The number can be recorded on a pad. The "number picker" then says, "I have picked a number between one and five. You have three guesses to figure out the number that I have picked." If the guesser is incorrect on the first or second guess, the number picker has to indicate if the guessed number is greater (more) (bigger) or less (fewer) than the picked number. If the guesser says a number greater than five, the number picker says, "Sorry, the number is either one, two, three, four, or five." If the guesser is incorrect on the third guess, the number picker shows the guesser (the pad with) the number picked. If the guesser correctly guesses the picked number on any one of the three tries, the guessers are awarded a point. The players then switch roles. The game ends after each player (team) has had a prescribed number of turns. (The game can end in a tie.)

By making a judicious first guess (picking the middle number, three) and using the feedback provided, a player can be virtually certain of being correct each time. For example, if the picked number is five, the guesser would know after the first try that the number could not be less than three (one or two) but has to be more than three (four or five). If the guesser did not pick the correct number on the second try, success would follow on the last try.

Even if a player does not think or discover this efficient strategy, he or she can still use incorrect guesses wisely to narrow down choices. Another highly efficient strategy is to always pick the number two first. If the feedback indicates that the number is bigger, the child then can choose four. If four is not the correct term, the feedback will tell the player which term (three or five) has been picked. A relatively inefficient strategy is to randomly guess or start with one (five) and add (subtract) one on each guess.

The game can be made more difficult by reducing the number of guesses to two or by increasing the range of allowable choices to 6, 7, 10, or more.

The game can be played over a period of time so that as many students as possible are given the opportunity to discover for themselves more efficient strategies and learn about more-less relationships. The game can also be played only once and serve as the basis for discussing the nature of problems, problem-solving strategies, reasoning logically, using information from errors, and so on.

Example 5–11   Little-Number Game

Objective: Practice mentally making gross comparison of less 1 to 10.

Grade Level: K.

Participants: One child or two teams of one to a few children.

Procedure: Explain, "In the Little-Number game, the goal is to pick the *smaller* number." Pose questions such as: "Arlene has a bag with ten coins, and Barb has a bag with one coin. Who has less? Who has fewer, Arlene with 10 or Barb with 1?"

Gross Comparisons 11 to 100

After remedying any deficiencies in the prerequisite skills (counting to 100 and gross comparisons 1 to 10), instruction should focus on developing greater familiarity with the number sequence to 100. Practice with number comparisons 11 to 100 can be done by using various games, such as the **Big-Number Game: 1–100**, **Baseball More Than** (Example 5–12), and **Dice More Than** (Example 5–13). Encourage children to think about and share their observations about the number sequence to 100 and comparing the magnitude of these larger numbers. If necessary, help the child to see the connection between his or her existing number-after knowledge and making gross comparisons of numbers 11 to 100.

Example 5–12 Baseball More Than

Objective: Mental gross number comparisons 11 to 100.

Grade Level: 1.

Participants: Two players or two small teams.

Materials: A baseball diamond (e.g., 1 × 1 foot piece of cardboard with four bases drawn in); objects ("pieces") to represent the batter, base runners, and runs; cue cards on which are printed two numerals (the numbers to be compared).

Procedure: The player or team "at bat" places a piece at home plate to represent the batter. The other player or team draws a cue card from a deck of cards and announces the comparison (e.g., "Which is more: 54 or 27?"). If the player (team) at bat correctly picks the larger number, the batter advances to first base. The player or team at bat then places another piece at home plate for the next batter. If the child (team) at bat is incorrect, an out is recorded. (Like baseball, three outs retire the side, and the other player or team takes their turn at bat.) If the player (team) at bat gets the next comparison correct, the piece representing the batter is advanced to first base; the piece already on first base is advanced to second. A run is scored when the player at bat has the bases loaded and then gets another comparison correct (the piece representing the runner on third is forced home).

Alternative Procedure: The cue cards can be made up to indicate whether a correct response results in a single (batter advances to first), a double (batter advances to second), a triple (batter advances to third base and forces all runners to score), or a home run (batter and all runners score). Indeed, the difficulty of comparisons can be matched to the outcome. For example, an easy comparison like 24 or 98 might only be worth a single. Whereas more difficult comparisons, like those involving a 28 or 73 (a child who focuses on the ones digits 8 and 3 would be misled and pick 28) or 73 or 63 (a child must know that the seventies are more than the sixties) might be worth a triple or home run.

The game can be adapted in various ways to meet the needs of individual players. With children who make few mistakes, the side can be retired by one mistake or by putting a limit on the number of runs that can be scored in an inning (e.g., maximum = 5 runs).

Example 5–13 Dice More Than
_____

Objective: Mental gross number comparisons 44 to 99.

Grade Level: 1.

Participants: Two to five players.

Materials: Two dice with the numerals 4 to 9 for each player; paper and pencil, or hand calculators, depending on the method of scoring used.

Procedure: On their turn, players throw the dice. They can arrange the dice in the order they desire (e.g., if a player rolled a 4 and a 6, the player could rearrange the dice to read 64). With two players, the child with the larger number wins a point. The players can alternate who makes the comparison to determine the larger number. With three to five players, the player(s) with the largest number win(s) a point. To make the comparing process more manageable with this number of players, have the children place their dice in front of them. Have one child start and compare his or her roll to that of the child to the left. The child with the smaller number then goes on to compare his or her roll to the next child to the left. This process is repeated until only the child with the largest roll has dice remaining.

Alternative Scoring Procedure: Instead of the winner scoring a point, the winner can be awarded the number of points equal to his or her roll. Using this scoring procedure, each player would need a calculator to keep track of his or her tally.

_____

Perception of Fine Differences with Sets 1 to 4

First ensure that a child understands the term more (masters the prerequisite perception of more). Then turn to the case of fine comparisons of one to four objects or pictured items, as in the **More-Cookie Game** (Example 5–14).

Example 5–14 More-Cookie Game
_____

Objective: Perception of fine differences with pictured sets of 1 to 4 items.

Grade Level: PK.

Participants: One child or a small group of children.

Materials: Cards such as those shown below.

A. ○   ●●●●●●   F.   ○   ●

                                                      ○

                                                      ○   ●

B. ○○○   ●●

                                         G.   ○   ●

                      ●   ○   ●●

                                                      ○   ●

C. ○

            ●

                                         H.   ○   ●

                                                                        ●

                                                      ○   ●

D. ○ ○   ●● ●●

    ○ ○   ●

                                         I.   ○   ●

                                                      ○

                                                                        ●

E. ○   ○   ●●●   ○

                                                      ○   ●

Procedure: Use the same procedure described for perception of more. Use Card A to explain the rules.

Inequivalence: Fine Comparisons

As with gross comparisons, fostering skill with fine comparisons should basically entail providing informal learning opportunities. Children should be given experiences with small numbers (1 to 5) first and then progressively larger ones. Instruction should proceed from the concrete (with objects) to the semiconcrete (using counting or number-after skills to make the comparison explicitly) and then to the abstract (mentally and efficiently making comparisons).

Fine Comparisons 1 to 5

First ensure that the prerequisite skills are mastered: perception of more and perception of fine differences with 1 to 4. Introduction of the skill should focus on helping children see that the numbers one, two, three represent increasingly larger sets. Begin by comparing very small sets of objects (one to three items). The **Store Game** (with objects version) and the **More-Fingers Activity**, described in Examples 5–15 and 5–16) are useful introductory activities. As children grasp the idea that each successive number in the count sequence represents a larger set, instruction can be expanded to include the somewhat larger sets of four and five.

Initially, collections of objects should be arranged so that, spatial cues are consistent with and highlight the difference in magnitude. That is, the collection with more should clearly (a) be longer, (b) cover more area, or (c) be more tightly (densely) packed:

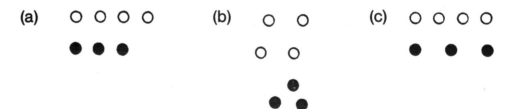

Typically, children spontaneously discover the key idea that appearances are not always a true indication of more. To encourage this discovery, introduce collections where the spatial cues are at odds with a correct magnitude comparison.

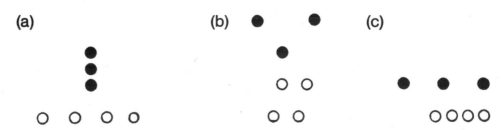

Most children will count spontaneously or employ their number-after knowledge to make comparisons, such as 3 vs. 4 or 5 vs. 4. For some children, especially children with learning handicaps, it may be helpful to point out explicitly the connection between counting and making number comparisons. During the course of instructional games, a teacher can use his or her turn to model a counting-based comparison procedure: "Which is more: five or four things? Let me see. When I *count*—one, two, three, *four, five*—five follows four so five things are more than four things." On their turn, children can be encouraged to verbalize the procedure as they figure out their answer. Moreover, it may be helpful with some children to point out explicitly the connection between their existing number-after knowledge and making fine number comparisons. For example, a teacher might ask, "What number comes after four?" After the child responds, the teacher can follow up with, "So which number is more: four or five things?" The basic count-from-one procedure and the more direct number-after procedure can be explained and practiced during the course of **Cards More Than**, described in Example 5–7, or the **Store Game** (Example 5–16) and the **Age-Comparison Activity** (Example 5–17) described below.

Example 5–15   More-Fingers Activity

Objective: Fine comparisons of 1 to 5 that involve counting objects.

Grade Level: PK.

Participants: One child or a small group of children.

Procedure: Initially, children can be encouraged to put up the fingers on one hand as they count. Stop the count at various points and say, for instance, "Which is more fingers: two fingers or one finger?" If need be, point out that more fingers go up the further we count. A variation of this activity involves representing one number with the fingers of one hand and another number with the fingers of the other hand. The child is then asked, for example, "So, which is more: four or five fingers?" As with all comparison tasks, sometimes give the smaller number first and sometimes the larger.

Example 5–16   Store Game

Objective: Fine comparisons of 1 to 5 objects either by counting (with-objects version) or mentally (without-objects version).

Grade Level: PK.

Participants: One or a small group of children.

Materials: Prizes like chalk, paper clips, stars, stickers, or rubber bands and envelopes in which to put the prizes.

Procedure: Explain, "In the Store game you can shop in the store and keep the prizes you pick. We will put the prizes you pick in your shopping bag [envelope]." Give the shopper(s) various choices such as the examples noted below. In the with-objects version, *actually put out* the items *as* the comparison question is asked. For example, for Question 1 below, put out two pieces and one piece of chalk.

1. Would you like two pieces of chalk or one piece of chalk? Which is more: 2 or 1?

2. Would you like three paper clips or four paper clips? Which is more: 3 or 4?

3. Would you like two stars or three stars? Which is more: 2 or 3?

4. Would you like five stickers or four stickers? Which is more: 5 or 4?

5. Would you like three rubber bands or two rubber bands? Which is more: 3 or 2?

Example 5–17   Age-Comparison Activity

Objective: Application of mentally making fine comparisons of numbers 1 to 5.

Grade Level: PK.

Participants: One child or a small group of children. The activity could also be adapted as a game between two small teams of players.

Materials: Picture cards of children (or animals) with numerals indicating their age in one of the corners.

Procedure: Say, for instance, "Here is Sally; Sally is 3 years old. Here is Teri; Teri is 2 years old [place to the right of the picture of Sally]. Sally is 3 and Teri is 2. Who is older: the 3-year-old or the 2-year-old?" Pick up the cards, and continue with other comparisons.

It is often useful to encourage children to discuss their current age in relationship to their age the previous year, their age at their next birthday, the age of an older or younger sibling or friend, and so on.

Fine Comparisons 6 to 10

First ensure that the more basic prerequisite skills (gross comparisons 1 to 10, fine comparisons 1 to 5, and number after 5 to 9) are *automatic* before beginning the training of fine comparisons 5 to 10. Children, including some mentally handicapped children, will spontaneously transfer their comparison skills for 1 to 5 to the somewhat larger numbers 5 to 10. If transfer does not occur spontaneously, recommend to the child the procedure taught for making fine number comparisons 1 to 5. **Cards More Than** (Example 5–7) and the **Big-Number Car-Race Game** (Example 5–18) or the **Enough-to-Buy Activity** (Example 5–19) can be used to practice this skill (or other number-comparison skills).

Example 5–18 Big-Number Car-Race Game: 1–10

Objective: Mentally making fine comparisons with numbers 6 to 10.

Grade Level: K.

Participants: Two players or two small teams of players.

Materials: Deck of number-comparison cards, spiral race-track board, and two miniature racing cars.

Procedure: Give the children their choice of racing car. Explain, "When it is your turn in the Big-Number Car-Race game, you will be given two numbers. The number you pick tells us how many spaces your car moves. The other number is how many spaces the other player's (team's) car can move. So try to pick the bigger number." Have the players take turns picking a number-comparison card from the deck or have a judge read the comparisons to the players.

Example 5–19   Enough-to-Buy Activity

Objective: Application of mentally making fine comparisons 5 to 10.

Grade Level: K.

Participants: One to five children.

Materials: Play dollar bills, price tags, and assorted store items.

Procedure: Explain, "Cookie Monster needs some help shopping. Would you help him by telling him if he has enough money to buy the things he picks out?" Put out an item, such as a ball. Have Cookie Monster put seven dollars in a pile. Point out the price tag ($8) and ask, "Cookie Monster has seven dollars, and this ball costs eight dollars. Is seven dollars enough to buy a ball that costs eight dollars?"

Fine Comparisons of Less 1 to 10

After remedying any deficiencies in the prerequisite skills (gross comparisons of less 1 to 10 and number before 2 to 10), training can focus on helping a child to see that their number-before knowledge can be used to specify fine comparisons of less than. **Golf** (Example 5–20) is an interesting way to provide practice mentally deciding which of two numbers between 1 and 10 is less.

Example 5–20   Golf

Objective: Mentally make fine comparisons of less involving numbers 1 to 10.

Grade Level: 1.

Participants: One to five players.

Materials: Scoresheet, pencil, deck of question cards, and hand calculator.

Procedure: Explain to the players that in golf, the idea is to get the lowest score possible. In this game, a player draws a card that has two numerals printed on it. To get the lowest golf score possible, a player should pick the smaller of the two numbers. The score is recorded on the hand calculator. Subsequent scores are added. At the end of the game, the child with the lowest overall score is the winner.

Fine Comparisons 11 to 100

After remedying any deficiencies in the prerequisite skills (fine comparisons 1 to 10 and number after 10 to 99) instruction should focus on developing greater familiarity with the number sequence to 100. This skill can be practiced by playing the football game described below (Example 5–21) or by adapting one of the games described for the other comparison skills. Encourage children to think about and share their ideas about the number sequence to 100 and comparing the magnitude of these larger numbers. If necessary, help the child to see the connection between his or her existing number-after knowledge and determining the larger of two adjacent two-digit numbers.

Example 5–21   Larger-Number Football

Objective: Practice mentally making fine comparisons 11 to 100.

Grade Level: 1.

Participants: Two players or two small teams.

Materials: Game board with 11 field lines (G, 10, 20, 30, 40, 50, 40, 30, 20, 10, G), deck of cards with number comparisons, deck of good-outcome cards (e.g., gain 10 yds., gain 50 yds., touchdown), deck of bad-outcome cards (e.g., no gain, lose 10 yds., fumble), and football marker.

Procedure: Say, "You're going to play Larger-Number Football. I'll flip a coin to see who gets the football first." Place the ball on the 20-yard line to start (eight lines from the child's goal and a touchdown). The defensive player draws a number-comparison card. If the offensive player (the child with the ball) responds correctly, he or she may draw a good-outcome card. If wrong, the offensive player draws a bad-outcome card.
  If an offensive player advances the ball to or across the opponent's goal line, a touchdown can be scored simply as 1 point.

To provide experience or practice with hand calculators, touchdowns can be scored as 7 points. For football purists, a touchdown can be scored as 6 points. The player can score the extra point by correctly answering an additional question. On the other hand, if the offense moves back to or across its own goal line, then the defense is awarded 1 point. (If a realistic scoring system is desired, a "safety" can be scored as 2 points). The game continues until the deck of comparison cards is exhausted or a time limit is reached.

Fine Comparisons of Less 11 to 100

After remedying deficiencies in the prerequisite skills (fine comparisons of more 11 to 100, fine comparisons of less 1 to 10 and number before 11 to 100) training should focus on developing greater familiarity with the descending order of the number sequence to 100. This skill can be practiced by changing the rules of Larger-Number Football to create **Smaller-Number Football**. If necessary, help the child to see the connection between his or her existing number-before knowledge and determining the smaller of two adjacent two-digit numbers.

SUMMARY

Understanding the numerical relations between two sets builds on direct-perception and numbering skills. Preschoolers can see that very small sets of one, two, and perhaps even three items are equivalent. Experiences in numbering such sets teaches them that the same (cardinal) label indicates the same number—despite differences or changes in appearance. Kindergartners may need training in establishing the equivalence of sets larger than three. Initially, they should be encouraged to count each set to determine "same number." Matching, which is a somewhat more abstract process, should be introduced later.

Likewise, when two sets clearly differ in number, children can see which has "more." As a result of numbering experiences, particularly with very small sets, preschoolers recognize that the number sequence represents quantities of increasing magnitude. This allows them to identify the larger of two widely separated numbers (make "gross" comparisons). For very small sets, preschoolers can see which set is more even when they differ by only one item. This provides a basis for using their number sequence to make "fine" comparisons: judge which of two neighboring numbers is more. Some kindergartners, however, may need training to make such comparisons up to 10 or even 5. Children naturally extend both gross and fine comparison skills as they learn more of the count sequence. Comparisons of "less" may be more difficult for some children than comparisons of "more."

Chapter 6

Informal Arithmetic

Gradually, young children extend their oral counting and numbering skills to the task of calculation. At first, a child may see that if one block is added to one already present, the result is "two." Next, the child may see that if another block is added to the two, the result is "three." There is only a thin line between counting and adding (Baroody and Ginsburg, 1986). Similarly, young children may see that if one cookie is taken away (subtracted) from the three present, only two are left. Addition and subtraction in this way are familiar experiences to preschool children (e.g., Gelman and Gallistel, 1978; Ginsburg, 1982).

Indeed, before they receive formal arithmetic instruction or master the basic addition and subtraction facts, young children can solve simple arithmetic word problems by using self-invented calculational procedures (e.g., Carpenter, 1986; Riley, Greeno, and Heller, 1983). Counting serves as the basis for this *informal addition* and *informal subtraction*. Initially, children rely on using objects to perform addition and subtraction calculations. In time, children abandon their object-counting (*concrete addition* and *concrete subtraction*) procedures in favor of more advanced procedures. With sufficient computational experience, children *spontaneously* invent *verbal-count procedures* to calculate sums and differences (e.g., Baroody, 1987b; Groen and Resnick, 1977). In brief, whether they use objects or not, counting is the natural medium for children's informal addition and subtraction.

Later, children assimilate multiplication in terms of their existing counting and addition knowledge and rely on informal procedures to calculate products. As with addition and subtraction, children are capable of *informal multiplication* before they master the basic times facts.

LEARNING

Informal Addition

Concrete Addition

Preschoolers have numerous experiences that involve adding something more to an existing collection to make it larger. An informal "incrementing" view of addition provides a basis for understanding and solving simple addition problems. Indeed, if given objects such as blocks or allowed to use their fingers, many kindergartners and even some preschoolers can solve word problems like that below (e.g., Carpenter and Moser, 1984; Hebbeler, 1977; Lindvall and Ibarra, 1979).

> Alice has two candies. Her brother gives her four more. How many candies does Alice have altogether?

Children use objects to model the incrementing process reflected in such "change problems." Specifically, children invent a counting-all procedure: They count out objects (blocks, fingers, marks, etc.) to represent the initial amount. Then they produce a number of objects to represent the amount added. Finally, they count the total number of objects. For example, to solve the word problem above, a child could (1) count out two blocks; (2) produce four more; and (3) starting with one again, count all the blocks put out. (Frame A of Table 6–1 shows this process with fingers.)

Children commonly use finger patterns to represent addends and compute small sums. For $2 + 4$, say, a child could automatically put up two fingers on the left hand and four fingers on the right. Once the finger patterns representing each term are produced, the child determines the sum by counting all the fingers.

With little or no instruction, primary-level children frequently can accurately *count-all with sets 1 to 5* (e.g., Baroody, 1984a; Ilg and Ames, 1951; Siegler and Shrager, 1984). *Count-all with sets more than 5* is more difficult, because each addend cannot be represented on the fingers of one hand. Even if other objects are available to model the problem, it is relatively difficult to produce sets greater than 5 and accurately count more than ten objects to determine the sum. Indeed, it is not uncommon for children to be off by plus or minus one because of a counting error (Ilg and Ames, 1951).

Verbal-Count Procedures

Without instruction or prompting, young children typically invent verbal procedures for calculating sums (Resnick, 1983). These procedures model their incrementing view of addition and exploit their highly familiar

Table 6–1 Concrete and Verbal Addition Procedures with Fingers and the Example 2 + 4

Procedure	Step 1	Step 2	Step 3
A. (Concrete) Count all	Count out 2 fingers "1, 2."	Count out 4 fingers "1, 2, 3, 4."	Count all 6 fingers "1, 2; 3, 4, 5, 6"
B. (Verbal) Count from one (basic version)	Count up to the first term 2 "1, 2;	Count-on 4 more times, keeping track of each additional count with a finger 3(+1), 4(+2), 5(+3), 6(+4)"	
C. (Verbal) Count from one (advanced version)	Count up to the larger term 4 "1, 2, 3, 4;	Count-on 2 more times, keeping track of each additional count with a finger 5(+1); 6(+2)"	
D. (Verbal) Count-on from the larger addend	Start with the larger term 4 "4;	Count-on 2 more times, keeping track of each additional count with a finger 5(+1), 6(+2)"	

knowledge of the number sequence. Indeed, even before arithmetic is formally introduced in school, most children can *mentally add one more.* For example, many 4½-year-olds can mentally calculate that three cookies and one more cookie is four cookies (Starkey and Gelman, 1982). Young children can add one more mentally because they can draw on their well learned number-after knowledge (Resnick, 1983). For instance, children can readily calculate that four and one more is five, because they know that five is the next number after four.

In time, children invent their own verbal-count procedures for calculating more difficult problems and, in the process, abandon their concrete procedures for calculating non-one problems. At first many children *count from one to add 2 to 5.* The more basic form of this procedure involves starting with "one," counting up to the cardinal value of the first addend, and then adding on the second addend (e.g., 2 + 4: "1, 2; 3 [is 1 more], 4 [is 2 more], 5 [is 3 more], and 6 [is 4 more]—so the answer is six"). In Frame B of Table 6–1, note that such a mental procedure uses objects in a different way than does the counting-all procedure. Objects, such as fingers, are used to keep track of how much must be added on. This keeping-track process can be simplified by ignoring the order of the addends and counting out the larger addend first (Baroody, 1984a). This advanced version of the count-from-one procedure is illustrated in Frame C of Table 6–1.

To save more effort, children invent an even more sophisticated verbal-count procedure. Counting-on from the larger addend involves starting with the cardinal value of the larger addend and counting-on the smaller term (e.g., 2 + 4: "4, 5 [is 1 more], 6 [is 2 more]—so the answer is six"). This sophisticated calculational procedure is shown in Frame D of Table 6–1. By the end of first grade, most children *count on 2 to 5 from the larger addend.* (Children sometimes count on from the first addend, but this happens infrequently and/or for a brief period of time.)

It is relatively difficult for children *mentally to add 6 or more.* Problems like 6 + 7 or 9 + 8 require a sophisticated and highly efficient keeping-track process. To mentally add 2 to 5, the child can easily keep track by counting the fingers of one hand. To mentally add 6 or more, the child must think to use, say, the fingers of both hands to keep track of the longer counting-on process.

Informal Subtraction

Concrete Subtraction

Preschoolers have numerous experiences where something is taken from an existing collection to make it smaller. An informal "take-away" view of subtraction serves as a basis for understanding and solving simple subtraction problems. In fact, if given objects such as blocks or allowed to use their fingers, most first graders and many kindergartners can solve take-away word problems like that below (e.g., Riley, Greeno, and Heller, 1983).

Helen had five postage stamps. She gave three to her sister. How many stamps does Helen have left?

Children use objects to model the take-away process implied by such problems. Specifically, they concretely represent the minuend (larger number) with objects (e.g., blocks, fingers, or marks), remove the number of objects equal to the subtrahend (the smaller number), and count the remainder to determine the answer. For example, to solve the word problem above, a child might automatically put up five fingers, then count and bend down again three fingers, and count the remaining fingers to determine the difference. Children commonly devise such an informal procedure and can *take away with objects* with little or no formal instruction.

Some children may know the take-away-with-objects procedure but may count inaccurately. For the word problem above, for example, a child may have difficulty representing the minuend accurately (put up four fingers or put out four blocks instead of five), take away one object too many or too few, or misenumerate the remaining objects. Such counting errors often lead to answers that are off only by plus or minus one.

Verbal-Count Procedures

Typically, children devise their own verbal-count procedures for modeling the take-away process. As with addition, young children can mentally calculate simple differences because they use their highly familiar knowledge of the number sequence. Early on, their number-before knowledge permits children to mentally take away one. For instance, many kindergartners can readily determine that four candies take away one candy is three, because they know that three precedes four in the count sequence.

In time, children spontaneously invent verbal-count procedures that replace their concrete procedure for calculating differences of more than one: *take away 2 to 5* and *take away 6 to 9* (e.g., Baroody, 1984b; Fuson, 1984). Initially, many children use a verbal-count procedure called *counting-down* that—like the concrete procedure—directly models "taking away" (e.g., Carpenter and Moser, 1982). Counting-down entails starting with the cardinal value of the minuend, counting backwards the number of times equal to the subtrahend, and announcing the last number counted (e.g., 5 − 2: "5; 4 [that's one taken away], 3 [that's two taken away]—so the answer is 3"). This procedure can be used with ease when subtracting two and three or even four and five. By the end of first grade, most children can efficiently take away 2 to 5.

With subtrahends greater than 5, keeping track of the counting-down process becomes increasingly difficult. As children are introduced to more difficult symbolic problems (e.g., 9 − 7) and take-away word problems (e.g., Hope had \$9 and spent \$7; how many dollars does she have left?), they resort to another verbal-count procedure that does not directly model taking away but does minimize the keeping-track process. Counting-up involves starting with the cardinal value of the subtrahend, counting forward until the minuend is reached—while keeping track of the number of steps in the forward count (e.g., 9 − 7: "7; 8 [that's 1 more], 9 [that's 2 more]—so the difference is two"). By third grade, many children discover that counting-down is relatively easy to use when the difference is greater than the subtrahend (e.g., 9 − 4 = 5), especially when the subtrahend is very small (e.g., 9 − 2 = 7). They recognize that counting-up is relatively more efficient otherwise (e.g., 9 − 7 = 2, 5 − 4 = 1, 19 − 12 = 7). At this point, children switch between the two informal subtraction procedures—choosing whichever one requires the least effort (Woods, Resnick, and Groen, 1975). The ability to flexibly choose between counting-down and counting-up better enables children to *take away from teens* (e.g., 11 − 4, 13 − 9).

Informal Multiplication

Typically, counting is also children's initial basis for determining multiplication products (e.g., Allardice, 1978; Kouba, 1986). Multiplication is often interpreted by children as the repeated addition of like terms. Usually, children just learning multiplication are already accustomed to *adding like sets of 2 to 5* objects (e.g., three groups of four objects: OOOO OOOO OOOO). The total number of objects can be determined by starting with one and counting all the objects, skip counting ("4, 8, 12"), or a combination of skip counting and counting by ones ("4, 8 is two fours; 9, 10, 11, 12, is the third four"). Children may also use known addition combinations to figure out such problems ("4 + 4 is 8; 8 + 4 is 12") or a combination of known addition facts and counting (e.g., "4 + 4 is 8 [that's two fours], 9, 10, 11, 12 [that's three fours]—so the answer is 12").

Many children quickly invent an object-counting procedure that involves representing one of the like sets with objects (e.g., fingers), and repeatedly counting this set as needed (e.g., for three groups of 4 objects: Put up four fingers and count, "1, 2, 3, 4 [that's four counted one time] 5, 6, 7, 8 [that's two times]; 9, 10, 11, 12 [that's three times]—so the answer is 12"). Table 6–2 illustrates this procedure. Note that in the illustration, fingers are used in two ways. The fingers of one hand are used to represent the counted set, and the fingers of the second hand are used to keep track of how many times the first set is counted.

Table 6–2 A Semiconcrete Multiplication Procedure Using Three Groups of Four as an Example and Fingers to Keep Track

Step	Left Hand	Right Hand
1	"Four."	"That's one four."
2	"5, 6, 7, 8."	"That's two fours."
3	"9, 10, 11, *12*."	"That's three fours."

Adding like sets with terms greater than 5 is rather difficult for children who rely on informal procedures. For eight groups of seven, for example, skip-counting and repeated-addition methods are difficult because skip counts of seven and addition facts involving seven are relatively less familiar to children than those involving smaller numbers. An object-counting procedure is difficult because 7 cannot be represented on one hand and a child cannot keep track of 8 counts of 7 on the other.

Table 6–3 summarizes the developmental sequence of the informal addition, subtraction, and multiplication procedures described above.

Table 6–3 A Suggested Sequence of Informal Arithmetic by Grade Level

Level	Informal Addition		Informal Subtraction		Informal Multiplication
	Concrete Addition	*Verbal-Count Procedures*	*Concrete Subtraction*	*Verbal-Count Procedures*	
K	Count all: Sets 1 to 5	—	—	—	—
	—	Mentally add one more	—	—	—
	—	—	Take away with objects	—	—
	—	—	—	Mentally take away one	—
1	Count all: Sets more than 5	Count from one to add 2 to 5	—	—	—
	—	Count-on 2 to 5 from the larger addend	—	—	—
	—	—	—	Take away: 2 to 5	—
	—	Mentally add on 6 to 9 more	—	—	—
2	—	—	—	Take away: 6 to 9	—
	—	—	—	Take away from teens	Adding 2 to 5 like sets
3	—	—	—	—	Adding more than 5 like sets

INSTRUCTION

In general, the operations should be introduced in contexts that are meaningful to children. Word problems and games are ideal media. The operations should be introduced concretely in terms of counting objects. Though some children will spontaneously model the meaning of word problems with objects, others may need to be encouraged to do so. Egyptian hieroglyphics are a useful vehicle for modeling word problems pictorially or semiconcretely. (Sets of 1 to 9 are depicted with tallies, which is a natural form of representation for many children.) Introduce the operations with small numbers (1 to 5); introduce numbers greater than 5 after they have achieved proficiency with smaller sets.

Instruction for preschool and kindergarten children should focus on concrete informal addition. Some children will invent verbal adding strategies before first grade, and this should not be discouraged. Teachers probably should wait until first grade before actively encouraging verbal counting strategies for addition—particularly the relatively sophisticated counting-on strategy.

Introduce informal subtraction after children are familiar with informal addition. Many children will find subtraction relatively difficult. Although multiplication is often postponed until third grade, informal multiplication can be introduced any time after children have mastered informal addition concepts and skills. Indeed, because it builds directly on their informal addition, children may find informal multiplication easier than informal subtraction.

Informal Addition: Concrete

Count-All: Sets 1 to 5

First ensure adequate proficiency with such prerequisite skills as enumeration of sets 1 to 10, production of sets 1 to 5, and fine comparisons of 1 to 10. Skill with finger patterns 1 to 5 or mentally adding one more would be helpful but is not necessary. For children who do not know a counting-all procedure, use simple word problems and a demonstration like that described in Example 6-1. Word problems are used to foster meaningful learning of the procedure.

Example 6-1 Using Word Problems to Teach a Basic (Count-All) Addition Procedure

---

If a child does not know a count-all procedure, read the following word problem and demonstrate how it can be figured out using pennies:

"Cookie Monster reached into a bag of cookies and pulled out two yummy cookies. He was so hungry, he then turned the bag upside down, and three more cookies fell out. How many cookies did Cookie Monster get? How much are two cookies and three more altogether?" Then say, "Put out two pennies to show how many cookies he grabbed first. Now put out three more pennies to show how many fell out of the bag. To find out how many there are altogether, count all the pennies."

After this demonstration, present Problem 1 below and encourage the child to use pennies, blocks, fingers, or other countable objects to calculate the answer. If the child remains silent or guesses incorrectly, reteach the counting-all procedure as done in the demonstration. Whether or not the child spontaneously uses the counting-all procedure to solve Problem 1, proceed with Problem 2. Many kindergarten-age children and even some elementary-level mentally handicapped children will need only a single demonstration of the concrete addition procedure to learn to count-all. In any case, monitor follow-up word-problem exercises and reteach the procedure as necessary.

1. "Cookie Monster's mother put out four cookies for Cookie Monster. Because he was very hungry, Cookie Monster took two more cookies out of the cookie jar while his mother was not looking. As he walked out of the kitchen, his mother asked: 'Cookie Monster, how many cookies do you have?' He had four cookies, and he got two more. How many cookies did Cookie Monster have altogether? You can figure out the answer any way you want: You can use these pennies, this paper and pencil, or your fingers." If necessary, repeat the problem. If the child remains silent, guesses incorrectly, or verbally calculates incorrectly, prompt with, "Use these pennies or your fingers to figure out how much four cookies and two more cookies are altogether."

2. "Cookie Monster went to the store to buy cupcakes for his mother. He picked out five cupcakes with chocolate frosting and three with strawberry frosting. When he went to the check-out counter to pay for the cupcakes, the check-out girl said, 'How many cupcakes do you have?' He got five cupcakes with chocolate frosting and three cupcakes with strawberry frosting. How many cupcakes did he have altogether? You can figure out the answer any way you want: You can use these pennies, this paper and pencil, or your fingers." If necessary, repeat the problem. If the child remains silent, guesses incorrectly, or verbally calculates incorrectly, prompt with, "Use these pennies or your fingers to figure out how much five cupcakes and three cupcakes are altogether."

Particularly with children who have had little or no previous addition experience, it is important to check for and immediately correct the error commonly made when children are first required to add sets. After producing sets to represent each addend, a child may start with one each time and simply enumerate the sets of objects separately. To help children understand that addition involves joining two collections, push the objects representing each addend together and then request the child to count to determine the answer. If necessary, explain that to find out how many there are altogether, we have to count all the objects without beginning again with one.

Counting all can be practiced in the context of any game that uses dice, such as the **Racing-Car** and the **Jungle-Trip** games described in Examples 6–2 and 6–3. A number of games from the Wynroth Math Program (e.g., **Animal Spots** described in Example 2–1) can be used for addition training by using two dice. Note that the dots on the dice should be large enough for the children to enumerate them with relative ease. If a child tries to count each die separately, push the dice together and point out that all the dots need to be counted to find out how many there are altogether.

Example 6-2 Racing-Car Game

Objective: Practice counting-all with addends 0 to 5.

Grade Level: K or 1.

Participants: Two to six players.

Materials: Race-track board (with at least 21 squares large enough to accommodate toy race cars), differently colored miniature race cars (or other markers for each player), and dice with 0 to 5 dots.

Procedure: Give the players their choice of race car and place the cars on the square marked Start on the race-track board. Explain, "In the Racing-Car game, we start here and race around the track. The car that goes furthest wins. To find out how many spaces we can move on our turn, we throw the dice, and add the two amounts shown."

Example 6-3 Jungle-Trip Game

Objective: Practice counting all with addends 0 to 5.

Grade Level: K or 1.

Participants: Two to six children.

Materials: Jungle-Trip game board (see below), markers, and dice with 0 to 5 dots.

Procedure: Have the players place their markers on the square marked Start on the Jungle-Trip game board. Explain, "In Jungle Trip, start here, try to avoid the jungle dangers, and make your way to a pyramid treasure. When it's your turn, we roll these dice to see how many spaces you can move."

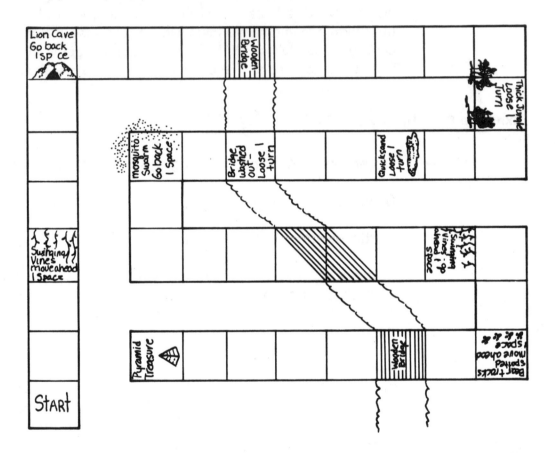

After children have learned a counting-all procedure with objects and how to use Egyptian hieroglyphics to represent a single set, verbally present word problems that are *accompanied* by a hieroglyphic representation (see Frame A of Example 6–4). Next, ask the students to record with Egyptian hieroglyphics verbally presented word problems (see Frame B of Example 6–4). Solving these pictured problems can easily be done by counting all and provides additional practice using this procedure.

Example 6–4 Addition Story Problems with Egyptian Hieroglyphics

A. Story problem accompanied by Egyptian hieroglyphic representation.

Teacher reads, "The pharaoh received three gold crowns for his birthday, which his scribe recorded in the royal record. The next day, two more gold crowns came. The scribe recorded these in the royal record also. According to the royal record, how many gold crowns did the pharaoh have altogether?"

Child records his or her answer (5) on the worksheet:

Royal Record

B. Story problem that students depict with Egyptian hieroglyphics and then solve.

Teacher says, "Pretend you are the intelligence officer of an Egyptian army. One of your jobs is to keep records of how many prisoners your army captures. Listen to the following story and use Egyptian hieroglyphics to make a record of the prisoners captured."

Story: "The Egyptian soldiers captured four enemy soldiers during the battle. They found three more after the battle. How many prisoners were captured altogether?"

Child depicts addends and records the sum on the worksheet:

Count-All: Sets More than 5

First ensure that prerequisite skills (enumeration and production of large sets and counting-all with small numbers) are mastered. The games used for counting all with sets 1 to 5 can be used to practice adding numbers 5 to 10 by substituting larger dice (five to ten dots on a side). When solving word problems, make available blocks, pencil and paper for making marks (tallies or Egyptian hieroglyphics), or other concrete or semiconcrete means for calculating sums. For some children, introducing larger problems will be a powerful incentive to invent verbal-count procedures or other more advanced means of determining sums.

Informal Addition: Verbal

Mentally Add "One More"

First ensure that a child is fairly proficient with such basic skills as number after 1 to 5 and enumeration of sets 1 to 5. For a child with little or no understanding of addition, introduce the addition of one in terms of counting and with sets of one to three objects. This training can take the form of a **Prediction Game**. For example, put out three pencils and ask the child to count the set. Next, add one more pencil and ask the child to predict how many there are now. If it makes the game more interesting, cover the set until the child makes the prediction. Then have the child count the set to check the prediction. As he or she makes progress, make the game more challenging by starting with somewhat larger sets. After the child is proficient with this concrete form of the game, introduce the less-concrete version: the **Behind-the-Screen Activity** (Example 6–5).

Example 6–5   Behind-the-Screen Activity

Objective: Mental addition (and subtraction) of one in a concrete context.

Grade Level: PK or K.

Participants: One child, small group of children, two small teams of children, or a whole class.

Materials: Pennies and a screen (e.g., 8½″ × 11″ piece of thin cardboard supported by a base). Prizes are optional.

Procedure: For example, say, "Here's one penny [put one penny in front of the child or children]. Now I'll hide the one penny with this screen [place the card in front of the penny]. Now I'll put out one more penny. [Do not allow the participant(s) to view the addition of the extra penny.] Without looking behind the screen, how much is one penny and one more altogether?" Then proceed with additional $n + 1$ questions in a similar manner. After an object is added to the collection behind the screen and the child has made his or her prediction, the screen can be removed, and the child can count to check the prediction. To provide variety, include $n + 0$ questions (cases where nothing is added to the hidden set) and $n - 1$ questions (cases where one is removed from the hidden set).

Count from One to Add 2 to 5

First ensure proficiency with the developmentally more basic strategy: counting all with sets 1 to 5. If given the opportunity to practice addition with objects, a child—when ready—may invent this more sophisticated verbal strategy. This process can be facilitated, though, by using word problem exercises, or (as discussed in Chapter 8) dice with numerals. In these situations, children may find it more convenient to use a verbal procedure than to produce and enumerate objects as required by a count-all strategy.

Counting-On 2 to 5 from the Larger Addend

First ensure that a child has mastered concrete addition: counting all with sets 1 to 5. If a child cannot make fine number comparisons automatically, have him or her master this prerequisite for calculational procedures that involves picking the larger addend. Once this skill is automatic, most children will spontaneously apply this number-comparison skill to make their informal arithmetic easier—to invent (the advanced form of counting from one to add 2 to 5 or) counting on 2 to 5 from the larger addend.

To maximize the chances that children will invent counting-on, ensure that they have mastered the prerequisite skills: count from one to add and mentally add one more. To facilitate the invention of counting-on, encourage mastery of the number patterns on dice (recognition of sets 1 to 5) and provide them ample opportunity to sum two dice patterns (see Frame A of Figure 6–1). To help prompt counting on, substitute a numeral die for one of the dot dice (see Frame B of Figure 6–1). A training procedure for directly encouraging the invention of counting-on is described in Figure 6–2.

Mentally Add 6 or More

First ensure that a child has mastered a keeping-track method and can count on with small problems (counting on 2 to 5 from the larger addend). If the prerequisite skill is automatic, training can focus on helping the child to extend the keeping-track process to count on 6 to 9. For a child who only makes minor errors, all that may be necessary is computational practice and encouragement to calculate carefully. Use a die with five to nine dots and a die with the numerals 5 to 9 to play any of the games listed earlier for

Figure 6–1   Using Dice to Foster Counting-On Using 5 + 4 as an Example

A. Using recognition of dice patterns.

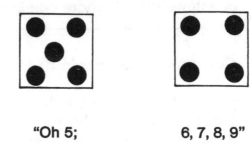

"Oh 5;   6, 7, 8, 9"

B. Using a numeral die and a dot die.

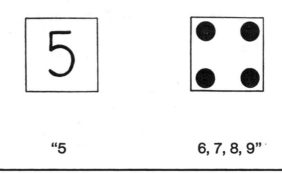

"5   6, 7, 8, 9"

Figure 6–2   Counting-On Training*

1. Present the child with a concrete representation of each addend and ask the child to add the sets. For example, say: "Let's add 5 and 3. Here's five [put out a card with five dots] and here's three [put out a card with three dots]. How much are five dots and three dots altogether?"

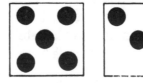

2. Before the child has a chance to count from one, hide the representation of the first addend and restate the problem: "How much are five and three altogether?"

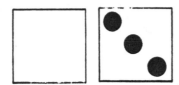

*This method was suggested to me by Ed Rathmell of North Iowa State University.

counting all: sets 1 to 5. For a child experiencing great difficulty in keeping track of six to nine, point out that the fingers of both hands can be used, or tape a number list from 1 to 9 on the child's desk to make keeping track easier (e.g., 8 + 6: "8, 9 [point to the 1 on the number list], 10 [point to the 2] . . . 14 [point to the 6 and stop]").

Informal Subtraction: Concrete

Take Away with Objects

First ensure adequate proficiency with more basic skills (counting all with sets 1 to 5 and mentally take away one) and component skills (production of sets 1 to 5 and 6 to 10, finger patterns 1 to 5 and 6 to 10, and enumeration of sets 1 to 5 and 6 to 10). For children who do not know take-away-with-objects procedure, use simple word problems and a demonstration like that described in Example 6–6. As with addition, word problems are used to foster meaningful learning and should involve small numbers (one to five) initially. As the child makes progress, problems with terms up to 10 (or even larger) can be introduced.

Example 6–6 Using Word Problems to Teach a Basic (Take-Away) Procedure

If a child does not appear to know a take-away-with-objects procedure, read the following word problem and demonstrate how it can be solved using pennies.

"Cookie Monster got six candy bars as a present. Because he had just eaten a huge meal and dessert, he only ate two candy bars and saved the rest for his bedtime snack. If Cookie Monster had six candy bars and he munched up two, how many does he have left for his snack?" Then say, "Put out six pennies to show how many candy bars he started with. Now take away two, because he ate two. To find out how many are left for his snack, just count the remaining pennies."

After the demonstration, present Problem 1 and encourage the child to use pennies again to calculate the answer. If the child remains silent or guesses incorrectly, reteach the take-away-with-objects procedure as done in the demonstration. Whether or not the child spontaneously uses the take-away-with-objects procedure to solve Problem 1, proceed with Problem 2. Many kindergarten-age children will need only a single demonstration of the concrete subtraction procedure to learn to take away with objects.

1. "Cookie Monster baked five cookies as a present for his sister on her birthday. The cookies looked so good when they came out of the oven that Cookie Monster ate three on the spot. If Cookie Monster made five cookies and ate three, how many are left for his sister? You can figure out the answer any way you want: You can use these pennies, this paper and pencil, or your fingers." If necessary, repeat the problem. If the child remains silent, guesses incorrectly, or verbally calculates incorrectly, prompt with, "Use these pennies or your fingers to figure out how much five take away three is."

2. "Cookie Monster was supposed to bring seven cookies to school for the holiday party. On the way to school, Cookie Monster could not resist sampling the cookies. He did not stop eating until he had swallowed four cookies. If Cookie Monster started out with seven cookies and he ate four, how many were left for the holiday party? You can figure out the answer any way you want: You can use these pennies, this paper and pencil, or your fingers." If necessary, repeat the problem. If the child remains silent, guesses incorrectly, or verbally calculates incorrectly, prompt with, "Use these pennies or your fingers to figure out how much seven take away four is."

By a simple rule change, take away with objects can be practiced with small groups of children by using the games suggested for concrete addition: **Animal Spots** (Example 2–1); **Racing-Car** and **Jungle-Trip** (Examples 6–2 and 6–3). In the most basic form of these games, have a player roll dice with 0 to 5 dots, choose the die with the larger number of dots, and take away (by covering up) dots on that die equal to those on the die with the smaller number of dots. A more advanced form can include a die with 0 to 5 dots and one with 5 to 10 dots.

Additional meaningful practice can be provided by reading children word problems (with minuends up to 9) and asking them to represent them with Egyptian hieroglyphics. This would entail representing the minuend with one-symbols (tallies) and the take-away process with cross outs (see Example 6–7). Such a procedure is very similar to the informal method with tallies that children often naturally rely on when doing subtraction assignments.

Example 6–7   Take-Away Story Problems

Teacher reads, "You are the pharaoh's scribe and royal record keeper. Your job is to keep track of the pharaoh's possessions. Listen to the following story about the pharaoh's horses and use Egyptian hieroglyphics to make a record of what happened."

Story problem: "The pharaoh had five horses [pause to allow students to represent with tallies]. He gave two to a visiting king [pause to allow students to represent with cross outs]. How many did the pharaoh have left in his stable?"

Pupil's depiction:

𝅸 𝅸 𝅸 𝅒 𝅒

Informal Subtraction: Verbal

Mentally "Take Away One"

First ensure that a child is fairly proficient with such basic skills as mentally adding one more and number before 1 to 5. For a child with little or no understanding of subtraction, introduce take away of one in terms of counting and with sets of 1 to 3 objects. This training can take the form of a

Prediction Game. For example, put out three pencils and ask the child to count the set. Then take away one and ask the child to predict how many there are now. If it makes the game more interesting, cover the set until the child makes the prediction. Then have the child count the set to check the prediction. As the child makes progress, make the game more challenging by starting with somewhat larger sets.

Behind-the-Screen (Example 6–5) is also a good activity to employ. Children who have not mastered number before or who have little or no understanding of subtraction may respond to $n - 1$ questions by stating the number of the set originally hid or by *adding* one to this number. If checking indicates the child has mastered number before, demonstrate the take-away process with objects in the context of a story.

A teacher, older children, or even the pupils themselves can put on **Mysterious-Disappearance Skits** in which, for example, Cookie Monster is supposed to bring five cupcakes to school for a party. However, the hungry Muppet hides behind a tree and eats one of the cupcakes. The audience can figure out how many he has left.

Take Away 2 to 5

First ensure that a child has mastered prerequisites (e.g., mentally takes away one, counting on from the larger addend, and counts backwards from 10). To foster counting-down, present word problems that entail taking away one followed by those that involve taking away two. As the child is ready, introduce problems that involve taking away three to five. If necessary, help the child to find ways of keeping track. For instance, model the counting-down procedure, using fingers to keep track. Other methods are discussed in Chapter 8 of Baroody (1987a) (see in particular Figure 8–6). If a child starts the keeping-track process too soon, explicitly point out, for example, "When we take two from five, five is how many we begin with. After we take away one, there are four left. After we take away two, there are three left." If necessary, have the child compare the outcomes of his or her incorrect verbal procedure with the outcomes of a take-away-with-objects procedure. If a child is prone to rush through the verbal-count procedure, reassure the child that accuracy is more important and that counting (and using fingers to keep track) is a sensible and widely used method.

Take Away 6 to 9

First ensure that a child has mastered the more basic skill: take away 2 to 5. For a child who relies on a counting-down procedure and has difficulty accurately calculating take away 6 to 9, encourage the child to devise a counting-up procedure (e.g., **The Balance Activity** described in Example 8–1 of Baroody, 1987a). In addition, help the child to see that counting-up is interchangeable with and can be used as a substitute for counting down (see Chapter 8 for details). If needed, reassure the child that it is not necessary to rush this informal calculating procedure. If indicated, help the child to start the keeping-track process in the correct place as suggested for the section entitled Take Away 2 to 5.

Take Away from Teens

First ensure that the child has mastered the more basic skills (take away 2 to 5 and 6 to 9, cite the number before the teens, and counting backwards from 20). As with take away 6 to 9, instruction should focus on helping children to see that counting-down and counting-up are interchangeable procedures.

Informal Multiplication

Adding 2 to 5 Like Sets

First ensure that a child has mastered foundational concepts and skills. At the very least, the child should be proficient with counting all with sets 1 to 5 and more than 5. It would be helpful if the child could count on from the larger addend. If the child has not mastered skip counting yet, counting by twos, fives, and so forth can be remedied in conjunction with training aimed at adding like sets.

To help children understand the idea of repeated addition of like terms, use word problems such as those in Example 6–8 (Kouba, 1986; Quintero, 1985). Encourage children to use objects or make drawings (with tallies or Egyptian hieroglyphics) to model concretely or semiconcretely the meaning of the problems. In addition to helping children understand the problem, such models may help children to discover shortcuts for finding solutions to such problems. For example, with three groups of five

$$\begin{array}{l} \text{OOOOO} \\ (\ \text{OOOOO}\ ), \text{most children abandon rather quickly a count-all-the-items-} \\ \text{OOOOO} \end{array}$$

by-one strategy in favor of more efficient methods such as skip counting ("5, 10, 15") and known addition combinations ("5 and 5 is 10 and 5 more is 15") (see Baroody, 1987a). The game described in Example 6–9 (**How Many Dots?**) can provide practice in estimating products as well as encouraging this shortcutting process.

Example 6–8   Using Word Problems to Introduce Repeated Addition of Like Terms

Have children solve word problems, such as these space stories. Explain that they may figure out the answers any way they want—including objects or making a drawing.

1. "The crew of the starship was assigned to collect rock samples on the newly discovered planet Orb. If each of the five crew members collected three rock samples, how many rock samples were brought back? You can figure it out by using these pennies, your fingers, this paper and pencil, counting out loud, or any way you want." If necessary, repeat the problem. If correct, congratulate the child and proceed with the next problem. If the child is silent, indicates that he or she does not know, interprets the problem as addition (answers: "five"), or verbally calculates the product incorrectly, prompt with, "Use these pennies to figure out how many rock samples were collected if five crew members *each* collected three rock samples." If the child remains silent or still indicates that he does not know, suspend testing.

2. "On their flight back from Orb, the starship crew received a coded message from home base. The message consisted of two beeps repeated four times. How many beeps did the message consist of?" If necessary, repeat the problem. If the child is silent, indicates that he or she does not know, interprets the problem as addition (answers: "six"), or verbally calculates the product incorrectly, prompt with, "Use these pennies to figure out how many beeps were in the message if two beeps were repeated four times."

Example 6–9   How Many Dots?

Objectives: Estimation of products up to 25 (Basic Version), illustrate multiplication as the repeated addition of like terms, provide practice in finding the solution to such problems, and furnish an opportunity to discover and practice shortcuts such as skip counting.

Grade Level: 2 or 3.

Participants: Two children or two small teams of players. (Up to about six children or teams can play if, instead of the procedure described below, the teacher acts as a judge and decides the winner.)

Materials: Dot cards, materials for recording estimates (optional), numberline from 0 to 25, measuring strip (strip of paper as long as the numberline and some means to keep score (see below).

A. Gauging the accuracy of the first player's estimate.

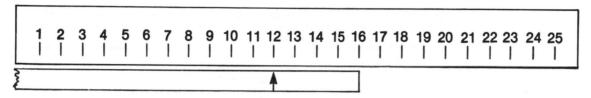

B. Gauging the accuracy of the second player's estimate.

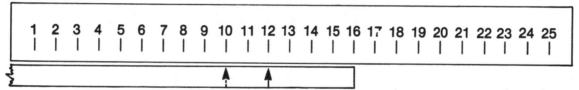

Procedure: A judge or one of the players turns over a card in the dot-card deck. Each player has about three seconds to guess how many dots are on the card. Recording answers on a magic slate, small chalkboard, or piece of paper is recommended. (To minimize disagreements, players should ensure that previous answers are not evident.) After estimates are noted, then the players should determine the exact number of dots. If a player does not give (record) an estimate within the time limit, his or her answer is disqualified and the other player wins the round. Otherwise, the winner is the player whose estimate is closer to the exact answer.

The relative closeness can be determined by using a numberline and a measuring strip. The judge or one of the players places the measuring strip under the numberline so that an end is at the mark for the exact answer (e.g., for 4 dots by 4 dots: 16). The first player's estimate (e.g., "12" in Frame A of the figure) is found on the numberline and its position is marked on the measuring strip. The same is done for the second player's estimate (e.g., "10" in Frame B of the figure). The player with the shorter mark is the winner and gets one point. Play continues until one player gets a predetermined winning total, a predetermined number of rounds as played, or a set amount of time runs out.

Adding More than 5 Like Sets

First ensure that a child has mastered the prerequisite skill (adding 2 to 5 like sets). Then help the child master the skills for informally figuring or reasoning out larger combinations: skip counting and adding-on or counting-on. For six groups of five items each, adding-on would entail: "Five groups of five is 25, so six groups of five is 25 and five more or 30." Similarly counting-on would involve: "Five groups of five is 25, so a sixth group is five more; 26 is one more, 27 is two more, 28 is three more, 29 is four more, *30* is five more." This can be done while playing **How Many Dots? (Advanced Version)**. (This version will require a numberline that runs from 0 to 81.)

For larger combinations, particularly, Wynroth (1986) suggests a vertical keeping-track method, which encourages children's natural tendency to use skip counting, adding-on, or counting-on. For a problem like five groups of six items each, a child would put out six objects or make six tally marks, and record a 6. Then the child would recount the six objects or tallies starting with seven and record the result of the second count: 12. This process would be repeated until the child has counted the six objects or tallies five times and recorded each result as shown below:

(1)	6
(2)	12
(3)	18
(4)	24
(5)	30

When introduced to another problem involving groups of six, the child would be encouraged to use his or her "six chart." For example, for six groups of six items each, the child would be encouraged to add or count on six from the fifth six or 30. This result would be recorded. In time, use of the chart would breed familiarity with skip counting by six as well as provide a basis for adding or counting on larger combinations.

Calculating the nine-times combinations, in particular, may seem insurmountable to children. Example 6–10 illustrates a finger-based device for figuring out the products of such combinations. This method has a number of advantages. Typically, third graders can master the strategy after only a couple of demonstrations. Children are often delighted that a teacher would show them a strategy that utilizes their natural medium for calculating: their fingers. (In effect, the teacher endorses the students' informal methods and thinking, which is important for building confidence.) The strategy also

Example 6–10 An Informal Means for Determining the Products of Nine

Fingers can be used to answer single-digit nine-times problems (e.g., "3 × 9" or "9 × 3") by means other than computing. Follow these steps:

1. Extend the fingers of both hands. Beginning with the left-most finger, count the fingers until the term multiplied by nine is reached. For example, with the palms facing away, the product of three times nine can be determined by beginning with the little finger of the left hand and counting this finger and the next two.

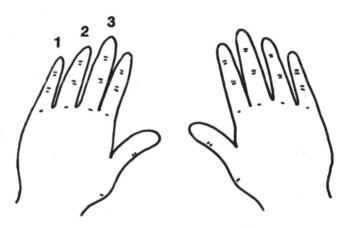

2. Fold down the last finger counted in Step 1 (e.g., for 3 × 9, the third finger from the left).

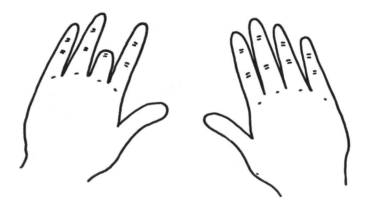

3. The number of fingers to the left of the folded finger specifies the tens digit of the product. The number of fingers to the right of the folded finger specifies the ones

digit. For 3 × 9, for instance, this process yields two and seven or "27."

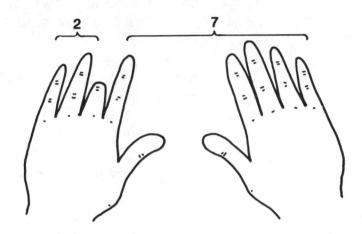

Note that for problems like 9 × 3, the order of the addends is disregarded. Thus 9 × 3 would be figured out in the very same manner as shown for 3 × 9.

The figures below illustrate Step 3 for 2 × 9 (9 × 2) and 7 × 9 (9 × 7).

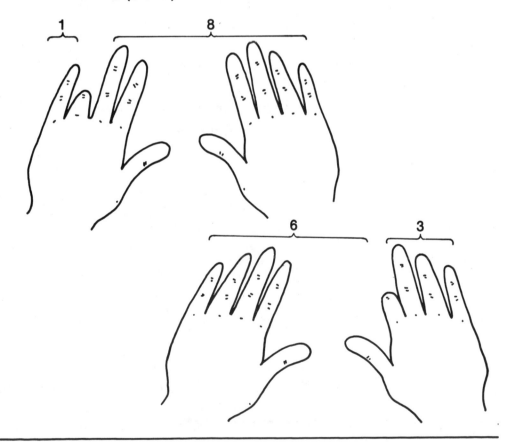

reinforces base-ten place-value concepts (the fingers represent so many tens and so many ones), and it is fun (Struck, 1987).

The idea of adding like sets can be applied to the task of gauging how many (like) groups a whole can be decomposed into. The activity **How Many Groups?** (Example 6–11) requires children to look at an array and *estimate* how many groups of a given number can be made. For Exercise A

Example 6–11 How Many Groups?

Objectives: Estimation of factors, group-in-like-sets concept, figuring out missing factor, fair-sharing concept, and missing-factor approach to figuring out division combinations. This activity could also be used to practice adding like sets of 2 to 5 as well as 6 to 9[+].

Grade Level: 3 to 4.

Participants: One child, small group of children, or whole class.

Materials: Worksheets like those in Figure 6–3 and stopwatch or watch with second hand (optional).

Procedure: At your signal have the participants turn over and examine their worksheet. Adjust the amount of time allowed to make an estimate according to the difficulty of the problem and the sophistication of the pupils. Enough time should be allowed to enable pupils to think about the problem and make a reasonable estimate but not so much time that they can determine an exact answer by counting by ones and grouping.

After children have recorded their estimate, have them circle the items in whatever groups the exercise calls for. Encourage children to compare the exact answer to their estimates. Ensure that a child is not belittled for his or her estimate. Emphasize that estimates are supposed to be (quick) educated guesses, rather than exact answers (figured out). It might be helpful to encourage a discussion of how to make better educated guesses (estimation strategies).

Children can practice honing their estimation skills with each other. One child can act as the teacher and briefly show one or several pupils an array. After the estimates are recorded, the teacher and pupil(s) can check the estimate by grouping.

Figure 6–3 Sample Worksheets for How Many Groups?

Exercise A

Estimate of how many bags of ___6___ can be made from the pile of 42 apples:

Number of groups of ___6___ circled: _____

```
O   O   O   O   O   O

O   O   O   O   O   O

O   O   O   O   O   O

O   O   O   O   O   O

O   O   O   O   O   O

O   O   O   O   O   O

O   O   O   O   O   O
```

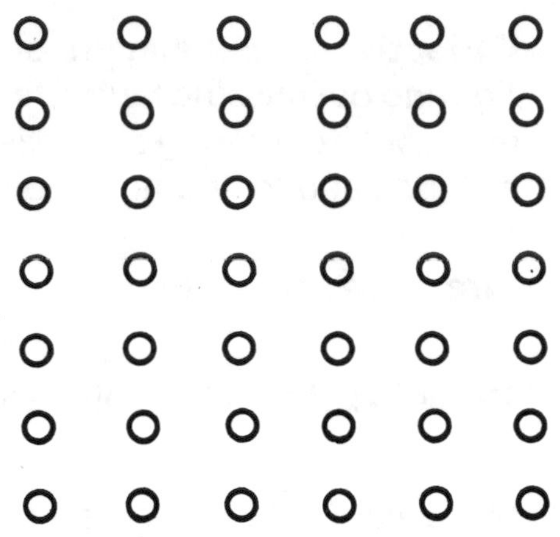

Exercise B

Estimate of how many bags of ___6___ can be made from the pile of 42 apples:

Number of groups of ___6___ circled: _____

```
O   O   O   O   O   O   O   O   O   O

O   O   O   O   O   O   O   O   O   O

O   O   O   O   O   O   O   O   O   O

O   O   O   O   O   O   O   O   O   O

O   O
```

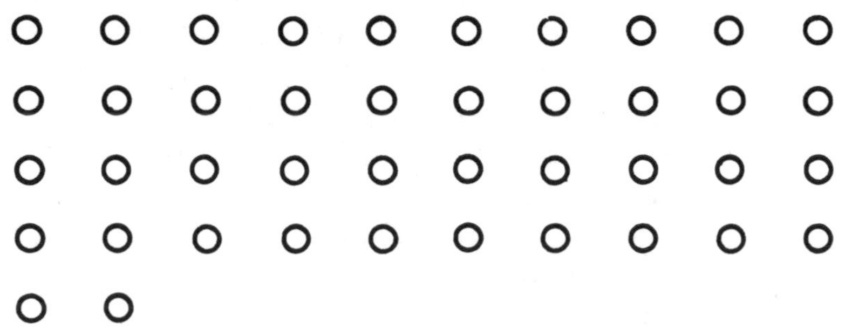

Exercise C

Estimate of how many bags of ___6___ can be made from the pile of 45 apples:

Number of groups of ___6___ circled: _____

O O O O O O O O O O
O O O O O O O O O O
O O O O O O O O O O
O O O O O O O O O O
O O O O O

Exercise D

Estimate of how many bags of ___6___ can be made from the pile of 45 apples:

Number of groups of ___6___ circled: _____

Estimate of the number of apples left over: _____

Actual number of apples left over: _____

O O O O O O O O O O
O O O O O O O O O O
O O O O O O O O O O
O O O O O O O O O O
O O O O O

in Figure 6–3, a child would have about ten seconds to look at the 6×7 array of data and gauge how many groups of six are present. Children should discover that with such arrays, they simply have to count the number of rows (of six) to determine the answer. Estimates can be checked by drawing circles around groups of six and counting the number of circles.

After a couple of introductory exercises like Exercise A, more difficult problems like Exercise B can be given. By checking their estimates by circling groups, children should gradually become familiar with the factors of a product (the basic multiplication combinations). Such an exercise also lays the concrete ground work for understanding division. For example, if we divide up a basket of 42 apples into bags of 6 apples each, how many people can share the apples fairly? It also provides a means for reasoning out and then mastering division combination (e.g., 42 divided by 6: How many groups of 6 do I need to make 42: seven).

Exercise C illustrates the next step that can be taken: grouping that leaves something leftover. This is helpful in illustrating the fact that numbers mesh (divide evenly) with only some factors (e.g., 6, 12, 18, 24, 30, 36, and 42 can be divided fairly into groups of 6 but 45 cannot). Such an exercise can also serve as a concrete lead into division with remainders. Exercise D addresses this issue even more directly.

SUMMARY

Initial arithmetic instruction should be based on counting—first with objects and then verbally. It can be made even more meaningful by using simple word problems. Moreover, it should focus first and at some length on problems with addends zero to five. Children should be encouraged to find or may need help finding more efficient strategies for coping with problems with terms greater than five.

Children typically come to school with the idea that addition involves incrementing. This provides the basis for inventing or readily grasping a concrete counting-all strategy or mentally adding one more. In time, children invent verbal strategies for larger problems. Initially, they may count from one to compute sums. Nearly all children invent counting on. The invention of this relatively sophisticated informal strategy can be accelerated or fostered by careful manipulation of a child's practice.

Children typically come to school with the idea that subtraction involves "taking away." This provides the basis for inventing or readily adopting a take-away strategy with objects and mentally taking one away. In time, children elaborate on their informal subtraction knowledge and invent verbal procedures for taking away two or more.

Children frequently interpret multiplication as repeated addition of like terms. As a result, they can bring to bear a number of informal calculational strategies including skip counting, using known addition combinations, or counting-on.

Chapter 7

Reading and Writing Symbols

Typically, children learn oral counting and numbering skills before they learn how to interpret, make, and use written representations of numbers (e.g., Ginsburg, 1982). Written representations of numbers, such as 5, 12, 47, and 106, are called numerals (see Figure 7–1). This chapter will focus on single-digit numerals: 1 to 9. Skills with multidigit numerals (e.g., 12, 47, 106, or 1,420) will be discussed in Chapter 10 along with other place-value skills and concepts.

Verbal skills with numerals include *numeral recognition* and *reading numerals*. Numeral recognition involves identifying the written form of a

Figure 7–1　Numbers or Numerals?

Should a teacher refer to a written number as a *number* or a *numeral*? Technically, 7, for example, is *not* a number. It is a numeral that represents the abstract concept, seven. Technically, 7 and other numerals are *labels* or *names for numbers*. Other names for (representation of) seven are $||||||\,|$, 5 + 2, and 8 − 1. Purists would insist that teachers use the technically correct terminology numeral to refer to written numbers. Others (e.g., Ginsburg, 1982) dismiss the distinction as unimportant. After all, children will tend to call numerals numbers in any case.

I recommend a compromise. Teachers should make an effort to use the terms *number* and *numeral* correctly so that children can learn from their example. However, I would be willing to call, say, 7 a number for the sake of clear communication (e.g., if a child were puzzled by the term *numeral*).

spoken number. This can be tested by reading a numeral to a child and asking the child to pick the numeral from several choices. Numeral reading involves naming a written form. This can be tested by showing a child a numeral and asking him or her what it is. Recognizing and reading numerals not only lags behind but depends on a child's oral-counting skill. Basically, children must learn which arbitrary written symbol represents the terms "one" to "nine" in their oral-count sequence.

Graphic skills with numerals require children to make the written forms of numbers and include *copying numerals* and *writing numerals*. Copying involves showing a child a numeral and asking him or her to draw a likeness of the model. Writing numerals involves reading a number to a child and asking him or her to draw its symbol.

Recognizing numerals is a first step in the *symbol recognition* skills required by school mathematics; children must also learn to identify the operation signs (+, −, ×, ÷). In addition, children must learn to recognize and use relational signs (symbols that denote important mathematical relationships, such as = signifies "equals").

LEARNING

Verbal Skills with Numerals

Numeral Recognition

In order to *recognize the one-digit numerals,* a child must be able to distinguish among the numerals. To do this, the child must know the defining characteristics of each numeral: the component parts and how the parts fit together to form a whole (Gibson and Levin, 1975). For example, the component parts of 6 are a curved line and a single loop. These component parts fit together in a particular way: The loop attaches at the bottom and to the right of the curve, which faces to the right. The curved line distinguishes a 6 from numerals that contain only straight lines (1, 4, and 7). The single loop distinguishes 6 from all other numerals except 9. The relative position of the loop and the direction of the curve are the only features that separate written sixes and nines.

Children sometimes confuse numerals with letters that share defining characteristics (e.g., read 5 as S). They frequently confuse numerals that share defining characteristics: 2 and 5 or 6 and 9. Many young children have difficulty discriminating between 6 and 9 (e.g., read 6 as "9"), because these numerals are similar except for the orientation of their parts. Reliably labeling orientation or direction (e.g., "the loop of a nine is at the top left") is a relatively difficult skill for young children to master. As a result, some children continue to have difficulty distinguishing these numerals in first and even second grade.

Reading Numerals

Like numeral recognition, *reading one-digit numerals* requires children to know the defining characteristics of the numerals. Unlike numeral recognition, reading numerals requires that children recall the verbal name for the represented number. Thus, numeral reading is somewhat more difficult than numeral recognition because children must remember verbal labels as well as what the written forms of numbers look like. Many children learn to distinguish among the single-digit numerals and thus learn to recognize and read these numerals before kindergarten.

Graphic Skills with Numerals

Copying Numerals

In order to *copy one-digit numerals,* it would seem that all children need is eye-hand and fine-motor coordination. Yet even after young children can demonstrate these perceptual-motor skills, an ability to copy numerals is not guaranteed. A child might repeatedly copy a five backwards: Ƨ . What they need is a systematic plan of execution: a motor plan for translating into motor actions what he or she sees (Kirk, 1981). A motor plan consists of a set of rules. These rules specify where to start and how to proceed (Goodnow and Levine, 1973). For example, to write a 7, children must know they should start at the upper left, draw a horizontal line from left to right, change direction, and make a diagonal line that ends up in the lower left. Before or soon after they enter school, children typically either figure out or are taught how to make numerals.

Without a motor plan, children will have difficulty properly forming a numeral—even with a model numeral in front of them or with repeated demonstrations. A common problem is starting off in the wrong direction. For example, if a child starts to copy the "hat" of the five and goes from left to right, the result is a backwards five: Ƨ . Even though he or she can see that the numeral is backwards and incorrect, a child may continue to copy fives backwards. The error will persist if the child does not recognize how to correct the incorrect motor plan.

Various difficulties can arise from an inaccurate or incomplete motor plan. Some children mimic the reading process by consistently drawing from left to right. As a result, such children regularly reverse fives (Ƨ) and nines (ρ). Because their orientation is difficult to define, diagonals are relatively difficult for young children to draw. When copying diagonals, young children often have difficulty in reproducing the direction of the model diagonal (e.g., / is incorrectly copied as ❘ , ╲ , or ▬). Common copying errors with sevens then, are the absence of a diagonal (┐) or a misdirected diagonal (╲). Eights are relatively difficult to copy because of the relatively sophisticated preplanning required to make the numeral. Many errors are due to the unsophisticated motor plans children use to copy numerals. For example, instead of a motor plan that is executed in a single motion, younger children tend to copy numerals by drawing the parts separately. If this is not done carefully in a preplanned manner, the child may not put the parts into a proper and recognizable part-whole relationship (e.g., copy 7 as ⌐| or 9 as ⵁ).

Writing Numerals

Like copying numerals, *writing one-digit numerals* requires that children have a motor plan to direct the writing process. Unlike copying numerals, writing numerals must be done without model numerals present—without any clues as to their appearance. Thus, children must *remember* (1) what the written form looks like (the defining characteristics of a numeral) as well as (2) the step-by-step plan for translating this mental image into motor actions (the motor plan for the numeral).

Because it requires that children not only know what a numeral looks like but have a motor plan that directs the writing process, writing single-digit numerals lags behind recognizing and reading numerals. The typical grade level and developmental order for verbal and graphic skills with numerals are summarized in Table 7–1.

Symbol Recognition

Operation Signs

With minimal training, children typically learn to recognize the + *sign,* − *sign,* and × *sign.* However, sometimes a child does poorly on written assignments because he or she does not know the sign for an arithmetic operation. For example, a child may know how to subtract (at least informally) but not know what the written symbol "−" means. As a result, instead of subtracting, the pupil may use the familiar operation of addition.

Relational Signs

Children must also learn to read and write commonly used symbols such as = (equals), ≠ (not equals), > (greater than), and < (less than). The = *sign*

Table 7–1   Sequence of Numeral Skills and Symbol Recognition Skills by Grade Level and Developmental Order

Level	Verbal Skills with Numerals	Graphic Skills with Numerals	Symbol Recognition	
			Operations Signs	*Relational Signs*
PK	Recognition of one-digit numerals	—	—	—
	Reading one-digit numerals	—	—	—
K	—	Copying one-digit numerals	—	—
	—	Writing one-digit numerals	—	—
1	—	—	—	= and ≠ sign
	—	—	—	> and < sign
	—	—	+ sign	—
	—	—	− sign	—
2	—	—	—	—
3	—	—	× sign	—

and ≠ *sign* usually cause little problem. The > *sign* and < *sign* are the source of much confusion, because it is difficult for children to remember which symbol represents more than and which represents less than. Note that these symbols have the same defining characteristics except one: (left-right) orientation.

INSTRUCTION

Verbal Skills with Numerals

Recognition of One-Digit Numerals

First ensure that a child has mastered counting by ones from 1 to 10. Remedial efforts should then focus on *pointing out* the numerals' defining characteristics: the component parts *and* how they fit together. It may facilitate learning to have the child describe the component parts and the part-whole relationships. If the child has not mastered the vocabulary that describes defining characteristics (e.g., top, bottom, right, and left), this deficiency should be remedied first. To some extent, a vocabulary deficiency can be circumvented. For example, for right-handed children, "toward your pencil hand" can be substituted for "right" and "toward your free hand" for left. Or, use easily identifiable pictures on the child's paper to identify position (e.g., see Figure 7–2). Note that easily confused numerals, such as 6 and 9 or 2 and 5, should be taught together. By placing the numerals side by side and explicitly noting how they differ, the child has a better chance of learning the features that distinguish the numerals.

Various games (Examples 7–1 through 7–7) for fostering recognition of numerals 1 to 9 are listed below.

Figure 7–2 Copying Paper with Pictures to Help Identify Position

Example 7–1   Number-List Race

Grade Level: PK or K.

Participants: Two to five or two teams of a few each.

Materials: Number list 1 to 9, number-pattern cards, miniature cars (see below).

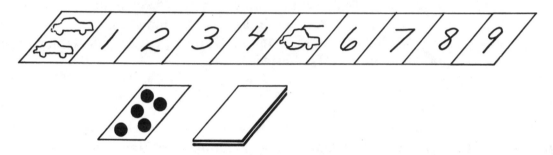

Procedure: Have each player pick a number-pattern card. Tell them (basic version) or have them count (advanced version) the number of dots on the card. Each player can then move his or her car to the number on the number list indicated by the card. The child whose car is further along the number list wins.

Example 7–2   Find the Number

Grade Level: PK or K.

Participants: One to five or two teams of a few each.

Materials: Number list 1 to 9 and sheath (see below).

Procedure: In random order, ask a child to uncover the numbers 1 to 9. If played as a competitive game, award a player (or team) for each correct answer.

Example 7–3 Clue Game

Grade Level: PK or K.

Participants: One.

Materials: Clue number-pattern cards and numeral cards 1 to 9.

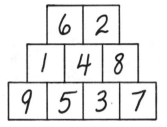

Procedure: In the advanced version, put out the numeral cards in random order. (This eliminates counting the numeral cards as a means of identifying the correct numeral.) Say, "In the Clue Game, you have to figure out what number I'm thinking about. Here's a clue" [point to the number-pattern card]. If necessary, say, "Count the dots to figure out the number I am thinking about." Then have the child point to the corresponding numeral card. In the basic version, put out the numeral cards in sequence (to make choosing the correct numeral easier) and count the number-pattern cards for the players. To practice larger numerals, include the appropriate numeral cards.

Example 7–4 Bingo

Grade Level: PK or K.

Participants: Two or more.

Materials: Bingo board with numerals 1 to 9, numeral cards 1 to 9, and colored markers (see below).

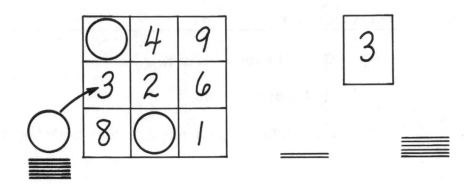

Procedure: Randomly call off numbers by drawing cards from a shuffled deck of numeral cards. Players place colored markers on their board on the appropriate square. The first player to get three in a row wins.

Example 7–5   Number Race

Grade Level: PK or K.

Participants: Two to six.

Materials: Deck of number-pattern cards 1 to 9, deck of numeral cards 1 to 9, and miniature race cars (see below).

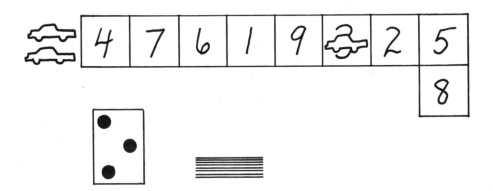

Procedure: In order (basic version) or random order (advanced version), put out the deck of numeral cards to make a track. A player draws a number-pattern card and moves his or her car to the space indicated. Whoever is closest to the finish line at the end of the round is the winner.

Example 7-6 Score Keeping

Grade Level: PK or K.

Participants: Two or two teams.

Materials: Game materials and numerals (numeral cards or magnetic numerals) to keep score (see below).

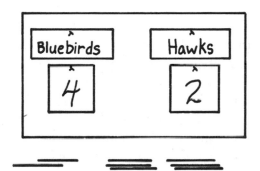

Procedure: High-Low (with dice or cards) or any other game that requires keeping score. State a score and ask a child to use numeral cards or magnetic numerals to post the score.

Example 7-7 Number-Search Game

Grade Level: PK or K.

Participants: Two teams of one to four children each.

Materials: Nine 3″ X 5″ cards, each of which has a numeral 1 to 9 printed on it. Play money for prizes is optional.

Procedure: Say, "Let's play the Number-Search game. Here are some cards with numbers on them. I'll put them out here so that you

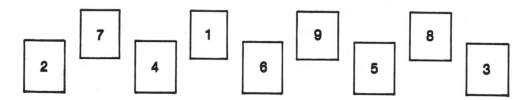

can see." Then place the 3″ × 5″ cards before the child face up either in order (basic version) or as shown above (advanced version). Continue by saying, "I'll read you a number and if you can point to the number I say, your team wins a play dollar. The team with the most money at the end of the game wins the game."

Reading One-Digit Numerals

Training should focus on helping children recognize the numerals: to learn the defining characteristics of each numeral. Point out that, as with identifying letters (e.g., *b, d*), orientation is very important in distinguishing between numerals. If a child continues to confuse certain numerals with other symbols (e.g., often reads 5 as S or confuses 6 and 9), point out how the symbols differ. It may help to give children mnemonics (memory aids) for remembering distinguishing characteristics. For example, "Nine is bigger than six; so when nine and six wrestle, nine always comes out on top. A nine's loop is on the top then, and a six's loop is on the bottom."

Try a variety of games to practice numeral reading. Use cards with numerals instead of dots for **Animal Spots** (described in Example 2–1), **Soccer** (described in Example 4–4), and **Cards More Than** (described in Example 5–7). Likewise, substitute numerals for dots on the cards used for **Moon Invaders**, described in Example 6–3 of Baroody, 1987a. Several additional games (Examples 7–8 through 7–10) are noted below. Continue to use the games that work best with a child.

Example 7–8   Zip Race

Grade Level: PK or K.

Participants: Two to six players.

Materials: "Zip-Race" Board (see below), two markers, and a deck of numeral cards.

Procedure: Give the children their choice of marker color and say, "In Zip Race, first we put our markers on Start. Then we read a card with a number on it. The number tells us how far we can move our marker. The player who goes the furthest wins. Let's see to what space you can move your marker." On their turn, have the players draw a card from the (shuffled) deck. As necessary, say, "Read this number." After the child responds, help move the child's or your marker to the appropriately numbered square on the board.

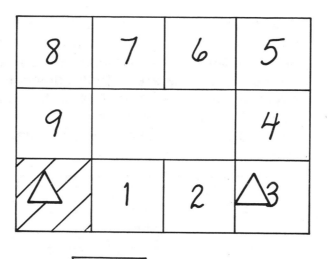

Example 7–9 Tic Tac Toe

Grade Level: PK.

Participants: Two players.

Materials: Tic-tac-toe board, O markers, X markers, and numeral cards 1 to 9 (see below).

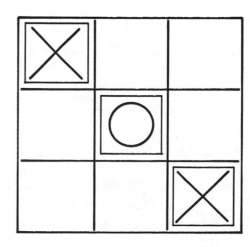

Procedure: Flip a coin or otherwise determine which player goes first and who gets the Xs and Os. On their turn, players draw a numeral card. If the numeral is read correctly, they place their marker on the square of their choice. If necessary, point out the distinguishing characteristics of the numeral or help the child to name the numeral. The game can be altered by numbering the squares. A drawn numeral card indicates on what square a player may place his or her marker.

Example 7–10   Car Race

Grade Level: PK or K.

Participants: Two to six.

Materials: Numeral cards 1 to 9, race track, and miniature cars (see below).

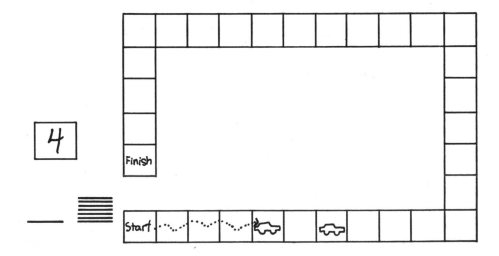

Procedure: The players draw and read a numeral card to see how many spaces to advance on their turn.

Graphic Skills with Numerals

Copying One-Digit Numerals

If a child cannot identify numerals, work on this skill and copying numerals can proceed hand in hand. Efforts in this case should focus on helping the child to identify and remember the defining characteristics of the numeral. If a child can identify but not copy a numeral, instruction should focus on teaching the child a motor plan for the numeral.

Because directional terms such as *right* and *left* may be unfamiliar or confusing to some children, pictures of common objects can be placed on writing paper to facilitate in direction giving. The special writing paper shown in Figure 7–3 is adapted from that suggested by Traub (1977). In using the special writing paper to help children to learn the (defining characteristics and) motor plan, first ensure recognition of the parts of the special paper: They should be familiar with the names "top, middle, and

Figure 7–3 Writing Paper with Direction Cues

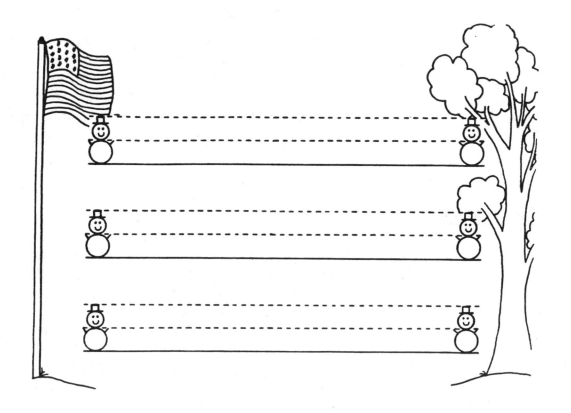

bottom line." If necessary, use the analogy: "The top line is the top of the snowman's tophat; the bottom line is the ground (line); and the middle line is the neck line of the snowman." Make sure the children can also successfully identify the flag side (left side) and tree side (right side). Also check to see if the child knows the concepts up, down, and across, because these directional terms are common in the instructions. Note that if a child consistently refers to the lines by other suitable names (e.g., calls the top line "sky"), substitute the more familiar term.

After a child is familiar with the special writing paper, motor-plan training can proceed using the following steps:

1. On the special writing paper, draw the numeral while describing the motor plan. An example of a motor plan for each numeral is detailed in Figure 7–4.

2. After describing and demonstrating the motor plan, define the starting point by drawing a dot.

3. Talk the child through the process (i.e., have the child execute each step of the plan as you present it). Provide feedback and correction as necessary.

4. If the child experiences difficulty, place the child's hand over yours and write the numeral as you describe its motor plan. Then place your hand over the child's and guide the child's writing as you talk through the motor plan. (These hand-over-hand techniques can be used until the child can copy the numerals independently.)

5. Encourage the child to verbalize that motor plan as he or she copies a model numeral.

Figure 7–4   Motor Plans for the Numerals 1 to 9

The numerals are presented in the following order so that instruction builds on previous learning. Easily confused numerals, such as 5 and 2 or 6 and 9 are taught one after the other so that differences in their execution can be highlighted.

For the sake of completeness, the motor plans below are rather detailed. Many children will *not* need such elaborate instructions. As long as the child has enough guidance to make the numeral accurately, the simpler the motor plan the better.

1. 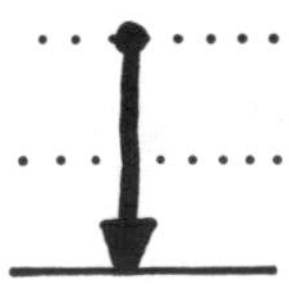   "One starts at the top line and drops straight down to the bottom line (ground). It goes all the way to the ground but not below it."

7.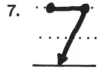

"Seven starts at the top line, walks along the top line toward the tree side, *stops,* and then slides down toward the bottom line and back toward the flag side. Like the one, it goes all the way to the ground but not below it."

Note that some children may lift the pencil between the two strokes. This produces results like

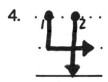

. Therefore, emphasize keeping the pencil in contact with the paper.

4.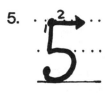

(1) "Four starts at the top line, drops straight down to the middle line, *stops,* then walks along the middle line toward the tree side, and stops. (2) Then down to the ground, crossing the first line that goes along the middle."
along the middle."

Note that it is important to emphasize the stopping points for some children.

5.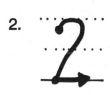

(1) "Five starts at the top line, drops straight down to the middle line, stops (like the four), and then makes a big tummy towards the tree side that ends up on the ground. (2) Five also has a hat. Go back to the top line where you started, walk along the top line toward the tree side, and stop."

2.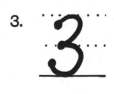

"Two starts below the top line (at the rim of the hat); now it makes an ear by traveling up to the top line toward the tree side, curving around all the way down to the bottom line, stopping underneath where it begins; and then it adds a tail by walking along the bottom line toward the tree side."

3.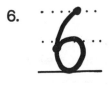

"Three starts below the top line (at the rim of the hat like the number two) and travels up to the top line toward the tree side, touches the top line, makes a tummy that rests on the middle line, makes a bigger tummy toward the tree side that touches the bottom line (ground), and curls up toward the flag side."

6.

"Six starts at the top line, curves down toward the flag side until reaching the middle line, continues to curve down but now toward the tree side until it reaches the bottom line, and then makes a ball at the bottom that touches the middle line before it closes."

Note that if a curve is too difficult, try a stick and ball. Specifically: "Six starts at the top line, drops straight down to the ground (just like the one), and then adds a ball that comes up toward the tree side, touches the middle line, and closes."

9.  "Nine starts below the top line (at the rim of the hat), makes a ball above the middle line that first goes toward the flag side and returns to the start, and then curves down toward the tree side until it reaches the bottom line (ground). So six has a ball at the bottom that faces the tree side, and nine has a ball at the top that faces the flag side."

Note that if a curve is too difficult, use a ball and stick approach. Specifically: "Nine starts below the top line (at the rim of the hat), makes a ball above the middle line that first comes toward the flag side and then returns to the start. Now, from where you started, a line drops straight down to the bottom line (ground)."

8. "Eight starts at the top line and it makes a small belly that goes down to the middle line and faces the flag side. Without lifting the pencil, make another belly that goes from the middle line to the bottom line and faces the tree side. Without lifting the pencil, make yet another belly that goes from the bottom line to the middle line and faces the flag side. Without lifting the pencil, make one final belly that goes from the middle line back to the start and faces the tree side."

 Note that if making one continuous motion is too difficult, use a simpler motor plan that involves making two circles one on top of the other. Specifically: "Eight starts at the top line, and it makes a ball that touches the middle line and then closes. Then it makes a second ball (circle) that touches the first one at the middle line, travels all the way down to the ground, and finishes by closing. (It looks like a snowman).

Note that some children make the bottom circle considerably smaller than the top. The snowman image sometimes helps.

Listed below in order of relative difficulty are a number of tracing and copying activities.

1. Trace finger over sandpaper or felt numerals.

2. Trace numerals with magic markers.

3. Connect the dots that are gradually faded out (see Figure 7–5 below).

4. Copy the numerals in sand or with finger paints using a finger.

5. Make clay copies of numerals.

6. Copy a numeral with a magic marker or colored chalk.

Games such as **Fishing for Numbers** (Example 7–11) and the **Target Game** (Example 7–12) can also provide copying practice.

Figure 7–5 Exercise in Which the Numeral 9 Is Faded-Out

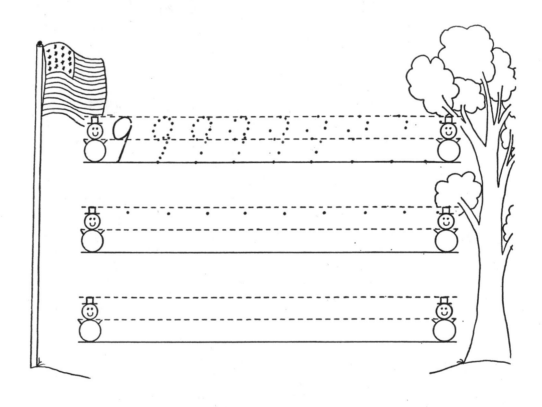

Example 7–11   Fishing for Numbers

Grade Level: PK or K.

Participants: One or several.

Materials: Four fish cutouts each with a numeral and a hole by which the fish can be hooked, pole with string and paper-clip hook, barrier and "fishing card" (see figure).

Procedure: Say, "Behind this barrier are number fish. Use this pole to see what number fish you can catch" (see Frame A). Either attach a number fish yourself or have a helper who is sitting behind the barrier attach one. Give the line a yank and say, "There's something on your line. Reel it in, and let's see what you have caught." Unhook the number fish, place it next to a square or the "Fishing Card" (see Frame B) and say, "So that we can remember what number fish you caught, let's write the number fish's number here on your fishing card." After the child has finished copying the numeral of the number fish, put the number fish aside and out of sight. Repeat this procedure for the remaining number fish.

A.

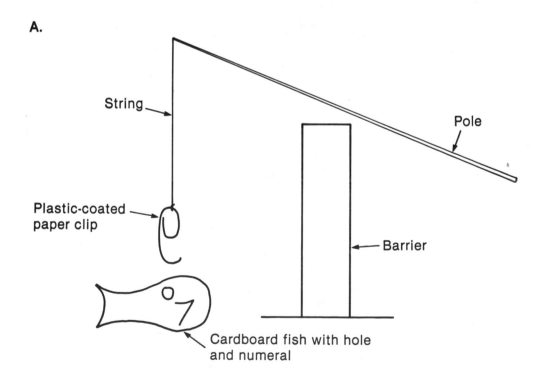

String

Pole

Plastic-coated paper clip

Barrier

Cardboard fish with hole and numeral

Alternative: Use magnetic plastic numerals and tie a magnet to the pole.

B.

It is important to remember that the practice provided by these tracing and copying exercises is not—in many cases—enough in itself to foster numeral-writing mastery. It is important that these activities be accompanied by descriptions of the defining characteristics and/or the motor plan. For example, if a child is having difficulty learning to copy numerals, one method that may be helpful is **Follow Me**. Using tracing paper with fading dots, the teacher traces the numeral with a marker while describing the step-by-step motor plan. The child follows the teacher's marker with a pencil. To the extent possible, have the child keep his or her pencil point in contact with the guiding marker.

Writing One-Digit Numerals

If a child is deficient in recognizing and/or copying, then remedial efforts should first focus on these skills. Once a child begins to copy a numeral successfully, begin writing training. That is, have the child try to write the numeral *without a model in view*. Continue to practice copying as needed, but fade out copying practice in favor of writing training as quickly as the child can handle it. If a child can recognize and copy a numeral, training can begin directly with remedying the writing deficiency. Taking into account individual needs, numeral-writing instruction can proceed in the sequence

Example 7–12 Target Game

Grade Level: K.

Participants: One to six.

Materials: A target (such as the one shown below) that is either flat on the ground or hung against the wall, and a supply of projectiles (e.g., plastic checkers) or darts with suction cups.

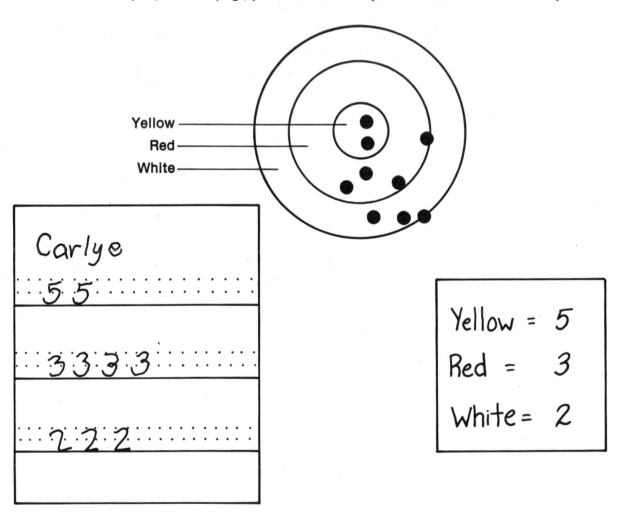

Procedure: A player throws the projectiles at the target. Each color band on the target is assigned a value (e.g., white = 2, red = 3, and yellow = 5). The child then records the results of his or her turn on a score sheet (e.g., in the figure, the child hit the yellow band twice, so two fives were recorded). After all the scores are recorded, the total score can be tallied by the teacher.

indicated in Figure 7–4. Writing training should focus on providing children an *explicit motor plan* for each numeral (see Figure 7–4). Encourage the child to describe the *essence* of the motor plan before and during practice. Have the child write numerals in the air with broad strokes as he or she describes the steps of the motor plan. By talking themselves through the steps required by the task, children should more readily internalize the motor plan for each numeral.

To make numeral-writing practice more interesting, use any game that requires a child to keep score. For example, if a child needs to practice the numeral 3, play **Soccer** (see Example 4–4) and make *every* goal worth 3 points. Likewise, with bowling games (the **Strike Game** described in Example 3–7 or the **Strike-and-Spare Game** described in Example 3–17), a strike can be defined arbitrarily as any number of points. For instance, if a child needed to practice writing fives, a strike could be worth 5 points. The **Target Game**, described in Example 7–12, can be easily adapted for this purpose. Simply remove the Point Chart and *verbally define* what each ring is worth. Games for *general* practice are listed here (Examples 7–13 and 7–14).

Example 7–13   Pick-Up

Grade Level: K.

Participants: Two to six.

Materials: Deck of pick-up cards (index cards with 1 to 9 dots), pencil, and paper for score sheet.

Procedure: Say, "This game is called Pick-Up. We'll put this deck of cards face down on the table. When it's your turn, you pick a card from the deck. The number of dots on the card is the number of points you get. We'll keep score and if you get the most points, you win the game." After drawing a card on their turn, some children, in the beginning, may need the prompt: "How many dots do you have on your card?" Make sure the child counts correctly. If necessary, say, "I see you have *x* dots on your card." Then continue with, "You get *x* points. Write *x* on your score sheet." Continue the game for two to five rounds. After completing the task, say, "Let's add up your scores. Use a hand-held calculator, abacus, tallies, or whatever to sum the score.

Example 7–14 Break-Out

Grade Level: K.

Participants: One to four players.

Materials: Cards with dots 1 to 9, cowboy figure, block, pencil and paper.

Procedure: Set up cards dot side down to form a "wall." Tell the player(s) that the cowboy is trapped on one side of the wall and has to "escape" to the other. A player tosses a block against the "wall" of cards. If the block lands on a card, turn the card over and announce, "You get *n* (number of dots on the card) points." Then have the child record the number on a score sheet. Continue until all the cards are turned over. Use a hand calculator to tally the final score.

Symbol Recognition

Recognition of the +, −, ×, =, ≠, >, and < Signs

First ensure that a child has an informal understanding of the concept represented: an incrementing view of addition (+); a take-away concept of subtraction (−); a repeated-addition-of-like-terms notion (×); same number and gross and fine comparisons of more (=, ≠, >), and gross and fine comparisons of less (<). Mnemonics (memory aids) may help some children to associate correctly symbols with informal concepts. The plus sign can be thought of as two sticks that have been joined. With the minus sign, one of the sticks has been removed. The times sign is the plus on its side (multiplication is related to addition). The equals sign is two lines that are *the same*. This analogy can foster the correct "relational" interpretation of equals (see Chapter 8).

    A memory aid for the greater-than and lesser-than signs is especially important because they are so similar in appearance. One analogy that can be used is that the small number goes on the small side of the sign and the large number on the large side. For >, the small end faces the right, so a small number goes on the right. Because a large number goes on the left, the expression must be read: "(Big number) is more (greater) than (small number)." For <, the small end (number) is left, so the expression is read: "(Small number) is less than (big number)." Wynroth (1986) suggests another analogy: Cookie Monster's mouth is always opened toward the larger number of cookies.

SUMMARY

Learning to work with written representations of numbers (numerals) should build upon children's oral- and object-counting experience and entails acquiring whole new sets of skills. Recognizing numerals and naming (reading) numerals each requires learning the defining characteristics of each number symbol. Instruction, especially for easily confused numerals such as 6 and 9, should focus on how the symbols differ. Writing numerals involves learning a motor plan: a step-by-step guide for translating the mental image of a numeral into motor actions. Even copying numerals from a model is difficult if a child lacks a motor plan. As with recognizing numerals, recognition of operation signs and relational signs depends upon learning the defining characteristics of these symbols.

Chapter **8**

Concepts and Their Formal Representations

Recognizing, reading, and writing symbols (discussed in the last chapter) are necessary skills for the more important objective of using formal representations. For example, children must learn to complete number sentences, which are expressions that summarize basic mathematical relationships or characteristics of arithmetic operations, such as $3 \_\_ 3$, $3 \neq \_\_$, $2 + 1 = \_\_$, and $2 + \_\_ = 3$. Mathematical symbols are conventions for representing mathematical ideas. They are socially agreed-upon, shorthand devices for precisely storing and communicating information about mathematical properties and relationships. To use and apply mathematical symbols effectively, children must understand the ideas or processes that the symbols represent.

Children's informal counting experiences (discussed in Chapters 3, 4, and 5) provide a basis for interpreting and using *prearithmetic symbols* (e.g., the numeral 7 or the number sentences: $7 = 7$, $7 \neq 8$, $7 < 8$, $7 > 6$) in a meaningful manner. Children's informal arithmetic (discussed in Chapter 6) provides the basis for interpreting and using common arithmetic expressions, *familiar number sentences,* such as $7 + 2 = ?$ or $\begin{smallmatrix} 7 \\ +2 \end{smallmatrix}$. Children's informal arithmetic also serves as the groundwork for learning the basic *arithmetic concepts* taught in primary curricula. The formal representations of some concepts are relatively unfamiliar to children. The (relatively) *unfamiliar number sentence* $5 + 5 + 5 + 5 = 5 \times 4$, for example, embodies a key relationship between addition and multiplication: Multiplication can be thought of as the repeated addition of like terms. This chapter will discuss the learning and teaching of a number of key mathematical concepts and their formal representations.

LEARNING

Prearithmetic Symbols

Most children just beginning school have some success representing or naming a single set (*cardinal value*), informally (e.g., with tallies) or even formally (with numerals) (Allardice, 1977; Sinclair and Sinclair, 1986). For example, if shown four buttons and asked to show on paper "how many things there are," kindergartners will typically make four tally marks (| | | |) or write the numeral 4.

The mathematical meaning of = is quite elusive for children. Because of the way it is commonly presented in such arithmetic expressions as $5 + 3 = ?$, children tend to interpret = as an "operator" symbol—as meaning "adds up to" or "produces" (e.g., Baroody and Ginsburg, 1983; Behr, Erlwanger, and Nichols, 1980). Because children interpret = as an operator symbol, they think that such expressions as $8 = 8$ and $9 = 9$ are incorrect. After all, how can eight add up to or produce eight! A common reaction to expressions like $8 = 8$ is: "Something is missing. They forgot to tell you what was added to the 8. It should be eight plus zero equals eight." Actually, = denotes an *equivalence relationship* ("the same number as"). Thus, $8 = 8$ is mathematically correct and means eight is the same number as eight. The symbol $\neq$ represents an *inequivalence relationship*. For example, $8 \neq 9$ means eight is "not the same number as" nine.

Most children just beginning school have difficulty representing relations between sets (e.g., *magnitude relationships*) and specified orders (*ordinal relations*). For instance, when asked to represent how two sets such as five marbles and three marbles compared in number (relative magnitude), young children typically just represented the larger quantity. When asked to show the order in which a frog jumped from one rock to a second and then to a third, most young children simply drew three rocks in a row—failing to present information about the order in which the frog jumped from rock to rock (Allardice, 1977).

Familiar Number Sentences

Children assimilate formal arithmetic expressions in terms of their informal arithmetic knowledge (e.g., Ginsburg, 1982; Hiebert, 1984). Children interpret *symbolic addition* expressions such as $2 + 5 = ?$ in terms of their informal incrementing view of addition: "Two and five more" (Baroody and Gannon, 1984; Weaver, 1982). Thus when asked to solve such number sentences, they use an incrementing (counting) strategy (e.g., "one, two, three is one more, four is two more, five is three more"). Likewise, children tend to assimilate *symbolic subtraction* such as $6 - 2 = ?$ in terms of their informal take-away concept and use a counting down strategy to solve the difference (e.g., Baroody, 1984b; Carpenter and Moser, 1982).

If a child does not see the connection between the formal symbolism and their informal concepts and strategies, then he or she does not have a basis for understanding and solving their written arithmetic work. Such a child may not comprehend formal expressions like $2 + 5 = ?$ or $6 - 2 = ?$ and perform very poorly on written arithmetic assignments. (Given verbally presented word problems with the identical terms, the same child may well compute the correct answer to these problems.)

Young children may have trouble representing addition and subtraction transformations. For example, asked to represent the story of a boy who had three marbles and then bought two more, young children have a tendency to simply record the sum. They make no effort to preserve information about the initial state (three marbles) or the transformation (the addition of two marbles).

Children often assimilate *symbolic multiplication* expressions such as $5 \times 3 = ?$ to their informal notion of repeated addition of like sets. This enables a child to solve such expressions by means of an informal procedure (e.g., using known addition facts, skip counting, or counting-on) well before they have mastered the multiplication facts.

Arithmetic Concepts

Because children tend to interpret $=$ as an operator symbol, they view (relatively) unfamiliar arithmetic expressions such as $8 = 5 + 3, 5 + 3 = 4 + 4$, or $5 + 3 = 9 - 1$ as incorrect. How can eight add up or produce $5 + 3$! Children who understand that $=$ also means the "same number as" are more comfortable with such expressions. Because a relational meaning of equals (equals is the same number as) is not emphasized in elementary school, many students hold on to an operator view of equals well into high school and even college (e.g., Byers and Herscovics, 1977; Kieran, 1980).

Because they view them as very different problems, it is a surprise to many children that $5 + 3$ has the *same-sum-as*, say, $4 + 4$ or $7 + 1$ (Baroody, 1987a). Indeed, because they informally view addition as an incrementing process, children initially do not realize that addition is commutative (Baroody and Gannon, 1984). For example, because they interpret $5 + 3$ as five and three more and $3 + 5$ as three and five more (as different problems) and do not know their sums, children naturally assume the combinations will have different answers. By the end of first grade, however, most children spontaneously discover that the order of the addends does not affect the sum (Baroody, Ginsburg, and Waxman, 1983). That is, from computational experience and reflection, they recognize the *commutativity of addition*.

At a very young age, children learn that addition and subtraction are related (inverse) operations (e.g., Gelman, 1972). Even preschoolers know that the addition of one can be undone by taking one away and vice versa (e.g., three cookies and one more is four but if one is removed we are back where we started: three). Later, children learn that this inverse relationship also applies to the addition and subtraction of larger numbers (e.g., Gelman, 1977). A general *addition-subtraction inverse principle* entails understanding that the addition of any n can be undone by the subtraction of n and vice versa. This principle provides the underlying rationale for a checking procedure sometimes taught for subtraction (e.g., the difference of $17 - 9$ should, when 9 is added, produce the original amount 17).

The discovery of same-sum-as and commutativity are steps toward a formal conception of addition. Formally, addition is defined as the *union of sets*. This conceptualization of addition is reflected in joining word problems like the one below:

> Miss Natalie's class had 12 boys and 14 girls. How many children did her class have altogether?

The differences between this more abstract formal conceptualization of addition and children's more concrete (incrementing) view are subtle but not unimportant. Psychologically, $12 + 14$ and $14 + 12$ imply different situations—and are different problems (Kaput, 1979). It is one thing to start with, for example, 12 marbles and to buy 14 more as opposed to starting with 14 and buying 12 more. Mathematically, the distinction between $12 + 14$ and $14 + 12$ is unimportant (Kaput, 1979). The terms 14 and 12 are subclasses that can be combined to form a class (26). The order in which they are combined is unimportant; $12 + 14$ and $14 + 12$ are equivalent.

A real grasp of the union-of-sets concepts (formal addition), then, entails an understanding of part-part-whole relationships (Piaget, 1965a). For example, with the expression $12 + 14 = 26$, 12 and 14 are the parts that form the (larger) whole 26. The elaboration of this part-part-whole concept is a key developmental aspect in the primary years (Resnick, 1983). This is discussed further below.

In time, children extend their grasp of part-part-whole relationships (and their understanding of formal addition). In particular, they learn that the order in which terms like 1, 2, 3 are grouped is irrelevant to the outcome. *Associativity of addition* implies that, for example, the sum of $1 + 2 + 3 = ?$ is the same whether 3 is added to the sum of 1 and 2 or 1 is added to the sum of 2 and 3: $(1 + 2) + 3 = 1 + (2 + 3)$. Like commutativity, the associativity is an important property of the operation of (formal) addition.

A key application of the part-part-whole concept is reasoning about situations in which there is a *missing part*. Research (e.g., Riley, Greeno, and Heller, 1983) indicates that as early as the first grade, some children have sufficient command of part-part-whole relationships that they can reason out problems in which the amount added is unknown (missing-addend problems) such as:

> Joey had three marbles. He bought some more marbles at the store. Now he has five marbles. How many marbles did he buy at the store?

More difficult for children are missing-augend problems in which the initial amount is missing (Briars and Larkin, 1984; Riley, Greeno, and Heller, 1983):

> Joey had some marbles. He bought three marbles at the store. Now he has five marbles. How many did he begin with?

Children often figure out both types of missing-part problems by counting up (e.g., in the problems above: "three, four is one more, five is two more").

Children's natural tendency to interpret expressions such as $5 - 3 = ?$ as five take away three is often reinforced in school by referring to such expressions as take-away problems. Actually, such subtraction expressions have several meanings. Another meaning is *additive-subtraction*: Subtraction is missing-part addition. For instance, the expression $5 - 3 = ?$ can be thought of as: What must be added to three to make five? (What is the missing part that must be added to the given part, three, to make the whole, five?) A word problem that illustrates this addition-subtraction meaning is:

> Margaret has five points and Fred has three. How many points does Fred need to score to catch up to Margaret?

At first, children often concretely model such problems by adding on (e.g., Carpenter and Moser, 1983). For example, they produce three objects and then add objects and count the result until they get to five. The number of objects added is given as their answer. Later, they solve such problems by counting up. Even later, children reason out such problems by using known addition combinations (e.g., three plus . . . two is five).

Subtraction can also have a comparative or *difference* meaning. A word problem that captures this meaning is:

> Margaret has five points and Fred has three. How many more points does Margaret have than Fred?

At first, children concretely model and solve such problems by matching sets. For the problem above, a child would produce a set of five and then one of three in one to one correspondence. The (two) unmatched items indicate the answer. Later, children use a counting up strategy to compute differences.

Though they realize that addition is commutative, children do not necessarily realize that two factors have the same product despite the order in which they appear (e.g., both 6×3 and 3×6 produce 18). When it comes to multiplication, children by and large have to rediscover or relearn that the order of the terms does not affect the outcome. Once the operation is introduced, though, children usually recognize the *commutativity of multiplication* quickly.

Unfamiliar Number Sentences

Though children usually have little difficulty interpreting familiar arithmetic sentences, such as $5 + 3 = ?$ or $8 - 5 = ?$, the same may not be true for relatively unfamiliar arithmetic sentences like $5 + ? = 8$ (e.g., Weaver, 1973). Unfamiliar number sentences express mathematical relationships such as:

- Children typically identify a number (a concept of the quantity seven) with the numeral used to designate it (in this case the numeral 7). Actually, the numeral 7 is but one name or label for the number seven. Seven could also be labeled $6 + 1$ or $7 + 0$. It also goes by the name of $5 + 2$ and $8 - 1$. In other words, there are many *other names for a number*. This idea is captured by expressions such as $7 = 6 + 1$, $4 + 3 = 5 + 2$, and $1 + 6 = 8 - 1$.

- *Commutativity of addition* can be represented formally by the expression $5 + 3 = 3 + 5$. The principle can be represented more generally (algebraically) by the expression $a + b = b + a$.

- The *addition-subtraction inverse* principle can be represented by the examples $5 + 3 - 3 = 5$ or $5 - 3 + 3 = 5$ and algebraically as $a + b - b = a$ or $a - b + b = a$.

- The *associativity of addition* can be illustrated symbolically by expressions like $(1 + 2) + 3 = 1 + (2 + 3)$. The principle can be represented more generally by the algebraic expression $(a + b) + c = a + (b + c)$.

- Missing-addend word problems (like the first story about Joey described above in which the amount added is unknown) can be expressed in terms of a *missing-addend* number sentence: $a + ? = c$ (e.g., $3 + ? = 5$). Note that an expression such as $3 + ? = 5$ actually summarizes an infinite number of specific stories that have the same numerical relationships. For instance, it also represents:

  Tyrone has a bag of five blue and red marbles. Three are blue and the rest are red. How many red marbles does Tyrone have?

- Missing-augend word problems (like the second story about Joey described above in which the original amount is unknown) can be expressed in terms of a *missing-augend* number sentence: $? + b = c$ (e.g., $? + 3 = 5$).

- The fact that multiplication can be thought of as the repeated addition of like terms is captured in such symbolic expressions as $5 \times 3 = 5 + 5 + 5$ (*equivalent + and × number sentences*). More abstractly, any number times 3 can be expressed $a + a + a = a \times 3$.

Table 8–1 outlines a suggested sequence of basic concepts and their representation, which is based, in part, on developmental research and current practice.

INSTRUCTION

In general, instruction should cultivate an understanding of number and arithmetic concepts first and then introduce the formal representation of these ideas. Prearithmetic symbols (e.g., $7 > 6$) and familiar arithmetic sentences (e.g., $5 + 3 = ?$) should be related or connected to children's informal mathematics. An understanding of new arithmetic concepts should be built up out of informal or counting-based experiences. By relating it to this more concrete experience (e.g., by connecting $5 + 3 = 3 + 5$ to children's knowledge of commutativity), unfamiliar number sentences can be made sensible to children. Translating word problems into number sentences and vice versa are important devices for fostering meaningful use of mathematical symbols.

Prearithmetic Symbols

Cardinal Value

First ensure that a child has mastered prerequisite concepts and skills (e.g., enumeration of sets, cardinality rule, and identity-conservation and order-irrelevance principles). Recognition of sets 1 to 3 and production of sets 1 to 5 would make for a more solid base but are not essential.

As a transition from informal to formal representations of numbers, a die or cards with both dots and numerals (see Figure 8–1) can be used before introducing numeral die or cards. Combination dot-and-numeral die or cards can be used to play games such as **Number-After Dominoes** (Example 3–18), **Soccer** (Example 4–4), and **Cards More Than** (Example 5–7).

Helping children learn how to interpret and use numerals should go

Table 8–1 Suggested Sequence of Concepts and Their Representations by Grade Level

Level	Prearithmetic Symbols	Familiar Number Sentences	Arithmetic Concepts	Unfamiliar Number Sentences
K	Cardinal value	—	—	—
1	Equivalence and inequivalence relationships	—	—	—
	Magnitude relationships	—	—	—
	Ordinal relationships	—	—	—
	—	—	Same-sum-as and Commutativity of addition	—
	—	Symbolic addition	—	—
	—	—	Union of sets and Part-part-whole	—
	—	Symbolic subtraction	—	—
	—	—	Addition-subtraction inverse	—
	—	—	—	—
	—	—	Associativity of addition	—
2	—	—	Missing part	Addition-subtraction inverse
	—	—	—	Missing addend
	—	—	Additive-subtraction and Difference	—
	—	—	—	Other names for a number and Commutativity of addition
	—	—	—	Associativity of addition
3	—	—	—	Missing augend
	—	Symbolic multiplication	—	—
	—	—	Commutativity of multiplication	—
	—	—	—	Equivalent + and X

Figure 8-1   Die with Both Dots and Numerals

hand in hand with their training on recognizing, reading, and writing numerals. The following games, described in Chapter 7, can help children connect numerals (formal cardinal representations) with concrete examples (informal understanding): **Numeral-List Race**, **Clue Game**, and **Number Race** (Examples 7-1, 7-3, and 7-5).

In addition to recognizing and understanding the meaning of specific symbols, use of symbols entails understanding that mathematical expressions are conventions for expressing mathematical ideas—a communication tool. Young children may need help learning the purposes of (formal) symbols. Specifically, they need to realize that mathematical symbols are convenient, if not necessary, shorthand devices for precisely storing and communicating information about mathematical properties and relationships. Children just entering school need the social knowledge and experience that will allow them to use written representations to communicate to others effectively. They need to know when and how to use symbols to get mathematical ideas across to others. For example, children must learn that what they put down on paper does not automatically communicate what they mean. It is important to take the perspective of the symbol reader.

Because most children can already use tallies and numerals to represent sets, exercises that involve the storing and communicating of cardinal information is a good starting point for teaching children the value of recording information (information is not lost because of, say, forgetting) and using formal symbols (numerals are easier to use than tally marks or drawings) (Hiebert, 1984). For example, in **Grapevine**, the teacher whispers a number to the first child in a chain, who records the number. The child then whispers the number to the next child, the second child whispers the number to the third child, and so forth. The last child reports the number that he or she heard, and the report is compared to the original number. Very often the oral communications will be distorted, and the wrong number will be reported. To dramatize this point, repeat the activity a number of times and note the number of "miscommunications." The process can then be repeated using written representations. With children who can write the numerals, the teacher tells the first child in a chain a number. The child records the appropriate numeral and shows it to the next child. The second child records the number and shows it to the third child, and so forth. The last child then compares the numeral he or she has recorded with that of the first child. The relative precision of written and oral communication can then be discussed. If desired, the activity involving numerals can be repeated a number of times so that the number of miscommunications using numerals can be compared to that resulting from oral communication. To demonstrate the advantage of formal symbols over informal ones, repeat the process with tallies.

Exercises that involve Egyptian hieroglyphics are an ideal vehicle for (1) bridging concrete and abstract representations of number and (2) helping children to see that formal symbols serve as a shortcut for communicating mathematical ideas. The exercise in Example 8–1 illustrates how the ancient Egyptians represented sets 1 to 9 with tallies. This system is basically the same as children's own informal tally method for representing sets. By asking children to translate Egyptian hieroglyphics into Arabic numerals (as Exercise A and Question 1 of Exercise B in Example 8–1 require), children can see the connection between their informal tallying system and the formal representation of numerals. By translating Arabic numerals into Egyptian hieroglyphics (as Question 2 in Exercise B of Example 8–1 requires), children again can relate formal symbols to their informal knowledge of numbers.

Example 8–1   Representing One to Nine with Egyptian Hieroglyphics and Arabic Numerals

---

Exercise A

The ancient Egyptians used a number system that is like our own (Arabic system) in some ways and in other ways is very different. The Egyptians used pictures (hieroglyphics) to represent numbers.

Hieroglyphics of Ancient Egypt	Our Arabic Numerals
Λ	1
Λ Λ	2
Λ Λ Λ	3

1. Tut took out his marbles to play and put them in a row:

○   ○   ○   ○   ○

To help him keep track of his marbles, Tut decided to record how many he had.

a. Using hieroglyphics, note below how many marbles Tut had.

b. How would we write this number of marbles?

2. Tut liked the idea of keeping a record so much, he decided to write down how many of each toy he had. For each toy, write down how Tut would have written in Egyptian hieroglyphics and what we would write today.

Toy	Egyptian Hieroglyphics	Our (Arabic) Numerals
a. ☐☐☐☐☐☐☐ (blocks)	_____	_____
b. △△△△△△△△ (toy pyramlds)	_____	_____
c. ◇◇◇◇◇◇◇ (toy dlamonds)	_____	_____

Exercise B

1. Pretend that a pharaoh (ancient Egyptian king) has appointed you as his tax collector and keeper of records. Translate the following tax record written in Egyptian hieroglyphics into our (Arabic) numbers.

a. Ace Reed Products, Inc.   Λ Λ Λ Λ   _____

b. Block Haulers, Inc.   Λ Λ Λ Λ Λ Λ Λ   _____

c. Cultured Cats, Inc.   Λ Λ Λ Λ Λ   _____

d. Durable Salves, Inc.   Λ Λ Λ Λ Λ Λ   _____

2. The following merchants received tax bills. Translate how much they owe into Egyptian hieroglyphics.

Merchant	Tax Owed	Egyptian Hieroglyphics
a. Ace Reed Products, Inc.	9	_____
b. Block Haulers, Inc.	6	_____
c. Cultured Cats, Inc.	8	_____
d. Durable Salves, Inc.	7	_____

In follow-up discussions of the exercise, ask the children to compare the advantages and disadvantages of each symbol system. Some children may prefer the Egyptian hieroglyphics because the tally system more directly models the sets of objects it represents. It is semiconcrete (more concrete than our Arabic numeral system). Moreover, it is a simpler system in that only a single symbol is used to represent all the numbers 1 to 9. Thus learning to write numbers is easier with Egyptian hieroglyphics than it is with Arabic numerals, in which nine different symbols must be learned. An advantage of Arabic numerals is their compactness. For example, writing a 9 is considerably easier than making nine tallies.

Equivalence and Inequivalence Relationships

First ensure that a child has mastered prerequisite competencies, particularly same number 1 to 5. Matching sets is not necessary.

Introducing the symbols during prearithmetic instruction can help children master an accurate meaning of $=$ as the same as and $\neq$ as not the same as. Use of these symbols can first be illustrated with sets. For example, a teacher can note that drawing in an equal sign between two groups of objects (e.g., $\overset{O}{O\,O} = OOO$) means one group has the same number as the other. To make the point, use small sets that children can readily recognize or count. Illustrate $\neq$ in a similar way (e.g., $\overset{O}{O\,O} \neq OOOO$). Exercise A of Example 8–2 illustrates an exercise that provides practice in using $=$ and $\neq$. Exercise B introduces the lesson without examples and thus requires children to remember that $=$ denotes equals and $\neq$ represents not equals. Exercises that involve numerals (such as Exercise C) can then be introduced.

Example 8–2 Exercises for Introducing = and ≠ Symbols

Exercise A

For each box below, put in an = or ≠ sign.

Example 1	O	**≠**	O O
Example 2	O	**=**	O
1	O O O	☐	O O O
2	O O	☐	O O O
3	O O O O	☐	O O O O
4	O O O	☐	O O O
5	O O O O O	☐	O O O O
6	O O	☐	O O O
7	O O O O O	☐	O O O O O
8	O O O O	☐	O O O O
9	O O O O O	☐	O O O O O
10	O O O O O	☐	O O O O O

Exercise B

For each box below, put in an = or ≠ sign.

1   ⚬⚬⚬   ☐   ⚬⚬⚬

2   ⚬⚬   ☐   ⚬⚬⚬

3   ⚬⚬⚬⚬   ☐   ⚬⚬⚬⚬

4   ⚬⚬⚬   ☐   ⚬⚬⚬

5   ⚬⚬⚬⚬⚬   ☐   ⚬⚬⚬⚬

6   ⚬⚬   ☐   ⚬⚬⚬

7   ⚬⚬⚬⚬⚬   ☐   ⚬⚬⚬⚬⚬

8   ⚬⚬⚬⚬   ☐   ⚬⚬⚬⚬

9   ⚬⚬⚬⚬⚬   ☐   ⚬⚬⚬⚬⚬

10   ⚬⚬⚬⚬⚬   ☐   ⚬⚬⚬⚬⚬

Exercise C

For each box below, put in an = or ≠ sign.

1. 7 ☐ 7

2. 8 ☐ 6

3. 9 ☐ 9

4. 5 ☐ 6

5. 7 ☐ 9

Magnitude Relationships

First ensure that a child has mastered prerequisite concepts and skills, particularly gross comparisons of more and less 1 to 10, and fine comparisons of more and less 1 to 10.

The > and < signs can be introduced as a shorthand for "is more than" and "is less than." Children can be asked to complete sentences like those in Example 8–3 with more than or less than. After children have started the exercise, note that symbols were used in place of first son, second son, and so forth to make recording easier. Encourage children to discuss how they can make recording "is more than" or "is less than" easier. Children may invent and agree upon their own symbols. Either during this or subsequent exercises, point out that the symbol for "is more than" is > and the shortcut for "is less than" is <.

Example 8–3   Indicating More Than and Less Than in Egyptian Hieroglyphics

Read to the class: "The first son of an ancient Egyptian King was very jealous of his brothers and sisters. As the first son, he felt that he should be the King's favorite child. To see who the King favored the most, the boy sneaked into the royal treasury. There he found the royal record books, which recorded the treasures set aside for each of the King's children."

The symbol ⬡ means first son; ⬡ means second son, ⬡

means third son; ⬡ means first daughter. For each item, show whether the first son's treasure:

IS MORE THAN
OR
IS LESS THAN

that of his brothers or sister.

Gold Coins

is greater than

Silver Coins

Jewels

Scrolls

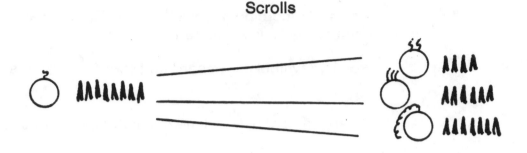

Such an exercise can then be repeated using numerals. For example, pupils can be instructed to complete the following by filling in "is more than" or "is less than":

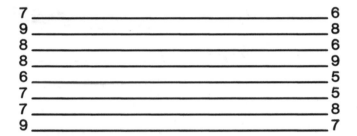

7 _____ 6
9 _____ 8
8 _____ 6
8 _____ 9
6 _____ 5
7 _____ 5
7 _____ 8
9 _____ 7

With any luck, children will quickly apply the lesson learned with the Egyptian hieroglyphics and shortcut the process by using > and < symbols.

Ordinal Relations

First ensure that a child has mastered the oral counting terms 1 to 10 in the proper sequence. A key concept for understanding relations is that items are ordered (ordinal designations are determined) in terms of a reference point. For example, in the row below, which item is first and which is last depends on whether the count begins on the right or left—whether the reference point is the right- or left-hand margin. The importance of reference point can be brought home to children by having them line up side-by-side. Pose the apparently innocent question: "Who's first?" The differences in opinion should help to make it clear that order—including first and last—is defined in terms of a reference point.

The **Frog-Hopping Activity** requires children to represent ordinal relations informally. Using a frog hand puppet or stuffed animal, demonstrate a frog hopping from one lilly pad (circle made of green construction paper) to another. Initially, begin with just three or four lilly pads in a row and have the frog hop end to end. Ask the children to make a record of the frog's travel and discuss their representations. One way to represent the order of hopping is with an arrow:

$$O \longrightarrow O \longrightarrow O \longrightarrow O$$

Another way to represent clearly the reference point and the sequential order of the hopping is with numbers:

$$\begin{array}{cccc} 1 & 2 & 3 & 4 \end{array}$$

Familiar Number Sentences

The key to introducing formal number sentences in a meaningful manner is to relate them to children's informal arithmetic knowledge. After children acquire an informal mastery of an operation, some children may benefit by seeing arithmetic expressions that involve both objects and numbers. Then introduce purely symbolic expressions.

Symbolic Addition

First ensure that children are adept at informal arithmetic (e.g., can calculate sums efficiently by some informal strategy). There are various ways of helping children to connect symbolic addition to their informal addition. With a simple modification, any of the games used to practice informal addition can be used. Instead of dot dice, use dice with both dots and numerals (as shown in Figure 8–1). Alternatively, a deck of cards can be drawn up with both concrete and numerical representations of addition combinations. Figure 8–2 illustrates a card that uses dice patterns. Beside helping them to see the link between their informal addition and formal representations of addition, using both concrete and numerical representa-

Figure 8–2   A Card Representing 2 + 5 Semiconcretely and Symbolically

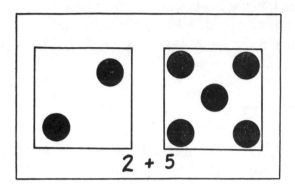

tions also permits children to solve for sums using a concrete counting-all procedure. The child merely has to count the dots. (This may be especially important for children still prone to making errors in counting out sets or enumerating sets greater than five.)

A next step is to have children play various games using dice or cards with just numerals. (This is appropriate for children who have mastered production and enumeration skills.) If a child does not spontaneously use an informal strategy to compute the sum, demonstrate concrete counting-all and have him or her practice the strategy. As Frame A of Figure 8–3 shows, have the child produce a number of blocks (or other countable objects) for each addend. Place the set directly below the addend. After both sets have been represented with objects, the child can proceed to count all of the items to determine the sum. Children can also be encouraged to represent the addends of symbolic problems on their fingers or on an abacus-like device (see Frame B of Figure 8–3).

Formal representations of addition can also be introduced to children as a means for recording the elements of a word problem. The teacher can note that written expression can help us remember the starting amount and what was added as well as the result. For practice, a teacher can present word problems to children and have them record the problem (and solution) as a number sentence.

Initially, semiformal representations, such as $5 + 3 \rightarrow 8$, should be accepted and even encouraged. *After* children have been introduced to a union-of-sets concept, they can be encouraged to use the conventional symbols 5 + 3 = 8. This progression is recommended to promote a relational view of equals and minimize reinforcing an operational interpretation.

After children can represent word problems with semiformal or formal number sentences, try reversing the process. Present pupils with a number sentence and ask them to make up a word problem that fits it. For example, ask a group of students to make a word problem for the expression 7 + 3 = ? Have the students share their word problems. This should help them see that the same formal expression represents a wide variety (infinite number) of specific stories. Encourage children to play the game with each other. Children often enjoy playing teacher and checking or outguessing another. Such an activity is useful in cultivating creativity and practicing writing skills.

Egyptian hieroglyphics are an ideal semiconcrete or pictorial medium to practice writing and interpreting number sentences for addition. Several exercises are illustrated in Example 8–4. Note that Question 5 in Exercise A is "impossible" (cannot be answered).

Figure 8–3 Linking Informal and Formal Addition: Using Counting-All to Solve Symbolic Addition Using 3 + 2 as an Example

A. Using blocks.

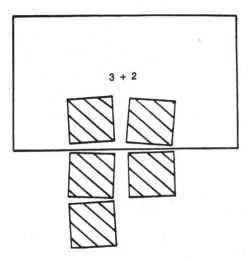

B. Using an abacus-like device.

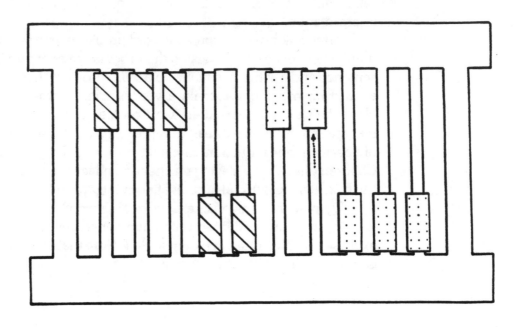

Example 8–4   Using Egyptian Hieroglyphics to Practice Writing and Interpretating Number Sentences for Addition

Exercise A

Follow along as your teacher reads a story about ancient Egyptians. Write a number sentence about the story using numbers, a plus sign, and an arrow (an equals sign). Then solve the problem.

Kingly's Gold and Silver Trinkets had the following supplies on hand:

Gold rings: Λ Λ Λ

Silver rings: Λ Λ Λ Λ Λ

Gold bracelets: Λ Λ Λ Λ Λ Λ

Silver bracelets: Λ Λ Λ Λ Λ Λ Λ

They received a shipment from the port of Alexandria of the following items:

Gold rings: Λ Λ Λ Λ

Silver rings: Λ Λ Λ

Gold bracelets: None.

Silver bracelets: Λ

1. How many gold rings did they have altogether?

2. How many silver rings did Kingly's Gold & Silver have altogether after the shipment?

3. How many gold bracelets did they have altogether when more were added?

4. How many silver bracelets did they have when the new shipment was added to their supply on hand?

5. How many necklaces did they have altogether after the shipment?

Exercise B

1. Make up your own story about the Pyramid Rock Quarry that would fit the number sentence $4 + 3 = ?$

2. Make up your own story about Kingly's Gold & Silver Trinkets that would fit the number sentence 2 + 5 = ?

Number sticks are another good semiabstract medium for introducing formal addition. Number sticks (see Frame A of Figure 8–4) can be made of popsickle sticks, tongue depressors, oaktag, or construction paper. Their lengths should be proportional to magnitude (e.g., a one stick can be ½-inch long; a two stick, 1 inch long; a three stick, 1½ inches long, and so forth). They should be identified with a numeral and may be color coded (e.g., white for one, red for two, orange for three, yellow for four, green for five, blue for six, purple for seven, brown for eight, grey for nine, and black for ten). Number sticks are similar to Cuisinaire rods with two significant differences: They are numbered, and (like Dienes blocks) a notched line separates each unit. Frame B of Figure 8–4 illustrates how they can be used to represent an addition word problem or symbolic problem (number sentence) and to figure out the sum.

Symbolic Subtraction

First ensure that children are adept at informal subtraction (e.g., can calculate differences efficiently by some means). As with addition, have children solve word problems concretely with fingers, blocks, or other objects (or semiconcretely with tallies or Egyptian hieroglyphics) and then represent the problems symbolically as number sentences. Note that Example 8–5 mixes addition and subtraction problems. Next, give number sentences and ask them to make up stories that fit the expression. Number sticks can also be used to model take-away story problems such as $\begin{array}{r} 5 \\ -3 \\ \hline \end{array}$ and to solve for the difference (see Frame C of Figure 8–4).

Figure 8–4 Using Number-Sticks to Represent Arithmetic Problems and to Find Their Solutions

A. Number Sticks 1 to 10

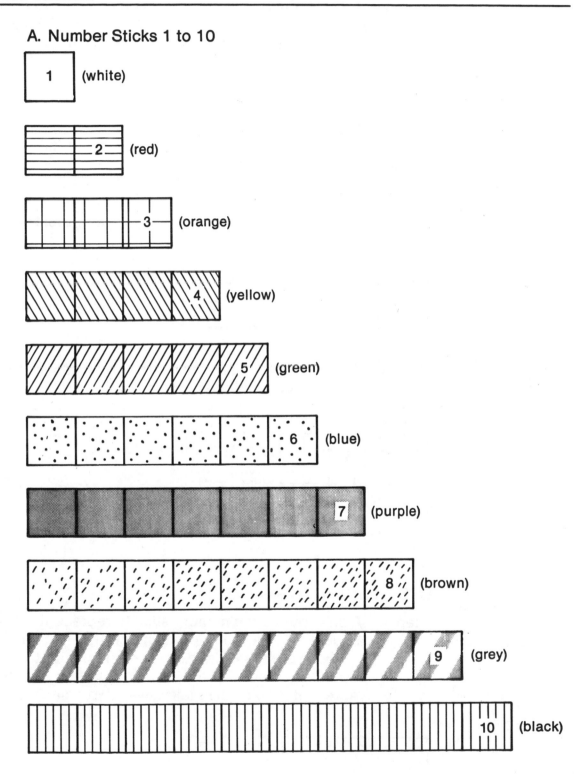

B. Addition

Step 1: A child represents each addend of a story problem or symbolic problem with the appropriate number stick. Illustrated below is the semiconcrete representation for "three and two more items" or $\begin{array}{r} 3 \\ +2 \\ \hline \end{array}$:

   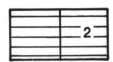

Step 2: The child pushes the number sticks together to represent the sum.

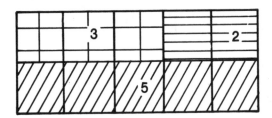

Step 3: The child determines the sum by finding the number stick that matches their combined lengths.

C. Subtraction (Take-Away)

Step 1: A child puts out a number stick to represent the starting amount in the word problem or the minuend in the symbolic problem. Place on it a number stick to represent the subtrahend. Illustrated below is the semiconcrete representation of "five take away two objects or $5 - 2$:

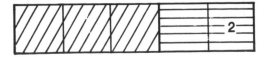

Step 2: The child places the number of one-sticks equal to the length of the larger stick (the minuend). Then he or she takes away the number of one-sticks that equal the length of the smaller stick representing the subtrahend.

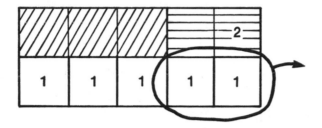

Step 3: The child replaces the remaining two number-ones sticks with a number-two stick to represent the answer.

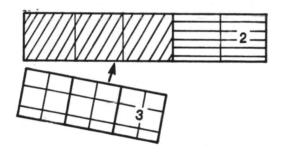

D. Multiplication

Step 1: A child makes a (semiconcrete) representation of four groups of twos.

Step 2: The child finds a number stick to represent the total.

Step 3: The child summarizes the semiconcrete representation with a formal addition sentence.

$$2+2+2+2=8$$

Step 4: The child devises an informal shortcut for representing four two's.

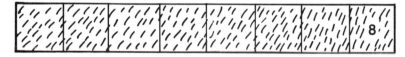

$$2+2+2+2=8$$

$$②+4 \rightarrow 8 \text{(or } 4②\longrightarrow 8)$$

Step 5: A teacher helps to connect the formal or conventional representation for multiplication with the informal models and representations.

$$2+2+2+2=8$$

$$②4 \rightarrow 8 \text{(or } 4②\longrightarrow 8)$$

$$2\times4=8 \text{ (or } 4\times2=8)$$

Example 8-5 Addition and Subtraction Problems with Egyptian Hieroglyphics

1. As the minister of business for an Egyptian pharaoh, you have the job of keeping employment figures. Each year you must update the records on each business: This involves noting how many helpers a business hired or lost, and how many they now have. Below is part of the employment record. For each business, indicate how many helpers it now has.

Business	Number of Helpers Last Year	Number of Helpers Hired or Lost	Number of Helpers the Business Has
a. Nile River Damage Control	ΛΛΛΛΛΛ	← ΛΛΛ	_____
b. Izzie's Idols & Graven Images	ΛΛΛΛΛ	ΛΛ	_____
c. Swampy Surveyors & Land Markers	ΛΛΛΛ	ΛΛΛ	_____
d. Pyramid Rock Quarry	ΛΛΛΛΛΛ	← ΛΛ	_____
e. Kingly's Gold & Silver Trinkets	ΛΛΛΛΛΛ	ΛΛΛ	_____
f. Futures Foretold	ΛΛΛΛΛ	ΛΛΛΛ	_____

2. For each merchant above, use our Arabic numerals to write a number sentence to summarize or represent what happened in the story.

3. Make up your own story that would fit the number sentence: $7 - 4 = 3$.

Symbolic Multiplication

First ensure that the child has mastered the prerequisite skill of adding like 2 to 5 sets. Introduce symbolic multiplication by relating number sentences like $4 \times 3 = ?$ to word problems and to children's informal representations (concrete models) of the problems (see Example 2–5). Initially, encourage informal strategies for determining the product of formal expressions such as $4 \times 3 = ?$. For example, explain, "In order to 'multiply' two numbers, you add one of the numbers to itself as many times as indicated by the other. . . . (This says four times three or 'four, three times,' so) 'hold up [four] fingers and count those fingers [three] times'" (Wynroth, 1986, p. 28). With the other (free) hand, the child can keep track of the number of times the first number is counted. Encourage skip counting and the use of mental addition as well. If the child has not mastered skip counting and single- and two-digit mental addition, remedial efforts with these related skills can proceed simultaneously with training in informal multiplication learning key multiplication combinations like the double $6 \times 6 = 36$. If necessary, point out informal methods for figuring or reasoning out larger products.

Example 8–6 illustrates how Egyptian hieroglyphics and word problems can be used to relate symbolic repeated addition and symbolic multiplication in a semiconcrete manner. By helping them see that the same problem can be represented by each, children may understand better the connection between repeated addition of a like term and multiplication.

Example 8–6   Multiplication with Hieroglyphics

1. As the accountant for Ace Pyramid Inc., your records show that you made 4 shipments of 5 granite blocks each:

    a. How many blocks were shipped altogether?

    b. Represent the problem above as an addition sentence (using Arabic numerals).

   c. Represent the problem above as a multiplication sentence (using Arabic numerals).

2. According to the records of Shaddy Shippers and Disreputable Deliveries, who picked the blocks up and brought them out to the Pyramid building site, they only made 3 shipments of 5 granite blocks each!

   a. How many blocks do they claim they picked up altogether?

   b. Represent the problem above as an addition sentence.

   c. Represent it as a multiplication sentence.

The same thing can be accomplished by having children score target games. For example, bean bags can be tossed at a target with each "hit" assigned a value. Take a child who manages to toss five of six bean bags onto a target that is presently valued at 3 points per hit. The child scores the target informally by, say, counting by threes. The player then records his or her score as an addition sentence ($3 + 3 + 3 + 3 + 3 = 15$) and as a multiplication sentence (3×5).

Number sticks provide another semiconcrete method for introducing multiplication, because they can be used to clearly point out the connection between a multiplication sentence (e.g., $4 \times 3 = ?$) and repeated addition ($4 + 4 + 4 = ?$). Begin by asking children to model a word problem with number sticks (e.g., see Step 1 in Frame D of Figure 8–4) and determine how may that is altogether (Step 2). The answer can be found by skip counting by twos *or* by matching the length of larger number sticks to the combined length of the two-sticks in a trial-and-error fashion. Then instruct the participants to write a number sentence to represent the situation above (e.g., see Step 3). After several such problems, encourage the child to use shortcuts for representing the problems (see Step 4). Then explain that our culture has a standard notation for such situations—a convention that is recognized world wide (see Step 5).

Multiplication with number sticks can be extended to products beyond 10 by making up additional number sticks to represent products greater than 10 (12: 6 inches long, pink; 14: 8 inches long, cream; 16: 10 inches long, aqua; etc.) or by encouraging informal solution s(e.g., skip counting, adding on, or repeated addition).

Arithmetic Concepts

Same Sum as and Commutativity of Addition

First ensure that children can informally calculate sums by some means. These concepts can be learned before written arithmetic is introduced. These concepts are embodied semiconcretely in the **Tower of Same-As** (Example 8–7) and **Fill In** (described later in Example 8–12). These regularities are ideally suited for guided discovery learning. For example, with no direct instruction, children of almost all ability levels, including those labelled mentally handicapped, will notice, exploit, and remember that addend order does not affect a sum (Baroody, 1987a). **In-Out Machine** exercises, such as those illustrated in Examples 8–8 and 8–9, are useful.

Example 8–7   Tower of Same-As
_____

Objectives: Same-sum-as and commutativity-of-addition concepts; practice basic addition combinations.

Grade Level: 1.

Participants: This game can be played by two children, two (or more) small teams of children, or individual children competing against their own record. The activity can also be adapted for instruction with an individual child, small group of children, or a class.

Materials: If used as a game, two sets of number sticks, like those in Frame A of Figure 8–4 are needed for each player or team. A set consists of two sticks representing each of the numbers 1 to 9 (18 sticks total). Also needed is some device for picking a number such as a deck of cards, numeral die, or spinner. For beginners, the numbers picked (the number-picking device) can range from 2 to 6. With more advanced players, the numbers can range from 2 to 10, or even 2 to 18.

Procedure: To begin play, a number is drawn from the deck, and participants must compose combinations that sum to the number (see the figure). The player (or team) with the larger number of combinations (tallest tower) is the winner.

There are several ways the rules can be implemented. First of all, the amount of time allowed for composing combinations can be varied from a number of minutes to fifteen seconds. A long (or, in effect, unrestricted) playing time permits more exploration and is useful when introducing the concept to children. A brief playing time is useful after children are familiar with the concept and need to practice basic combinations.

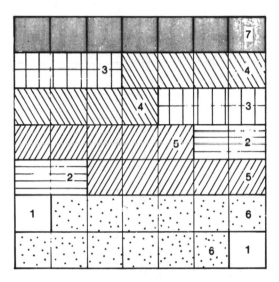

The rules governing how players obtain number sticks for making the combination can also be varied. Players can begin the game by choosing their own set of number sticks or drawing them from a pile of overturned sticks. The first method is always useful, but particularly so when introducing the concept. The second method introduces an element of chance and excitement and is useful when the game is used to practice the basic number combinations. If this method is used, players should take turns drawing two number sticks. (Optional rule: A third number stick can be drawn on a turn if a previously drawn number stick is traded in. Number sticks that are traded in are left up so that an opponent can see it—and take it if so desired.) Unlike the first method in which participants work simultaneously, this method does not have a time limit. Instead, play continues a prespecified number of turns. Note that some children will spontaneously begin using three (or more) sticks to make a tower level or floor. Unless it interferes with an objective to practice larger combinations, this should be encouraged by providing each player with a third set of number sticks.

Example 8–8   In-Out Machine Exercise for Facilitating the Discovery or Application of the
Commutative Property of Addition

Fill in the blanks for the In-Out Machine below.

In	Out
(2,1)	3
(1,2)	3
(1,8)	9
(8,1)	
(7,3)	10
(3,7)	
(5,4)	9
(4,5)	
(2,6)	
(6,2)	8
(3,9)	12
(9,3)	
(17,4)	21
(4,17)	

1. What does this machine do to the input?

2. Did you notice any rules this machine seems to follow?

Example 8–9   In-Out Machine Exercise for Facilitating the Discovery of Same Sums

Fill in the blanks for the In-Out Machine below.

In	Out
(8,1)	9
(1,8)	
(5,4)	9
(3,6)	
(7,2)	
	9
(5,2)	7
(2,5)	
(4,3)	7
(1,6)	
	7

Union of Sets and Part-Part-Whole

First ensure that children can informally calculate sums by some means and can use the equals and unequals sign correctly in comparing two sets or numbers. The aim of instruction should be to supplement children's incrementing view of addition with a more formal conception. (*Replacing the informal view with a mathematically correct conception is counter-productive—even if it were psychologically possible.*)

Solving combine word problems (e.g., Jose has four pennies and three nickels. How many coins does he have altogether?) can serve as an introduction to the part-part-whole concept integral to the union-of-sets concept. Because such problems are similar to change (incrementing) problems, they are easily assimilated and readily solvable by first-graders (Briars and Larkin, 1984; Riley, Greeno, and Heller, 1983). A semiconcrete introductory exercise to combine problems is illustrated in Example 8–10.

Example 8–10   A Combine Word Problem Involving Egyptian Hieroglyphics

Follow along as your teacher reads a story about ancient Egyptians. If possible, write a number sentence about the story using numbers, a plus sign, and an equals sign. Then solve the problem.

After the spring floods, one partner from Swampy Surveyors and Land Markers went north up the river to see which farms had been flooded and would have to be resurveyed. As he passed each flooded farm, he made a mark. When he returned he had found the following number of farms flooded: ΛΛΛΛΛΛ

Another partner went south down the river. He recorded the following number of flooded farms: ΛΛΛΛΛΛ

How many farms did the partners find flooded along the Nile River altogether?

The aim of the exercises in Example 8–11 is to introduce children to both familiar and *unfamiliar* number sentences in a semiconcrete manner. Such an approach is consistent with a formal (union-of-sets or part-part-whole) view of addition. It helps minimize an operator interpretation of equals and foster a relational interpretation. Note that Problems 1 and 3 in Exercise A parallel the format of familiar number sentences for addition. Children should be instructed to read Problem 1, for example, as "Four and three are the same number as what?" Problems 2 and 4 parallel an unfamiliar format. Problem 2, for instance, can be thought of as what number can be decomposed (split up into) parts of one and two? It can also be read "What is the same number as one and two?" (Exercises B, C, and D are described in more detail in the section on missing addends below.)

Example 8–11   Semiconcrete Addition in Familiar and an Unfamiliar Format

Exercise A: $a + b = ?$ and $? = a + b$ Formats

1.

2.

3.

□□□ (3) + □ (5) = □

4.

□ = □ (3) + □ (1)

Exercise B: $a + ? = c$ Format

1.

□□□ (3) + □ = □ (4)

2.

□ (4) + □ = □ (6)

3.

□ (1) + □ = □ (3)

4.

□ (5) + □ = □ (6)

5.

□□□ (3) + □ = □ (5)

Exercise C: $a + b = b + ?$ and $a + b = c + ?$ Formats

1.

2.

3.

4.

5.

6.

Exercise D: $a + ? = c$ and $? + b = c$ Formats

1. + [ ] =

2. [ ] + =

3. + [ ] =

4. [ ] + =

5. [ ] + =

Though the exercises in Example 8–11 could be made up as worksheets and given as written seatwork, they can also be used to play a game such as **Fill In** (Example 8–12) or **Supposed to Be** (in Wynroth, 1986).

Example 8–12   Fill In

Objectives: Same-as (relational) interpretation of the equals sign, practice computing addition, and same-sum-as.

Grade Level: 1.

Participants: Two to five players.

Materials: A different worksheet of problems (see Example 8–11) for each player. The same format(s) should be used on each worksheet. These can be laminated for reuse. Large number of fill-in tiles can be made from square pieces of paper, oaktag, or light cardboard on which there are 0 to 10 dots. The fill-in tiles should be the same size as the empty box on the worksheet.

Procedure: Each player draws a worksheet and puts it down in front of his or her position for all to see. The fill-in tiles, which have been turned over, are put out. Players (blindly) draw five tiles. On their turn, a player may place a fill-in tile in a box that would appropriately complete the expression. For example, if a player had Worksheet (Exercise) A and had drawn tiles with no, one, three, eight and nine dots, he or she could not use the no-dot, three-dot, and nine-dot tiles. The one-dot tile could be used to complete Problem 2 and the eight-dot tile to complete Problem 3. Whether or not they place a tile on the worksheet to complete an expression, players may trade in any tile they have for another tile. The discarded tile, however, must be left face up and can be obtained by an opponent when he or she trades in. This means a player should consider what his or her opponents need to complete their worksheets before discarding a tile.

Addition-Subtraction Inverse Principle

First ensure that children have the prerequisite counting skills (oral counting to 10, number after 1 to 9, number before 2 to 10, and enumeration or pattern recognition 1 to 10). Children should also be able to add and subtract one mentally and recognize that adding one is undone by taking one away and vice versa. If necessary, these two informal arithmetic competencies can be encouraged by playing the basic version of the **Modified Magic Show** (Example 8–13). In this version, all changes in the hidden set should involve the special cases of adding or subtracting one. In the advanced version, changes of more than one are made.

Example 8–13 Magic Show

Objectives: General addition-subtraction inverse principle (i.e., the addition of more than one is undone by the subtraction of that number and vice versa) and, if necessary, the specific rule that adding one is undone by subtracting one and vice versa.

Grade Level: 1 (advanced version); PK or 1 (basic).

Participants: One child, a small group of children, or a whole class.

Materials: Magic Show Curtain Card and a number of pennies or other countable objects.

Procedure: Explain, "In the Magic Show, I will show you some pennies. Remember how many there are because I will hide the pennies and do some things to them. Your job is to tell me how many pennies I am hiding after I am all through." Present the children with sets of one to nine, remove the set from view and add (or subtract) one to eight items, and (still out of view) reverse the last step. An example is detailed here:

Put out pennies and say, "Here are five pennies." Put the "Magic Show Curtain Card" in front of the pennies to conceal them from the child and say, "How many pennies am I hiding?" If the child is wrong, take away the card, help the child to count the pennies, rehide the pennies, and say, "How many pennies am I hiding?" For all children, say, "Now I am adding four pennies to the five pennies. Now I'm taking away four pennies. How many pennies am I hiding now? Remember: I started with five, I added four, then took away four."

If a child has difficulty with the task described above, try using sets of one to four and adding or subtracting one to three. If the hiding procedure with just small numbers is still too difficult, try the procedure in full view of the child. Show them the initial set, add (or subtract) one or a few, and then reverse the second step. After *each* step, have the child determine how many items are in the set.

Associativity of Addition

By requiring that participants use three number sticks to make a number, the **Tower-of-Same-As** can be used to introduce *informally* the associative principle of addition. For example, a child can see that a two-stick, a four-stick and a five-stick made the same sum as a four-stick, a five-stick, or a two-stick.

Missing Part

First ensure that children can solve simple change and combine word problems and can compute sums by some informal means. A missing-part concept can then be introduced with missing-addend word problems (stories in which the amount added is missing). Example 8–14 illustrates such an exercise. Note that the missing-addend problems are mixed with regular change problems. After children are comfortable with this type of missing-part problem, then introduce missing-augend word problems (stories in which the initial amount is not given).

Example 8–14   Addition and Missing-Addend Problems with Egyptian Hieroglyphics

---

As an Egyptian King's tax collector and tax recorder, you must make sure the correct amount is paid by each merchant. Each merchant should have paid 7 coins in taxes. For each of the following merchants indicate whether they paid too little in taxes and owe the king more money in taxes *or* paid too much and should get money back. Show how much money they should pay or should get back.

a. Nile River
   Damage
   Control   Λ Λ Λ Λ Λ Λ Λ Λ Λ   pay more/get back_____coins

b. Izzie's Idols &
   Graven Images   Λ Λ Λ Λ Λ Λ   pay more/get back_____coins

c. Swampy
   Surveyors &
   Land Markers   Λ Λ Λ Λ   pay more/get back_____coins

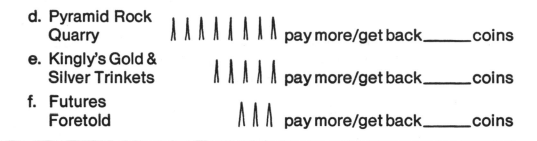

d. Pyramid Rock
Quarry   Λ Λ Λ Λ Λ Λ Λ Λ   pay more/get back_____coins

e. Kingly's Gold &
Silver Trinkets   Λ Λ Λ Λ Λ   pay more/get back_____coins

f. Futures
Foretold   Λ Λ Λ   pay more/get back_____coins

The game **Fill In**, described in Example 8–12, can provide practice solving for a missing part in a semiconcrete context. Use a missing-part worksheet like those illustrated in Exercise B, C, or D of Example 8–11 for each player. Exercise B contains relatively easy missing-part problems: missing addend ($a + ? = c$) format. Note that all the terms in these problems are relatively small and that the missing part, in particular, is one, two, or three. Such an exercise is appropriate for introducing missing-parts. Exercise C (with $a + b = b + ?$ and $a + b = c + ?$ formats) may be somewhat more difficult for children. Note that Exercise C semiconcretely embodies commutativity and same-sum-as concepts.

Encourage children to solve the missing-term expressions by counting up. For Problem 2 in Exercise B, for example, comment, "Four and what makes six?" If the child does not spontaneously count up, prompt with, "Try counting to see." If necessary, illustrate the counting-up procedure, "Four, five is one, six is two—four and two make six." For many children, it may be more meaningful to encourage a "systematic trial-and-error" approach. Have a child first try a fill-in tile of one, count all the dots to be added, and compare it with the sum. For Problem 2 in Exercise B, this would result in a mismatch (four dots and one dot are not the same number as six dots). Have the child then try increasingly larger fill-in tiles until he or she finds one that produces the sum. For Exercise C, a child could count to determine the sum on the left-hand and then—if need be—add dots by trial and error to the box on the right-hand side until that side reaches the same total as the left-hand side.

Number sticks can be used to represent and solve word problems with a missing part in a semiformal manner. For instance, for a story involving an initial amount of four toys, an unknown added amount, and a total of six toys, a child would put out a four stick and a six stick directly below it. The child should quickly discover that a two stick needs to be added to the four stick to match the length of the six stick. By using a similar procedure with missing-augend problems, the child may discover the similarity or connection between the two types of problems.

Additive-Subtraction and Difference

First ensure that children have a basic understanding of subtraction (e.g., can take away with objects). They should also have mastered the skills children commonly use to solve such problems concretely (counting-on and matching).

The objective of formal instruction should be to build upon and *supplement* children's informal view of subtraction as take away. One method for broadening children's view of subtraction is to help them see that familiar subtraction sentences such as $7 - 4 = ?$ actually represent a variety of problem situations. Fuson (1988), who developed the method, uses a chart like the one in Table 8–2 to make the point. Note that for difference problems, the chart illustrates the informal method of matching the sets and counting the remainder. For additive-subtraction, the informal strategy of adding on is not illustrated but can easily be imagined. For example, in Table 8–2, Allison has to add on three to have the same number of stickers as Cyndi. Children should be given a variety of subtraction word problems and asked to summarize them as number sentences. To require thoughtful analysis, (change and combine) addition problems should be intermixed. First concrete strategies and then counting up should be encouraged for additive-subtractive and difference problems.

Example 8–15 illustrates a method that uses the familiar take-away situation to highlight part-part-whole and introduce additive-subtraction.

Table 8–2 Facilitating a Broader View of Subtraction*
(All of these story situations can be solved by subtraction)

Name	Story Problem	Picture		Symbols
Take away	Cyndi has 7 stickers. She gives 4 to Allison. How many does she have left?	Cyndi: Allison:	O O O O O O O	7−4=? or 7 −4
Difference	Cyndi has 7 stickers. Allison has 4. How many more stickers does Cyndi have?	Cyndi: Allison:	O O O O O O O O O O O	7−4=? or 7 −4
Additive-subtraction	Cyndi has 7 stickers Allison has 4 stickers. How many more stickers does Allison have to get to have the same as Cyndi?	Cyndi: Allison:	O O O O O O O O O O O	7−4=? or 7 −4

*Based on Fuson (1988).

Example 8–15 Combining Take-Away and Part-Part-Whole Instruction*

Step 1: Show the child a set of objects and ask how many items there are.

Step 2: Cover the set. (If necessary, ask again how many items are in the covered set.)

Step 3: Remove a number of items from beneath the cover, place the removed items beside the cover, and ask: "How many are left under the cover?"

Note that it may be easier to begin instruction (a) with even-numbered sets of objects (e.g., 2, 4, 6, 8, or 10) and (b) by removing half the items covered (1, 2, 3, 4, and 5 respectively). This exploits children's knowledge of the addition doubles ($1 + 1 = 2, 2 + 2 = 4, 3 + 3 = 6, 4 + 4 = 8$, and $5 + 5 = 10$). Next, try removing more than half the items from either evenly or oddly numbered sets (e.g., removing three from a covered set of five). This should reinforce children's tendency to count up (e.g., in the problem above: three, four is one five is two—two are left). As soon as pupils are ready, remove the concrete support for computing the answer (i.e., simply tell the pupil how many items have been removed and keep the items out of sight). After children are proficient with smaller sets, graduate to sets with 11 to 18 items. Again it may be helpful to start with evenly numbered sets and remove half (e.g., $12 - 6, 18 - 9$).

*Based on a suggestion provided by Ed Rathmell, Northern Iowa University.

Note that though the situation involves subtraction (taking away objects), the solution involves determining the missing part, which when added to the given part yields a given whole. This training procedure is particularly useful with children who can count-on. In Step 3 of Example 8–15, a child could count, "Three; four is one more, five is two more, six is three more—three."

Number sticks are a useful semiformal device for developing familiarity with additive-subtraction and difference meanings of subtraction. They can be used to model additive-subtraction and difference word problems. For instance, for the problem listed in Table 8–2, a child would put out a seven-stick to represent the number of stickers Cyndi has and a four-stick to show how many Allison has. The child can solve the problem simply by finding the number-stick that added to the four-stick makes the same length as the seven-stick. *This method can also be substituted for the* more cumbersome

(take-away) procedure for solving symbolic problems such as $\begin{array}{r} 7 \\ -4 \\ \hline \end{array}$ *outlined in Frame C of Figure 8–4.*

Commutativity of Multiplication

The prerequisites for a meaningful grasp of the principle are the repeated addition of like sets (Chapter 7) and symbolic multiplication (this chapter). Learning that multiplication is commutative can be facilitated by working with small combinations like three twos (3 × 2) or two threes (2 × 3), because such combinations can easily be represented with manipulatives or calculated informally. (This leaves more attention free to notice the regularity.)

The commutative property of multiplication can be illustrated in a semiconcrete manner by playing a multiplication version of the **Tower of Same-As**. In this version, players can use two *or more like* number sticks to produce a drawn number (e.g., see Frame A of Figure 8–5). To draw attention to the commutative property, have the children record their results informally (e.g., see Frame B of Figure 8–5).

Though some children need such semiconcrete models of the concept, it may not be necessary for many children. Especially if given the opportunity to calculate pairs symbolic problems like 4 × 2 = ? and 2 × 4 = ?, a child will often discover and comprehend the regularity. Even so, concrete activities, such as the Tower of Same-As, may deepen children's understanding of multiplication and its commutative property.

Unfamiliar Number Sentences

Children should master the relevant concept first. Unfamiliar number sentences should be introduced as a way of formally representing the

Figure 8–5 The Commutative Principle of Multiplication: A Semiconcrete Model*

A. Tower of Same-As Solution for 12

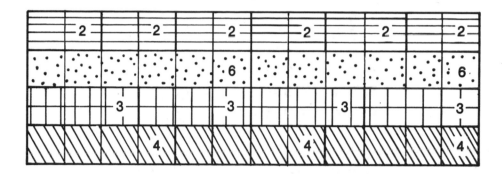

B. Informal representation of the solutions

② 6 → 12
⑥ 2 → 12
③ 4 → 12
④ 3 → 12

*Note that this example is contrived to highlight this commutative property. Children, of course, may construct their answer in a different order. Even so, there is the *opportunity* to discover the commutative regularity.

arithmetic concept. To further foster meaningful learning, relate unfamiliar number sentences to word problems (e.g., Bebout, 1986; Carpenter and Bebout, 1985).

Addition-Subtraction Inverse

First ensure that a child can solve semiconcrete addition-subtraction inverse problems, such as those described for the Modified Magic Show. Written assignments or the game **Fill In** involving worksheets like that in Exercise A of Example 8–16 can be used to highlight the principle. (To play the symbolic version of **Fill In**, substitute fill-in tiles with numerals for fill-in tiles with dots.)

Example 8-16   Unfamiliar Number Sentences with Numerals

Exercise A

1. $5 + 3 - 3 = $ _____
2. $7 - 4 + 4 = $ _____
3. $6 - 5 + 5 = $ _____
4. $8 + 2 - 2 = $ _____
5. $9 + 6 - 6 = $ _____
6. $9 - 5 + 5 = $ _____

Exercise B

1. $5 + $ _____ $ = \ 8$
2. $6 + $ _____ $ = \ 7$
3. $4 + $ _____ $ = \ 9$
4. $3 + $ _____ $ = \ 7$
5. $9 + $ _____ $ = 12$
6. $8 + $ _____ $ = 10$

Exercise C

1. $5 + 3 = $ _____
2. _____ $ = 2 + 4$
3. $5 + 1 = 3 + $ _____
4. $4 + 2 = 2 + $ _____
5. $5 + 2 = 7 + $ _____
6. $8 = 6 + $ _____

Exercise D

1. $5 + 3 + 2 = $ _____ $ + 5 + 3$
2. $4 + 1 + 3 = $ _____ $ + 4 + 1$
3. $6 + 2 + 3 = 2 + 3 + $ _____
4. $5 + 1 + 6 = 1 + 6 + $ _____
5. $8 + 4 + 6 = 4 + 6 + $ _____
6. $5 + 3 + 7 = 3 + 7 + $ _____

Exercise E

1. _____ $+ 3 = 5$
2. _____ $+ 6 = 7$
3. _____ $+ 5 = 8$
4. _____ $+ 1 = 6$
5. _____ $+ 3 = 6$
6. _____ $+ 2 = 9$

Exercise F

1. $5 + 5 + 5 + 5 = 5 \times$ _____
2. $2 + 2 + 2 + 2 + 2 = 2 \times$ _____
3. $4 + 4 + 4 = 4 \times$ _____
4. $8 + 8 = 8 \times$ _____
5. $3 + 3 + 3 + 3 =$ _____ $\times 4$
6. $5 + 5 + 5 + 5 + 5 + 5 =$ _____ $\times 6$

Missing Addend

First ensure that a child can solve semiconcrete, missing-addend problems. Word problems are a useful mechanism for helping children to understand notations such as $6 + ? = 9$. Example 8–17 illustrates how word problems can be used to bridge the gap between semiconcrete and formal representations. Written assignments or the game **Fill In** involving worksheets like those in Exercise B of Example 8–16 can provide practice for solving missing-addend problems.

Example 8–17 Missing-Addend Problems with Egyptian Hieroglyphics

---

1. All of these merchants should have paid 10 coins in taxes. How many more coins does each have to pay to the king?

   a. Ace Reed Products   ΛΛΛ ΛΛ Λ Λ   _____

   b. Block Haulers   Λ Λ ΛΛ Λ Λ   _____

   c. Cultured Cats   ΛΛΛΛΛ   _____

   d. Durable Slaves   ΛΛ Λ Λ Ι Λ Ι   _____

2. For each merchant above, use our arabic numerals to write a number sentence that shows what they paid, what they still owe, and the amount they owe in taxes altogether. Use a ? to indicate the unknown amount the merchant still owes.

3. Make up your own story that would fit the number sentence: $7 + ? = 13$

4. Make up your own story that would fit the number sentence: $5 + ? = 8$

Other Names for a Number and Commutativity of Addition

First ensure that children have mastered the same-sum-as, commutativity-of-addition, union-of-sets, part-part-whole, and missing-part concepts in a semiconcrete context. Worksheets like that in Exercise C of Example 8–16 can be used as written exercises or to play the game **Fill In**. Unfamiliar number sentences of the form $? = a + b$ (e.g., Problem 2 in Exercise C of Example 8–16) can be related to word problems where a whole is *decomposed* into its parts:

Kenny had a bag of marbles. He poured them out onto the ground and sorted them. His collection of marbles consisted of two cat's eyes and four solids.

Unfamiliar number sentences in the form of $a + b = c + ?$ (same-sum-as expression such as Problem 3) or $a + b = b + ?$ (commutativity equations such as Problem 4) can also be related to word problems such as those below:

1. Ariane claimed that she could play a bowling game as well as her brother Alexi. On his first turn Alexi knocked down 5 pins, and on his second turn he knocked down 1. On her first turn, Ariane knocked down 3 pins. How many pins does she have to knock down on her second turn to get the same number of points as her brother?

2. In the first day of the School Olympics, Alison won 4 blue ribbons and 2 red ribbons. On the second day, she won the same number of ribbons again, but this time she won 2 blue ribbons. How many red ribbons did she win on the second day?

Associativity of Addition

It may be helpful if the child understands the principle at a semiconcrete level—for example, if he or she is familiar with the Tower-of-Same-As (three stick version). The exercise described in Chapter 2 (Example 2–10) can be used to introduce the idea with written expressions. Written exercises or the game **Fill In** involving worksheets like that in Exercise D of Example 8–16 can be used to highlight the principle further.

Missing Augend

First ensure that a child can solve semiconcrete missing-augend and symbolic missing-addend problems. As with symbolic missing-addend expressions, relate missing-augend number sentences to missing-augend word problems. Worksheets like those in Exercise E in Example 8–16 can be used to practice solving symbolic missing-augend problems either as written assignments or as part of the game **Fill-In**.

Equivalent + and ×

First ensure that a child understands symbolic multiplication—specifically, that multiplication is simply repeated addition of like terms. Written exercises or the game **Fill In** involving worksheets like that in Exercise

E of Example 8–16 can be used to reinforce the formal representation of this equivalence relationship.

SUMMARY

Children should understand the underlying concept of a symbol before the mathematical symbol itself is introduced. This can be done by introducing a concept in terms familiar to children: counting or informal arithmetic. Formal representations should be introduced later as, say, shorthand devices for describing what children already know (Holt, 1964). Teachers should help make clear the link between the formal symbol and the children's existing (informal) ideas.

Most school children will already have a solid informal basis for understanding prearithmetic symbols such as numerals and the greater-than signs. Care needs to be taken with introducing the equals sign as the "same number as"—so as to avoid the tendency to interpret it as "produces." Children should master informal arithmetic before familiar number sentences such as $5 + 3 = ?$, $5 - 3 = ?$, and $5 \times 3 = ?$ are introduced.

An important goal of primary instruction is to deepen children's understanding of the arithmetic operations by helping them see patterns, relationships, or new meanings. This broadening of mathematical concepts can be facilitated by building upon children's informal arithmetic and using manipulatives. Once children understand the arithmetic concept at a concrete level, then their formal representation in the form of unfamiliar number sentences can be introduced. For example, once children recognize from their computational experience that addend order does not affect the sum, *then* expressions like $5 + 3 = 3 + 5$ can be introduced to represent the commutative property of addition.

Chapter 9

Basic Number Combinations

Even after arithmetic is formally introduced, children frequently rely on informal methods to figure out sums, differences, or products for a considerable period of time. During this phase of informal exploration, children usually discover important relationships that underlie the number combinations and that help them to remember this basic information. Children only *gradually* master the basic number facts (single-digit number combinations).

The basic number combinations embody numerous relationships and patterns that children can exploit to master whole groups or families of combinations (e.g., Folsom, 1975; Jerman, 1970; Rathmell, 1978; Trivett, 1980). For example, one rule (adding zero does not change a number) underlies the 19 single-digit combinations involving zero. This chapter will describe the various *addition, subtraction,* and *multiplication families* and the relationships that can serve as the basis for mastering them.

Even in this day of computers and calculators, mastery of the single-digit number facts remains one of the most basic objectives of primary schooling. The quick and accurate production of sums, differences, and products is important for three (interrelated) reasons. First, it makes written and mental multidigit calculation easier, if not possible. Second, it permits the discovery of relationships, which can facilitate the mastery of other basic combinations. For example, if a child knows that $7 + 1 = 8$, he or she is more likely to discover that $1 + 7$ and $7 + 1$ are equivalent—that addend order does not affect the sum. By exploiting this (commutative) relationship, children can more readily master unknown commuted versions of already learned combinations. Third, mastery of basic combinations is a key to mastering multidigit combinations. By relating multidigit combinations, such as $100 + 100 = ?$ or $300 + 200 = ?$, to known single-digit combinations ($1 + 1 = 2$ or $3 + 2 = 5$), children can more quickly master an array of multidigit combinations. This will be discussed further in Chapter 11.

LEARNING

The basic number combinations are not merely a "basket of facts" that children simply and quickly absorb (memorize by rote) (Anderson, 1984). Instead, they—quite sensibly—learn the single-digit combinations as a system of interrelated facts (Brownell, 1935; Carpenter, 1985; Olander, 1931). To learn and use the relationships or patterns underlying these combinations, children often need a period of informal calculation and reflection.

Indeed, children commonly invent "thinking strategies": devices for reasoning out (unknown) combinations. For example, if a child knows $5 + 5$ is 10, he or she can reason that $5 + 6$ must be one more than 10 or 11. Likewise, the child can use other known "doubles" like $4 + 4 = 8$ or $6 + 6 = 12$ to reason out other "doubles plus one," such as $4 + 5 = ?$ or $7 + 6 = ?$. Thinking strategies are children's informal way of exploiting relationships or patterns.

As the example above illustrates, children use "easier facts" to figure out and then remember "harder facts." Mastering the number combinations is essentially a building process. Children master many new combinations by "seeing" how they are connected (related) to previously learned combinations (Baroody, 1987a).

Like computing sums by counting, thinking strategies are meaningful to children and not quickly abandoned (Brownell, 1935). In fact, children frequently do not memorize all the basic addition facts until second or even third grade; the basic subtraction facts until third or even fourth grade; and multiplication facts by fourth grade or so (e.g., Ashcraft, 1982; Carpenter and Moser, 1984; Lankford, 1974; Svenson, 1974; Woods, Resnick, and Groen, 1975). Indeed, even many adults still use informal procedures to compute or reason out sums and do so rather quickly (e.g., Browne, 1906; Svenson, 1985). Delineated below are the relationships or patterns that can serve as thinking strategies for reasoning out and learning various families of combinations.

Addition Families

Commuted Pairs

The discovery of commutativity may greatly facilitate mastery. By practicing and mastering a combination such as $5 + 3$, a child can also respond to $3 +$

$5 = ?$ efficiently. By exploiting commutativity, the child cuts by nearly half the number of combinations that must be memorized. The discovery and use of this general principle may occur early but perhaps not until after children have mastered more specific relationships—combinations involving one and zero (Baroody, 1987a; Resnick, 1983).

$n + 1$ and $1 + n$

Informal knowledge permits children to master the family of combinations involving the addition of one relatively quickly. Many already have a basis for responding efficiently to a symbolic combination such as $4 + 1 = ?$. They can mentally add one more because they have discovered a "number-after" rule (e.g., the number after 4 is 5, so four and one more is five). Once they see a connection between formal addition and their existing informal knowledge, children can automatically recall any $n + 1$ combination for which they know the next number—even single-digit and multidigit combinations (such as $86 + 1$) that they have *not* practiced previously (Baroody, 1983, 1985).

Children may then have to learn that $1 + n$ combinations are equivalent to $n + 1$ combinations (that the number-after rule applies to something-added-to-one problems also). Because this is usually accomplished with a minimum of computational experience, children can also master the range of $1 + n$ combinations without practicing each individual fact (Baroody and Ginsburg, 1986).

$n + 0$ and $0 + n$

The family of combinations involving zero is among the earliest mastered because children quickly recognize the $n + 0$ or $0 + n = n$ rule.

$n + 2$ and $2 + n$

The family of combinations involving two is learned fairly early, in part perhaps because children can exploit the skip-the-next-number relationship (e.g., $6 + 2$: *6,* skip 7, 8).

Small $n + n$

The "doubles" with sums no larger than 10 ($1 + 1, 2 + 2, 3 + 3, 4 + 4,$ and $5 + 5$) are among the earliest combinations memorized. This may be due partly to the fact that there are many naturally occurring pairs or "doubles" (e.g., five fingers on each hand, 10 digits altogether).

Small Miscellaneous

Other combinations with sums no greater than 10 are learned only gradually. "Near doubles" such as $3 + 4$ are often learned by exploiting known $n + n$ facts $(3 + 4 = [3 + 3] + 1 = 6 + 1 = 7)$. Some combinations such as $3 + 5$ can be recomposed as a known double $(3 + 5 = [3 + 1] + [5 - 1] = 4 + 4 = 8)$.

Large $n + n$

Typically, the larger doubles $(6 + 6, 7 + 7, 8 + 8,$ and $9 + 9)$ are learned somewhat later than small doubles.

Equals Ten

The sums-to-10 family (e.g., $6 + 4$ or $7 + 3$) may have special significance to some children because of our base-ten place-value system and their natural endowment of ten fingers.

$n + 8$ and $8 + n$ or $n + 9$ and $9 + n$

The family of combinations involving eight or nine are relatively difficult for children. However, many discover that the sums can be reasoned out by exploiting problems involving 10.

Large Miscellaneous

Other combinations with sums larger than 10 are relatively difficult for children to learn.

Subtraction Families

Complements

A direct implication of the additive-subtraction concept (discussed in the previous chapter) is that subtraction combinations have addition complements. For instance, because the expression $5 - 3 = ?$ can be thought of as what must be added to three to make five, $5 - 3 = 2$ and $3 + 2 = 5$ are complementary combinations.[1] Research (Baroody, Ginsburg, and Waxman,

---

[1]At a deeper level, children might recognize that $5 - 3 = ?$ and $5 - 2 = ?$ are also related. With a well developed part-part-whole concept, a child would recognize that the parts 3 and 2 can combine in any order to constitute the whole 5 $(3 + 2 = 2 + 3 = 5)$. They would also recognize that removing one part from the whole leaves the other part: $5 - 3 = 2$ and $5 - 2 = 3$.

1983; Buckingham, 1927; Carpenter and Moser, 1984; Knight and Behrens, 1928; Siegler, in press; Steinberg, 1985) in fact, indicates that mastery of addition facts and the learning of subtraction combinations are psychologically related. It seems that *once* children recognize the over-arching relationship between addition and subtraction and have mastered the addition counterparts, they can proceed to learn quickly the remaining unmastered subtraction combinations (Baroody and Ginsburg, 1986; Thornton and Smith, 1988). Apparently, though, children do not readily discover that subtraction combinations have addition complements. And, of course, it takes time before they master the larger addition combinations, which provide the basis for learning the larger subtraction counterparts.

$n - 1$

Most children may learn the minus-one family of facts by using their existing counting (just-before) knowledge. As with addition involving one, once they see the connection between symbolic subtraction and their existing informal knowledge, children can respond efficiently to a range of single-digit (and multidigit) $n - 1$ combinations without practicing each fact separately. Children can exploit a number of other relationships that makes rotely memorizing individual facts unnecessary.

$n - 2$

With the minus-two family, children can also exploit the well-learned count sequence.

$n - 0$

The minus-zero family is learned early because children quickly come to appreciate the principle that if nothing is taken away, a number remains unchanged.

$n - n$

The easily recognized pattern underlying this family (e.g., $4 - 4$ and $9 - 9$) is: A number reduced by itself leaves nothing.

$m - n = n$

This family is composed of combinations in which the minuend is twice the subtrahend (e.g., $6 - 3 = 3$ or $12 - 6 = 6$). These combinations are learned before many other combinations because their complementary addition doubles (e.g., $3 + 3 = 6$ or $6 + 6 = 12$) are learned relatively early.

Difference of 1

The subtraction of number neighbors (e.g., $3 - 2 = 1$ or $9 - 8 = 1$) forms a special class of facts: "The difference of neighboring numbers is always one."

$10 - n$

Combinations with 10 as a minuend (e.g., $10 - 3$, $10 - 6$) may have a special status for some children because of our natural endowment of 10 fingers.

Teen $- n$

These combinations (e.g., $15 - 8$) may not be mastered by most children until after third grade. The *teen* $- 9$ (*teen* $- 8$) family can be solved by converting the problem to a more familiar teen $- 10$ problem and then adding one (two). The remainder (large miscellaneous combinations) can be reasoned out by using the complement principle.

Multiplication Families

$n \times 1$ and $1 \times n$

Children readily grasp the times-one family of facts because of the obvious rule: Any number times one is that number.

$n \times 0$ and $0 \times n$

The times-zero family is often learned quickly because the principle underlying this group of facts is easily noticed and internalized: Anything multiplied by zero is zero.

$n \times 2$ and $2 \times n$

The times-two family often builds upon a child's knowledge of the addition doubles (e.g., "3×2 is 6 because 3 and 3 is 6") or counting by twos.

$n \times 5$ and $5 \times n$

The five-times family is often learned before other facts because children are familiar with the count-by-fives sequence.

Other Small Times

Other combinations are typically mastered later. For example, the $n \times 3$ and $3 \times n$ or $n \times 4$ and $4 \times n$ families are relatively difficult because skip counting by three or four is not especially familiar to children.

Other Large Times

Combinations with both factors greater than five are especially difficult for children to master. Children may not completely master families such as $n \times 9$ and $9 \times n$ until fourth grade or even later.

Though a number of factors can determine the rate and order in which children acquire mastery of basic-combination families, approximate the developmental sequences for the operations of addition, subtraction, and multiplication are delineated in Table 9–1.

Table 9–1 A Suggested Sequence of Basic Number-Combination Skills by Grade Level

Level	Addition Families	Subtraction Families	Multiplication Families
1	$n + 1$ and $1 + n$, $n + 0$ and $0 + n$	—	—
	$n + 2$ and $2 + n$ and Small $n + n$	—	—
	—	$n - 1$, $n - 0$ and $n - n$	—
	—	$n - 2$	—
2	Small misc.	$m -$ small $n = n$	—
	Large $n + n$ and	Difference of one	—
	Equals 10	Small misc.	—
	$n + 9$ and $9 + n$	$m -$ large $n = n$	—
3	Larger misc.	$10 - n$	—
	—	Teen $- 9$ or 8 and Large misc.	—
	—	—	$n \times 1$, $1 \times n$, $n \times 0$ and $0 \times n$
	—	—	$n \times 2$ and $2 \times n$
	—	—	$n \times 5$ and $5 \times n$
	—	—	Other small and large times*

*These combinations can be introduced and practiced in third grade. It may not be realistic to expect that all or even most children will recall these combinations by the end of third grade. Third graders can be encouraged to use informal methods and thinking strategies to find these products.

INSTRUCTION

Because it involves more than rote memorization, mastery of the basic number combinations requires more than just practice. It requires meaningful instruction because—at heart—internalizing basic number combinations entails recognizing and exploiting relationships. In fact, some research (e.g., Brownell and Chazal, 1935; Steinberg, 1985; Swenson, 1949; Thiele, 1938; Thornton, 1978; Thornton and Smith, 1988) indicates that a meaningful approach is more effective in facilitating retention and transfer than a drill approach (Suydam and Weaver, 1975). This helps explain why so many teachers find a drill approach so unproductive. Besides being uninteresting and uninspiring, it fails to teach the key component needed for mastery: noting and using relationships. Meaningful learning of the basic combinations requires time. Children should be given ample opportunity to compute sums, differences, and products. During this initial and necessary stage, children should be encouraged to look for and exploit patterns or relationships. Moreover, teachers should foster children's natural inclination to invent and use thinking strategies. After all, thinking strategies are children's informal way of searching for and exploiting patterns and relationships. This crucial intermediate stage in the meaningful memorization of basic number combinations should not be rushed either.

Practice plays an important role in helping children to recall specific facts or to use relationships automatically. However, it should play a secondary role to discovering relationships and inventing thinking strategies. Moreover, practice should come after such experiences. By using games, practice can actually be *interestng* and meaningful.

Teaching Thinking Strategies

Even *if* it were no more effective in promoting mastery than drill, there are a number of advantages to encouraging and teaching thinking strategies. An approach that emphasizes thinking strategies is inherently more interesting and enjoyable. It validates children's informal mathematical thinking (your approach to mathematics is useful) and makes basic arithmetic and number-fact mastery less threatening and overwhelming for children. It illustrates in a personally meaningful way that arithmetic problems can be solved in various ways. Such an approach encourages children to look for relationships and reason about numbers. It more accurately reflects the nature of mathematics than does a rote memorization approach. A meaningful approach to number-fact mastery is more likely to foster analytic-thinking and problem-solving skill than will a drill approach. Such an approach is useful even with children with mathematical learning difficulties (Thornton and Toohey, 1985).

Table 9–2 outlines thinking strategies for the operations of addition, subtraction, and multiplication. How should teachers promote the learning of thinking strategies? Should they point them out directly, allow children to discover them in due course, structure practice to foster their discovery, or have children who have invented a strategy share it with others? There are no pat answers to these questions. A mix of each method may prove the most helpful. The exact mix will depend on such things as the level of ability, the personalities of the pupils, time constraints, and so forth.

By sharing a few thinking strategies, a teacher endorses looking for and exploiting patterns. Do not be disappointed if all children do not pick up and use the examples. After all, not all will be ready to benefit from this direct instruction, and some may favor alternative methods that are more familiar. In any case, encouraging *thinking* strategies should not become another memorize-math-by-rote routine. Simply endorsing children's informal approach is important enough.

The invention of thinking strategies should be applauded. After all, it is a sign that a child is really thinking about mathematics. Asking the child to share his or her ideas with others will serve as recognition and may help the other children learn that specific thinking strategy and encourage them to invent ones of their own.

Encouraging the Discovery and Exploitation of Patterns

Children should be encouraged to look for and exploit patterns. One way this might be done is to give them a table of basic facts, such as the times table in Example 9–1, and challenge them to find patterns. This type of unstructured-discovery-learning exercise might work well as seatwork for some young, primary-level children (particularly those who are gifted) but might be more suitable for older elementary children. At the primary level, such an exercise might better be done as a small-group problem-solving exercise.

Various devices can be used to structure practice in such a way that children are more apt to discover key patterns, relationships, or rules. For each of the arithmetic operations, **Math-Detective** and **In-Out Machine Exercises** can help highlight a variety of patterns (see Examples 9–2 and 9–3). Moreover, such exercises can provide the basis for small-group or class discussions of number-combination patterns.

Table 9-2 Thinking Strategies for Addition, Subtraction, and Multiplication Families of Facts

Family	Thinking Strategy	
$n + 0$ or $0 + n$	*$n + 0 = n$ rule:	Addition in which zero is a term that does not change the other number.
$n + 1$ or $1 + n$	*n-after rule:	The sum of $n + 1$ (or $1 + n$) is the number after n in the count sequence.
$n + 2$ or $2 + n$	*Skip-next-n rule:	The sum of $n + 2$ ($2 + n$) is the number after the next number after n in the count sequence.
Small or Large Misc.	*Commutativity:	Addend order does not affect the sum. For example, because the sum of $5 + 3$ is 8, the sum of $3 + 5$ must also be 8.
	*Doubles plus one:	Combinations like $3 + 4$ can be recomposed as $3 + (3 + 1)$ or $(3 + 3) + 1$. Because $3 + 3$ is six and 4 is one more than 3, then $3 + 4$ must be six and one more, or 7. Likewise, a relatively difficult combination like $8 + 7$ can be thought of as $(1 + 7) + 7$ or $1 + (7 + 7)$. Because the double $7 + 7$ is 14, one more makes $8 + 7$ equal to 15.
	*Doubles minus one:	A combination like $3 + 4$ can be recomposed in terms of the double $4 + 4$. Because 3 is one less than 4, then $3 + 4$ is one less than 8, or 7.
	*Doubles by recomposition:	Combinations like $5 + 3$ can be converted into doubles by taking away one from the larger term and giving it to the smaller term ($5 + 3 = [5 - 1] + [3 + 1] = 4 + 4 = 8$). Likewise, larger, relatively difficult combinations like $7 + 9$ can be converted to $8 + 8$. Because it is not readily apparent to many children, this is one thinking strategy that a teacher might want to point out to children.
$n + 8$ or $8 + n$ $n + 9$ or $9 + n$	*Recomposition to 10:	The relatively difficult combinations involving eight or nine can be recomposed as the relatively easy combinations involving 10. For $9 + 4$, for example, nine can be made into 10 by adding one, which is

Table 9–2 Continued

Family	Thinking Strategy	
		taken from the 4 making it three $(9 + 4 = [9 + 1] + [4 - 1] = 10 + 3 = 13)$. Similarly, combinations involving eight can be recomposed into combinations involving 10 by transferring two (e.g., $8 + 4 = [8 + 2] + [4 - 2] = 10 + 2 = 12$).
$n - 0$	*$n - 0 = n$ rule:	Zero subtracted from a number leaves it unchanged (subtractive-identity principle).
$n - 1$	*n-before rule:	To subtract one from the number, state the number in the count sequence that comes before it.
$n - n$	*$n - n = 0$:	A number subtracted from itself leaves nothing.
Difference of One	*The difference-of-one rule:	Whenever neighbors in the sequence (e.g., 6 and 7) are subtracted, the difference is one $(7 - 6 = 1)$. (The rule also applies to cases where the smaller number is the minuend, e.g., $6 - 7$. In this case, though, the difference is *minus* one.)
$n - 2$ $m - n = n$ Small Misc. $10 - n$ Large Misc.	*Complements:	Any subtraction combination can be figured out by recalling its related or complementary addition combination. For instance, $8 - 5$ can be thought of as what do I need to add to five to make 8: three (because $5 + 3 = 8$). This might be introduced with the $n - 2$ and $m -$ small $n = n$ combination because of children's relatively greater familiarity with $n + 2$ or $2 + n$ and small $n + n$ combinations.
Teen $- 9$ Teen $- 8$	*Recomposition to 10:	The relatively difficult minus-nine (or eight) family can be recomposed as the relatively easy minus-10 family. For example, $17 - 9 = (17 - 1) - (9 + 1) = 16 - 10 = 6$.
$n \times 0$	*$n \times 0 = 0$ rule:	Any number times zero is zero.
$n \times 1$ or $1 \times n$	*$n \times 1$ or $1 \times n = n$ rule:	The multiplicative-identity principle states that a number times one is the number itself.

Table 9–2 Continued

Family	Thinking Strategy	
$n \times 2$ or $2 \times n$	*Equivalent addition double:	Recall the equivalent addition double (e.g., 7×2 or 2×7 is equivalent to $7 + 7 = 14$). Note that the product of all such combinations are even numbers.
$n \times 5$ or $5 \times n$	*Skip count by five:	Count by five n times (e.g., 5×3 is 5, 10, *15*). Note that five times an even-number ends in 0; five times an odd number ends in 5.
Other Small and Large Times	*Commutativity:	Except for the doubles, all multiplication combinations are related to another by the principle of commutativity (e.g., if $8 \times 7 = 56$, then $7 \times 8 = 56$).
	*Doubles plus (or minus) one:	Near doubles can be reasoned out in terms of known doubles. For example 7×8 is 7×7 plus another seven $49 + 7 = 56$ (seven sevens plus an eighth seven). It could also be thought of as 8×8 minus an eight: $64 - 8 = 56$.
	*Doubles by recomposition:	A combination such as 8×6, that can be converted to a double (7×7) by compensating addition and subtraction of one has a product that is one less than the product of the double ($49 - 1 = 48$). Likewise 6×4 can be reasoned out by subtracting one from the product of 5×5: $25 - 1$ or 24.[1]
$n \times 9$ or $9 \times n$	*Times-nine rule:	The product of nine and a number is composed of a number with a tens-place digit equal to $n - 1$ and a ones place digit that sums to 9 (e.g., for 9×7, the tens place digit is $7 - 1$ or 6 and the ones place digit is six plus what makes nine: 3).

[1]This can be demonstrated by algebra: If $n =$ the factor of a double, then the double like 7×7 can be represented as $n \times n$. A problem like 8×6 can be represented as $(n + 1) \times (n - 1)$. The product of cross multiplication yield $n^2 + n - n - 1$, which reduces to $n^2 - 1$ or $(n \times n) - 1$.

Example 9-1 Product-Patterns Exercise

PRODUCT PATTERNS

Can you find five patterns in the products of the basic multiplication facts?

0X0	0X1	0X2	0X3	0X4	0X5	0X6	0X7	0X8	0X9
0	0	0	0	0	0	0	0	0	0
1X0	1X1	1X2	1X3	1X4	1X5	1X6	1X7	1X8	1X9
0	1	2	3	4	5	6	7	8	9
2X0	2X1	2X2	2X3	2X4	2X5	2X6	2X7	2X8	2X9
0	2	4	6	8	10	12	14	16	18
3X0	3X1	3X2	3X3	3X4	3X5	3X6	3X7	3X8	3X9
0	3	6	9	12	15	18	21	24	27
4X0	4X1	4X2	4X3	4X4	4X5	4X6	4X7	4X8	4X9
0	4	8	12	16	20	24	28	32	36
5X0	5X1	5X2	5X3	5X4	5X5	5X6	5X7	5X8	5X9
0	5	10	15	20	25	30	35	40	45
6X0	6X1	6X2	6X3	6X4	6X5	6X6	6X7	6X8	6X9
0	6	12	18	24	30	36	42	48	54
7X0	7X1	7X2	7X3	7X4	7X5	7X6	7X7	7X8	7X9
0	7	14	21	28	35	42	49	56	63
8X0	8X1	8X2	8X3	8X4	8X5	8X6	8X7	8X8	8X9
0	8	16	24	32	40	48	56	64	72
9X0	9X1	9X2	9X3	9X4	9X5	9X6	9X7	9X8	9X9
0	9	18	27	36	45	54	63	72	81

Pattern

Example 9–2   Using Math-Detective Exercises to Discover
Number-Combination Relationships

Math Detective Exercise A

a. What number comes after each of the following when we count?

4 _____   2 _____   5 _____   7 _____

b. Find the sums for each of the following problems in any way you
   wish. You may calculate sums by using blocks, fingers, an
   abacus or a calculator.
   What do you notice about these problems?

4	1	2	1	5	1	7	1
+1	+4	+1	+2	+1	+5	+1	+7

4 + 1 = ☐   2 + 1 = ☐   5 + 1 = ☐   7 + 1 = ☐

1 + 4 = ☐   1 + 2 = ☐   1 + 5 = ☐   1 + 7 = ☐

Math Detective Exercise B

Find the sums for each of the following problems in any way you
wish. You may calculate sums by using blocks, fingers, an
abacus or a calculator.
What do you notice about these problems?

6	3	0	9	0
+0	+0	+4	+0	+2

1	0	5	0	2
+0	+3	+0	+9	+0

Math Detective Exercise C

Find the sums for each of the following problems in any way
you wish. You may calculate sums by using blocks, fingers, an
abacus or a calculator.
What do you notice about these problems?

2	3	4	5	3	4
+2	+2	+4	+4	+3	+3

$$
\begin{array}{cc} 2 \\ +2 \end{array}\quad
\begin{array}{cc} 2 \\ +3 \end{array}\quad
\begin{array}{cc} 4 \\ +4 \end{array}\quad
\begin{array}{cc} 4 \\ +5 \end{array}\quad
\begin{array}{cc} 3 \\ +3 \end{array}\quad
\begin{array}{cc} 3 \\ +4 \end{array}
$$

1 + 1 = □   4 + 4 = □   1 + 1 = □

2 + 1 = □   5 + 4 = □   1 + 2 = □

Math Detective Exercise D

Find the sums for each of the following problems in any way you wish. You may calculate sums by using blocks, fingers, an abacus or a calculator.

What do you notice about these problems?

2 + 2 = □   4 + 4 = □   3 + 3 = □

1 + 3 = □   3 + 5 = □   4 + 2 = □

$$
\begin{array}{cc} 4 \\ +4 \end{array}\quad
\begin{array}{cc} 5 \\ +3 \end{array}\quad
\begin{array}{cc} 2 \\ +2 \end{array}\quad
\begin{array}{cc} 3 \\ +1 \end{array}\quad
\begin{array}{cc} 3 \\ +3 \end{array}\quad
\begin{array}{cc} 2 \\ +4 \end{array}
$$

Math Detective Exercise E

Find the sums for each of the following problems in any way you wish. You may calculate sums by using blocks, fingers, an abacus or a calculator.

What do you notice about these problems?

$$
\begin{array}{cc} 10 \\ +2 \end{array}\quad
\begin{array}{cc} 9 \\ +2 \end{array}\quad
\begin{array}{cc} 10 \\ +6 \end{array}\quad
\begin{array}{cc} 9 \\ +6 \end{array}\quad
\begin{array}{cc} 10 \\ +4 \end{array}\quad
\begin{array}{cc} 9 \\ +4 \end{array}\quad
\begin{array}{cc} 5 \\ +10 \end{array}\quad
\begin{array}{cc} 5 \\ +9 \end{array}
$$

$$
\begin{array}{cc} 10 \\ +6 \end{array}\quad
\begin{array}{cc} 9 \\ +6 \end{array}\quad
\begin{array}{cc} 7 \\ +10 \end{array}\quad
\begin{array}{cc} 7 \\ +9 \end{array}\quad
\begin{array}{cc} 8 \\ +10 \end{array}\quad
\begin{array}{cc} 8 \\ +9 \end{array}\quad
\begin{array}{cc} 10 \\ +9 \end{array}\quad
\begin{array}{cc} 9 \\ +9 \end{array}
$$

4 + 10 = □   3 + 10 = □   6 + 10 = □   7 + 10 = □

4 + 9 = □   3 + 9 = □   6 + 9 = □   7 + 9 = □

10 + 4 = □   10 + 3 = □   10 + 6 = □   10 + 7 = □

4 + 10 = □   9 + 3 = □   9 + 6 = □   9 + 7 = □

Math Detective Exercise F

Find the sums for each of the following problems in any way you wish. You may calculate sums by using blocks, fingers, an abacus or a calculator.

What do you notice about these problems?

$$
\begin{array}{ccccc}
9 & 8 & 7 & 6 & 5 \\
+1 & +2 & +3 & +4 & +5 \\
\end{array}
$$

$$
\begin{array}{c}
4 \\
+6 \\
\end{array}
$$

$$
\begin{array}{c}
3 \\
+7 \\
\end{array}
$$

$$
\begin{array}{c}
2 \\
+8 \\
\end{array}
$$

$$
\begin{array}{c}
1 \\
+9 \\
\end{array}
$$

Math Detective Exercise G

a. What number comes before the following numbers when we count?

_____ 5 _____ 3 _____ 9 _____ 7 _____ 4 _____ 8

b. What is the difference between the following?

$$
\begin{array}{cccccc}
5 & 3 & 9 & 7 & 4 & 8 \\
-1 & -1 & -1 & -1 & -1 & -1 \\
\end{array}
$$

Math Detective Exercise H

What pattern is shown below?

$$
\begin{array}{cccc}
7 & 5 & 8 & 6 \\
-6 & -4 & -7 & -5 \\
\end{array}
$$

$$4 - 3 = \square \qquad 9 - 8 = \square$$

Math Detective Exercise I

What *two* patterns are shown below?

3	6	9	7	7	4
−0	−6	−0	−0	−7	−4

$8 - 0 =$ ☐ $5 - 5 =$ ☐ $6 - 0 =$ ☐ $4 - 0 =$ ☐

Math Detective Exercise J

What *patterns* are illustrated below?

4	2	5	0	5	1
×2	×4	×0	×5	×1	×5

3	6	0	6	1	6
×6	×3	×6	×0	×6	×1

8	4	8	0	8	1
×4	×8	×0	×8	×1	×8

Math Detective Exercise K

Do you notice anything about the products of the nondoubles?

3	4	6	7	4	5	8	9
×3	×2	×6	×5	×4	×3	×8	×7

$2 \times 2 =$ ☐ $7 \times 7 =$ ☐ $5 \times 5 =$ ☐ $9 \times 9 =$ ☐

$1 \times 3 =$ ☐ $8 \times 6 =$ ☐ $6 \times 4 =$ ☐ $10 \times 8 =$ ☐

Example 9–3   Using In-Out Machine Exercises to Highlight Relationships Among Number Combinations

Exercise A

In	Out
1	2
4	5
9	10
7	
3	
5	
	9
	3
2	
0	

Exercise B

In	Out
3	3
6	6
9	9
5	
1	
8	
	4
	2
	7
0	

Exercise C

In	Out
(2,1)	3
(1,2)	3
(1,7)	8
(7,1)	
(5,1)	6
(1,5)	
(9,1)	10
(1,9)	
(8,1)	
(1,8)	

Exercise D

In	Out
(3,3)	6
(4,3)	7
(2,2)	4
(2,3)	
(3,3)	6
(4,3)	
(8,8)	
(8,9)	
(7,7)	
(8,7)	
(5,5)	
(6,5)	

Exercise E

In	Out
(3,3)	6
(4,2)	6
(5,5)	10
(6,4)	
(6,6)	12
(7,5)	
(7,7)	
(8,6)	
(8,8)	
(9,7)	
(4,4)	
(5,3)	
(2,2)	
(3,1)	

Exercise F

In	Out
(3,3)	6
(2,4)	6
(5,5)	10
(4,6)	
(6,6)	12
(5,7)	
(7,7)	
(6,8)	
(8,8)	
(7,9)	
(4,4)	
(3,5)	
(2,2)	
(1,3)	

Exercise G

In	Out
5	4
3	2
9	8
7	
4	
8	
	4
	1
	5
	0

Exercise H

In	Out
(5,4)	1
(3,2)	1
(9,8)	1
(7,6)	
(4,3)	
(6,?)	1
(8,?)	1
(2,?)	1

Exercise I

In	Out
3	3
6	6
9	9
7	
4	
8	
18	
	6
	5

Exercise J

In	Out
7	0
9	0
12	0
5	
8	
18	
42	
	0

Exercise K

In	Out
4	8
5	10
1	
3	
25	
0	
	8
	4
	20

Exercise L

In	Out
(4,2)	8
(5,3)	15
(6,2)	12
(2,4)	
(3,5)	
(2,6)	
(8,3)	24
(3,8)	
(7,2)	14
(2,7)	
(8,7)	56
(7,8)	
(6,9)	54
(9,6)	
(3,9)	
(9,3)	
(3,7)	
(7,3)	

In Example 9–2, the aim of Math Detective Exercise A is to help students discover that $n + 1$ and $1 + n$ combinations are equivalent (the sum of both is the number after n in the count sequences). Exercises B, I, and J underscore the rules for adding, subtracting, and multiplying with zero ($n + 0$ or $0 + n = n$, $n - 0 = n$, and $n \times 0$ or $0 \times n = 0$, respectively). (In addition, Exercise I illustrates the $n - n = 0$ rule; Exercise J, the $n \times 1$ or $1 \times n = n$ rule and the commutative principle of multiplication.) Exercise C is set up to help children discern the doubles-plus-or-minus one pattern; Exercise D is arranged to help students recognize that some combinations can easily be redistributed to form doubles; Exercise E illustrates that relatively easy combinations with 10 can be used to reason out those with 9. Exercise F highlights the sums to 10. Exercise G gives children practice in using the number-before rule for $n - 1$ combinations, and Exercise H highlights the differences-of-one relationship. Exercise K hints at the relatively difficult doubles-by-recomposition thinking strategy for multiplication.

In Example 9–3, In-Out Machine Exercise A could provide the basis for discussing the relationship between the number sequence and addition involving one. After completing the exercise, ask students to discuss their answers and what they think the invisible process inside the machine is doing. Some children may note that the machine is just adding one. With any luck, some students will see a connection with the number-after items. Then discuss the relationship between addition involving one and the number-after pattern. Encourage the children to state the relationship explicitly: When we add with one, the sum is just the number after (the other addend).

Exercise B highlights the effect of adding zero: the $n + 0 = n$ rule. Exercise C underscores the equivalence of $n + 1$ and $1 + n$ combinations. The purpose of Exercise D is to help students discover the doubles-plus-one thinking strategy; Exercises E and F help students discover the doubles-by-compensation thinking strategy.

Exercises G, H, I, and J can be used to highlight the subtraction thinking strategies of $n - 1 =$ the number before n when we count, difference of 1, $n - 0 = n$, and $n - n = 0$, respectively. Note that for the last item in Exercise J, there are any number of acceptable answers. For Exercise I, the invisible process of the machine could be "adding with zero" or "multiplying by one" as well as "subtracting zero." Thus the exercise can serve as the basis for discussing the fact that each of the operations is governed by an identity principle. Exercise J can also be used to highlight the multiplication patterns $n \times 0$ or $0 \times n = 0$. Therefore, with children familiar with multiplication, Exercises I and J can be used to reinforce the idea that there can be more than one correct solution to In-Out Machine exercises (some mathematical problems).

Exercise K can be used to illustrate the relationship between the addition doubles (e.g., $4 + 4 = 8$) and times-two combinations ($4 \times 2 = 8$). Again, group discussions can be used to highlight the connection between the operations (and the point that some problems may have more than one solution). Exercise L can be used to highlight the commutative principle of multiplication. It could also be used to highlight the equivalence of repeated addition (e.g., 5, 3 = 5 + 5 + 5 = 15) and multiplication (e.g., 5, 3 = 5 × 3 = 15).

One way to help children formalize their discovery is to encourage them to make up an "album of combination families." As a child discovers or learns about a new pattern, a page can be added to the album (see Example 9–4). It may be appealing to note each entry in a distinctive color. Collecting

Example 9–4 Sample Entry of an Album of Combination Families

ADDITION PATTERNS

0+0	1+0	2+0	3+0	4+0	5+0	6+0	7+0	8+0	9+0
0+1	1+1	2+1	3+1	4+1	5+1	6+1	7+1	8+1	9+1
0+2	1+2	2+2	3+2	4+2	5+2	6+2	7+2	8+2	9+2
0+3	1+3	2+3	3+3	4+3	5+3	6+3	7+3	8+3	9+3
0+4	1+4	2+4	3+4	4+4	5+4	6+4	7+4	8+4	9+4
0+5	1+5	2+5	3+5	4+5	5+5	6+5	7+5	8+5	9+5
0+6	1+6	2+6	3+6	4+6	5+6	6+6	7+6	8+6	9+6
0+7	1+7	2+7	3+7	4+7	5+7	6+7	7+7	8+7	9+7
0+8	1+8	2+8	3+8	4+8	5+8	6+8	7+8	8+8	9+8
0+9	1+9	2+9	3+9	4+9	5+9	6+9	7+9	8+9	9+9

CODE	PATTERN
	Double plus or minus one

new entries might provide incentive for some children to discover new patterns. If necessary, challenge your pupils to find other patterns. Finding less obvious patterns may be especially interesting for gifted children. In the course of constructing their album of number-combination families, some children may notice that some combinations can belong to more than one family.

Encourage children to compare the exercise sheets and their findings for the various operations. The exercise sheet for subtraction shown in Example 9–5 may even prompt some children to ask about the empty cells on the top right and bottom left. Questions about the first are a natural lead into negative numbers (e.g., the cell to the right of $8 - 8$ represents $8 - 9$). Exploring the combinations with negative differences can reinforce mastery of the basic subtraction combinations and minimize the use of small-from-

Example 9–5   Families-of-Subtraction-Combination Exercise

SUBTRACTION PATTERNS

0–0									
1–0	1–1								
2–0	2–1	2–2							
3–0	3–1	3–2	3–3						
4–0	4–1	4–2	4–3	4–4					
5–0	5–1	5–2	5–3	5–4	5–5				
6–0	6–1	6–2	6–3	6–4	6–5	6–6			
7–0	7–1	7–2	7–3	7–4	7–5	7–6	7–7		
8–0	8–1	8–2	8–3	8–4	8–5	8–6	8–7	8–8	
9–0	9–1	9–2	9–3	9–4	9–5	9–6	9–7	9–8	9–9
10–0	10–1	10–2	10–3	10–4	10–5	10–6	10–7	10–8	10–9
	11–1	11–2	11–3	11–4	11–5	11–6	11–7	11–8	11–9
		12–2	12–3	12–4	12–5	12–6	12–7	12–8	12–9
			13–3	13–4	13–5	13–6	13–7	13–8	13–9
				14–4	14–5	14–6	14–7	14–8	14–9
					15–5	15–6	15–7	15–8	15–9
						16–6	16–7	16–8	16–9
							17–7	17–8	17–9
								18–8	18–9

large bug later when multidigit subtraction is introduced. Questions about the empty cells in the lower left are a natural lead into new and recurring patterns among multidigit combinations.

Basic Addition Combinations

The **Addition-Pattern Activity** helps children to visualize sums to 10 in terms of patterns based on five (Easley, 1983; Flexer, 1986; Hatano, 1980). For example, as shown in Frame A of Figure 9–1, the combination $4 + 2$ is transformed into the problem $5 + 1$, which is easily identified as 6. This activity lends itself to the task of mastering the sums of 10 in particular. The

Figure 9–1 Addition-Pattern Activity

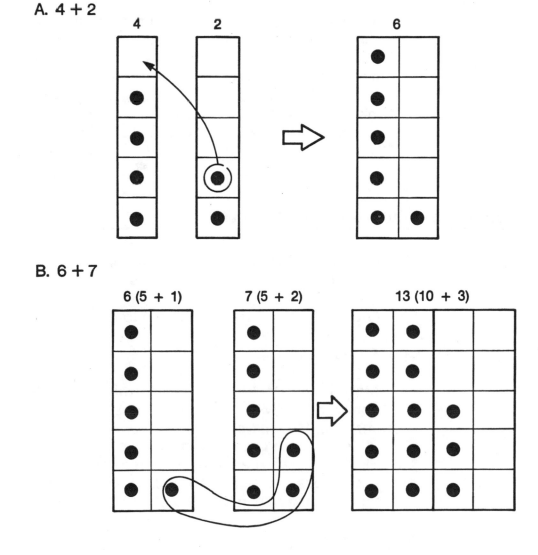

A. $4 + 2$

B. $6 + 7$

C. 9 + 7

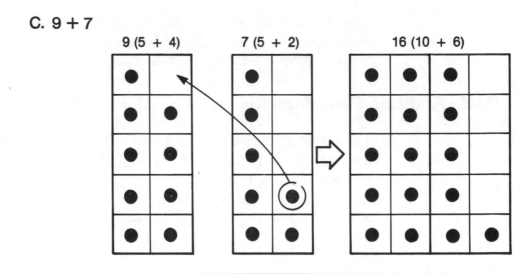

advanced version (illustrated in Frames B and C of Figure 9–1) helps children to visualize sums to 18 in terms of patterns based on five and ten (Thompson and Van de Walle, 1984; Wirtz, 1980). It is an especially useful means for helping children to discover the recomposition to 10 thinking strategy. **Addition-Pattern Estimates** (Example 9–6) combines practice in making estimates of single-digit addition combinations and using visual patterns to facilitate the remembering of basic facts.

Example 9–6   Addition-Pattern Estimates

Objectives: Practice estimating and computing sums to 10 (basic version) or to 18 (advanced version).

Grade Level: 1 (basic version) to 3 (advanced version).

Participants: One to five children.

Materials: Deck of cards on which are printed the addition combinations with sums 1 to 10 (basic version) or to 18 (advanced version); 10 chips, pennies, or other small countable objects; and a 2″ × 10″ card divided into ten one-inch squares (see Step 1 of Figure 9–2). Also needed are colored pattern-plates for the numbers 1 to 10 (basic version) or to 18 (advanced version). The pattern plate for 7 is illustrated in Step 2 of Figure 9–2. Lastly, materials to keep score are needed (chalkboard, paper, etc.).

Procedure: On their turn, the players draw a card and immediately make a guess (estimate) of the sum. If the child to the player's left counts "one Mississippi, two Mississippi, three Mississippi" before an estimate is given, the player must give up his or her turn. If the player makes an estimate within the time limit, he or she continues his or her turn as detailed in Figure 9-2.

Figure 9–2 Addition-Pattern Estimates

Step 1: Child draws card and (immediately) estimates the sum.

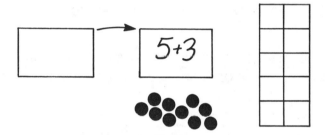

Erin turns over the top card of the deck and responds, "Seven."

Step 2: The pattern-plate for the estimate is placed on the player's card.

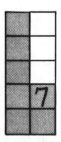

Erin places the pattern-plate for 7 on her card.

Step 3: The child then counts chips to represent the first addend and does likewise to represent the second addend.

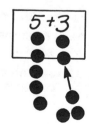

Erin has counted out five chips and is completing the process for the 3.

Step 4: The chips are transferred to the players card.

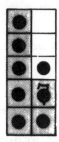

Step 5: The estimate is compared to the computed sum for accuracy.

Erin notes that there is one chip beyond the template. Because the estimate is off by one, she records one point on the chalkboard.

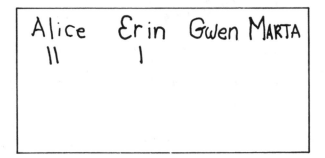

Indeed, a wide variety of games can provide all the practice children need to master basic addition combinations and do so in an entertaining manner. A number of games already described can be used or adapted for this purpose. For example, the **Tower of Same-As**, described in Example 8–7, would be appropriate for first graders in practicing sums to 10 and for second graders in practicing sums to 18. With numeral dice and a spiral race track, the **Racing-Car Game** described in Example 6–2) and the **Dinosaur Race** (Wynroth, 1986) could be used in first-to-third-grade to practice sums to 10 (dice with numerals 0 to 5) or sums 8 to 18 (dice with numerals 4 to 9). For more specific practice, decks of cards can be drawn up that include the combinations of just one or a few combination families (e.g., an eight-nine deck can include $n + 8, 8 + n, n + 9,$ and $9 + n$ combinations).

Dicey Baseball and **Dicey Football** (Examples 9–7 and 9–8) also provide entertaining practice. **Adds To** (Example 9–9) is more abstract the The Tower of Same-As.

Example 9–7   Dicey Baseball

Objective: Practice basic addition combinations with sums to 10 (basic version) or 18 (advanced version).

Grade Level: 1 (basic version) to 3 (advanced version).

Participants: Two children or small teams of players.

Materials: Two dice with the numerals 0 to 5 (basic version), 1 to 6 dots, or numerals 4 to 9 (advanced version); outcome chart (see below); and markers (blocks) or other materials for keeping score (e.g., chalk for making tallies).

Procedure: The number of runs a player (team) scores in the inning is determined by the roll of the dice. The player sums the numbers rolled and consults the outcome chart. The players then record the number of runs indicated by the outcome chart. The player's opponent does the same to complete the inning. After nine innings, the players count up their score (markers, tallies, etc.).

	Sum of Dice Roll		
Basic Version	*With Regular Dice*	*Advanced Version*	*Outcome: Points Scored*
0	2	8	6
1	3	9	4
2	4	10	2
3	5	11	1
4	6	12	0
5	7	13	0
6	8	14	0
7	9	15	1
8	10	16	2
9	11	17	3
10	12	18	5

Example 9–8   Dicey Football

Objectives: Practice (a) basic addition combinations with sums to 10 (basic version) or 18 (advanced version) and (b) use of hand-held calculators.

Grade Level: 1 (basic version) to 3 (advanced version).

Participants: Two children or small teams of players.

Materials: Two dice with the numerals 0 to 5 (basic version), 1 to 6 dots, or numerals 4 to 9 (advanced version) outcome chart (see below); hand-held calculator; and materials for keeping score (paper and pencil, chalk and chalkboard, etc.)

Procedure: The number of points a player (team) scores in a quarter is determined by the roll of the dice. The player sums the numbers rolled. The opponent checks the sum given on the hand-held calculator. If there is no disagreement, the player consults the outcome chart. If the player gives an incorrect sum, he or she scores 0 points that quarter. If the opponent incorrectly calculated the sum on the calculator, the player scores the number of points indicated on the outcome chart *plus* a bonus of three points. The opponent's turn completes the quarter. After the game is completed, the calculator can be used to determine the final scores of the two players (teams).

Sum of Dice Roll

Basic Version	With Regular Dice	Advanced Version	Outcome: Points Scored
0	2	8	17
1	3	9	14
2	4	10	7
3	5	11	6
4	6	12	0
5	7	13	0
6	8	14	3
7	9	15	7
8	10	16	10
9	11	17	14
10	12	18	21

Example 9-9 Adds To

Objectives: Practice basic addition combinations with sums to 10 (basic version) or 18 (advanced version) and illustrate same-sum concept (with number sentences).

Grade Level: 1 (basic version) to 3 (advanced version).

Participants: Two to six players.

Materials: Deck of cards, each with a number 0 to 9, and a spinner, die or other device for selecting sums.

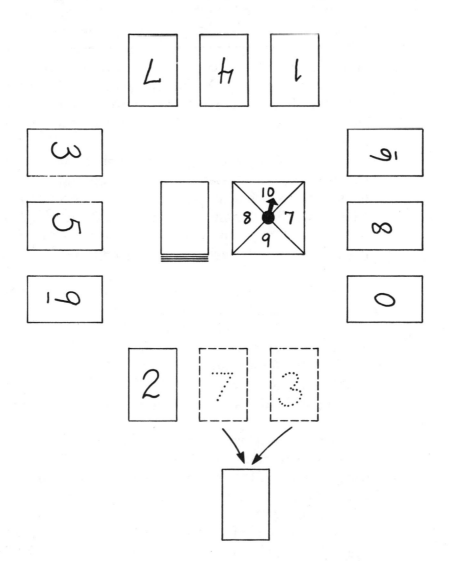

Procedure: Using a spinner or die, the dealer selects "the sum." Each player is dealt three cards face up. In turn, the players check their cards to see if two of their numbers "sum to" the selected number. If so, the two cards are placed face down in a player's point pile. If not, the player may discard and draw a new card. After the round is completed, the dealer selects a new number (sum). Play continues for a predetermined number of rounds or until a player or players obtain a predetermined cards in their point pile.

Guess-What-Adds-Up-To is a relatively sophisticated game that is based on the Number-Guess Game, described in Chapter 5. Two to six children can play the game, but first-graders, especially, will probably need supervision and help. In the basic Guess-What-Adds-Up-To version, one player ("the picker") picks a number card from a deck with cards 0 to 10. (With more advanced players, the numbers can range from 0 to 18.) The other player(s) ("the guessers") then try to figure out the number by posing addition combinations. After a guesser has posed a combination, the picker indicates whether it produces the chosen sum or not. And if not, he or she indicates whether the sum of the posed combination is more or less than the chosen number.

If two children are playing with number cards 0 to 10, then the guesser can be given four guesses. With two players and number cards 0 to 18, the guesser has six chances. The guesser scores a point for figuring out the chosen number. Otherwise, the picker gets the point. The roles are then reversed and the game continues for a prescribed number of turns. (A tie is possible.) A sample exchange is detailed below:

Abjul: Shuffles deck and picks a card (8) without showing it to Bess.
Bess: Is it 3 plus 2 equals 5?
Abjul: No, it's more than 5.
Bess: How about 4 plus 3 is 7?
Abjul: No, its more than 7?
Bess: Is it 5 plus 4 is 9?
Abjul: No, it's 8. (Shows the card.) I score a point.

If more than two children play, the guessers take turns (e.g., going in a clockwise direction) registering their guesses until someone figures out the chosen number. That person is awarded a point and must make the first guess of the next round. Play continues for a prescribed number of rounds. (Ties are possible.)

By simply modifying the rules, Guess What Adds Up To can be used to practice a particular combination family. For example, if the $n + 2$ or $2 + n$

family needs to be practiced, the number cards (the number picked) should range from 2 to 11, and the guesser must pose his or her guesses in terms of combinations involving two (e.g., "Is the number 2 + 3 or 5").

Basic Subtraction Combinations

The games used to practice the basic addition combinations can easily be adapted to practice subtraction combinations. Addition-Pattern Estimates can easily be modified to create the game **Subtraction-Pattern Estimates.** Sums To can become **Subtracts To** by simply changing the rules and using a number selecting device that includes numbers from 0 to 9. The deck of number cards for the basic version would range from 0 to 9; for the advanced version, from 0 to 18. **Racing-Car**, and the like, can be played with a deck of cards on which are printed the combinations that need to be practiced. Guess-What-Adds-Up-To can be converted to **Guess-What-Subtracts-To** to practice combinations with minuends from 1 to 10 (basic version) or 11 to 18 (advanced version). As with addition, a particular subtraction family (e.g., minus fours) can be practiced by including the appropriate number cards to define the range of the choice (0 to 6 or 0 to 13) and requiring the guessers to state problems in terms of the family of interest (as a minus-four combination).

Several other games for practicing subtraction combinations are described below. **What's Related?** (Example 9–10) calls attention to the relationship between addition and subtraction. **Two-Dice Difference** (Example 9–11) is based on the Difference Game (see Example 9–1 in Baroody, 1987a). Though both games have the same objectives, the latter can be played by only two children or two small teams of players.

Example 9–10 What's Related?

Objectives: Reinforce explicitly the addition-subtraction complement principle and provide practice of the basic subtraction combinations with single-digit minuends (basic version) or teen minuends (advanced version).

Grade Level: 1 or 2 (basic version); 2 or 3 (advanced version).

Participants: Two to six players.

Materials: Deck of subtraction combinations with single-digit minuends (basic version) or teen minuends (advanced version) and a deck of related addition combinations.

Procedure: From the subtraction deck, the dealer deals out three cards face up to each player (see figure). The dealer places the addition deck in the middle of the table and turns over the top card. The player to the dealer's left begins play. If the player has a card with a subtraction combination that is related to the combination on the addition card, he or she may take the cards and place them in a discard pile. The dealer then flips over the next card in the addition deck and play continues. The first player(s) to match (discard) all three subtraction cards wins the game (short version) or a point (long version). (Unless the dealer is the first to go out, a round should be completed so that all players have an equal number of chances to make a match.)

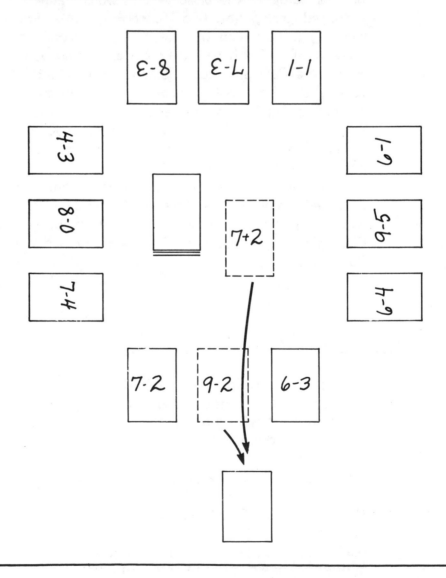

Example 9–11   Two-Dice Difference

Objectives: Practice basic subtraction combinations with single-digit minuends (basic version) or teen minuends (advanced version) and reinforce a "difference" meaning of subtraction.

Grade Level: 1 or 2 (basic version); 2 or 3 (advanced version).

Participants: Two to six players.

Materials: Dice with numerals 0 to 5 and 4 to 9 (basic version) or dice with single-digit numerals (0 to 5 or 4 to 9) and teen numerals (10 to 15 or 13 to 18). Each player will need a mechanism to keep track of his score. Concretely, this can be done with Dienes blocks as illustrated in Figure 10–3. Symbolically, players could keep a running score using paper and pencil or on a hand-held calculator.

Procedure: On their turn, players roll the dice. The difference between the two numbers is their score that round. The game ends when one or more players achieve a predetermined score on a round or after a predetermined number of rounds have been completed.

Basic Multiplication Combinations

To practice the basic times combinations, Adds To can easily be converted to **Factors Of. Racing Car** can be played with a deck of cards on which are printed combinations with factors 0 to 5, 0 to 9, or specific multiplication families. In the multiplication version, the winner is the first player to complete a predesignated number of laps around the board. Some mechanism should be provided to keep track of each player's laps.

SUMMARY

The basic number combinations are replete with relationships. Discovering patterns and reasoning out answers are key means by which children naturally and sensibly master the "basic facts." Instruction also should foster meaningful memorization, not memorization by rote. This can be accomplished by permitting a prolonged period of informal calculation during which children are encouraged to discover relationships and use thinking strategies. Because learning the basic number combinations is a building process, it is particularly important for instruction to help children "see" the connection between new combinations and existing knowledge (e.g., between adding one and number-after knowledge, between subtraction combinations and related addition combinations, between times two combinations and addition doubles). Practice should follow meaningful instruction and, by using games, can be done in an entertaining fashion. In brief, instruction on the basic number combinations is an ideal occasion for encouraging discovery and invention and fostering thinking, excitement, and confidence.

Chapter 10

Base-Ten Place-Value Skills and Concepts

As the range of children's oral counting expands to 100 and beyond, the stage is set for learning *multidigit numeration skills*. This includes *reading multidigit numerals* (e.g., a child sees 13 and says "thirteen") and *writing multidigit numerals* (e.g., a child hears "thirteen" and writes 13).

Our written numbers are a base-ten place-value system. It is a place-value system because the position of a digit determines its value (e.g., the digit 4 in 4,038, 1,421, 2,947, and 3,654 represents different values by virtue of its position). Ours is a base-ten numeration system because, moving from right to left, each place increases in value by a factor of 10. For example, in 3,654, 4 represents 4×1 or 4×10^0 (four units that cannot be grouped into a ten); 5 represents 5×10 or 5×10^1 (five groups of ten); 6 represents 6×100 or 6×10^2 (six groups of ten tens); and 3 represents 3×1000 or 6×10^3 (three groups of ten hundreds). Base-ten place-value concepts are important because they provide the underlying rationale for multidigit numeration skills and written arithmetic procedures. (The latter are discussed in Chapter 12.)

Place-value skills and concepts include recognizing the ones, tens, hundreds, and thousands place (*place recognition*) and judging the value of a digit within a multidigit term (*place-value notation*). For instance, place recognition entails understanding that the 4 in 4,038 is in the thousands place; place-value notation involves knowing that the 4 stands for four thousands or four thousand.

Base-ten concepts and skills include *base-ten equivalents*: 10 ones (units) form a group of ten, 10 groups of ten form a group of one hundred, and so forth. Identifying the *smallest and largest* (one-, two-, three- or four-digit) *term* involves recognizing a key regularity that stems from the fact that our numeration system groups by ones, tens, hundreds, thousands, and so forth. *Flexible enumeration* is the facility to switch among counting by ones, tens, hundreds, etc., to count a set consisting of different denominations.

LEARNING

Multidigit Numeration Skills

Reading Multidigit Numerals

Once they can read the single-digit numerals 0 to 9, children can proceed to learn how to interpret combinations of these digits. Young children, especially those not familiar with the number sequence beyond 10 or so, may not realize that multidigit numerals such as 63 represent *a* number. As a result, they simply read the digits of such terms separately (e.g., 63: "Six; three" or "Six and three"). As they learn and use larger count terms, young children quickly grasp the notion that multidigit numerals correspond to these numbers and must be read as a whole.

The next step in learning to read multidigit numerals involves discovering the rules for accurately translating our written system into the verbal number sequence. That is, children must learn how our base-ten place-numeration system uses *position* to encode information concerning magnitude. For example, to decode 63 correctly, a child must realize that the order of the digits must be considered (e.g., 36 and 63 represent different numbers) and that such terms are read from left to right (e.g., 63 translates into sixty + three or sixty-three, not thirty + six or thirty-six). The teens, though, are treated somewhat differently (e.g., 16 translates into six + teen or sixteen, not teen + six, ten + six, or sixty-one). In effect, the child must learn the rules (and exceptions) for how our written positional notation system matches up with the rules for generating the count sequence.

Reading *teen numerals* involves connecting the highly regular written forms (one + the one-digit numerals: 11, 12, 13, 14, 15, 16, 17, 18, 19) to the appropriate but not entirely regular verbal counterparts in the count sequence ("*eleven, twelve, thirteen,* four*teen,* fif*teen,* sixteen . . ."). Thus, for example, 17 translates in a straightforward manner into "seventeen," but 15 translates into fifteen rather than "five-teen."

Reading the remaining *two-digit numerals* likewise involves connecting the written forms with the corresponding verbal sequence terms (e.g., 50 with "fifty" and 62 with "sixty-two"). Reading *three-digit numerals* requires learning a special hundreds rule: The left-hand term is read as a single-digit term with the term "hundred" tacked on (e.g., *132* translates into "*one +* hundred thirty-two" or *346* translates into "*three + hundred* forty-six"). It also involves learning special rules for handling zeros (e.g., 708 = "seven hundred [no decade term] eight"). Reading *four-digit numerals* requires realizing that four digits specifies using a thousand rule (e.g., *1,432* = *"one + thousand four hundred thirty-two"* or *2,432* = *"two + thousand* four hundred thirty-two"). The rules for using zero as a placeholder are even more complicated at this level.

Writing Multidigit Numerals

Once they can write single-digit numerals, children then must learn how to combine these digits to represent larger numbers. In particular, they have to learn that the arrangement in which digits are written is of the utmost importance. Because order is important, multidigit numerals cannot be written as they are heard (e.g., "seventeen" cannot be written 71—a common error among children just beginning school). Moreover, because place designates value, other numbers such as "forty-eight" cannot be written as they are heard: 408—a common error early in the first grade. By the end of first grade, most children have mastered writing *teen and two-digit numerals*.

In time, children master the rules for writing *three-digit numerals* and, then *four-digit numerals*. One rule they must appreciate is that hundred terms contain only three digits (e.g., five hundred three is written 503 not 5,003). Moreover, they must learn, in effect, to use zero as a placeholder.

Place-Value Skills and Concepts

Usually, children begin acquiring multidigit numeration skills by rote (e.g., Ginsburg, 1982; Resnick, 1983). Children are introduced and many learn to read and write two-, three-, and even four-digit numerals without really understanding their underlying base-ten place-value rationale. This helps to explain why primary-level children make as many numeral-reading and numeral-writing errors as they do. It explains why—even among children who master the rules for reading and writing multidigit numerals—many young pupils have such difficulty explaining what component digits mean (e.g., "The 2 in 3,248 is two one hundreds or two hundred").

Despite its central importance for understanding multidigit numeration *and* computational skills, research suggests that children generally have a weak grasp of place-value ideas throughout the primary years (Ross, 1986). What place-value knowledge is learned in the early grades is often limited and rote. An incomplete or inadequate understanding of place value is a key reason children have learning difficulties at higher grade levels.

Children's counting-based view of numbers is a major obstacle to their understanding and use of multidigit numeration and other base-ten place-value skills. Because of their informal concept of number, children interpret the numeral 13, for example, as "13 things" or "13 units," not as a composite of one ten and three ones. Indeed, they are so accustomed to thinking of multidigit numerals such as 13 as a single group, many children have great difficulty assimilating the qualitatively different base-ten place-value conception of numbering taught in school.

Place Recognition

Even after children learn to read two-digit numerals, they may not be able to point out the ones and tens place. Because of their informal conception of number, they treat two-digit numerals as a whole and do not realize that multidigit numerals actually have components. For example, the digits in 27 are treated as a unit not as an amalgam of ones and tens.

With instruction, children begin to recognize that the digits in two-digit numerals can be considered separately and each occupy their own special place. Some children, though, may confuse the names of the ones and tens place and incorrectly identify, say, the right-hand digit as the tens (Ross, 1986). This may help to account for the common reversal error (e.g., reading 72 as "twenty-seven"). Children, though, readily learn to recognize the *ones, tens, and hundreds place* and later the *thousands place*.

This is a necessary first step in mastering place value. However, children can learn to identify place names by rote. Therefore, this skill does *not* necessarily imply an understanding of place value (e.g., Resnick, 1982). For example, even after they can recognize the ones and tens place, children may not be able to answer correctly a question like: How many tens are in 27?

Place-Value Notation

With instruction, children do learn to "note place value" for two-digit numerals (e.g., the 2 in 27 means two tens) and to extend this skill to larger numbers (e.g., 243 represents 2 hundreds, 4 tens, and 3 ones). Noting place value is another important step. However, because it can be done by rote, this skill does not guarantee a deep understanding of place-value. A child who has mechanically mastered this skill can successfully answer place-value questions usually found in textbooks and standardized tests, such as: 27 = ____ tens and ____ ones or 2 tens + 7 ones = ____. However, they do not really recognize that, say, the 2 in 27 is a multiple of 10 and represents groups of ten rather than ones or units. As a result, such children do not realize that the component parts of 27 must sum to make the whole: $20 + 7 = 27$, and they make a variety of errors (Ross, 1986). For example, some children interpret the 2 in 27 as two objects and the 7 as seven objects and indicate that the sum of the parts is nine.

A deep understanding of place value requires that a child comprehend that digits in the tens place represent multiples of 10—are a different kind of unit than those in the ones place. A child at this level realizes that the sum of the parts of a multidigit must equal the whole represented by the numeral (Ross, 1986). A child who understands that the "digit values equal the whole," know, for example, that 27, can be decomposed into two different kinds of units (tens and ones) and that they (20 + 7) must sum to 27. A deep understanding of place value also entails realizing that "zero is a place-holder." In brief, real mastery of *place-value notation of ones and tens* and then *hundreds* implies understanding that digit values equal the whole and that zero serves as place holder—as well as the skill of noting place value.

Place-value notation that involves renaming (e.g., 12 ones and 3 tens is 42 or vice versa) is a particularly difficult application of place value. It appears to require a deep understanding of place-value and develops relatively late (e.g., Resnick, 1982).

Base-Ten Skills and Concepts

To understand multidigit numerals and arithmetic algorithms, it is important to grasp the idea that our number system regroups by ten: 10 ones can be regrouped to form a larger unit called ten, 10 tens can be regrouped to form an even larger unit called hundred, 10 hundreds can be regrouped to form an even larger unit called thousand, and so forth. Thinking in terms of ones, tens, hundreds, and so on, also gives children flexibility in coping with a wide range of tasks such as comparing and ordering numbers, mental figuring, estimating, and checking (e.g., Payne and Rathmell, 1975).

Base-Ten Equivalents

A basic base-ten notionis an appreciation of the base-ten equivalents: 10 ones constitute 1 ten (*ones in 10*), 10 tens constitute 1 hundred (*tens in 100*), and 10 hundreds constitute 1 thousand (*hundreds in 1000*).

Smallest and Largest Terms

A key characteristic of our base-ten place-value system is its repetitive nature. For the non-negative numbers, the smallest and largest *one- and two-digit terms* are 0, 9, 10 and 99. This pattern is echoed with *three-digit terms* (100 and 999) and *four-digit terms* (1,000 and 9,999). Recognizing these benchmarks suggests a relatively sophisticated understanding of the base-ten place-value system.

Flexible Enumeration

Flexible enumeration is relatively difficult because it requires a child to quantify (count) a set in terms of tens, hundreds, and so on, as well as ones. Though third graders can, for example, count 5 $100 bills by one hundreds or count 3 $10 bills by tens, many have difficulty combining such counts if the 5 $100 bills and 3 $10 bills are put together (Resnick, 1983). Some children count: "100, 200, 300, 400, 500, 501, 502, 503"; some: "100, 200, 300, 400, 500, 600, 700, 800."

A suggested instructional sequence for base-ten place-value skills and concepts is summarized in Table 10–1.

INSTRUCTION

Primary-level children can be helped to extend their informal conception of number if base-ten place-value training is done concretely with size embodiments such as Dienes blocks[1] or interlocking blocks (e.g., Fuson, 1988; Resnick and Omanson, 1987). This instruction should begin by helping children understand the ideas of grouping by 10 and of using position to distinguish among different denominations. The grouping-by-10 idea can be introduced by the **Wood-Trading Activity**, described in Figure 10–1. The position-defines-value concept can be introduced with the **Basic Version of the Larger-Number Game**, the **Basic Version of the Largest-Number Draw Game**, and **Target Game 100**, described later in this chapter. In Figure 10–2, note that multidigit numeration skills, such as reading and writing two- or three-digit numerals, are introduced in a meaningful manner—hand in hand with base-ten place-value instruction.

After experiences representing multidigit numbers with concrete size embodiments, Egyptian hieroglyphics are an ideal pictorial device for practicing multidigit numeration and base-ten skills. This semiconcrete system is a straightforward base-ten system. Moreover, working with Egyptian hieroglyphics readily lends itself to children's informal methods, particularly counting by ones and tens. Though the Egyptian hieroglyphics are not a place-value system, *translating* these symbols into Arabic numerals and vice versa can help children understand the idea of positional notation underlying our written number system. For all these reasons, exercises with Egyptian hieroglyphics are an ideal vehicle for bridging children's informal knowledge and formal (base-ten place-value) representations of number.[2]

---

[1]Dienes (1960) blocks include units ($1 \times 1 \times 1$-cm blocks), longs ($1 \times 10 \times 1$-cm bars obviously consisting of 10 units), flats ($10 \times 10 \times 1$-cm squares consisting of 100 units), and cubes ($10 \times 10 \times 10$-cm blocks representing 1000 units).

[2]In addition to being a pictorial system, the Egyptian hieroglyphics are a more abstract representational system than size embodiments in another way. Unlike Dienes blocks, in which a long is clearly made up 10 units, the Egyptian hieroglyphic for ten (∩) does not depict units. Presented with the symbol for ten, a child must mentally equate 10 units and 1 ten. Likewise, a deep understanding of our positional notation entails recognizing that the *1* in 10 represents a ten: a group of 10 units. (The 0 can be interpreted to mean that there are no units left after the grouping process.)

Table 10-1 A Suggested Sequence of Base-Ten Place-Value Skills and Concepts by Grade Level*

Level	Multidigit Numeration Skills		Place-Value Skills and Concepts		Base-Ten Skills and Concepts		
	Reading Multidigit Numerals	*Writing Multidigit Numerals*	*Place Recognition*	*Place-Value Notation*	*Base-Ten Equivalents*	*Smallest/ Largest Term*	*Flexible Enumeration*
1	Teen	Teen	Ones, tens, and hundreds	—	Ones in 10	—	—
	Two-digit	Two-digit	—	Ones and tens	Tens in 100	—	—
	—	—	—	—	—	One- and two-digit	—
2	Three-digit	Three-digit	Thousands	Hundreds	Hundreds in 1000	—	—
3	—	—	—	—	—	Three-digit	Ones and tens
	Four-digit	Four-digit	—	—	—	Four-digit	Ones, tens, and hundreds
	—	—	—	With renaming	—	—	—

*This suggested sequence is debatable. It approximates how these skills and concepts are currently taught. Some evidence (e.g., Resnick, 1982, 1983) suggests that even with manipulative-based instruction, it takes time for children to develop a deep knowledge of base-ten place-value—knowledge that can be related to various embodiments, tasks, and problems. In contrast to the prolonged developmental scheme depicted above, Fuson (e.g., 1986) argues that with an integrated approach that uses size embodiments, even average-ability first graders can learn base-ten place-value skills and concepts with up to four-digit terms. Advantages of such an approach include making clearer the 10-for-1 trading-in pattern and the role of zero as a place holder. Fuson, then, recommends greatly compressing the time for instruction on base-ten place-value skills and concepts. Indeed, she adduces some evidence that with effective instruction, children acquire an unusually deep understanding of such ideas (e.g., many can explain related renaming procedures). Thus compressing such training may be educationally sound for some children, perhaps most. Given the uncertain evidence, it may be advisable to take a middle course between the prolonged and compressed approaches. Thus it is recommended that such instruction begin in earnest in the first grade with two-digit terms (with size embodiments). Teachers can then judge how quickly to proceed with three- and four-digit instruction. With integrated and meaningful instruction, there may be little reason why many children cannot begin work on most of the competencies including reading and writing four-digit numerals by the end of first-grade. It is recommended that different embodiments (e.g., Dienes blocks, hieroglyphics) and tasks be introduced throughout the primary years and that teachers help children to see the connections among them all.

Figure 10–1 Wood-Trading Activity

A. Player's existing score (nine longs and seven units or "ninety seven").

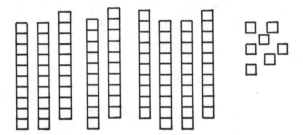

B. Player rolls a five and collects five more units.

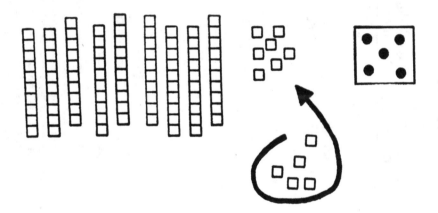

C. Trades in 10 units for a long (a ten).

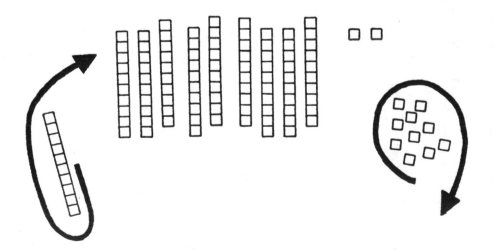

D. Trades in 10 longs (tens) for a flat (a hundred).

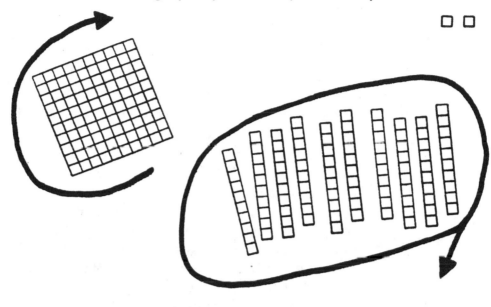

Figure 10–2 Size Embodiments to Teach Place Value Using the Target Game as an Example

---

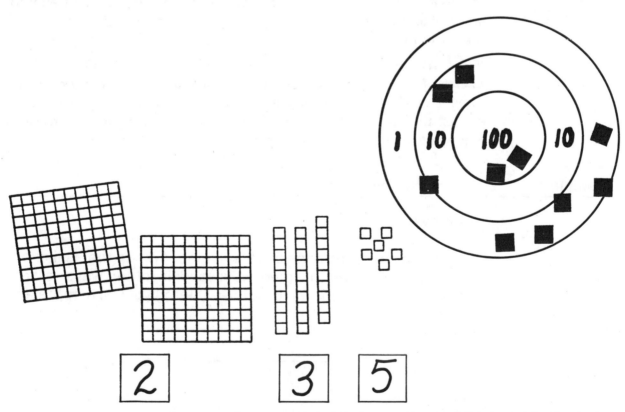

The concrete models of the target and Dienes blocks helps make clear that 235 ("two hundred thirty-five") is a composite of two hundreds, three tens, and five ones.

Exercise A of Example 10–1 introduces students to the Egyptian hieroglyphic representations of 1 (Λ) and 10 (⋂). In Question 1a, three is represented in a straightforward manner with three one-tallies: ΛΛΛ

For 1b, some children will record 10 as: ΛΛΛΛΛΛΛΛΛΛ . Help them to reflect on such an answer by asking, "Is there an easier way to show 10 in Egyptian hieroglyphics?" A teacher can summarize the discussion by saying, "Instead of writing out 10 one-symbols, which is a lot of work, the early Egyptians used a special symbol to represent *a* group of ten." Questions 1c–1f are an effort to draw attention to the fact that teens are a composite of ten and ones. Question 2 of Exercise A does the same by asking a student to translate Egyptian hieroglyphics into Arabic numerals.

After such introductory exercises with the teens, students are ready for more advanced exercises with larger two-digit terms. Question 1 of Exercise B asks students to translate two-digit numerals into hieroglyphics. For example, 12 translates into ⋂ ΛΛ ; 21, into ⋂ ⋂ Λ . Such translations concretely highlight a very important point about our numeration system: position (place) defines value. A comparison of the four representations makes it clear that the 2 in 12 represents 2 ones and the 2 in 21 stands for something different: 2 tens. Moreover, such exercises provide a concrete model for the idea of zero as a place holder. For example, in translating 20 into ⋂ ⋂ , a student can see that the 2 implies two tens and the 0, no ones. Exercise C extends the students' grasp of hieroglyphics by introducing the symbol for 100 and three-digit terms. Question 3 is an effort to make more explicit the idea of place-value notation. Note that Exercise D requires among other things, flexible enumeration.

Example 10–1   Egyptian Hieroglyphics

Exercise A

The ancient Egyptians used a number system that is like our own (Arabic system) in some ways and in other ways is very different. The Egyptians used pictures (hieroglyphics) to represent numbers.

Egyptian	Arabic
Λ	1
Λ Λ	2
⋂	10

1. Pretend that a pharaoh (ancient Egyptian king) has appointed you as his tax collector and keeper of records.

   a. If a poor merchant paid 3 coins in taxes, how should this be recorded in Egyptian hieroglyphics?

   b. If the king raised his taxes and demanded that the poor merchant pay 10 coins in taxes, how should this be recorded?

   c. If another merchant had to pay 4 coins in taxes, how would this be noted?

   d. If this merchant's taxes were raised and he had to pay 14 coins, how would this be recorded?

   e. A third merchant had to pay 8 coins in taxes, how would this be noted?

   f. If his taxes were raised and he had to pay 18 coins, how would this be recorded:

2. Translate the following tax record written in Egyptian hieroglyphics into our (Arabic) numerals.

   a. Ace Reed Products, Inc.   ∩ Ⅰ Ⅰ Ⅰ Ⅰ   _____

   b. Block Haulers, Inc.   ∩ Ⅰ Ⅰ Ⅰ Ⅰ Ⅰ Ⅰ Ⅰ _____

   c. Cultured Cats, Inc.   ∩ Ⅰ Ⅰ Ⅰ Ⅰ Ⅰ   _____

   d. Durable Slaves, Inc.   ∩   _____

Exercise B

1. As the pharaoh's tax collector and keeper of records, you have to check the records to make sure all merchants have paid the right amount.

   a. Nile River Damage Control, Inc. is supposed to pay 12 coins in taxes this tax period. What would 12 look like in Egyptian hieroglyphics?

   b. Izzie's Idols & Graven Images, Inc. is supposed to pay 21 coins. Show this in hieroglyphics.

   c. Swampy Surveyors & Land Markers, Inc. should have 48 coins in taxes recorded. What should the tax record show?

   d. Pyramid Rock Quarry owed 84 coins. What should be noted?

   e. Kingly's Gold & Silver Trinkets, Inc. should have 20 coins in taxes, and their record should reflect what?

   f. Futures Foretold, Inc. should have on the records 40 coins. Show this.

2. You check the tax records. For each of the following, translate the Egyptian hieroglyphics into our own Arabic numerals.

   a. Nile River
      Damage Control   ∩∩∩ΙΙ   _____

   b. Izzie's Idols &
      Graven Images   ∩∩ΙΙΙ   _____

c. Swampy Surveyors
   & Land Markers   ∩∩∩∩⋀   _____

d. Pyramid Rock
   Quarry   ∩∩∩∩∩∩   _____

e. Kingly's Gold &
   Silver Trinkets   ∩∩∩∩   _____

f. Futures Foretold ∩∩∩∩∩∩⋀⋀⋀⋀⋀ _____

Exercise C

In addition to the pictures (hieroglyphics) for 1 (⋀) and 10 (∩) that you already learned about, the ancient Egyptians also had a symbol for 100: ℓ .

1. The pharaoh's (king's) army won a battle and brought back many things won in the battle. The king wants you to make a record of his winnings. Make up a symbol for each thing on the list and record the number of those things in hieroglyphics.

   a. 100 battle axes _____

   b. 148 helmets _____

   c. 176 horses _____

   d. 250 wagons _____

   e. 304 swords _____

   f. 400 prisoners _____

2. The following record was made of the battle. Translate the Egyptian hieroglyphics into our (Arabic) numerals.

   a. ℓ ℓ ℓ ℓ   ✗   _____ spears lost

   b. ℓ ∩ ∩ ⋀⋀⋀⋀⋀⋀ ⬧ _____ helmets lost

c. ℰ ∩ ∩ ∩ ∩ ∩   ⇻   _____ horses lost

d. ℰ ∧ ∧ ∧   ⇻   _____ wagons lost

e. ℰ ℰ   ⇻   _____ swords lost

3. a. How many hundred symbols are in ℰ ℰ ∩ ∧ ∧ ∧ ? _____ Ten symbols? ____ One symbols? ____. How would this number be written in our (arabic) system? ____. Do the same for each of the following:

b. ℰ ∧ ∧ ∧ ∧ ∧ = ___ hundred(s), ___ ten(s), & ___ one(s) = _____

c. ℰ ℰ ∩ ∩ ∩ = ___ hundred(s), ___ ten(s), & ___ one(s) = _____

d. ℰ ℰ ℰ ∧ ∧ = ___ hundred(s), ___ ten(s), & ___ one(s) = _____

e. ℰ ℰ ℰ ℰ ℰ = ___ hundred(s), ___ ten(s), & ___ one(s) = _____

Exercise D

Below is a record of the size of forms along a portion of the Nile River. Translate the recorded area into arabic numerals.

A. ℰ ℰ ℰ ℰ ∩ ∩ ∧ ∧ ∧

B. ℰ ℰ ℰ ∩ ∩ ∩ ∩ ∩ ∧ ∧

C. ℰ ℰ ℰ ℰ ℰ ℰ ∧ ∧ ∧ ∧

D. ℰ ℰ ∩ ∩ ∩ ∩ ∩ ∩

E. ℰ ℰ ℰ ℰ ∩ ∩ ∩ ∧ ∧ ∧ ∧ ∧

Base-ten place-value concepts and skills can be further reinforced by playing games that involve using objects to keep track of scores that exceed 10 (see Figure 10–3). In **High Card 100**, **Shuffleboard 100**, and **Draw 100** (Examples 10–2 through 10–4), the first child or team to accumulate 100 points win. Note that the scoring procedure illustrated in Figure 10–3 achieves a number of important objectives: (1) recognition of ones, tens, and hundreds place; (2) place-value notation, with ones, tens, and hundred, including zero as a placeholder; (3) digit values equal the whole; (4) reading and writing teen and two-digit numerals; and (5) base-ten equivalents (ones in 10 and tens in 100). In addition to providing a concrete model for these base-ten place-value concepts and multidigit numeration skills, such a scoring procedure provides a concrete embodiment for the multidigit addition (renaming) procedure. Other activities that provide interesting, concrete, and *integrated* training include **Space Wars** (described in Chapter 12) and the Wynroth (1986) Program's **Forward Bowling** and **Backward Bowling**[3] (described in Chapter 12 of Baroody, 1987a).

Example 10–2 High Card 100

Grade Level: 1.

Participants: Two to six players.

Materials: Deck of cards with a numeral 0 to 10 on each (a standard deck can be used).

Procedure: Each player draws a card from the deck and places it face up in front of him or her. The player(s) with the highest card wins the round. The face value of the winning card would be the winner's score for that round. It is possible for the game to end in a tie.

[3]The trading-in process used in these Wynroth game is more abstract than the scoring procedure with Dienes blocks described here. With the latter, 10 units is traded in for a long that clearly shows it is made up of 10 units, and so forth. In the Wynroth games, 10 unit blocks are traded in for a *single* block that is put on the tens post; 10 tens are traded in for a *single* block that is put on the hundreds post. Thus 182 is represented as one block on the hundreds post, eight blocks on the tens post, and two blocks on the ones post. This is a more abstract model for multidigit numbers than that provided by size embodiments.

A variety of materials can be used to illustrate this more abstract regrouping process. For example, with **High Card**, **Shuffleboard**, or **Draw 100**, players could win play money instead of points and trade 10 $1 bills for a $10 bill. The first player(s) to trade in 10 $10 bills for a $100 would be the winner. This "scoring procedure" exploits many children's familiarity with money (e.g., Lampert, 1986; Lawler, 1981). Pictorially, tallies could be used to illustrate the relatively abstract process of trading in 10 ones for 1 ten. A player's chalkboard (or scoresheet) would have three columns labeled *hundreds, tens,* and *ones.* After collecting 10 tallies in the ones column a player could erase (cross out) these marks and enter *a* tally in the tens column.

Figure 10–3 A Scoring System for Teaching Base-Ten Place-Value Skills and Concepts

Materials: Miniature chalkboard, chalk, and Dienes blocks for each player or team. Each chalkboard needs ones, tens, and hundreds labels printed in chalk or written on masking tape, mailing labels, and so on. An oaktag scoreboard could be used instead of a chalkboard. This would require a supply of "number squares": two of each numeral 0 to 9 printed on a separate card for each player or team.

A. Player's existing score.

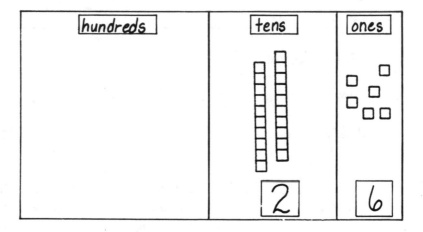

B. Player scores 7 points; counts out 7 unit blocks, and adds them to the ones column.

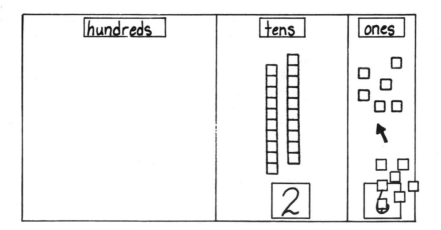

C. Because of "overcrowding," the player trades in 10 ones for a long that is put in the tens column.

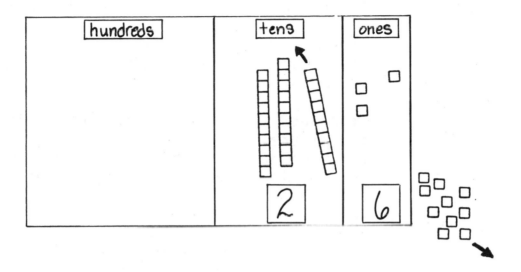

D. The numeral designation is now corrected to reflect the new (concrete model) of the score.

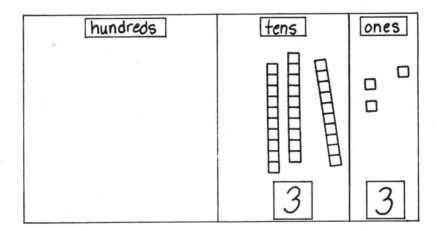

Example 10–3   Shuffleboard 100

Grade Level: 1.

Participants: Two players or two small teams of players.

Materials: Shuffleboard equipment *or* table-top substitute (e.g., checkers and an unsharpened pencil). Using masking tape, a board can be laid out on the floor or a table-top (see figure).

Procedure: To keep the scoring procedure simple, each player gets just one shot per round. At the *end* of the round, each player with a checker on or touching a box "records" their score. For the sake of fairness, the order in which players shoot should be alternated.

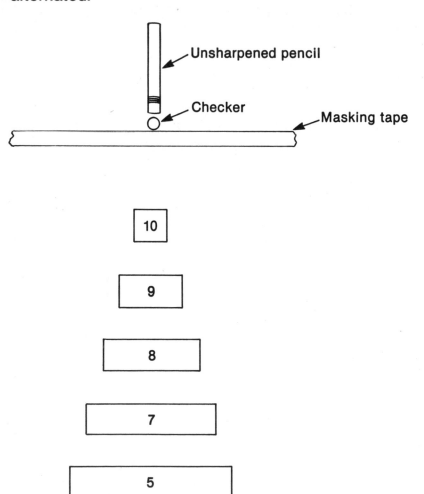

Example 10–4 Draw 100

Grade Level: 1.

Participants: Two to five players or two small teams.

Materials: Cards that state how many ones and tens can be added to a player's score (e.g., ADD 1 ten and 3 ones, ADD 0 tens and 9 ones, and ADD 3 tens and 0 ones).

Procedure: On their turn, players draw a card and add the values stated on the Draw Card to the score on their scoreboard. Play continues until the round when one or more players obtain a score of 100. By allowing everyone to complete the last round, the game is fair to all players and allows for ties.

With minor adjustments, the scoring procedures and games described above can be used to work on three- and four-digit skills and concepts, including: (1) recognition of the thousands place; (2) place-value notation with hundreds and thousands, including zero as a placeholder; (3) digit values equal the whole; (4) reading and writing three- and four-digit numerals; and (5) base-ten equivalents (hundreds in 1000). A teacher will need to include higher values in the card decks for High Card and Draw, and the boxes for Shuffleboard. For example, for **Draw 500** or **Draw 1000**, add cards like ADD 1 hundred, 3 tens, and 6 ones or ADD 0 hundreds, 9 tens. Simply add a thousands column to the scoreboard and provide a size embodiment for 1,000 (Dienes block cube). The winning score can be reset to 500 or 1,000 for three-digit work and 5,000 or 9,999 for four-digit work.

Multidigit Numeration Skills: Reading Multidigit Numerals

Instructional points specific to reading multidigit numerals and several games for practicing these skills are discussed below. The following may be unnecessary if instruction in reading multidigit numerals is done in a meaningful manner. The following techniques—used in conjunction with size embodiments—may be useful in remedial instruction.

Reading Teen Numerals

Ensure that prerequisite skills (oral counting to 19, recognition of numerals 1 to 9, and reading one-digit numerals) have been mastered first. If necessary, point out that teen numerals stand for *a* number and that, for example, 15 stands for and is read as the count term "fifteen." If need be, point out that the second term provides the clue for deciding which teen term the numeral represents (e.g., 14: the second term is four, so this teen term is "fourteen"). Practice for reading the teen numerals specifically can be done with the **Zip Race**, described in Example 10–5.

If a child has difficulty learning to read teen numerals, work on the somewhat easier skill of numeral recognition. That is, use games or activities in which a teen number is stated and the child has to pick out the correct numeral from a number of choices (e.g., Which of these is fourteen: 12, 17, 71, 14, 70, 41?).

Example 10–5   Zip Race: 11–19

Objective: Reading the teen numerals.

Grade Level: K or 1.

Participants: Two to six players.

Materials: Zip-Race Board (see figure), race cars (or markers) for each player, and numeral cards 11 to 19.

18	17	16	15
19			14
START	11	12	13

Procedure: Give the children their choice of marker color and explain, "In the Zip Race we put our race cars on 'Start.' Then we pick a card with a number on it. The number tells us how far we can move our race car. The player who goes the furthest wins." Shuffle the deck of numeral cards. On their turn, have the players draw and read a card. If necessary, say, "Read this number for me." If the child simply reads the individual digits (e.g., "one, three" for 13 or "one, five" for 15), say, "How else can we say this number?"

The Zip-Race board can consist of a Start and nine squares labeled eleven, twelve, thirteen, and so forth. (This would provide practice reading the number names for teens.) Alternatively, each square could contain a set of dots one greater than that in the preceding square. (This would provide practice for enumeration of sets 11 to 19 and matching the set to its cardinal designation.) The simplest solution is to label the squares with numerals (11, 12, 13, and so forth). If labeled with numerals, make sure players read the card (and do not simply match the numeral on the card with the numeral on the board). To make the game somewhat more difficult for advanced players, the numerals on the Zip-Race board can be in a random order. Play can continue until every player has had a specified number of turns. Note that because the cards are in random order, a player may have to move backwards on a turn (e.g., a child might be on the eighteenth square and then draw 12).

Reading Two-Digit Numerals

Ensure that the prerequisite skills (oral counting to 100 and reading one-digit numerals) have been mastered first. If necessary, point out that two-digit numerals stand for *a* number and that a zero can act as a place holder. For example, with 40, the first term 4 *stands for* four tens or "forty" and *zero* stands for no ones (forty *and no more*). With 41, the first term stands for four tens or "forty" and one stands for one one (forty *and one more*).

The **Zip-Race** described above can be adapted to practice reading two-digit numerals specifically. Make up a deck of cards with the numerals 20 to 99. Use a board in which the squares spiral inward and are labeled with numerals.

Reading Three-Digit Numerals

Ensure that the prerequisite skills (rules for counting larger numbers and reading one- and two-digit numerals) are mastered first. If necessary, point out that the first term on the left of a three-digit numeral is read as a one-digit term + hundred (e.g., *1*37 as "one + hundred" and *6*37 as "six + hundred"). As needed, point out the role of zero as a placeholder (e.g., *6*07: the first term to the left is still read as *six* hundred not sixty as it looks). Moreover, it is important to help children discover that zero in the context of multidigit numerals cannot be disregarded but that it means none of a particular unit— *skip* the place designation for that position. In the case of 408, zero means no tens—skip from the hundreds designation ("four hundred") to the ones designation ("eight").

Reading Four-Digit Numerals

Ensure that the prerequisite skills (rules for counting larger numbers and reading one-, two-, and three-digit numerals) are mastered first. If necessary, point out that the first term on the left of a four-digit numeral is read as a one-digit term + thousand (e.g., 4,705 is read "four + thousand . . ."). As needed, point out the role of zero as a placeholder (e.g., 1,034: the first term on left is still read as one + thousand and not "one hundred" or "ten"). Moreover, it is important to help children discover that zero in the context of four-digit numerals means skip *that* place designation. With 1,034, for instane, zero means there are no hundreds; therefore skip the hundreds word: "one + thousand (no hundreds) thirty-four."

Multidigit Numeration Skills: Writing Multidigit Numerals

Even with teen terms, writing instruction should focus on helping children appreciate positional notation. It is critical that positional notation be taught in terms of the children's informal knowledge using concrete models.

Writing Teen and Two-Digit Numerals

First remedy any deficiencies in prerequisite skills (writing single-digit numerals, counting by ones to 99, and recognition of two-digit numerals). Help the children discover how our highly regular written symbol system "maps" onto their familiar but not entirely regular verbal number sequence. One rule for translating sequence terms from ten to ninety-nine into written numbers is that only two numerals are used (e.g., forty-two is written 42 not 402 because the 4 stands for four tens or forty). Encourage children to discover the regularities of the written system—the repetition of patterns: first decade and the single-digit sequence (10, 11, 12 . . .), second decade + the single-digit sequence (20, 21, 22 . . .), and so forth. Note that not only do the terms within a decade go up in sequence but that subsequent decades also follow the single-digit sequence (*10, 20, 30, 40, 50, 60, 70, 80, 90*).

Writing Three-Digit Numerals

First remedy any deficiencies in prerequisite skills (writing one-digit, teen, and two-digit numerals and rules for counting numbers in the hundreds). It may help to work next on recognition of three-digit numerals. Writing instruction should focus on helping children appreciate the positional notation system used to write terms between 100 and 999. If necessary, point out that hundred terms consist of three, and only three digits (e.g., three hundred sixty two is written *362* not *30062*). Encourage children to explore the repetitive patterns of three-digit numerals and how the written system corresponds to the verbal number sequence.

Writing Four-Digit Numerals

First remedy any deficiencies in prerequisite skills (writing one-digit, teens, two-digit, and three-digit numerals and rules for writing numbers in the thousands). It may help to work next on recognition of four-digit numerals. Writing instruction should focus on helping children appreciate the positional notation system used to write terms between 1,000 and 9,999. If necessary, point out that terms *"one* thousand . . ." to *"nine* thousand . . ." consist of four and only four digits. Encourage children to explore the repetitive pattern of four-digit numerals and how the written system corresponds to the verbal number sequence.

Place-Value Skills and Concepts

Place-Value Notation: Ones and Tens

The idea that position is crucial to defining value can be reinforced by playing the games **Larger-Number** and **Largest-Number Draw**, described in Examples 10–6 and 10–7). **Target Game 100** (Example 10–8) and **Target Game: 1 and 10** (described later in the chapter) can reinforce place-value notation skills and concepts.

Example 10–6   Larger-Number Game (Basic Version)

Objective: Make explicit that the position of a digit in a two-digit numeral defines its value.

Grade Level: 1.

Participants: For 2 to 30 players or two teams of players.

Materials: Nine cards, each with a digit 1 to 9, for each player or team. A spinner or other mechanism for picking numbers.

Procedure: Using a spinner, call out two different numbers in random order and ask which is larger. If needed, use a prompt such as, "When we count, which takes longer to count up to—sixty-eight [point to the arrangement 68] or eighty-six [point to the arrangement 86]?"

With a large group, ask the children to record the combinations they make. This will permit you to check later those responses that you do not have time to check during the activity. The players (teams) select these two number cards and arrange them any way they wish. If the arrangement is the larger of the two possible combinations, the player (team) is awarded a point. For example, if the numbers six and eight were called out, all who form the arrangement 86 would get a point. For children who made 68, point out the arrangement 86 and relate each to the pupils' verbal, number-sequence knowledge.

Example 10–7   Largest-Number Draw (Basic Version)

Objective: Position defines value.

Grade Level: 1.

Participants: One or more groups of two to four players.

Materials: A deck of 9 cards, each with a digit 1 to 9 (for each group of two or four players). The complexity of the game (size comparisons) can be increased by playing with a larger deck of, say, 18 or 27 cards.

Procedure: After shuffling the deck, each player draws two cards. The players may arrange their cards in any way they wish. The player who has the largest number wins the round and a point. Play continues until a preset number of points is obtained.

Example 10–8   Target Game 100

Grade Level: 1.

Participants: Two to five players or two small teams.

Materials: From six to ten bean bags, chips, checkers, pennies, or the like; target with rings worth 1 and 10. Concentric circles can be drawn on the floor or on a cardboard with chalk, or constructed of masking tape. Actually, the target can take any shape desired as long as there is a ones and a tens area.

Procedure: On their turn, players toss the bean bags onto the target and record their score (see Figure 10–2). The game ends with the round in which one or more players obtain a score of 100.

Place-Value Notation: Ones, Tens, and Hundreds and Zero as a Placeholder

The role of zero as a placeholder can be explored in the games **Larger-Number** and **Largest-Number Draw (Advanced Version)** by simply adding a zero card (for the two-digit version) or zero cards (two and three for the three- and four-digit versions, respectively). In the three-digit version of Larger Number, the combination 630 would beat 603, 360, 306, 063 or 036. **Target Game 500** (or **1000**), which can be created from **Target Game 100** by adding a hundreds ring, or **Target Game: 1, 10,** and **100,** which is described in Example 10–10, can reinforce place-value notation skills and concepts.

Place-Value Notation with Renaming: Ones, Tens, and Hundreds

Place-value notation with renaming can be practiced by playing **Advanced Draw**. This game is played exactly like Draw. However, the Draw Deck includes special cards such as: Add 1 hundred, 3 tens, 13 ones or Add 0 hundreds, 14 tens, 2 ones.

Base-Ten Skills and Concepts

Base-Ten Equivalents: Ones in 10, Tens in 100, and Hundreds in 1,000

That we regroup units by ten in our number system is an outcome of a natural endowment—our ten fingers. Our fingers provide a ready-made tallying system. Early in human history, herdsmen or merchants counted on their fingers to keep track of items. When they ran out of fingers but needed to continue their tally, something had to be done to represent the first ten items. So they put down a pebble or other marker to mark this group of ten. When tallying very large quantities, the number of "ten pebbles" ("ten markers") could be reduced by using a rock (or special marker) to represent 10 tens.

Wood-trading activities (see Figure 10–1) are an enjoyable way of introducing this trading-in process (e.g., Dienes, 1960). In the base-ten rendition of the **Wood-Trading** game, children learn to trade in 10 unit blocks for a long (a ten), 10 longs for a flat (100), and 10 flats for a cube (1,000). In the basic version of the game, the winning score can be defined as one (or several) longs. In the intermediate version, it can be defined as one (or several) flats. In the advanced version, the goal can be defined as one (or several) cubes. The advanced version, in particular, should help children see that the trading-in process (in base ten) always involves collecting 10 of a particular wood or number (Fuson, 1986). This should help children master the base-ten equivalents.

The Egyptian hieroglyphics are an excellent pictorial or semiconcrete model for the trading-in process and teaching base-ten equivalents.[4] When written tally systems were invented (e.g., the Egyptian hieroglyphics: Λ = 1), people continued to substitute *a* symbol for 10 tallies (units or ones) because it was more efficient. The Egyptians substituted $\cap$ for $\Lambda \Lambda \Lambda \Lambda \Lambda \Lambda \Lambda \Lambda \Lambda$. Likewise, as larger and larger quantities had to be tallied, it was important to have a large denomination symbol that could be substituted for many 10 symbols. The Egyptians used $\wp$ instead of $\cap\cap\cap\cap\cap\cap\cap\cap\cap\cap$. Likewise, $\mathcal{\S}$ was used instead of writing out 10 $\wp$ s. The Egyptian Hieroglyphics Exercises described in Chapter 12 for practicing multidigit calculation involve trading in and would be useful in teaching base-ten equivalents.

---

[4]The relatively abstract process of trading 10 units for a ten that bears no resemblance to 10 units can also be practiced with **Chip-Trading**. For example, white, red, blue, and purple chips can represent ones, tens, hundreds, and thousands, respectively. *Ten* white chips are traded in a *one* red chip, and so forth. This can be done as an optional activity after Wood-Trading and before the Egyptian Hieroglyphics if a teacher wishes. It is probably important for a teacher to ask the children while they play what the red chip represents.

Chip Trading can involve exchange rates other than 10, and these can be used to introduce other base systems. To introduce base five, for example, a white could be equated with ones, five whites could be traded for a red (a five), five reds could be traded for a blue (a twenty-five), and so on. The New Math and some curricula today introduce other base systems (bases for regrouping) before introducing base ten. Fuson (1988) argues that if the objective is to help children understand regrouping by ten, it is probably best to teach base-ten skills and concepts directly. Unfortunately, research does not clearly indicate which is the more effective approach.

Largest/Smallest One-, Two-, Three-, and Four-Digit Terms

Children need opportunities to reflect on the structure of our written number system. **Modified Largest-Number** (or **Smallest-Number Draw** (Example 10–9) can provide a context for discussing the smallest and largest two-, three- and four-digit terms. A teacher could casually ask, for example, "What do you think the best draw (for the three-digit version of Largest-Number Draw) would be?"

Example 10–9   Modified Largest-Number (Smallest-Number) Draw

Objective: Number patterns among three-digit (or two- or four-digit) numbers.

Grade Level: 1 to 3.

Participants: For two to twelve players.

Materials: A deck of thirteen cards: eight with a digit 1 to 8 and five with the digit 9 (for two or four players). An additional deck is needed for each additional group of two to four children.

Procedure: After shuffling the deck(s), each player draws three cards and arranges them in any order he or she wishes. In Largest-Number Draw, the child who has the largest number wins the round. (In Smallest-Number Draw, the reverse holds.) Play continues until a preset goal is obtained by a player (or possibly by more than one player). The game can be introduced with the two-digit version. Each player draws and arranges two number cards. After children are familiar with three-digit patterns, the game can be used to explore four-digit patterns.

Flexible Enumeration: Ones and Tens, or Ones, Tens, and Hundreds

Flexible enumeration with ones and tens (ones, tens, and hundreds) can be introduced relatively concretely by playing **Target Game: 1 and 10** (or **Target Game: 1, 10, and 100**), described in Example 10–10.

Example 10–10   Target Game: 1 and 10 (or 1, 10, and 100)

Objectives: (1) Reinforce place-value notation skills and concepts and (2) practice flexibly switching between counting by tens and ones (or hundreds, tens, and ones).

Grade Level: 3 (or perhaps lower).

Participants: Two to five players or two small teams.

Materials and Procedure: The materials and rules are the same as Target Game 100. However, a relatively abstract scoring procedure is used. Instead of recording their scores with manipulatives (e.g., Dienes blocks) and numerals, players note their score on a chalkboard or paper with just numerals (e.g., three bean bags on the hundreds ring, five on the tens ring, and none in the ones ring would be recorded 350). The player (or team) with the higher score wins the round and gets a point. The winning player (team) is the first to register a preset number of points (e.g., 5 points for a short game; 15 points for "period-length" game).

SUMMARY

Informally, children view multidigit terms such as 12 or 103 as representing a specific number of units. The underlying base-ten place-value rationale for such numerals is foreign to their thinking. As a result, children often learn to read and write multidigit numerals by rote, and, not surprisingly, many have difficulty with these skills. Place-value skills (e.g., recognition of the ones, tens, and hundreds place) and concepts (position defines the value of a digit) are central objectives of primary schooling. Also central are base-ten concepts (e.g., our numeration system is based on grouping by tens and so each position in a multidigit numeral increases by a factor 10). Abstract base-ten place-value lessons are difficult for children to grasp.

It is crucial that such instruction build upon children's informal mathematical knowledge. Work can begin with concrete models (size embodiments such as Dienes blocks) in which a ten is clearly a group of 10 ones. Numerals can then be introduced in terms of size embodiments and games that require regrouping objects in order to keep score or calculate sums or differences. Egyptian hieroglyphics are a powerful semiconcrete model for base-ten ideas and even place-value concepts. Such instruction enables children to master base-ten, place-value, multidigit-numeration, and multidigit arithmetic concepts or skills in an integrated and meaningful manner.

Chapter 11

Multidigit Mental Arithmetic

Mental arithmetic includes both mental computation, which entails finding exact answers, and estimation, which entails finding reasonable approximations of answers. These skills build on children's knowledge of the number sequence (discussed in Chapter 3), concepts of addition and subtraction (Chapter 8), single-digit combinations (Chapter 9), and place value and base ten (Chapter 10) (e.g., Resnick, 1983). Though mental arithmetic skills are not always adequately emphasized in school, they have as much if not more practical value as any aspect of the mathematics curriculum (Bell, 1974). Countless situations require the "addition" or "subtraction" of multidigit terms without the aid of paper and pencil or calculator. Adults routinely engage in *multidigit mental computation*.

Estimation of multidigit arithmetic is a particularly important skill in everyday life (Reys, 1984; Trafton, 1978). It is often used to do things such as figuring out tips in restaurants or at the hairdressers, or quickly checking the cost of items at the grocery or hardware store. With the widespread use of calculators and computers, estimation is more important than ever as a means of checking the reasonableness of answers (Hope, 1986).

In addition to their utility in adult life, there are other good reasons for cultivating mental computation and estimation skills. Children with good mental arithmetic skills may be more prone to check and correct their written work. The development of multidigit mental computation—like that of the basic number combinations—basically entails discovering and exploiting relationships and patterns. It can also be an important vehicle for encouraging mathematical thinking and problem solving (Driscoll, 1981). Indeed, estimation is at heart a problem-solving exercise and requires the thoughtful analysis and flexibility of such an endeavor.

LEARNING

Multidigit Mental Computation

Addition

To perform multidigit mental computation effectively, children must be able to generate basic (single-digit) and large-number (multidigit) combinations automatically. For example, to avoid becoming confused in adding 316 + 253, a child needs to recall effortlessly the basic fact that 6 + 3 = 9 and the large-number combinations 10 + 50 = 60 and 300 + 200 = 500. As with basic combinations, a key to mastering large-number addition combinations is discovering relationships and patterns. A key class of large-number combinations that children seem to learn in this way involves adding 10. Children learn quickly the pattern underlying the addition of 10 and a single-digit number (n) or a single-digit number and 10 (*10 + n or n + 10*): the sum is a teen that incorporates the single-digit term (e.g., 10 + 7 or 7 + 10 → seven + teen or 17).

Children can learn to add decades and 10 (*decade + 10 or 10 + decade*) automatically by exploiting the counting (count-by-ten) knowledge they already have (Resnick, 1983). Though children may know the decade sequence (10, 20, 30, 40 . . .) well and may be able to cite automatically the decade after another (e.g., the 10 after 70 is 80), they may not realize this knowledge can be used to solve, say, 20 + 10 = ? or 10 + 70 = ? Children have to see there is a connection between their existing knowledge of the decade sequence and such addition (e.g., the decade after 70 is 80, so the sum of 10 + 70 is 80). Once a child makes the connection, he or she can readily generate the sums to any problem involving a decade and 10. The memorization of combinations involving 10 and a decade may be facilitated by seeing how they parallel their single-digit counterparts (e.g., by comparing 10 + 70 = 80 with 1 + 7 = 8). After children discover the pattern above, they can exploit it to add automatically other two-digit numbers and 10 such as 32 + 10. In this case, the *two-digit n + 10* rule specifies: The sum is the decade after 30 with same ones place digit.

Children can exploit patterns or relationships to master other large-number combinations as well. For instance, they soon see that the 10 + n = n + teen pattern also applies to the addition of single-digit numbers and other decades (*decade + n or n + decade*) such as 20 + 7 = 27 or 7 + 20 = 27. Children can automatically add *decade and decade* (e.g., 40 + 30 = 70) by using their existing knowledge of the basic combinations (e.g., 4 + 3 = 7, so *four-ty* plus *thir-ty* is *seven-ty*). This connection can be used to respond efficiently to somewhat more complex combinations: *two-digit n and decade* (e.g., 30 + 42 = 72). Other *parallel addition facts* include combinations that involve a two-digit addend and a next-decade sum (e.g., $24 + 6 = 30$ parallels $4 + 6 = 10$).

Though children may not automatically see their application, the patterns for two-digit addition recur in the same or similar form with three-digit addition. In time, children either discover or learn that adding 100 and a single- or two-digit number (*100 + n or n + 100*) is a straightforward process (e.g., $100 + 7$ is "one hundred seven" and $76 + 100$ is "one hundred seventy-six"). Adding 10 to three-digit numbers (*three-digit n + 10*) requires knowing $10 + n$ or $n + 10$, decade $+ 10$ and two-digit $n + 10$ rules, and the rules for generating the number sequence to at least 1,000. For example, $103 + 10$ is an extension of the $10 + n$ or $n + 10$ rule: The sum is a teen that incorporates the single-term (13), prefaced by "one hundred" (one hundred thirteen). For a combination like $290 + 10$, the child must recognize that the decade $+ 10$ pattern applies (i.e., the sum is the next term in the count-by-10 sequence). Moreover, the child must know that the decade after 290 in that sequence is 300. Similarly, *three-digit n + decade* (e.g., $120 + 40$ or $123 + 40$) entails recognizing the application of decade $+$ decade and two-digit $n +$ decade patterns to three-digit addition. In cases, such as $160 + 40$ or $163 + 40$, the child must also have facility with the hundreds sequence (i.e., realize that the decade after 190 is the next hundreds term: 200). With *hundreds + 100* (e.g., $400 + 100$ or $100 + 400$), the child need only see a connection with the familiar $n + 1$ or $1 + n$ family (e.g., $4 + 1$ is 5 so *four*-hundred plus *one*-hundred is *five*-hundred). With $900 + 100$, the child would also have to appreciate that "ten-hundred" is called one thousand (the next hundreds term after 900 is one thousand). Likewise, adding hundreds, such as $400 + 300$, (*hundreds + hundreds*) entails seeing a connection with related basic combinations (e.g., $4 + 3 = 7$, therefore, *four*-hundred plus *three*-hundred is *seven*-hundred).

Subtraction

As with addition, efficient multidigit mental subtraction entails mastery of single-digit and large-number combinations. Like addition, mastering large-number subtraction combinations involves discovering new patterns or relationships with existing knowledge of the number sequence or basic combinations.

Mastering large-number subtraction facts begins with those combinations involving 10. Once children recognize that the sum of 10 and a number (*n*) is the teen counterpart of the number (*n* + teen), they should have no difficulty also recognizing the *teen* $- 10 = n$ pattern (e.g., $17 - 10 = 7$). Moreover, children's knowledge of the decade sequence (10, 20, 30 . . .) can serve as the basis for subtracting 10 from a decade (*decade* $-$ *10*). For example, to compute the difference of $30 - 10$, a child has only to think of the decade just before 30: 20. Remembering decade $- 10$

combinations may be facilitated by noticing the parallel between such combinations and single-digit minus-one combinations. In time, children also learn *two-digit n − 10* combinations (e.g., 42 − 10 = 32).

Children frequently use a variety of recurring patterns to master large-number combinations that do not involve 10 as well. Automatic recall of a basic fact like 7 − 4 can be extended to the subtraction of decades *decade − decade*: seven(+ty) minus four(+ty) is thir(+ty). This knowledge is then used to master *two-digit n − decade* combinations (e.g., 42 − 20 = 22). Other *parallel minus facts* include decade − n combinations (e.g., 30 − 6 is analogous to 10 − 6) and those governed by the number-before rule (e.g., 47 − 1 = 46), difference-of-one rule (e.g., 47 − 46 = 1), and identity principle (e.g., 47 − 47 = 0).

Estimation of Multidigit Arithmetic

Skillful estimating requires mental computation facility, sound conceptual knowledge of arithmetic and place value, flexibility, and knowledge of specific estimation strategies. Though children need not be good at estimation to be good at mental computation, they need to be good at mental computation to be good at estimation (Reys, 1984). Clearly, a child cannot make estimates quickly and accurately if he or she has inefficient mental computational skills.

Estimation skill grows as children's conceptual (particularly place-value) knowledge expands. As they understand more about arithmetic and place value, children can make more and more exact estimates (Trafton, 1978). Indeed, without formal instruction, first and second graders recognize that 50 is an absurd estimate for 52 + 26 ("because it is less than you started with"). Many would reject 60 as a good estimate because fifty something and twenty something ought to be at least seventy-something. That is, they have sufficient mental computation skill and arithmetic or place-value knowledge to recognize informally unreasonable and reasonable approximations.

Computational estimating requires the mental flexibility to risk exploration and giving inexact answers. Unfortunately, as early as first grade, children become so concerned with producing the correct answer that they refuse to make estimates. Even when asked to estimate quickly, children may insist on laboriously calculating the correct answer. Rigidity then is one of the primary barriers to good estimation skill.

Though children will informally acquire some estimation skill, instruction or specific strategies can extend their estimation facility. A simple estimation strategy, which does not require a deep understanding of place value, involves focusing only on the digits that will have the biggest impact on the sum (Reys, 1984). With the problem 56 + 43, the tens-place digits 5 and 4 will have the biggest impact on the sum and so they are added producing the estimate of 90-plus. Such a *front-end strategy with two-digit terms* is a natural bridge with children's informal estimation skill and is so straightforward that it can be taught readily to first graders. As children learn to add hundred terms, they can easily make *front-end* estimates with three-digit terms. For example, focusing on the most influential (the hundreds-place) digits for the problem below quickly leads to the estimate of 700 plus.

$$
\begin{array}{r}
432 \\
87 \\
296 \\
8 \\
+156 \\
\hline
\end{array}
$$

Rounding strategies are typically what are taught as estimation (Trafton, 1978). It is important to note that there is no one correct way to estimate (sums and differences) by rounding. How rounding is done depends upon the objective of the exercise (Reys, 1984). Consider the following problem.

To remodel a kitchen, five items were needed. Their costs are listed below:

$$
\begin{array}{r}
\$137 \\
\$\ 42 \\
\$592 \\
\$\ 56 \\
\$\ 89 \\
\hline
\end{array}
$$

If a rather precise estimate was needed (to, say, check whether or not the items were rung up accurately by the checkout clerk), it would be helpful to round to tens:

$$
\begin{array}{r}
140 \\
40 \\
590 \\
60 \\
90 \\
\hline
920
\end{array}
$$

If a gross estimate (for, say, estimating the total cost) was needed, then rounding off to hundreds might suffice.

```
        100
          0
        600
        100
        100
        ———
        900
```

If a very gross estimate was all that was needed (to ensure that, say, the cost did not exceed an upper limit of $1,200), rounding *up* to the nearest hundred would be useful.

```
        200
        100
        600
        100
        100
       —————
      1,100
```

Rounding, then, is very much a problem-solving activity that requires mental computation skill with tens and hundreds, place-value knowledge, and flexibility. *Rounding with two- and three-digits,* therefore, requires more sophistication than a front-end strategy.

Unfortunately, mental arithmetic skills in general and estimation in particular often are not given adequate attention in school (e.g., Carpenter, Coburn, Reys, and Wilson, 1976). Estimation training too often focuses exclusively on rounding (Trafton, 1978), and it is taught mechanically. Children are not helped to appreciate the value of estimating; they do not understand that the aim of estimation is to make difficult computations manageable. Because they learn estimation skills by rote and out of context, they do not realize that an estimation strategy is determined by a thoughtful analysis of task goals.

A suggested sequence of mental-arithmetic competencies by grade level is outlined in Table 11–1.

INSTRUCTION

Multidigit Mental Computation

The key ingredient in fostering mastery of large-number combinations is helping children to discover the underlying patterns of these combinations and how these patterns are related to existing knowledge. **Egyptian Hieroglyphics, In-Out Machine,** and **Math Detective Exercises** are well suited for this purpose. For instance, in Example 11–1, the first question

Table 11–1 Suggested Sequence of Mental-Arithmetic Competencies by Grade Level and Developmental Order

Level	Multidigit Mental Computation		Estimation of Multidigit Arithmetic
	Addition	*Subtraction*	
1	$10 + n$ or $n + 10$	—	—
	Decade $+ n$ or n decade	Teen $- 10$	—
	Decade $+ 10$ or $10 +$ decade	Decade $- 10$	—
	—	—	Front-end with two-digit terms
2	Decade $+$ decade	Decade $-$ decade	—
	Two-digit $n + 10$	Two-digit $n - 10$	—
	Two-digit $n +$ decade	Two-digit $n -$ decade	—
	Parallel addition facts	Parallel minus facts	—
	$100 + n$ or $n + 100$	—	—
3	Hundreds $+ 100$	—	Front-end with three-digit terms
	Hundreds $+$ hundreds	—	—
	Three-digit $n + 10$	—	—
	Three-digit $n +$ decade	—	—
	—	—	Rounding with two and three digits

in Hieroglyphics Exercise A helps focus attention on the effects of adding a single-digit number to 10. Such problems as $\cap$ + $\wedge\wedge\wedge\wedge$ and $\cap$ + $\wedge\wedge\wedge\wedge\wedge$ are a concrete embodiment of the $10 + n = n +$ teen pattern.

A group discussion may help some children to consciously recognize that the sum contains the same number of ones as the term added. Writing the number sentences (e.g., $10 + 4 = 14$) further reinforces this point and helps connect the idea to its formal representation.

The aim of Question 2, which entails adding a single-digit number to 10, is similar. Implicitly, it illustrates that $10 + n$ and $n + 10$ are equivalent. Question 3 more directly makes this point. Exercise B focuses on the teen $-$ 10 pattern. Exercise C illustrates that the number-after pattern is *repeated* at the decade level (e.g., the sum of $6 + 1$ is the *number* after six—seven— similarly, the sum of $60 + 10$ is the *decade* after 60—70). Note that these exercises complement the base-ten place-value training discussed in the previous chapter (e.g., a teen is actually a composite of a ten and ones and a two-digit term is an amalgam of tens and ones). In fact, instruction of large-number combinations ought to go hand in hand with base-ten place-value training.

Example 11–1 Egyptian Hieroglyphic Exercises that Highlight Patterns Underlying Large-Number Combinations

Exercise A

1. The Pharaoh asked the members of his court for a tribute of 10 gold pieces to help victims of the flood. This was not enough, so he asked court members to contribute again whatever they could afford. The record of the tributes is shown below. Figure out the number of gold coins each court member contributed altogether and record the result in hieroglyphics. Then write a number sentence in our Arabic numbers that shows the same thing.

Court Member	First Tribute		Second Tribute		Tribute Altogether	Number Sentence
Reb	∩	+	⋀⋀⋀⋀	→	_____	☐ + ☐ = ☐
Stef	∩	+	⋀⋀⋀⋀⋀⋀	→	_____	☐ + ☐ = ☐
Jer	∩	+	⋀⋀⋀⋀⋀⋀⋀	→	_____	☐ + ☐ = ☐
Shan	∩	+	⋀⋀⋀⋀⋀⋀⋀⋀	→	_____	☐ + ☐ = ☐
Obin	∩	+	⋀⋀⋀⋀⋀	→	_____	☐ + ☐ = ☐
Kare	∩	+	⋀⋀⋀⋀⋀⋀⋀⋀	→	_____	☐ + ☐ = ☐

2. Because it was his birthday, the Pharaoh wanted to make everyone happy. He decided to give court members silver pieces according to their rank. The highest ranking court member received nine pieces; the lowest ranking just one. After passing out the silver, he saw that everyone was so happy that he decided to give everyone ten more pieces of silver. Of course, as King's treasurer, you had to record all

the expenses and note how many silver pieces each person got altogether. Write a number sentence for each also.

Court Member	First Gift		Second Gift		Total Altogether	Number Sentence
Reb	‖‖‖‖‖‖‖‖	+	∩	→	____	☐ + ☐ = ☐
Stef	‖‖‖‖‖‖	+	∩	→	____	☐ + ☐ = ☐
Jer	‖‖‖‖‖	+	∩	→	____	☐ + ☐ = ☐
Shan	‖‖‖‖	+	∩	→	____	☐ + ☐ = ☐
Obin	‖‖‖	+	∩	→	____	☐ + ☐ = ☐
Kare	‖	+	∩	→	____	☐ + ☐ = ☐

3. The Pharaoh enjoyed playing games with his brothers. The scores for each game are shown below. As the official scorekeeper note the players' score altogether in hieroglyphics. Write a number sentence that shows what each player scored in the games and their total score.

Player	Game 1		Game 2		Total	Number Sentence
Pharaoh	∩	+	‖‖‖‖‖‖	→	____	☐ + ☐ = ☐
Brother 1	‖‖‖‖‖‖	+	∩	→	____	☐ + ☐ = ☐
Pharaoh	∩	+	‖‖‖‖	→	____	☐ + ☐ = ☐
Brother 2	‖‖‖‖	+	∩	→	____	☐ + ☐ = ☐

Exercise B

The Pharaoh organized a fair for all of the children in the kingdom to go to. It cost 10 gold pieces to get in to the fair. The children would have to take the 10 gold pieces from the allowance they have saved up. The number of gold pieces each child has saved is shown below in hieroglyphics. Figure out how many gold pieces each child will have after he or she pays the entrance fee to go to the fair. Then write a number sentence to represent the same thing.

Child	Allowance Saved	Entrance Fee	Gold Pieces Leftover	Number Sentence
Bet	∩ ΛΛΛΛ	– ∩ →	_____	☐ – ☐ = ☐
Joh	∩ ΛΛΛΛΛΛΛ	– ∩ →	_____	☐ – ☐ = ☐
Mar	∩ ΛΛ	– ∩ →	_____	☐ – ☐ = ☐
Cin	∩ ΛΛΛΛΛ	– ∩ →	_____	☐ – ☐ = ☐
Cha	∩ ΛΛΛΛΛΛΛ	– ∩ →	_____	☐ – ☐ = ☐
Bri	∩ ΛΛΛΛΛΛ	– ∩ →	_____	☐ – ☐ = ☐

Exercise C

It was Market Day in the Pharaoh's kingdom. There were two farmers present to distribute the corn to all of the families. To make sure they all receive some corn before the farmers ran out, the Pharaoh ordered each farmer to distribute a certain amount of corn to each family. Shown below is the amount of corn each farmer was to give to each family. Determine how much corn each family received altogether, and record your answer in hieroglyphics. Then write a number sentence that shows the same thing.

Family Name	Corn from Farmer #1	Corn from Farmer #2	Corn Altogether	Number Sentence
Waks	ΛΛΛΛΛΛ	+ Λ →	_____	☐ + ☐ = ☐
Bro	∩∩∩∩∩∩	+ ∩ →	_____	☐ + ☐ = ☐
Jons	ΛΛ	+ Λ →	_____	☐ + ☐ = ☐
Dur	∩∩	+ ∩ →	_____	☐ + ☐ = ☐
Maon	ΛΛΛΛΛΛΛ	+ Λ →	_____	☐ + ☐ = ☐
Haon	∩∩∩∩∩∩∩	+ ∩ →	_____	☐ + ☐ = ☐
Fak	ΛΛΛΛ	+ Λ →	_____	☐ + ☐ = ☐
Thom	∩∩∩∩	+ ∩ →	_____	☐ + ☐ = ☐
Reil	ΛΛΛΛΛΛ	+ Λ →	_____	☐ + ☐ = ☐
Wils	∩∩∩∩∩∩∩	+ ∩ →	_____	☐ + ☐ = ☐

In Example 11–2 In-Out Machine Exercise A can help focus attention on the effects of adding 10 to one- and two-digit numbers. (The invisible internal mechanism or function that children must uncover is + 10.) If desired, such exercises can be tailored to focus on one specific objective (e.g., n + 10, two-digit n + 10, or decade + 10). The aim of Exercise B is to help children see that the patterns of adding 10 with one- and two-digit numbers are *repeated* at the three-digit level. Note that to highlight these connections, unknown combinations are placed next to related known combinations. For instance, in Exercise B, 130 + 10 = 140 (a three-digit example) is introduced immediately after 30 + 10 = 40 (its two-digit counterpart).

Math Detective Exercises also can help students see that their knowledge of basic number combinations can be used to figure out large-

Example 11–2 Using In-Out Machine Exercises that Highlight Patterns Among Multidigit Combinations

Exercise A			Exercise B	
In	*Out*		*In*	*Out*
3	13		30	40
33	43		130	140
6	16		3	13
46	56		103	
7			46	56
27			146	
0			7	
70			107	
80			207	
84			80	
2			180	
12			280	
22			380	
32				15
42				115
52				215
	14			615
	24			
	50			
	52			

number combinations. For example, Exercise A in Example 11–3 highlights that the decade-before pattern for decade − 10 combinations, like 70 − 10, parallels the number-before pattern for $n − 1$ combinations, like 7 − 1. It also underscores the fact that the $n − 0$ rules apply to two-digit combinations as well as one-digit combinations, that decade − decade combinations echo the basic single-digit combinations, and that the difference-of-consecutive-decades-is-10 pattern parallels the difference-of-one pattern (e.g., 9 − 8).

Exercise B highlights the reappearance of the sums-to-10 combinations at the two-digit level as sums to the next decade (e.g., 8 + 2 produces the

Example 11–3 Using Math Detective Exercises to Extend Known Patterns

Exercise A

Find the sums for each of the following problems in any way you wish. You may calculate sums by using your fingers, an abacus, or a calculator. You may think out the sums if you wish.
What do you notice about these problems?

7	70	2	20	4	40	9	90
−1	−10	−1	−10	−1	−10	−1	−10

4	34	9	49	8	80	6	60
−0	− 0	−0	− 0	−0	− 0	−0	− 0

7	70	6	60	5	50	8	80
−5	−50	−2	−20	−3	−30	−4	−40

4	40	7	70	8	80	9	90
−3	−30	−6	−60	−7	−70	−8	−80

Exercise B

Find the sums for each of the following problems in any way you wish. You may calculate sums by using your fingers, an abacus, or a calculator. You may think out the sums if you wish.
What do you notice about these problems?

2	8	18	2	2	28	68	2	2	78	88	2
+8	+2	+ 2	+18	+28	+ 2	+ 2	+68	+78	+ 2	+ 2	+88

3	7	17	3	3	27	67	3	3	77	87	3
+7	+3	+ 3	+17	+27	+ 3	+ 3	+67	+77	+ 3	+ 3	+87

4	6	16	4	4	26	46	4	4	76	84	6
+6	+4	+ 4	+16	+26	+ 4	+ 4	+46	+76	+ 4	+ 6	+84

	5	15	5	5	25	45	5	5	75	85	5
	+5	+ 5	+15	+25	+ 5	+ 5	+45	+75	+ 5	+ 5	+85

decade 10 and similarly 68 + 2 produces the next decade after 60: 70). Once children recognize this pattern they can quickly generate add-to-next-decade sums. That is, they no longer laboriously have to calculate the sum mentally using the standard (carrying) algorithm.

In brief, Egyptian Hieroglyphics, In-Out Machines, and Math-Detective exercises can be crafted to encourage the discovery of a specific pattern or to practice a range of objectives. The next section details games that can be used to practice a range of large-number combinations.

10 + n or n + 10, Decade + n or n + Decade, Decade + 10 or 10 + Decade, Two-Digit n + 10, Teen − 10, Decade − 10, and Two-Digit n − 10

First ensure that prerequisite skills are mastered. For 10 + n or n + 10, children should have mastered a means to figure out such sums either by calculating, counting-on, or through pattern recognition (see the Addition Pattern Activity in Chapter 9). For decade + n, the child should first be familiar with n + 0 or 0 + n combinations. The psychological prerequisites for decade + 10 or 10 + decade is knowledge of the count-by-ten sequence and the decade after 10 to 90. It helps children master two-digit n + 10 if they were already proficient at decade + 10 or 10 + decade. If not, both skills can be worked on simultaneously, but efforts should focus on the decade + 10 or 10 + decade skill first and how two-digit n + 10 is simply an extension of it. For 34 + 10, for example, the next decade after 30 is 40 and ones digit comes along for the ride (40 + 4) = 44.

To master teen − 10 it would be helpful to know 10 + n or n + 10 combinations. If not, both can be worked on simultaneously but emphasis should be on the addition combinations, which can be more easily figured out informally. Decade − 10 requires a child to automatically cite decade before terms up to 100. It may be helpful but not entirely necessary for children to master decade + 10 first. For two-digit n − 10, it would be helpful to know decade − 10 and two-digit n + 10 combinations.

Grid Race (Example 11–4), **Card Game 99** (Example 11–5), and **Backward Grid Race** (Example 11–6) are entertaining ways to help children notice two-digit arithmetic patterns and practice these rules.

Example 11–4   Grid Race

Objectives: Mental two-digit addition, particularly with ⁺0 (basic version) and subtracting by 10 (advanced version).

Grade Level: 1 or 2.

Participants: Two to six players.

Materials: The basic version of the game requires tokens (place markers) for each player; deck of cards indicating +1 to +9 and large proportion of +10 cards (a standard deck of cards could be substituted with aces worth 1, 2 to 9 worth their face value and the rest worth 10); and 1 to 100 grid as shown below. For the advanced version, simply include a supply of −10 cards in the deck.

Finish	100								
	90	91	92	93	94	95	96	97	98	99
	80	81	82	83	84	85	86	87	88	89
	70	71	72	73	74	75	76	77	78	79
	60	61	62	63	64	65	66	67	68	69
	50	51	52	53	54	55	56	57	58	59
	40	41	42	43	44	45	46	47	48	49
	30	31	32	33	34	35	36	37	38	39
	20	21	22	23	24	25	26	27	28	29
	10	11	12	13	14	15	16	17	18	19
Start	0	1	2	3	4	5	6	7	8	9

S
t
a
r
t

Procedure: On their turn, players draw a card and add the number indicated to the number their token is resting on. All players start on 0. The first to get 100 wins. A player does not have to obtain the exact sum of 100 to win (e.g., if a player's token is on 96 and he draws a 7, the player would simply advance to the 100 grid and win).

Note that players will—initially—often count out their move. For example, a player with a token on grid 47 who draws a +10 will count ten spaces up to grid 57. After playing the game for a while, players should notice that when adding +10, they can avoid this laborious counting process and skip to the grid in the next column immediately above the one the token occupies. For instance, they can move directly from grid 47 to 57.

To help students connect an existing knowledge of the count by-tens sequence with addition, have the players try a warm-up exercise before the grid race. Starting with 0, have a pupil count by tens as he or she points to the appropriate grid. Have another pupil count by tens starting with 4, 6, 7, 8, or 9 (a single-digit number in which the next term is a regular ten).

Example 11-5   Card Game 99

Objectives: Two-digit mental addition and subtraction, particularly with 10 and including two-digit $n + n$.

Grade Level: 1 or 2.

Participants: Two to six players.

Materials: A deck of cards can be made with 3″ × 5″ cards. A beginner's deck would consist of about four of the following: +0, +1, +2, +3, +5, 99, and REVERSE. The deck should also include about 12 of the following: +10 and −10. An advanced-player's deck would consist of about four cards of each of the following: +0, +1 *or* +11, +2, +3, +4, +5, +6, +7, +8, +9, +10, −10, 99, and REVERSE. Blocks or any countable objects can be used for markers. There should be three markers for each player.

Procedure: The object of the game is to avoid being the player who discards a card that puts the discard-pile total over 99. Each player is dealt three cards and *a* card is turned over to start the discard pile. The player to the left of the dealer starts play by adding to the discard pile. The player announces the value of the discard pile, the value of his or her discarded card, and the sum of the two cards (or difference in the case of −10). Discarding a 99 card does not add 99 to the discard pile, it simply makes its value 99 automatically (regardless of its previous value). Discarding a REVERSE simply changes the direction of play (e.g., from clockwise to counterclockwise). After a player has discarded and announced the outcome of the discard, he or she may pick another card from the pile. A player loses this draw if the next player puts a card on the discard pile before the draw is made (if the player forgets to draw). Play continues until a player puts the discard pile total over 99. That player gets a point (marker). The cards are reshuffled and a new round is then begun. The game ends when a player has lost three rounds (collected three markers). The player or players with the fewest markers wins the game.

By starting with a beginner's deck, it will give children considerable practice adding and subtracting 10. Afterward, introduce the advanced-players deck that includes the more difficult mental addition of 4, 6, 7, 8, and 9.

Example 11–6   Backward Grid Race

Objective: Mental multidigit subtraction, particularly with 10.

Grade Level: 2 or 3.

Participants: Two to six players.

Materials: Tokens for each player, deck of cards indicating −1 to −9 and large proportion of −10 cards, and a 1 to 100 grid similar to that shown for Grid Race.

Procedure: This game is played like Grid Race except that players begin at the top of the grid and work down. A player's move is determined by taking the difference between the number of the space he or she is on and the card drawn.

To introduce multidigit subtraction gradually, first play the advanced version of Grid Race and/or Card Game 99. In this way, decade − 10 and two-digit n − 10 are practiced before more difficult multidigit subtraction combinations. The next step in the transition is to play Backward Grid Race with −1, −2, −3, and −10 cards only. Then introduce −4 to −9 cards when the children are ready.

Three-Digit n + 10, Three-Digit n + Decade, Hundreds + 100, and Hundreds + Hundreds

First ensure that prerequisite skills are mastered. This includes the two-digit combinations already discussed because they are component parts of three-digit n + 10 and three-digit n + decade. For instance, 140 + 10 entails automatic knowledge of decade + 10, and 253 + 40 involves efficiently generating a two-digit n + decade sum. Hundreds + 100 involves knowing the count by hundreds sequence and hundred-after terms. Perhaps more critical is mastery of n + 1 combinations and how these related to the hundreds + hundreds addition (e.g., 400 + 100 can be thought of as [4 + 1] + hundred or five + hundred). Likewise, hundreds + hundreds is dependent upon automatic recall of single-digit counterparts. **Card Game 999** (Example 11–7) provides an entertaining vehicle for noticing and practicing these rules.

Example 11-7   Card Game 999

Objective: Mental three-digit addition, particularly with +100 and +10. Optional: The game could also provide practice for −10 and/or −100.

Grade Level: 3.

Participants: Two to six players.

Materials: A deck would consist of about four cards of each of the following: +0, +10, +20, +30, +40, +50, +60, +70, +80, +90, +100, (−10, −100), 999, and REVERSE. Three markers for each player are also needed.

Procedure: Follow the procedures described for the Card Game 99, except that the critical total in this game is 999.

Estimation

Estimation training should be taught in a meaningful manner (Trafton, 1986). It is not enough to teach estimation skills like rounding in a vacuum. Children need to see the value of estimating. Thus it is essential to make clear the reasons for making estimates. One device for helping children to appreciate the uses of estimation is a story problem. In Example 11–8, the first story (Part I) illustrates that an exact answer is not always needed to answer a problem. The second story (Part II) highlights the value of estimation as a means of checking computed answers. The third story (Part III) underscores the fact that it is not always practical to determine an exact answer. Estimation makes manageable computations that are otherwise difficult if not impossible.

Example 11-8   Count Disorderly Stories That Illustrate the Value of Estimation

Part I of the Raisin King: Safe But Sorry

Count Orderly decided to visit his brother Count Disorderly. He arrived at Count Disorderly's castle to find his brother very, very sad. Count Orderly asked, "Dear brother why are you so upset?"

Count Disorderly explained that he wanted to be the new Raisin King at the Spring Fair. To become the new Raisin King, a person had to eat more raisins than anyone else in the kingdom. Count Glutton, who was crowned Raisin King the year before, had eaten 500 raisins. This meant that Count Disorderly would have to bring to the fair and eat at least how many? [Five hundred and one.]

Count Disorderly went on to explain that he had gone to the store and bought every box of raisins he could find. Sure enough, everywhere in the castle Count Orderly looked, there was a box of raisins. Just then a pile of boxes tumbled down. A box of raisins fell in Count Orderly's lap. He looked at the box and exclaimed, "Oh brother, it says right here on the box that each box contains at least 300 raisins. If you needed 501 raisins, why did you buy *all* of these boxes of raisins?"

Count Disorderly was a little embarrassed. He explained, "I saw that on the box but I wanted to make sure that I had 501 raisins. So I bought all of these boxes to make sure that I had enough raisins."

[What do you think of Count Disorderly's explanation? Did he need to buy so many boxes of raisins to become Raisin King? How many boxes did he really need and how could he have figured this out?]

Part II of the Raisin King: The Crazy Calculator

Count Orderly asked Count Disorderly, "Brother, is one box of raisins enough?"

Count Disorderly reasoned, "I don't think so. I need 501 raisins and a box has at least 300. If it had more than 400 or 500, it would probably say so."

Count Orderly agreed. "Yes, so one box probably has between 300 and 400 raisins. To make things simple, let's say 300 or 400." [If Count Orderly and Disorderly wanted to be safe and make sure they were not estimating too much, should they use 300 or 400?] "Let's use 300 to be on the safe side," he continued. "If one box has 300 raisins, it is not enough to become Raisin King. Will two boxes give you at least 500 raisins?"

Count Disorderly replied, "I don't know. I don't know how much 300 and 300 is altogether. I can't add that high yet. That's why I bought so many boxes."

"Let's use a calculator to find out how much 300 and 300 is," Count Orderly suggested. I have mine here in my shirt pocket." Count Disorderly eagerly took the calculator and tried to add 300 and 300. "Three hundred and thirty." he explained. "I knew two boxes wasn't nearly enough, I knew I needed all these boxes."

"Let me see the calculator," said a puzzled Count Orderly. "Maybe you're reading the calculator wrong." Count Orderly looked at the calculator. Sure enough the answer was 330.

[Why was Count Orderly puzzled by Count Disorderly's calculation on the calculator? Don't you always get the right answer when you use a calculator? For more advanced children follow up with: What is wrong with the answer of 330? About what should it be? What do you think Count Disorderly did wrong when he calculated the answer?]

Count Orderly thought a minute and then said, "I think two boxes should have more than 330 raisins altogether. If one box has 300, another hundred would make it 400. Two boxes should have at least 400.

Count Disorderly jumped up and down and shouted, "But I used the calculator, and *it* says 330. A calculator can't be wrong!"

Count Orderly replied, "That's not true. The calculator just does whatever you tell it to. If you make a mistake, the calculator may just make the same mistake." [What kinds of mistakes do you think people commonly make when using a calculator?] "For example, a common mistake is to forget a zero. Brother! I bet that's what you did. You added 300 and 30, not 300 and 300."

Count Disorderly said, "I didn't know you could make a mistake with calculators. Let me try adding 300 and 300 again. Now it says 600. Two boxes is enough to become Raisin King. What am I going to do with all these raisins?"

"You can give them away to people at the fair," Count Orderly suggested. "That would make a lot of people very happy."

Part III of the Raisin King: The Raisin Baron

The next day, Count Orderly stopped by to visit Count Disorderly. Again, he found his brother deep in despair. Count Disorderly was also knee-deep in raisins.

Before Count Orderly could ask what was happening, Count Disorderly explained, "Well, as long as I had all these boxes of raisins, I wanted to know how many raisins I did have. So I have been emptying the boxes and trying to count the raisins."

Count Disorderly was so upset that he began to cry. "It's been horrible!" he weeped. I count and count and count and then I forget what I've counted. Or a pile of raisins I've counted falls down and gets mixed up with the raisins I'm counting. I've been counting all day and finished only 10 boxes of raisins. I still have 990 more boxes of raisins to count."

[Do you think it wise for Count Disorderly to try to find out exactly how many raisins he has?]

"Brother, why bother?" asked Count Orderly.

"There will be a thousand people at the Spring Fair. If I pass out raisins to everyone as you suggested will I have enough? I don't want to run out and have some people mad at me."

"Brother, you have 1000 boxes of raisins with 300 raisins in each box. If there are a thousand people at the fair, you will have *plenty of* raisins for everyone—even if you eat two boxes yourself to become the Raisin King.

Estimation should be approached as a problem-solving task. Children should first be encouraged to consider thoughtfully the goal or aim of a task. The level of accuracy needed will determine whether an exact computation or estimated answer is needed and, if the latter, the precision of the estimate. (For example, if Count Disorderly had considered this in Part III, he would have saved himself considerable effort. A precise answer was not needed and was impractical to obtain. With 300 raisins per box and 998 boxes of raisins, Count Orderly knew there were "plenty" or raisins—more than 100 a person. A more precise estimate was not required.)

Estimation practice should be done on a regular basis and in an interesting and concrete manner. For example, virtually all children at some time or another have accompanied one or both of their parents on a trip to the grocery store. **Nervous Shopper** (Example 11–9) is based on such informal and concrete experiences. This game also highlights practical uses of estimation and its relationship to everyday life. The use of the calculator as a "cash register" is a fast, simple way for students to check their mental arithmetic.

In making estimates, children should be encouraged to make use of the arithmetic (and place-value) knowledge they have. (In discussing the reasoning processes of Count Orderly in Example 11–8, note that he did not simply make wild guesses or blindly accept what the calculator indicated. He used what he knew to make educated guesses and critical judgments.)

One of the most difficult objectives a primary teacher faces is helping children become flexible and secure enough to engage in estimation. It will help if children are given estimation experience all along: estimating the number of items in a set, measurements of quantity, and single-digit sums or differences. It helps if the teacher does not overemphasize getting *the*

Example 11–9   Nervous Shopper*

Objective: Practice estimating cost that entails multidigit addition for two to five children. The difficulty of the task can be adjusted by modifying the budget that a player is given and the prices of the items.

Grade Level: 2 or 3.

Materials: Calculator, one basket for each "shopper," play money, and various food items that one would have for dinner clearly marked with price tags (use either empty, clean containers collected from home or construct your own items).

Procedure: The object of this game is to put together a complete dinner without going over a predetermined budget. To play, one child must be designated as the cashier and the other children as shoppers. Each shopper will be given $10.00 with which he or she is to buy all the necessary ingredients for one evening's dinner. The cashier should be stationed at a desk or table with the calculator. When the shopper has made his or her selections, the child should go over to the check-out line where the cashier will add up the purchases on the calculator to see if the child has gone over his or her budget. Initially, the food items should be priced using whole numbers from one to five in order to develop mental calculation skills. When the children have become proficient at this level, price tags can be changed to numbers like $1.10, $4.99, and so on, and the budget can be increased.

---

*Sarah Scoville of Urbana-Champaign, Illinois, suggested this idea.

correct answer. Perhaps one of the most important things a teacher can do is *model* estimation skills for the class by "thinking out loud" (e.g., Our class will have about 20 at the picnic, and Mrs. Braun's will have about 25, so we need about 45 cups."). This provides concrete evidence that the teacher is comfortable with the process. Thoughtful efforts at estimation need to be praised and even discussed.

Furthermore, it is especially important at first to avoid the common practice of asking children to make an estimate, then determining the exact answer, and finally compare the estimating to the exact answer (Carlow,

1986). Children may sense that it is the exact answer that is *really* important. Initially, then, feedback can indicate whether or not an estimate would have accomplished an intended purpose. For example, the goal can be to gauge whether or not a set (or jar) of objects is enough for a group of ten children. After children make their estimate (yes, there is enough, or no, there's not enough), they can count to see if there are at least ten objects. Thus—at least in cases where there were more then ten objects—the children could evaluate the accuracy of their estimates without determining the exact number of objects present. In time, children do need to learn that some estimates are better than others. Here it is more important to measure estimates against an exact answer.

The games **Ready-Set-Add** and **Ready-Set-Subtract** (Example 11–10) can be adapted to practice estimation skills such as a front-end or a rounding strategy with problems of any size. The addition version with two-digit combinations is described below.

Example 11–10 Ready-Set-Add or Ready-Set-Subtract

Objective: Computational estimation with two-digit combinations.

Grade Level: 1 or 2.

Participants: The game can be played by individual pupils who would compete against their own records or an existing class record. It can be played competitively with two to six players or two small teams of players. A teacher or a child should serve as a judge.

Materials: Record sheets and answer keys (see next page). A calculator could be substituted for the answer keys.

Procedure: The judge presents a combination to the player(s) by saying, for example, "Combination A. Ready, set, add: 32 + 41." The judge gives players, say, two seconds to indicate their estimate. A player indicates an estimate by putting an X on Number List A on their record sheet. The judge then scores the players' estimates by comparing the answer key to their marked number list. If there is a match (e.g., for 32 + 41, if a player marked 70), then the player (team) is awarded a point. The player or team with the most points at the end of the game, wins.

A. Record Sheet

A	B	C	D	E	F
10—	10—	10—	10—	10—	10—
20—	20—	20—	20—	20—	20—
30—	30—	30—	30—	30—	30—
40—	40—	40—	40—	40—	40—
50—	50—	50—	50—	50—	50—
60—	60—	60—	60—	60—	60—
70—	70—	70—	70—	70—	70—
80—	80—	80—	80—	80—	80—
90—	90—	90—	90—	90—	90—
100—	100—	100—	100—	100—	100—
100+—	100+—	100+—	100+—	100+—	100+—

G	H	I	J	K	L
10—	10—	10—	10—	10—	10—
20—	20—	20—	20—	20—	20—
30—	30—	30—	30—	30—	30—
40—	40—	40—	40—	40—	40—
50—	50—	50—	50—	50—	50—
60—	60—	60—	60—	60—	60—
70—	70—	70—	70—	70—	70—
80—	80—	80—	80—	80—	80—
90—	90—	90—	90—	90—	90—
100—	100—	100—	100—	100—	100—
100+—	100+—	100+—	100+—	100+—	100+—

B. Sample Answer Key Card

32+41
10—
20—
30—
40—
50—
60—
70— X
80—
90—
100—
100+—

An excellent source of teaching ideas for estimation is the 1986 National Council of Teachers of Mathematics Yearbook (Schoen and Zweng, 1986). In addition to the front-end and rounding strategies described here, this reference describes other computational estimation strategies that are appropriate for elementary-level children (e.g., see Leutzinger, Rathmell, and Urbatsch, 1986; Reys, 1986).

Front-End with Two-Digit and Three-Digit Terms

First ensure that children have a basis for understanding two-digit (three-digit) addition and subtraction, including recognition of the ones, tens (and hundreds) place and place-value notation for two-digit (three-digit) terms. To learn the skill they do *not* have to produce basic facts automatically. However, to use the strategy with any efficiency, children should be able to generate single-digits sums rather quickly by recall, reasoning, or counting-on or counting-down.

If they have the prerequisites, children could be introduced to a front-end strategy with two-digit terms *and* three-digit terms simultaneously. For most, though, it may be helpful to introduce it with only two-digit arithmetic, which is less complicated and more familiar. The methods described below are illustrated with examples involving two-digit addition. They could just as easily be used with subtraction or three-digit arithmetic.

Specific estimation strategies can be pointed out as part of an estimation activity such as **Good or Bad Estimator**. Show the number sentence like $98 + 75 = 12$ and say, "Cookie Monster thinks 98 cookies and 75 cookies adds up to about 12 cookies. Is 12 a good guess or a bad guess? Is he about right or way off?" Have the participants discuss the reasons for their answer. Present a mix of number sentences that are good examples of estimation (e.g., $63 + 24 = 81, 74 + 3 = 76$) and those that are bad (e.g., $55 + 26 = 107, 73 + 22 = 23$). Be sure to include two-plus one-digit examples (e.g., $76 + 5 = 120$).

During the discussions of their answers, the key elements of a front-end approach may come up: The answer to two-digit problems must be at least as large as the sum of the tens digits. Some children will quickly pick up the front-end strategy with only a brief explanation and minimal encouragement.

For other children, it may be necessary to highlight the relative importance of the tens-place outcome by using a concrete model. In such cases, ask children to represent a problem such as $\begin{array}{r} 56 \\ +43 \end{array}$ on a concrete-computation board like that shown in Figure 12–1. Then ask, "If you could add just one of these columns, which would come the closest to giving us the correct answer?" Check the responses by first figuring out the correct answer concretely as shown in Figure 12–1. Then add just the ones digits (6 + 3 = 9). Next add just the tens digits (50 + 40 = 90). Compare the two with the exact answer.

Though a front-end strategy is relatively simple, it should not be learned and used mechanically. Like any problem-solving activity, estimation requires a thoughtful analyses of the problem. Consider the problems below:

A	B	C	D
126	128	168	125
341	10	399	99
+507	+ 7	+576	+ 86

A front-end strategy yields reasonably accurate estimates for Problems A (900+) and B (100+) but significantly underestimates Problems C (900+) and D (100+).

Have children discuss the merits of a front-end strategy with such problems. Solicit suggestions for how to improve estimates with Problems like C and D. One improvement is using a refined front-end strategy, where an estimator takes into account the first *two* most influential digits—in this case, the hundreds and tens place. A refined front-end strategy is illustrated below with Problems C and D.

C	D
160	120
390	90
+ 570	+ 80
1120	290

Exercises that entail analyzing the usefulness of a front-end strategy are a natural introduction to rounding. In this way, rounding can be introduced as a means for making even more precise estimates than a front-end strategy.

Rounding with Two and Three Digits

First ensure that children have a sound basis for understanding two- and three-digit arithmetic, including an ability to compute the answers of such problems by using manipulatives. Children also need a fairly sound understanding of place value—including recognition of the ones, tens, and hundreds place; place-value notation for two- and three-digit terms; zero as a place holder; and the sum of digit values equals the whole. Efficient application of rounding skills also requires accurate and quick mental computation skills with single- and multidigit combinations.

Rounding should be taught in a problem-solving context. Help children to see that rounding is another means for making difficult calculations more manageable. They also need to understand that how rounding is implemented depends on the aim of the task. Group discussions can be helpful in making decisions about the aims and thus the approach of an estimation effort.

A discussion can be facilitated by playing **Good or Bad Estimator**. Ask children to evaluate the rounding efforts of a fictitious character in terms of the aims of a task. Consider the story problem below:

> Joslin got $10 for her birthday. She went to a department store and bought items she liked. To make sure she did not overspend the $10 she had, Joslin estimated the cost of each item she picked out. Below is a list of the prices of the items and Joslin's estimates for them.

Item Price	Joslin's Estimate
$1.42	$1
$2.09	$2
$1.23	$1
$5.33	$5

> After picking out the fourth item, Joslin thought to herself: $1 + $2 + $1 + $5 is $9. Good, my $10 is enough.

After reading the word problem above, ask the children what they think will happen at the check out counter and whether her estimation strategy was effective or not. (The items actually cost $10.07—more than Joslin has. Her rounding-off-to-the-nearest dollar approach *underestimated* the total cost. Her strategy put Joslin in an embarrassing situation.) Ask what other estimation strategies might be more effective—given Joslin's goal of not spending more than $10. (She could have rounded up—overestimating the cost of each item: $2 + $3 + $2 + $6. This would have alerted her to the possibility that she didn't have enough money to buy all the items. Alternatively, she could have used a more sophisticated rounding strategy: $1.40 + $2.10 + $1.20 + $5.30. This would have signalled that she was critically close to the cut off point of $10 and possibly over the limit.)

Ready-Set-Add and **Ready-Set-Subtract** are interesting ways to practice rounding skills. The two-digit version of the game described above is useful in practicing rounding to the nearest decade. With the three-digit version, the record sheet can require players to round to the nearest hundreds (Frame A of Figure 11–1) or tens (Frame B). An alternative

Figure 11-1   Sample Answer-Key Cards for Ready-Set-Add (Subtract): Three-digit Version

A.	347 + 482	B.	347 + 482				
	100—		100—	400—		700—	
	200—		110—	410—		710—	
	300—		120—	420—		720—	
	400—		130—	430—		730—	
	500—		140—	440—		740—	
	600—		150—	450—		750—	
	700—		160—	460—		760—	
	800— X		170—	470—		770—	
	900—		180—	480—		780—	
	1000—		190—	490—		790—	
	1000+—		200—	500—		800—	
			210—	510—		810—	
			220—	520—		820—	
			230—	530—		830— X	
			240—	540—		840—	
			250—	550—		850—	
			260—	560—		860—	
			270—	570—		870—	
			280—	580—		880—	
			290—	590—		890—	
			300—	600—		900—	
			310—	610—		910—	
			320—	620—		920—	
			330—	630—		930—	
			340—	640—		940—	
			350—	650—		950—	
			360—	660—		960—	
			370—	670—		970—	
			380—	680—		980—	
			390—	690—		990—	
						1000—	
						1000+—	

scoring procedure also gives the judge practice rounding off. Instead of using a ready-made answer-key cards, the judge computes answers on a calculator and makes up an answer-key card by rounding off the calculated answer.

SUMMARY

Mental arithmetic, which includes the exact process of mental computation and inexact process of estimation, is widely used by adults but often is not adequately emphasized in school. Efficient multidigit mental calculation of sums and differences depends upon mastery of single-digit and multidigit combinations, particularly those involving 10 and factors of 10. A key element in mastering multidigit combinations is discovering how they are connected or related to existing knowledge. For example, adding 10 to another decade can become automatic by exploiting knowledge of the count-by-tens sequence. Subtracting combinations like $70 - 40 = ?$ and $90 - 80$ can be mastered quickly by building upon knowledge of the single-digit combinations such as $7 - 4 = 3$ and $9 - 8 = 1$.

Efficient multidigit estimates of sums and differences depends upon good mental computational skill, conceptual knowledge of arithemtic and place value, and flexibility (risk-taking ability). A front-end strategy, which focuses on the digits with the greatest impact, is sufficiently simple that it can be taught to first graders who do not have a deep understanding of place value. Rounding strategies can be introduced after children comprehend place value. It should be taught in a problem-solving context, because a thoughtful analyses of the task *goal determines how* the rounding is performed.

Chapter 12

Multidigit Written Calculation

Even in this age of hand-held calculators and personal home computers, it is important for children to learn about written calculational routines. Occasions arise when calculations must be performed without the aid of machines. In such cases, informal counting strategies are impractical. (They become increasingly difficult to use as the numbers involved in calculations become larger.) Written algorithms (step-by-step procedures), which make use of base-ten place-value ideas, provide an efficient means for performing arithmetic calculations with multidigit terms.

Moreover, knowledge about written algorithms can be useful in multidigit mental arithmetic—both estimation and mental calculation. For example, to check a cashier's total of 324 for 149 + 185, a shopper could mentally carry out the standard right-to-left addition algorithm. Finding that the ones-place digit should be 4 (9 + 5 = 14), the shopper sums the tens-place terms (1 + 4 + 8 = 13) to find that the tens-place digit should be 3, not 2.

Perhaps most importantly, children still need to *understand* how and why the multidigit algorithms work. Without a conceptual basis, their written or mental use of algorithms will probably be hampered or less efficient.

To master *written multidigit addition* and *written multidigit subtraction,* children must learn all the steps of the formal *procedure* in their correct order. One component is how to line up the terms correctly (*correct alignment*). For multidigit addition algorithms, children must also learn where to start, where to write the sums, and how to carry. When they comprehend the underlying base-ten place-value rationale for the algorithms, children are much more likely to learn the procedures efficiently, apply them to more complicated problems, and use them effectively in problem-solving contexts. However, learning and even understanding the step-by-step procedures of the algorithm does not itself guarantee *accuracy*. Children must be able to calculate or recall arithmetic combinations, and they must care enough to carry out all aspects of the procedure carefully.

LEARNING

Written Multidigit Addition

Correct Alignment

To execute the (vertical) multidigit addition and subtraction algorithm, terms should be lined up from the right side so that the ones-place digits form a single column, the tens-place digits line up vertically, and so forth. Children who do not understand the underlying place-value rationale for the procedure may make one of several errors. Some may make no effort to align terms correctly. Some may be confused and align on the left at times and on the right at other times. Perhaps because they are influenced by left-to-right reading procedures, some may consistently align on the left (Bug 1 in Table 12–1). Alignment difficulties may appear when children have to copy problems from a text, record verbally presented problems, or set up word problems. Alignment-related errors are especially likely to occur when a child is required to write or copy problems horizontally or do worksheet exercises in which the problems are printed horizontally (Bug 2 in Table 12–1). Children who have mastered *correct alignment with 2-digit terms* and who understand its underlying rationale of vertical addition should have no difficulty transferring the alignment procedures to horizontal problems, addition with *three-digit* terms, or subtraction.

Procedure and Accuracy

Children usually have little difficulty mastering a two-, three-, or even four-digit written addition procedure that does not involve carrying (*2-, 3- and 4-digit with no renaming*). The step-by-step procedure is rather straightforward and entails minimal knowledge of place value. The child simply starts with the ones digits, obtains their sum, and records it below the ones column. The same process applies to the tens-place digits, hundreds-place digits, and so forth. However, with or without carrying, written addition can be confusing for some children when it is not connected in a meaningful way to their informal mathematical experience. The result can be bugs like 3, 4, and 5 in Table 12–1.

Table 12-1 Some Common Addition Bugs

(1)	102 +19 ――― 292	193 + 88 ――― 1073		(5)	42 +13 ―― 73	91 +32 ―― 51
(2)	34 + 5 + 84 18 + 3 = 48 25 + 6 = 85			(6)	25 +17 ―― 32	21 18 +24 ―― 53
(3)	123 52 + 4 ―― 17	25 17 + 4 ―― 19		(7)	19 +13 ―― 41	22 +18 ―― 31
(4)	25 + 3 ―― 73	54 +23 ―― 95		(8)	77 +16 ―― 813	726 + 267 ――― 9813
				(9)	91 +32 ―― 24	72 +41 ―― 14

Explanations:
(1) *Vertical misalignment*—e.g., on 102 + 19, the child copied the problem such that 19 is under the '10' of 102. Then, beginning at the right, 2 + 0 = 2, 0 + 9 = 9, and 1 + 1 = 2 for an answer of 292.
(2) *Mental misalignment*—e.g., on 18 + 3, the child added the first digit of each term (1 + 3 = 4) and then added 8 + 0 = 8 for an answer of 48.
(3) *Adds all digits*—e.g., on 123 + 52 + 4, the child added 1 + 2 + 3 + 5 + 2 + 4 to get 17.
(4) *Adds across horizontally*—e.g., on 25 + 3, the child added 2 + 5 = 7, wrote this in the tens place, then added 0 + 3 = 3 and wrote 3 in the ones place for an answer of 73.
(5) *Adds digits criss-cross*—e.g., on 42 + 13, the child began by adding 4 + 3 = 7, wrote the 7 down, then added 2 + 1 = 3 for an answer of 73.
(6) *Ignores carried digit*—e.g., on 25 + 17, the child began by adding the digits in the ones column (5 + 7 = 12), put down the ones digit of the sum (2) but not the tens digit (1), and then added the digits in the tens column (2 + 1 = 3) to arrive at a final answer of 32.
(7) *Carries wrong digit*—e.g., on 19 + 13, the child began by adding 9 + 3 = 12, wrote down the wrong digit (1), carried the 2, and added the 2 to the tens column digits (2 + 1 + 1 = 4) to get 41.
(8) *Doesn't carry; writes all sums on bottom*—e.g., on 77 + 16, the child added 7 + 6 = 13, wrote both digits of the sum below, added 7 + 1 = 8 to get 813.
(9) *Adds from left to right*—e.g., on 91 + 32, the child began by adding 9 + 3 = 12, wrote 2 in the tens place, carried the 1 to the ones place and added 1 + 1 + 2 = 4 to get 24.

Though many children rotely master the two-digit addition algorithm that involves carrying (*2-digit with renaming*), often such learning does not transfer to that involving three or four digits (*3- or 4-digit with renaming*) or more (Ginsburg, 1982). Because they do not comprehend the purpose of such algorithms, some children fail to learn all (or any) of the steps (Engelhardt, Ashlock, and Wiebe, 1984). Quite often, the results are systematic errors such as Bug 6 in Table 12–1 (e.g., Ashlock, 1982; Brown and Burton, 1978). A lack of understanding or misconceptions can lead children to invent their own incorrect but systematic errors (e.g., Bugs 7, 8, and 9 in Table 12–1).

Though mastering an algorithm goes a long way toward ensuring accurate computation, it does not guarantee a child will use it efficiently. Children at this level may—for various reasons—make slips (minor mistakes or inconsistencies) (Buswell and Judd, 1925; Ginsburg and Mathews, 1984). Accuracy with any procedure may be delayed if a child has not mastered the basic addition combinations or cannot informally calculate sums efficiently. Children may also have difficulty completing written assignments accurately if they feel compelled to rush or see no point in the task.

Written Multidigit Subtraction

Similarly, children usually master the written subtraction procedure *with 2-, 3-, or 4-digits with no renaming* (borrowing)—even though they may not understand it. Nevertheless, some children have difficulty with the written subtraction when it is not tied to understanding. In some cases, children resort to using a familiar procedure (Bug 1 in Table 12–2). Subtracting with zero (in the subtrahend) often causes difficulty (see Bug 2 in Table 12–2).

Many children have enormous difficulty with problems that involve *2-, 3-, or 4-digits with renaming*. As a result, systematic errors, such as Bugs 3 and 4, are common. Subtraction that involves borrowing from zero is especially difficult for children (see Bugs 5, 6, and 7 in Table 12–2). Subtracting from zero is also a special source of difficulty, and children find all sorts of (incorrect) ways to arrive at some answers (see Bugs 8 and 9 in Table 12–2) (e.g., Brown and Burton, 1978; Buswell and Judd, 1925; Van Lehn, 1983).

If children still have difficulty recalling or computing differences (e.g., by separating from or counting-down), then they will continue to be inaccurate even after they have mastered a procedure. Note though that not understanding and remembering the algorithm accurately is the chief obstacle in achieving written subtraction accuracy with any of the subtraction algorithms.

Table 12-2 Some Common Subtraction Bugs

(1)	24 − 8 32	36 −17 53		(5)	103 − 45 158	101 − 56 145
(2)	128 −107 1	145 −120 20		(6)	205 − 36 269	101 − 56 45
(3)	24 −17 13	253 −118 145		(7)	208 − 49 69	304 − 75 139
(4)	40 −12 38	44 −36 18		(8)	140 − 21 121	130 − 93 43
				(9)	108 − 47 101	130 − 28 110

Explanations:
(1) *Adds instead of subtracts*—e.g., for 24 − 8, the child added 4 + 8 = 12, carried the 1 and added 1 + 2 = 3 to get 32.
(2) *Subtracts n − 0 = 0*—e.g., for 128 − 107, the child subtracted 8 − 7 = 1, answered 2 − 0 as 0, and subtracted 1 − 1 = 0 to get an answer of 1.
(3) *Subtracts smaller digit from larger*—e.g., for 24 − 17, the child subtracted 7 − 4 = 3, then 2 − 1 = 1 for an answer of 13.
(4) *Borrows without reducing*—e.g., for 40 − 12, the child borrowed from but did not reduce the 4 in the tens place. He or she subtracted 10 − 2 = 8 and 4 − 1 = 3 to get 38.
(5) *Borrows from 0 and changes to 9 without reducing*—e.g., for 103 − 45, the child "changed" the 0 to a 9 but left the 1 in the hundreds place, subtracted 13 − 5 = 8, 9 − 4 = 5, and brought the 1 down to get 158.
(6) *Borrows from 0 and changes to 9 without reducing except when 10 is on the left*—e.g., for 205 − 36, the child used Bug 5 described above. However, when 10 is on the left, as in 101 − 56, the child did reduce this final 10 and subtracted 9 − 5 = 4 to get the answer of 45.
(7) *Skips over 0 to borrow*—e.g., in 208 − 49, the child skipped over the 0 and borrowed from the 2, subtracted 18 − 9 = 9, borrowed from the 2 (now 1) again, and subtracted 10 − 4 = 6 to get 69.
(8) *Subtracts 0 − n = n (n = any number)*—e.g., for 140 − 21, the child subtracted 0 − 1 = 1, then completed the rest of the problem in the normal way to get 121.
(9) *Subtracts 0 − n = 0*—e.g., for 108 − 47, the child subtracted 8 − 7 = 1, answered 0 − 4 as 0, and brought down the 1 to get 101.

INSTRUCTION

Formal instruction on the arithmetic algorithms should be done in a meaningful manner by building on children's informal arithmetic knowledge. More specifically, multidigit addition and subtraction should be introduced to children in concrete ways—*using objects or manipulatives*—and *in conjunction with instruction on base-ten and place-value skills and concepts* (e.g., Fuson, 1986, 1987). Note that the scoring system shown in Figure 10–3 and used to teach base-ten place-value competencies in a meaningful manner *also concretely models a carrying procedure.*

The written exercises should be introduced *after* children have mastered concrete models for the processes. Moreover, it is essential for teachers to help children bridge the gap between concrete models and symbolic arithmetic. A teacher needs to *point out explicitly how each aspect of* the unfamiliar written procedure parallels the familiar concrete model for the algorithm (Bell, Fuson, and Lesh, 1976; Fuson, 1986, 1987, 1988; Resnick, 1982, 1983; Resnick and Omanson, 1987). Moreover, the written procedure should appear as an *easier* way of arriving at a solution (Holt, 1964).

There is no reason why learning and practicing arithmetic algorithms should be a tedious chore. Such efforts should be done with a *purpose* so that it is meaningful and interesting. Solving story problems and keeping score for games (e.g., **High Card**, **Shuffleboard**, **Draw**, and **Target Game** described in Examples 10–2, 10–3, 10–4, and 10–8) are two natural avenues for making this instruction and practice consequential and stimulating. Children should be given regular practice, but not so much at any one time that it becomes just something to get through (Holt, 1974).

Too often, a method is taught as the one and only correct procedure. It is important to help children realize that there is often more than one way of figuring out problems. Indeed, some alternatives are more efficient than a class- or textbook-taught "standard algorithm." Examples 12–1 and 12–2 illustrate several useful alternative procedures that side-step the difficult renaming process.

Table 12–3 outlines a traditional instructional sequence of multidigit calculational skills. Such a piecemeal approach has a number of *disadvantages* (e.g., Fuson, 1986). One, introducing algorithms without renaming before teaching those with renaming may foster a mindset that results in common bugs such as the does-not-carry and smaller-from-larger errors (Bug 8 in Table 12–1 and Bug 3 in Table 12–2, respectively). Two, it masks the power and the principles of the written algorithms. A child who *understands* the principles underlying the procedure for three-digit addition should have no difficulty applying the procedures to four-digit problems or larger. Moreover, working on problems with three-digits or more may help

Example 12–1   An Expanded Algorithm for Multidigit Addition*

The algorithm illustrated below side-steps the carrying process and reinforces place value.

Step 1	19 +13 ―― 12	765 +278 ―― 13
Step 2	19 +13 ―― 12 20	765 278 ―― 13 130
Step 3	19 +13 ―― 12 20 ―― 32	765 278 ―― 13 130 900
Step 4		765 278 ―― 13 130 900 ―― 1043

*This method was suggested by an anonymous reviewer.

Example 12–2   Equal-Addition Method for Multidigit Subtraction*

Just as it is sometimes easier to transform a relatively difficult combination into a relatively easy one for basic number combinations (e.g., $16 - 9 = (16+1) - (9+1) = 17 - 10 = 7$), so it is with much larger combinations ($306 - 199 = (306+1) - (199+1) = 307 - 200 = 107$).

If children have not learned this equal-addition method, they can be helped to discover it with an exercise like Exercise A below. Exercise B can be used to practice this skill.

Exercise A

Subtract each of the following.

- Is there anything you notice about the minuend (top number) from problem to problem?

- Is there anything you notice about the subtrahend (bottom number) from problem to problem?

- What do you notice about the difference from problem to problem?

15	25	35		115	215	415
−10	−20	−30		−110	−210	−410

14	24	34		114	214	414
− 9	−19	−29		−109	−209	−409

Exercise B

Use the equal-addition method to make the following subtraction combinations easier to figure out.

(a)	208	(b)	496	(c)	816	(d)	800
	−199		−198		−297		−477

(e)	201	(f)	403	(g)	488	(h)	807
	−192		−188		−198		−297

---

*Based on Grossman (1985).

Table 12–3 Traditional Sequence of Written Calculational Competencies

Level	Written Multidigit Addition		Written Multidigit Subtraction
	Correct Alignment	*Procedure and Accuracy*	*Procedure and Accuracy*
2	With 2-digit terms	2-digit without renaming	—
	—	—	2-digit without renaming
	—	2-digit with renaming	—
	—	—	2-digit with renaming
3	With 3-digit terms	3-digit without renaming	—
	—	—	3-digit without renaming
	—	3-digit with renaming	—
	—	—	3-digit with renaming

children to understand better the base-ten place-value principles that underlie these algorithms than work that focuses on two-digit arithmetic exclusively. Fuson has shown that meaningful and effective instruction on multidigit algorithms can be successfully compressed.

For these reasons, it is recommended that teachers try combining instruction on two-, three-, and four-digit addition—both with and without carrying.[1] Moreover, once they have mastered the algorithm, it appears that children really enjoy the challenge of figuring out even larger problems—even problems with ten digits (e.g., Fuson, 1986). For the same reasons, combined instruction is also recommended for subtraction.

Teachers may find that such an approach is not appropriate for all children. Or some may be locked into teaching specific objectives at their grade level. In such cases, the methods discussed below can easily be adapted for training at a specific level.

Correct Alignment and Written Addition Procedure and Accuracy: 2-, 3-, and 4-Digit with No Renaming and with Renaming

First ensure that children have mastered prerequisite skills (e.g., written addition procedures with one-digit terms) and can either recall *or* compute

---

[1] If instruction focuses on two-, three-, and four-digit addition in sequence, a teacher may want to give children the opportunity to "invent" algorithms for larger numbers. For example, after working on two-digit problems, introduce—without fanfare—word problems involving a three-digit addend into practice exercises for the two-digit algorithm. *Or* adjust upward from 100, the score needed to win a game. Some children will readily apply their renaming procedures to the new task of three-digit addition. Some children may be tentative or even disconcerted by the change. Encourage these children to apply what they do know to the new task. As a group, discuss and question their experiences with the "new" procedure.

single-digit combinations efficiently. Teaching the multidigit addition algorithm should be done in stages (e.g., Thompson and Van de Walle, 1980). (1) To begin with, it may be helpful to master a concrete model for the multidigit algorithm, such as that illustrated in Figure 10–3.[2] (2) Next, focus on computing with objects and numerals simultaneously. (3) Then practice computing with numerals only. It may be helpful to begin each of these three stages of instruction by solving story problems. Keeping score for games can then provide the practice necessary to master the procedure.

Figure 12–1 illustrates the key second stage, which involves both objects and written numbers. It is important that a teacher note *how each step in the written procedure corresponds to a step in the concrete model* (e.g., see Frame B of Figure 12–2). Explicitly pointing out the link between the steps of the written and concrete procedures is more effective than the common approach of working out the problem with manipulatives and then recording the answer symbolically as in the first stage (Bell, Fuson, and Lesh, 1976).

Note that correct alignment and the renaming procedure[3] are taught as integral and natural parts of the calculational or scoring procedure. This provides a meaningful and motivating context to learn these skills. Because carrying is not singled out for special attention ("Now we are going to study renaming. This is harder . . ."), the skill is introduced in a nonthreatening manner to children.

Egyptian hieroglyphics also provide an ideal pictorial or semiconcrete device for practicing multidigit addition (see Frame A of Figure 12–2).[4] Frame B of Figure 12–2 illustrates how the written algorithm can be *explicitly* related to this semiconcrete model. Exercises like those illustrated in Example 12–3 are a natural extension of the hieroglyphic exercises described in Chapter 10 for fostering an understanding of base ten and place value.

---

[2]Fuson (1986) notes that her research indicates that the first stage of computing with objects only may be unnecessary. She finds that introducing the written algorithm at the same time as the concrete model can be effective. Therefore, she argues that it is more efficient simply to begin with Stage 2. However, it may be less confusing for some children to learn the concrete procedure without simultaneously learning a second (written) procedure. Moreover, why postpone the base-ten place-value training (provided by the scoring procedure in Figure 10–3) until children are ready to learn multidigit addition procedures?

[3]Before introducing algorithms with written numbers only, it may be helpful for some children to learn a more abstract scoring (regrouping) procedure: representing a group of 10 ones with *a single* item (object or tally) in the tens place. In Figure 12–1, note that 10 units are traded in for a long, which is clearly composed of 10 units and which makes the trading-in process highly concrete. In the **Forward Bowling Game** (Wynroth, 1986), 10 blocks from the ones post is traded in for *one* block that is put on the tens post. This abstract procedure more directly models the written algorithm in which a single-digit (a 1 representing 1 ten) is carried to the next column.

[4]In particular, it introduces children to the relatively abstract idea of representing 1 ten with a single symbol (something that does not resemble 10 ones) (see footnote 3).

Figure 12–1   A Concrete Model for Teaching Correct Alignment and the Multidigit Addition Algorithm with or without Renaming, Using "2328 + 1714" as an Example*

A. Represent the addends.

Thousands	Hundreds	Tens	Ones

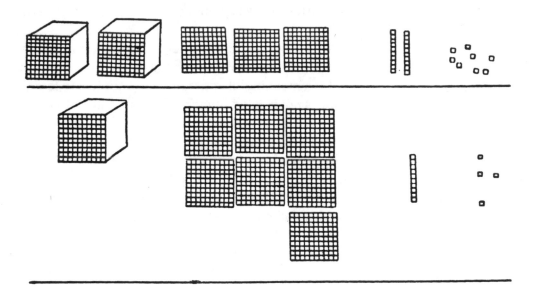

B-1. Combine the units in the ones place.

Thousands	Hundreds	Tens	Ones

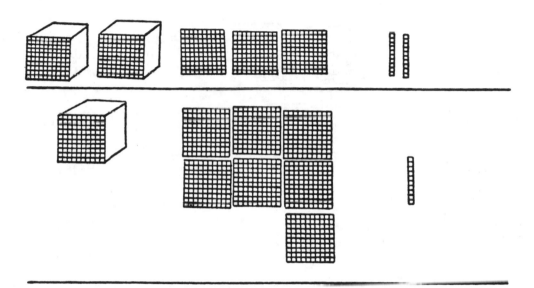

B-2. Group 10 unit blocks and exchange for a long.

Thousands	Hundreds	Tens	Ones

C. Combine the items in the tens column.

Thousands	Hundreds	Tens	Ones

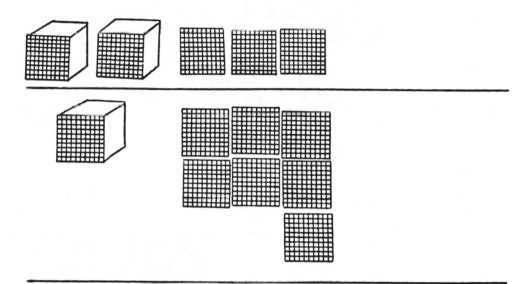

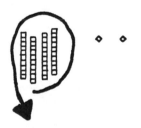

D-1. Combine the items in the hundreds column.

Thousands	Hundreds	Tens	Ones

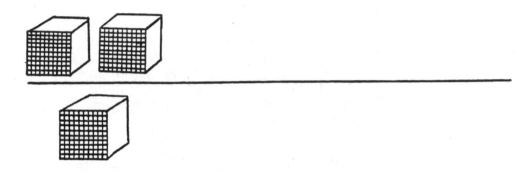

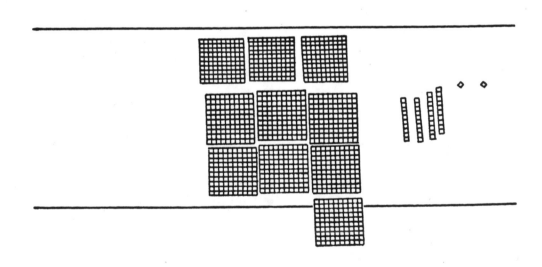

D-2. Group 10 flats and exchange for a cube.

Thousands	Hundreds	Tens	Ones

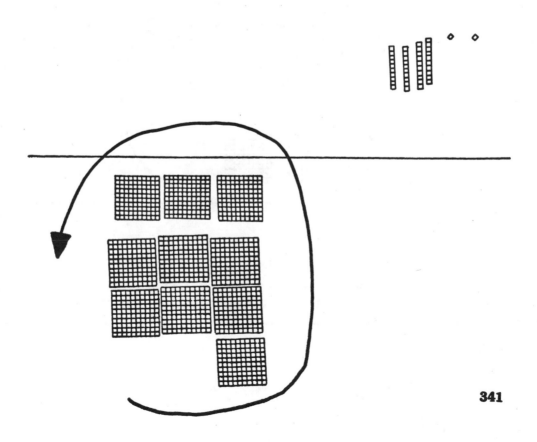

E. Combine the thousands items.

Thousands	Hundreds	Tens	Ones

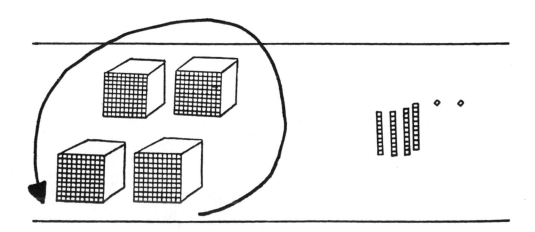

---

*This variation of Thompson and Van de Walle's (1980) transition board more directly mimics the standard carrying algorithm.

Figure 12–2   A Semiconcrete Method for Learning How to Carry

A. Teaching The Carrying Procedure with Egyptian Hieroglyphics

Step 1: Translate the symbolic problem into hieroglyphics.

47 ∩∩∩∩ΛΛΛΛΛΛΛ   57 ∩∩∩∩∩ΛΛΛΛΛΛ
+38   ∩∩∩ΛΛΛΛΛΛΛΛ   +48   ∩∩∩∩ΛΛΛΛΛΛΛΛ

Step 2: Combine the marks represents the ones terms. If this combining process produces a group of 10, circle the 10.

47 ∩∩∩∩ΛΛΛΛΛΛΛ   57 ∩∩∩∩∩ΛΛΛΛΛΛ
+38   ∩∩∩ΛΛΛΛΛΛΛΛ   +48   ∩∩∩∩ΛΛΛΛΛΛΛΛ

Step 3: Cross out the circled one-symbols and replace this group with the more convenient tens-symbol.

47 ∩∩∩∩ΛΛΛΛΛΛΛ   57 ∩∩∩∩∩ΛΛΛΛΛΛ
+38   ∩∩∩ΛΛΛΛΛΛΛΛ   +48   ∩∩∩∩ΛΛΛΛΛΛΛΛ

Step 4: Combine the tens-symbols. If this combining process produces a group of 10 circle the 10.

57
+48

Step 5: If needed, cross out the circled tens symbols and replace this group with the more convenient hundreds symbol.

57
+48

Step 6: Translate the hieroglyphics into numerals.

47
+38
―――
85

57
+48
―――
105

B. Explicitly Linking the Carrying Algorithm to the Semiconcrete Model

Step 1: Add the ones-place digits.

```
  47        ΛΛΛΛΛΛΛ
+ 38        ΛΛΛΛΛΛΛ
  15
```

Step 2: If the sum is 10 or more, regroup it in terms of a ten and the ones left over.

```
  47        ΛΛΛΛΛΛΛ
+ 38        ΛΛΛΛΛΛΛ
  05
```

Step 3: Place the symbol for the ten in the tens column.

```
  1          ∩
  47        ΛΛΛΛΛΛΛ
+ 38        ΛΛΛΛΛΛΛ
  5   05
```

Step 4: Add the tens-place digits.

```
  1               ∩
  47        ∩∩∩∩∩ ΛΛΛΛΛΛΛ
+ 38        ∩∩∩   ΛΛΛΛΛΛΛ
  85   05
```

Example 12–3   Addition with Hieroglyphics

1. As the owner of Felicitous Felines, you are delighted with the monthly sales of cats (a favorite and worshipped pet in ancient Egypt).

   Each of the following households bought a single cat at the regular price of 25 coins. Add this cost to their balance (the amount they owed from before) to find out how much to bill them this month. Represent the sum in hieroglyphics and then translate it into Arabic numerals.

𝑅 ∩ΛΛΛ _____ _____

𝑅 ∩∩∩ΛΛΛ _____ _____

𝑅 ∩∩ΛΛΛΛΛΛ _____ _____

𝑅 ∩∩∩∩ΛΛΛΛ _____ _____

2. As the librarian for the Alexandrian Library, one of the world's leading stores of knowledge, you have to record the new books added to your collection. Indicated below in hieroglyphics are the numbers of books that you had. The Arabic numeral indicates how many books were added this year. Indicate in hieroglyphics and then in Arabic numerals the total number of books in each collection.

Agriculture	∩∩∩ΛΛΛΛ	(+62)	_____ _____
Astrology	∩∩∩∩ΛΛΛΛΛ	(+45)	_____ _____
Geometry	∩∩∩∩ΛΛΛΛΛ	(+32)	_____ _____
History (military)	∩∩∩∩ΛΛΛΛ	(+28)	_____ _____
History (political)	∩∩∩ΛΛΛΛΛ	(+30)	_____ _____
Husbandry	∩∩∩∩	(+52)	_____ _____

Written Subtraction Procedure and Accuracy: 2-, 3-, and 4-Digit with and without Renaming, with and without Zero

Before introducing concrete models for two-, three-, or four-digit subtraction, first ensure that children have mastered analogous models for addition. Ensure facility with concrete models for subtraction before introducing written subtraction procedures. As with addition, problems that do and do not require renaming can be introduced together. Moreover, research (e.g., Fuson, 1986) suggests that with the use of size embodiments, training can proceed with problems involving two- to four-digits (or even more).

The concrete methods used to model addition can easily be adapted to model subtraction. In conjunction with story problems or a game like **Space Wars** (Example 12–4), the concrete scoring procedure for addition, such as that illustrated in Figure 12–1 could simply be reversed (see Example 12–5). Moreover, if desired, the games can be adjusted to practice a particular skill. For instance, to practice two-digit subtraction with and without renaming, a player or team could start at 99 instead of 0. As points are scored, unit blocks are removed from the ones column. If there are not enough blocks in the ones column to complete the removal process (e.g., a player's existing score is 32 and he or she scores 8 points), then a long from the tens column would have to be exchanged for 10 unit blocks that are put in the ones place. This enables the players to complete the removal process (e.g., eight blocks are removed from the 12 now sitting in the ones column).

Example 12–4 Space Wars
_____

Objective: The game can be used to practice either two-, three-, or four-digit subtraction.

Participants: Two players or two small teams of players. The game can be played so that three to six children compete.

Materials: Scoreboard like that in Example 12–5 and a spinner board. To practice two-digit subtraction, the spinner board would consist of two spinners, one labeled ones and the other tens, each divided into 10 sections labeled 0 to 9 (see figure). To practice three-digit subtraction, a third spinner labeled hundreds is added.

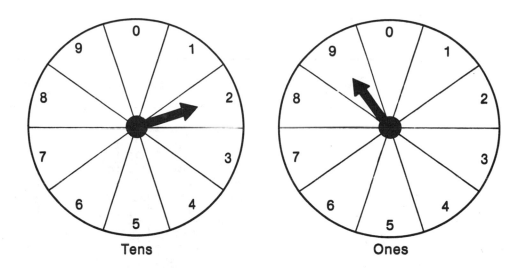

Tens   Ones

Procedure: For two-digit subtraction, play begins with a score of 99 for each player. Explain that each player has 99 space fighters in his or her squadron. On a player's turn, the child spins the spinner. The player's opponent loses that number of space fighters. The opponent then takes away that number of blocks from his or her scoreboard. (If the game is played in teams, then players should take turns spinning and adjusting the team's score. If three to six children play, all opponents lose the spinned number *or* the spinner can name *the* opponent he or she wishes to lose the spinned number.) The winner is the player who out survives his or her opponent(s).

For three-digit minus two-digit subtraction, the game can be started with a score of 199 or 299. Two (ones and tens) spinners are used. For three-digit minus three-digit subtraction, begin with a score of 999 and use three (ones, tens, and hundreds) spinners.

Example 12–5   Modeling a Multidigit Subtraction Word Problem

Word Problem: Rebecca's Girl Scout troop received 833 boxes of cookies. Her school needed 147 for a picnic. Rebecca checked the sales records and found that 684 cookies had been sold. Were there enough boxes of cookies left for her to fill the school's order?

A. Represent the minuend.

Thousands	Hundreds	Tens	Ones

$$\begin{array}{r} 833 \\ -684 \\ \hline \end{array}$$

B-1. Subtract the ones-digit terms first: Trade in a long for 10 units.*

Thousands	Hundreds	Tens	Ones

$$\begin{array}{r} 8\overset{2}{\cancel{9}}\overset{1}{3} \\ -\,684 \\ \hline \end{array}$$

*Note that for some children, it may be easier to *do all the regrouping first* (e.g., Fuson, 1986). In which case, a child would then check the tens column subtraction. Seeing that it requires regrouping also, the child would then proceed to trade in a flat for 10 longs.

B-2. Complete the ones-place subtraction.

Thousands	Hundreds	Tens	Ones

$$
\begin{array}{r}
8\overset{2}{\cancel{9}}\overset{1}{3} \\
-\ 6\ 8\ 4 \\
\hline
9
\end{array}
$$

C-1. Subtract the tens-digit terms: Trade in a flat for 10 longs.

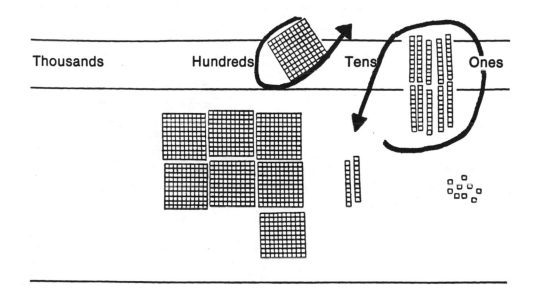

Thousands	Hundreds	Tens	Ones

$$\begin{array}{r} \overset{7\;\overset{12}{2}\;\overset{1}{}}{8\,\cancel{9}\,3} \\ -\,6\,8\,4 \\ \hline 9 \end{array}$$

C-2. Complete the tens-place subtraction.

Thousands	Hundreds	Tens	Ones

$$\begin{array}{r} 7\,121 \\ \cancel{8}\cancel{3}\,3 \\ -6\,8\,4 \\ \hline 4\,9 \end{array}$$

D-1. Subtract the hundreds-digit terms, clear the subtrahend (the portion taken away), and answer the question posed by the problem.

Thousands	Hundreds	Tens	Ones

$$\begin{array}{r} 7\;12\;1 \\ 8\,8\,3 \\ -\,6\,8\,4 \\ \hline 1\,4\,9 \end{array}$$

Yes, Rebecca can fill the school's order.

Figure 12–3 illustrates how Egyptian hieroglyphics can be used to model semiconcretely the multidigit subtraction procedure with borrowing.

Figure 12–3 The Borrowing Procedure with Egyptian Hieroglyphics

Step 1: Translate the minuend into hieroglyphics.

134
−86

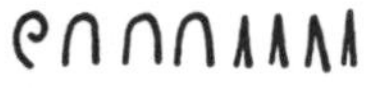

Step 2: Trade in a ten for 10 ones.

2 1
1~~3~~4
− 86

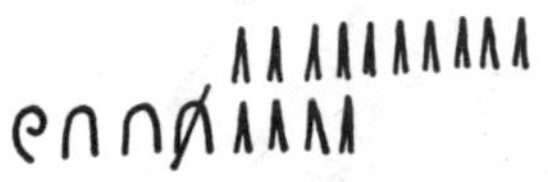

Step 3: Complete the take-away process for the ones digit.

2 1
1~~3~~4
− 86
8

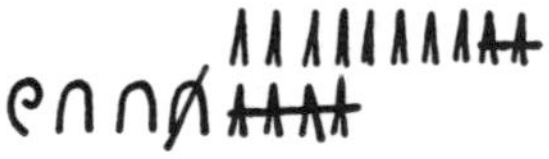

Step 4: Trade in a hundred for 10 tens.

12 1
~~1~~~~3~~4
− 86
8

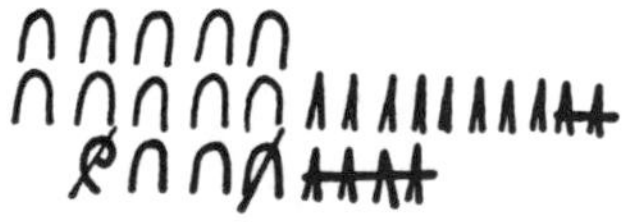

Step 5: Complete the take-away process for the tens digit.

12 1
~~1~~~~3~~4
− 86
48

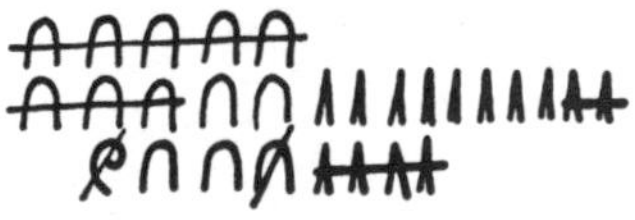

SUMMARY

Children often learn multidigit written calculation procedures for addition and subtraction without understanding the underlying base-ten place-value rationale for such algorithms. Though many children successfully memorize and use these formal arithmetic skills, many do not. Moreover, in the age of electronic calculators and computers, mere facility in computing is far less important than understanding the computational routine.

Instruction on the multidigit arithmetic algorithms should be done in tandem with base-ten place-value instruction—using size embodiments and concrete regrouping models. Egyptian hieroglyphics can provide an interesting semiconcrete model for these arithmetic algorithms. It is essential that a teacher help children to see the link between concrete models and their written work: The teacher should relate each step of a concrete (or semiconcrete) model to each step of the written algorithm. Practice of multidigit arithmetic can and should be meaningful and interesting to children.

Chapter 13

Geometry and Fractions

Chapters 3 to 12 described how children develop basic number, arithmetic, and base-ten place-value skills and concepts. These chapters illustrated how formal instruction can build upon children's informal knowledge to make it interesting, meaningful, and thought-provoking. Frequently, primary instruction also introduces geometry (e.g., shape identification) and fractions (e.g., identification of ½, ¼, and ⅓). Unfortunately, this initial instruction too often focuses on mastering skills by rote, which may not interest children or provide a solid basis for later learning (e.g., Davis, 1984; Hiebert, 1984). This chapter discusses how the cognitive principles of teaching can be applied to the topics of geometry and fractions so that initial instruction is engaging, understandable, and challenging, and so that it provides a solid foundation for later learning.

Unlike previous topics that dealt with sets of discrete (countable) entities, geometry deals with space and form. Elementary instruction in geometry entails learning the names and characteristics (attributes) of one-dimensional spatial entities such as a line, two-dimensional forms such as a square, or three-dimensional objects such as a cube. It should also involve learning the *relationships* among entities and their attributes.

Unlike previous topics that dealt with discrete quantities (whole numbers with no "in-betweens"), fractions deal with both discrete and continuous quantities (subdivisions of a whole: the parts in between wholes). Discrete quantities are clearly associated with one-to-one object counting, whereas continuous quantities are closely associated with measuring. Fractions belong to the category of numbers called *rational numbers*. (In this context, rational refers to a ratio or proportion, not reasonableness.)

Because whole numbers or integers like 1 or 3 can be thought of as rational numbers or ratios (e.g., $1/1 \rightarrow$ one *unit,* $3/1 \rightarrow$ three *units*), they fall under the category of rational numbers (see Figure 13–1).

GEOMETRY

Learning

Like other aspects of mathematical learning, children's knowledge of geometry proceeds gradually through a series of stages.[1] At an intuitive level, children learn to recognize geometric figures such as ☐ or ☐ by their shapes or physical appearance. At this level, they do not define geometric forms in terms of attributes or properties and do not see how different figures like a square and rectangle are related.

At an intermediate level, children begin to learn the characteristics of different geometric forms. However, they do yet see the relationships among properties of a figure and among different figures. In time, students achieve a more advanced level. They establish the interrelationships of properties both within figures (e.g., in a quadrilateral, parallel opposite sides necessitates equal opposite angles) and among figures (a square is a rectangle because it has all the properties of this figure) (Crowley, 1987).

Elementary-level instruction often focuses on shape recognition and perhaps the memorization of a few key terms such as line segment, angle, and congruence (Dana, 1987). Because such an approach does not promote understanding, children develop partial or even incorrect concepts. For example, Hershkowitz, Bruckheimer and Vinner (1987) found that many students (and some adults) had difficulty with the angle task depicted in Figure 13–2. Though they correctly identified E as a point within the angle, they failed to do the same with Points B, C, and D. Such children do not understand (or apply) the idea that an angle is a figure formed by two lines that extend *infinitely* from the same point.

An incomplete concept of angles may be fostered by text diagrams that depict angles as finite. A child's conception of angles may be further restricted if a teacher or text uses only one kind of angle (acute angles like ∠ . Because they see only a *single example* of the concept, children may

---

[1]A more complete description of the van Hiele model of the development of geometric thought can be found in Crowley (1987). The description in this book parallels the Level 0, 1, and 2 in the van Hiele model. Levels 3 and 4 are not described as they deal with the thinking of older children.

Figure 13-1   The Real Number System

I. Hierarchy of the Set of Real Numbers

A. Nonnegative numbers (0, 1, 2, 3...)

B. Negative numbers (− 1, − 2, − 3...)

C. Integers

(D. Fractions & decimals)

E. Rational numbers (e.g., 1/1, 1/2, 1/4, 1/8, 2/2)

F. Irrational numbers (e.g., $\sqrt{2}$)

G. Real numbers

II. Venn Diagram of the Set of Real Numbers

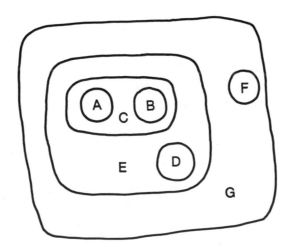

Set	Elements
A	Nonnegative integers (natural numbers 1, 2, 3, etc., and 0)
B	Negative integers
C	All integers
D	Fractions and decimals
E	Rational numbers (positive and negative)
F	Irrational numbers
G	Real numbers

Figure 13–2 Angle Task

In the following drawing, circle all the points which are inside the angle.

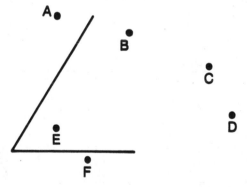

develop an intuitive or informal notion of angles that *excludes* obtuse angles like _ or even right angles L .

Instruction

Geometry instruction can and should be interesting, meaningful, and thought-provoking. Indeed, it affords numerous problem-solving opportunities. The instructional guidelines below follow from a cognitive perspective. Points 1, 2, and 3 apply to all children, though some examples illustrating the last point may be appropriate for more advanced students only. The application of Point 4 depends on a child's readiness and may not be applicable to most primary-level students.

1. Instruction should *first focus on building an intuitive knowledge and then informal knowledge*. At the primary level, visual patterns provide an ideal introduction to geometry and problem solving (DeGuire, 1987). The 1987 Yearbook of the National Council of Teachers of Mathematics (Lindquist and Shulte, 1987) contains numerous teaching suggestions involving patterns. Children might first copy patterns made of interlocking. colored paper or beads (see Frame A of Example 13–1, then look for patterns (Frame B of Example 13–1), and finally create their own patterns (Frame C of Example 13–1) (DeGuire, 1987).

Example 13–1   Copying, Finding, and Creating Patterns

A. Initial Activity: Copying Patterns

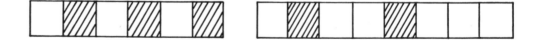

Copying patterns is a relatively simple task because the child has only to find a match for the next block. Begin with relatively easy patterns to copy like the one on the left and then introduce more complex patterns like the one on the right.

B. Analytic Activities: Finding a Pattern

In **Pattern Prediction**, a child must discern a pattern in order to predict what comes next. It can serve as an individual, a small-group, or a whole-class problem-solving exercise. It can be played as a game between two players or two teams. In the latter, team members can take turns solving patterns or work as a team.

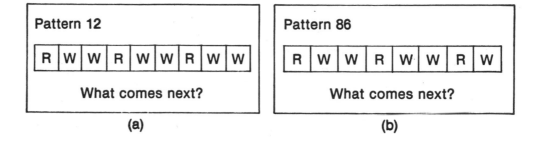

(a)   (b)

Two cards from a Pattern-Prediction deck are illustrated above. Note that the answer can be written on the back so that a player can check the correctness of his or her response immediately. Alternatively a child can record his or her prediction on a worksheet after the appropriate pattern-card designation and the teacher can check its correctness against an answer key.

The cards can be made up with patterns of varying complexity. The difficulty of the questions can also be varied by requiring children to predict a missing element from the middle of a repeating pattern (Card b above) rather than the first element of a new repetition (Card a).

Copy From Memory requires a child to examine a series of blocks, colored papers, or beads (as in Frame A) and *decipher* a pattern. After a prescribed time, the model is removed and the child must reconstruct it from memory. Again, this can serve as an individual, small group, or whole class problem-solving exercise. It can also be played as a game between two players or teams. By playing Copy From Memory, children may discover some important lessons about their memory. They may notice that simple patterns of a few elements may be recorded effortlessly in visual memory. They should find, however, that larger or more complex patterns require effort to identify and remember. With all but the simplest patterns, they may find that verbalizing and rehearsing the description of the pattern is helpful.

In **Pattern or Random?** a child, group, team, or class must determine if an array of colored interlocking blocks, paper blocks, or beads does or does not make a pattern. In the more advanced form of the activity or game (**What's My Rule?**), participant(s) must also describe any patterns noted.

C. Creative Activities: Making Patterns

Once children can distinguish between patterns and non-patterns, they are ready for the next challenge: creating their own patterns (DeGuire, 1987). Some children will need encouragement to take this step. All will need to be reminded that a pattern should be repeated three times to serve as a good example.

With geoboards, sticks, or pattern blocks, children can also be encouraged to copy, analyze, and create geometric forms. Example 13–2 illustrates several exercises with pattern blocks. Frame A illustrates the relatively straightforward task of making an exact copy. Frame B illustrates a somewhat more complicated copying task that requires a child to combine blocks to create the component geometric forms of the model. In Frame A of Example 13–3, note that the relatively "simple" task of copying a geometric involves careful observation and precise numbering skill: By counting or using pattern recognition, a child must discern that the apex is the third nail from the left on the top row and that the base begins and ends one unit on either side of the apex on the third row. Frames B and C illustrate how geoboards can be used to encourage children to analyze and create figures.

Example 13–2   Exercises with Pattern Blocks

A. Copying Geometric Figures with the Same Pattern Blocks

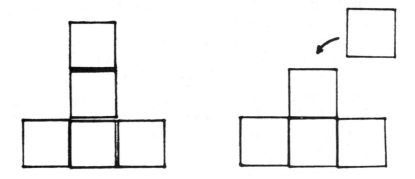

B. Copying Geometric Figures with Combinations of Pattern Blocks

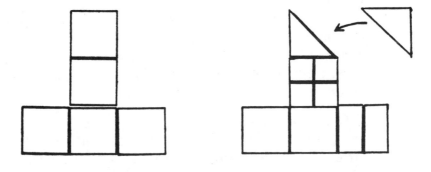

Example 13-3 Copying, Analyzing, and Creating Figures with a Geoboard* or Dot Matrix

A. Copying Figures

Use rubber bands to make the same shape on your geoboard.

B. Analyzing Figures

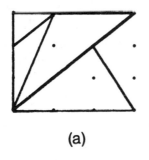

(a)

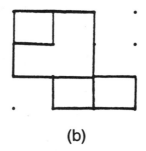

(b)

1. How many triangles can you find in Figure a?

2. How many squares can you find in Figure b?

C. Creating Figures

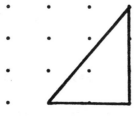

Example

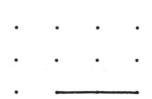

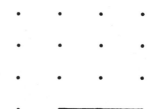

1. How many figures can you make by adding *two* lines to the one already shown. Note that like the figure in the example, all three lines have to join and extend from a dot in the matrix.

2. The example shows a triangle. With three lines can you make an enclosed figure that is not a triangle?

_____

*Geoboards can easily be constructed with nails and squares cut from a counter-top.

2. Formal knowledge of geometry should be introduced gradually and should build upon informal knowledge. The **Matching Figures Game**, described in Example 13–4, illustrates how an informal matching activity can help children with the formal terms *congruence* (two or more figures are congruent if they have the same shape and the same size) and *similarity* (two or more figures, which may or may not be the same size, are similar if they have the same shape).

Example 13–4   Matching Figures Game

Objective: Reinforce the definition of congruence and similarity.

Grade Level: 3 and up.

Participants: A group of two to six children.

Materials: Geometric-form blocks and a deck of cards depicting the geometric forms. For each block, there should be two cards. Half the cards should have forms congruent with the block forms; half with the same shape but smaller.

Procedure: Each player draws a specified number of geometric form blocks (e.g., three). The object of the game is to match blocks and cards. In the basic version of the game, a player gets two points for congruent matches, one point for similar matches, and no points for no match.

After the order of play has been determined, the first player turns over the top card of the deck. If the card form is similar or congruent to one of his or her blocks, the player may take the card and place the appropriate block on it. This serves to check for similarity and congruence. If the card form is only similar, a player may wish to pass in the hopes of getting a congruent card form later. (When a match is made the card and block are set aside and a new [congruent] card form may not be substituted.) If a player draws a card form that is neither congruent nor similar, the card is passed to the next player on the left. This player can then take the card if a match is found. If not, the card is passed on until a match is found or the card is returned to the player who drew it. In the latter case, the card is put on the bottom of the deck.

Whatever the outcome of the first draw, the second player (in a clockwise direction) turns over the next card. The round is played like that described above. Play continues in a similar fashion until one player has matched all (three) blocks with cards. The winner is the child with the highest point total. (Note that ties are possible and that the player with three matches will not necessarily win.)

An advanced form of the game (for gifted and upper-elementary children) can include a bidding mechanism. In this version, each player begins with $25 (five $1, two $5, and one $10). Congruent matches earn a player an additional $10 and similar matches, $5. The first player turns over the top card. If he or she wants the card, the player must make a bid. Each player in turn may make a bid. The player who drew the card can make one final bid if he or she wishes. The card goes to the highest bidder. If a player does not want the card, he or she enters a bid of $0. If all bids on a card are $0, the card is returned to the bottom of the deck and play continues with the second player drawing a card. The winner of the game is the player with the *largest* amount of money at the end of the game.

---

3. *Use a variety of examples and nonexamples to teach definitions or concepts.* For instance, when introducing triangles, use a variety of forms (equilateral: △ , isosceles: △ , right-angled: ◺ , scalene: △ , and obtuse angled: ◺). Example 13–5 illustrates an exercise with a variety of

examples and nonexamples to teach the definition of diagonal. This overcomes the narrow concept of diagonals that students typically develop because their text uses only a single example or a few examples like that illustrated in Figure A of Example 13–5.

Example 13–5 Definition-of-Diagonals Exercise

Consider the examples and nonexamples below.

1. This dotted line is a diagonal.

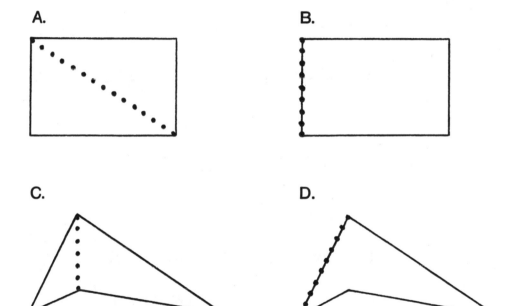

The dotted lines in Figures A and C are diagonals; those in Figures B and D are not.

1. How many diagonals does the figure below have?

2. Can a triangle have a diagonal?

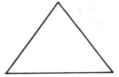

3. Is this dotted line a diagonal?

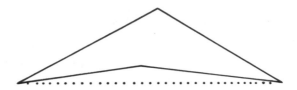

4. How many diagonals does the figure below have?

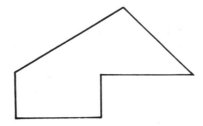

5. Define diagonal. Definition:

---

*After giving the students an opportunity to examine the examples and non-examples of a diagonal, proceed with Questions 1 to 5. After the students have answered a question—either individually or as teams—discuss their answers (reasoning) and indicate the correct answer (see the Key below). Then proceed to the next question. **Key.** *Question 1:* The quadrilateral has 2 diagonals. *Question 2:* No, a triangle does not have diagonals (because there are no nonadjacent angles). *Question 3:* Yes, the dotted lines are diagonals. Though counterintuitive, a diagonal may be external to the figure. *Question 4:* This polygon has 9 diagonals. *Question 5:* A diagonal is a line that extends between the vertices of two *nonadjacent* angles of a polygon (or polyhedral).

Example 13–6 illustrates an exercise that uses examples and non-examples to help children move toward a formal definition of rectangles. Most children are surprised by the answer to Question 13. Intuitively, rectangles and squares are different and unrelated figures. If the definition of rectangle is considered, a square logically is a rectangle—it is a rectangle in which all four sides are equal. Though we probably should not expect children to abandon their intuitive notions immediately, it is important to begin encouraging children to consider examples logically in terms of a definition. Question 13 also illustrates the next point—Point 4.

Example 13–6 What Is a Rectangle?*

Aim: This exercise uses examples and nonexamples to help students discover the critical attributes of a geometric form or concept and arrive at a concept definition.

Procedure: This exercise is suitable to individual or whole-class instruction. It is especially useful when used in conjunction with small-group discussions. After going over Steps 1 to 5 with the students, the exercise can be completed in several ways. Have the students complete Steps 5 to 11 and then discuss their answers to each step, discuss each step as a class, *or* have small groups discuss and reach a consensus on each step and then discuss their answers either after all groups have completed the exercise or after each step.

Discussion Questions and Points:

- If we are interested in describing what a rectangle is, why include Step 2? [Nonexamples help us to define which characteristics or attributes are necessary or critical and which are not.]

- What does Step 2 tell us? [Rectangles do not include three-sided or non-enclosed figures.]

- What does Step 3 tell us? [Orientation is *not* a critical attribute.]

- What do Steps 4 and 5 tell us? Hint: How is the figure in Step 4 [5] different from those in Steps 1 and 3? [The corners are not square or perpendicular. The same is true of the figure in Step 5, and—like the figure in Step 2—it has three, not four, sides.]

● The figure in Step 6 is not a rectangle because the corners are not square and the two sides are not parallel.

What Is a Rectangle?

1. This is a rectangle.

2. This is not a rectangle.

3. This is a rectangle.

4. This is not a rectangle.

5. This is not a rectangle.

6. Is this a rectangle?   Yes   No

7. Is this a rectangle?   Yes   No

8. Is this a rectangle?   Yes   No

9. Is this a rectangle?   Yes   No

10. Is this a rectangle?   Yes   No

11. Is this a rectangle?   Yes   No

12. Is this a rectangle?   Yes   No

13. Is this a rectangle?   Yes   No

14. What is the definition of a rectangle?

---

*Based on a method described by Herron, Agbeki, Cattrell, and Sills (1976) and Hershkowitz, Bruckheimer, and Vinner (1987).

4. *Focus on relationships among figures and attributes.* The exercise illustrated in Example 13–7 was designed to help highlight the logical or hierarchical relationships among a group of geometric forms. A polygon is any many-sided, enclosed figure. In this exercise, polygons are the broadest class of figures. (Note that in the Venn diagram in Figure 13–3, polygon includes the other forms.) Quadrilaterals are *four*-sided, enclosed figures and hence a subclass of polygons, which also includes the subclasses of three-sided figures, five-sided figures, and so forth. Parallelograms, in turn, are a subclass of quadrilaterals. Specifically, they are quadrilaterals in which the opposite sides are parallel. Rectangles are a subclass of parallelograms in which adjacent sides meet at a right angle. A square is that subclass of rectangle in which all sides are equal. Note that each subclass adds a defining attribute or characteristic that has the effect of cutting down the number of qualifying figures.

Example 13–7 Hierarchy of Forms

1. Which of the following is a polygon?

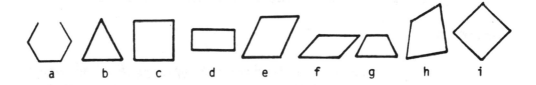

2. Which of the following is a quadrilateral?

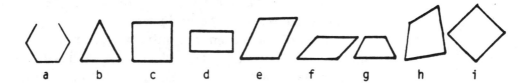

3. Which of the following is a parallelogram?

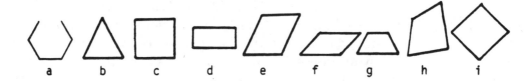

4. Which of the following is a rectangle?

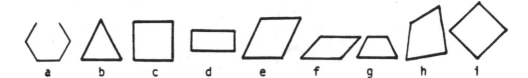

5. Which of the following is a square?

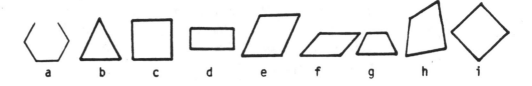

FRACTIONS

Learning

Even primary-level children typically have had some informal experiences with fractions. For example, there are numerous situations where they must share fairly a discrete quantity (e.g., a plate of cookies or box of crayons) or continuous quantities (e.g., a candy bar or a cake). As a result of such informal encounters, many primary children are familiar with the expression "one half." They may also intuitively recognize that a half share should be the same size—*a part of equal parts*.

In school, children are introduced to formal representations of fractions. In the primary grades, this often includes the symbols ½, ¼, and ⅓. These symbols are typically related to graphic representations ("pie diagrams") like that shown in Figure 13–4. Usually, operations on fractions (e.g., adding fractions with like denominators such as 1/4 and 2/4) are not introduced until fourth grade. Fractions are deemed a difficult concept, and indeed, many children have considerable difficulty with the topic (e.g., Behr, Lesh, Post, and Silver, 1983; Post, 1981).

Common errors among elementary school children include not recognizing that a fraction is a part of so many *equal-sized* parts (see Frame A of Figure 13–5). Another prevalent mistake is choosing as the larger fraction the one with the larger denominator (see Frame B). Because

Figure 13–3 Venn Diagram Representing the Hierarchical Relationships Illustrated in Exercise B

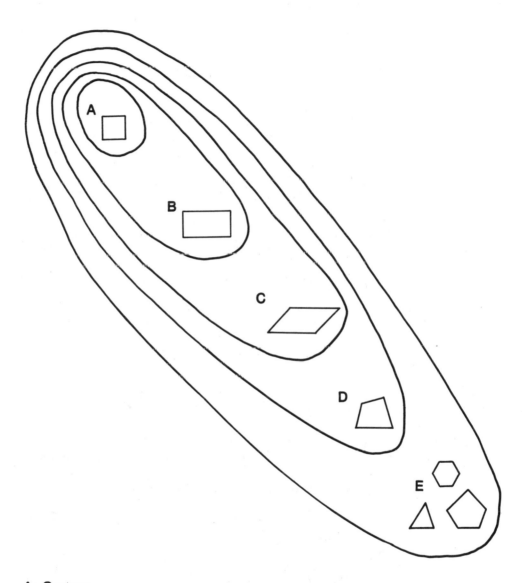

A: Square

B: Rectangle

C: Parallelogram

D: Quadrilateral

E: Polygon

Figure 13–4 Graphic Representations of ½, ¼, and ⅓

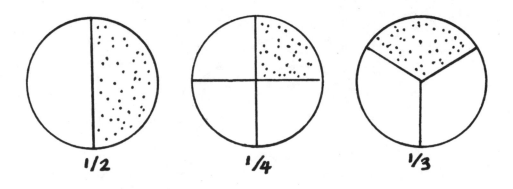

Figure 13–5 Common Errors in Children's Fraction Work

A. A part of so many depicted but not comparable parts.

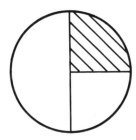

Write a fraction to show what part of the pie is shaded: _____ ⅓ _____

B. Choosing the fraction with the larger number.

   Circle the fraction that shows the larger amount.

   a. 1/3 or (1/4)

   b. (2/5) or 2/3

C. Defining all fractions as a part of one whole.
   For each diagram, color in ¼.

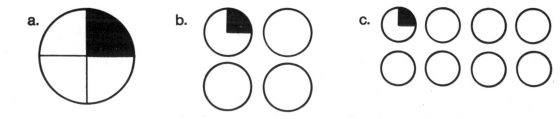

children do not really understand fractions, they incorrectly apply their magnitude comparison rules for whole numbers (e.g., Post, Wachsmuth, Lesh, and Behr, 1985). In Frame B, for example, the child reasoned that four is more than three, therefore one fourth must be bigger than one third.

In Frame C, the student confuses one-fourth *of four pies* (Question b) with one fourth *of a pie* (Question a). The error is repeated on the more difficult Question c (one fourth *of eight pies*). Children commonly fail to appreciate the difference between a fraction of one whole and a fraction of a group (a set of things) (Davis, 1984). This is not surprising given that, all too often, children are introduced to fractions with just one type of representation—typically continuous quantities (i.e., pie diagrams in which *a* whole is divided into parts) (e.g., Silver, 1983).

Instruction

Most primary-level children can learn about fractions in a meaningful manner *if* the topic is introduced carefully and informally. Indeed, it is essential to introduce fractions concretely before they are expected to cope with the formal instruction on the topic in fourth or fifth grade.

Fair-sharing activities are very useful for introducing children to fractions. Such activities allow children to see concretely a whole divided (equally) into parts. Begin by having two children share something equally between them. If necessary, introduce the term *one-half* to label each childs share. Next, do the same with four children to introduce *one-fourth*. Then work in groups of threes to introduce *one-third*. Other fractions like *one-fifth* or *one-sixth* can be introduced in time.

Note that such sharing activities can be done with either discrete or continuous quantities. Multiple representations may help children develop a broader and deeper understanding of fractions. Specifically, it should help them see that fractions can refer to a part of a group of things as well as to a part of a single whole.

Such fair-sharing activities are especially useful for highlighting the point that fractions are a part of so many *equivalent* parts. Most children are quick to comment when a collection of four marbles or a candy bar is not split evenly in two. In addition to taking advantage of fair sharing situations, a teacher can discuss stories like that in Example 13–8. When it comes time to introduce the formal symbolism of fractions, it will probably be helpful to remind children that fractions describe fair-sharing situations (e.g., ½ represents one part of two *equal* parts, ⅓ represents one share of three equal shares).

To help children develop an understanding of fractions and their comparative size, try activities like the game **Candy Store**. Present a player

Example 13–8 Unfair Shares

Count Fractious invited Count Denomination from a neighboring kingdom to play a new game called Dragon. Count Fractious ripped open the game box, grabbed all twelve dragon pieces inside the box, and proclaimed, "I'm the winner!"

Count Denomination said, "I have a good idea. Let's read the rules first." He then found the rules and began reading, "Step 1, split up the dragon pieces among the players. . . ."

"Ha!" commented Count Fractious as he placed two dragon pieces in front of Count Denomination and ten in front of himself. "There's your share. Now the game is fair," proclaimed Count Fractious.

"But, but, but that's not fair," protested Count Denomination.

"Frog bubbles," snapped Count Fractious. "Sure it is. I've *split up* the dragon pieces between the players."

"But, but, but something isn't right here," said a baffled Count Denomination.

[Why didn't Count Denomination think it was fair? How many dragon pieces should each of the two players have gotten?]

Before the matter could be settled, the players heard a knock on the door. It was Count Fractions, cousin of Count Fractious. Count Fractious was delighted to see him. "Good, good, good. We have another person to play my new game."

Count Fractious then took one of Count Denominator's dragon pieces and placed it before Count Fractions. "Here's your share," he said with a sly smile.

"Something isn't right here," said a puzzled Count Denomination.

"What's the problem now?" sneered Count Fractious. "I've split up the pieces among the players just like the rules say."

Count Fractions picked up the rule book in disbelief and read. "I think," he concluded, "the rules mean that the dragon pieces should be split up evenly so that each player gets an equal number."

[How many dragon pieces should each of the three players get?]

Count Fractions noted, "If we share twelve dragon pieces fairly among three players, let's see. . . ."* He placed one, two, three, and then four dragon pieces in front of each player. "Each player should have four pieces. All right, if you want to be picky about it," shrugged Count Fractious. "We'll give one third of the twelve pieces to each of the players."

---

*At this point in the story, the children can be given twelve objects and asked to figure out each player's share.

or team with, for example, six candies (or candy substitutes) and ask if they would like one-half or one-third. Show how many the player or team would have gotten if they chose the other number. For example, say, "You want one-third? Let's see how much one-half of six is. If we split six evenly into two shares, your share would have been three. Now one-third of six means we split six evenly into three shares. Your share is two." The player or team then receives two candies, markers, or points. Later, by relating the comparison of formal symbols of, say, ½ and ⅓ to such concrete situations, children will be less prone to consider ⅓ larger than ½.

When introduced to fractions, children should be taught the heuristic of "defining the whole" (Davis, 1984). (This should further help children to avoid confusing a fraction of *a* whole and a fraction of a group.) More specifically, they should be encouraged to first define for themselves what the whole is. Once the whole is defined, children can then proceed to divide it into the required number of equal parts. Example 13–9 illustrates a concrete lesson on "the whole." Example 13–10 describes an extension of this method to introduce adding unit fractions (⅓ + ⅓ = ⅔) and the idea of mixed fractions (4/3).

Example 13–9 Defining "The Whole"*

Have all children set out a specific strip, Cuisenaire rod, colored stick, or colored construction paper, which will be the *whole*. This term is used instead of one because it saves confusion between the one in fractions such as one-third. The lesson begins with a question: "Which strip is one-half of the whole?" Immediately it is emphasizing thinking skills, and focusing on discovering relationships. [The children must experiment with the strips until they come up with the appropriate answer.] Then, in turn, ask which is one-fourth and one-third. At the beginning the questions should represent unit fractions (numerator equals one). This makes it easier for the students in two ways: (1) the correct number of pieces equals the whole and (2) they all are the same size. The teacher should show nonexamples of this; even though 3 + 3 + 2 = 8, and it is in three parts, it still does not equal one-third. Stress that the three pieces are not the same size. This activity is repeated with several unit fractions, with different wholes. Explain each time that we have a new whole.

———
*Based on a method described by Davis (1984) and Thompson and Van de Walle (1984).

Example 13–10   Introducing More Complex Fractions*

Using the "whole" method described in Example 13–9, the teacher can introduce counting by unit fractions. After the students are able to pick one-third, introduce two-thirds, three-thirds, and so forth. For example, ask, "If one red strip equals one-third (of a whole represented by a dark-green strip), what should we call two red strips?" The strips should be laid out so the students can see the part "added on." Then add on a third, a fourth, a fifth, and a sixth part to illustrate three-thirds (which equals one whole), four-thirds, five-thirds, and six-thirds (which equals two wholes). Afterward, the teacher can go back and introduce other names for fractions (e.g., four-thirds equals [is the same as] one and one-third). The strips should be used to validate the information concretely. When switching to a new whole, the teacher should use both the improper-fraction and the mixed-fraction terms (e.g., five-fourths and one-and-one-fourth).

Note that in this activity children are manipulating concrete objects before any formal terms are introduced. Indeed, without knowing it, children are actually adding fractions. Thus, when adding unit fractions is formally introduced in fourth grade, children will have a concrete basis for assimilating this instruction.

---

*Based on a method described by Davis (1984) and Thompson (1984) and Van de Walle (1984).

SUMMARY

Geometry and fractions involve continuous quantities that must be measured or entail parts of wholes. Too often, instruction focuses on abstract symbols and rote memorization of names, definitions, and procedures. Frequently, the result is poor understanding and application.

Instruction in these areas should follow the same cognitive principles discussed in earlier chapters. That is, it should begin with and build on concrete experiences. Geometry instruction, in particular, should use a variety of examples and nonexamples to teach definitions or concepts. More advanced geometry instruction should focus on relationships among figures and attributes. Initial fraction instruction should focus on fair-sharing activities. It should help children to understand that a fraction is a part of so many *equivalent* parts and to define clearly what the whole is. Teachers should explicitly connect formal representations to concrete models or children's informal concepts. A cognitive approach to teaching geometry, fractions, and decimals can make these topics interesting, meaningful and thought-provoking for primary children and provide them a solid basis for further instruction later.

Chapter 14

Epilogue

The cognitive approach described in this book is dramatically different from the traditional approach of direct instruction-demonstration-and-drill. With the traditional textbook approach, the teacher's edition lays out what to tell and show children, and the workbook provides the practice. Unfortunately, the familiar tell-show-do approach is not well suited to how children really learn (e.g., Davis, 1984; Stodolsky, 1985).

In contrast, a cognitive approach cannot specify a single course of action that will work for every teacher in every situation for every child. Thus it is a difficult and demanding program to implement. However, such an approach is not only more educationally sound than the traditional direct-instruction-and-drill approach, it is more humane. Consider the following case studies described in Example 14–1.

Example 14–1　Case Studies: Arithmetic with Egyptian Hieroglyphics*

Incident 1

A student teacher introduced the characters for the ones and the tens in Egyptian number system to his primary math group on a Monday. The next day they practiced writing numbers with these symbols and worked on addition.

On Wednesday, he gave each student a piece of writing paper that had a unique hieroglyphic in the top right hand corner. He explained that the symbol represented students' names and that they were going to work for Pharaoh in his warehouse. That raised some questions, so they discussed who Pharaohs were and some background history about Egypt.

The first problem was then presented. They were to keep track of Pharaoh's inventory. In the morning, they received 24 gold bracelets from the Queen of Sheba. In the afternoon, they received a shipment of 35 gold bracelets from Babylon. That evening the Pharaoh wanted to know how many gold bracelets he had received during the day.

During the presentation of the problem, one of the students wrinkled her nose and said, "Hey, I thought we were supposed to be doing math."

The student teacher replied, "We are. It's kind of fun, isn't it?"

Incident 2

Several weeks later, the master teacher introduced the class to written, two-digit subtraction with renaming. To provide some informal basis for this classroom instruction, the student teacher introduced his tutees to subtraction with the Egyptian numbers. To enable them to subtract the ones-place digits, the children were helped to see that they could substitute 10 one-symbols for a ten-symbol. The term *borrowing* or *renaming* was not mentioned during the tutoring session.

Later in the day, one of the tutees was working on the math seat work assigned by the classroom teacher: a workbook page involving subtraction with renaming. The girl got stuck on the very first problem 43 − 18. After repeated efforts to compute the difference, she was frustrated to the point of tears and said, "You can't subtract eight from three!"

The pupil next to her said, "You have to borrow."

She shouted in exasperation, "I don't know how to borrow!"

The student teacher walked over and asked her what the problem was. She explained the difficulty. The student teacher suggested that she try to work it with the Egyptian numbers. They worked through the first two problems together. The girl then worked the next one as he watched. She completed the rest of the page by herself.

Later, as they were walking down the hall, the girl took the student teacher's hand, pulled him down to listen, and said: "You know what? Subtracting in Egyptian is really borrowing."

---

*These case studies were conducted and reported to me by Scott E. Cunningham of Urbana-Champaign.

Example 14–1 illustrates that mathematics can be readily integrated with other content areas (in this case, history), can actively engage children's thinking and natural curiosity, and can be fun. The second incident in Example 14–1 illustrates that gaps between formal training and children's informal knowledge makes mathematics unnecessarily difficult and frustrating to children. It underscores the need for concrete models and for explicitly connecting these models to symbolic mathematics. It highlights the value of individual diagnosis and prompt intervention. (In this case, the student teacher had provided an informal basis for the instruction. By then relating the written mathematics to the child's existing knowledge, the otherwise mysterious formal procedure suddenly made sense.)

In both of these case studies, the student teacher endeavored to teach mathematics in an interesting, meaningful, and thought-provoking manner. His pupils were also learning something more subtle about mathematics (it can be exciting), mathematical learning (it involves making connections), and themselves ("I am capable of learning mathematics"). Fostering reasonable beliefs, positive feelings, and confidence are at least as important as mastering facts and skills.

A cognitive approach to mathematical instruction is not easily or quickly implemented and it is sometimes an uncertain course for a teacher. Thus, some words of caution are probably in order. A cognitive approach to mathematics education requires considerably more knowledge, time, and energy than does a traditional approach. A cognitive approach requires a teacher to understand how children learn mathematics and to know specific methods for encouraging learning in a meaningful and interesting manner. It entails being sensitive to their readiness for instruction, not to mention their needs, feelings, and interests. Any effort toward meeting individual educational needs requires immense time, effort, and commitment.

A cognitive approach requires treating mathematics instruction as an ongoing, problem-solving activity. It requires more professional judgment than does a traditional approach. Because of the complexities of learning and teaching, there are not simple solutions for teaching mathematics to all children in every situation. The general guidelines outlined in Chapter 2 and the teaching ideas described in Chapters 3 to 13 are intended as suggestions or starting points. They may well have to be modified to meet the demands of a particular child, class, or situation. They are intended as a stimulus for further creative applications.

A cognitive approach requires a willingness to take risks. It requires the teacher to take on a different and perhaps somewhat more threatening role than does a traditional approach. As a facilitator, a teacher may have to resist the temptation of simply telling or showing chidlren how to do mathematics. Creating meaningful learning situations may put a teacher in a situation where he or she does not know all the answers to the children's questions. Some teaching ideas—no matter how good they appear to be—

may not work with a child, a group, or a class. A teacher must be willing to evaluate constantly his or her efforts and to change course if necessary.

A cognitive approach requires a teacher to trust children. It necessitates viewing children as much more capable than implied by a traditional approach. If the learning situation is prepared *effectively,* children can be thoughtful, inventive, and eager learners.

Because a cognitive approach is difficult and requires so much, a teacher cannot realistically expect to fully implement such a program immediately. The cognitive approach described in this book is an ideal vision to work toward. Worthwhile goals such as the creation of an effective mathematical instruction often take time—sometimes measured in years. Yet, a cognitive approach holds the promise of seeing children truly enjoying and thinking about mathematics.

Appendix A

Suggested Developmental Sequence of PK Skills and Concepts

Oral Counting	Numbering	Numerical Relationships
Count by ones 1 to 10	—	Perception of "same" and "more"
—	Enumeration of sets 1 to 5	Perception of fine differences 1 to 4
—	Cardinality rule	—
—	Identity-conservation principle	—
—	Recognition of sets 1 to 3	—
—	Order-irrelevance principle	—
Number after 1 to 9	—	—
—	—	Same number 1 to 5
—	Finger patterns 1 to 5	—
—	Production of sets 1 to 5	Gross comparisons 1 to 10
—	—	Fine comparisons 1 to 5
Count by ones 11 to 19	—	—

Note that for PK through Grade 3, problem solving is not treated as a separate topic but as an integral aspect of the topics at a given level. Similarly, estimation of quantity and single-digit arithmetic are not listed separately but are part of the training on numerical relationships, informal arithmetic, and number combinations. For example, **Quick Look Game: 1 to 3** (Example 4–6 on page 91) and **1 to 6** (page 93) can provide estimation experience as well as practice in recognizing number patterns. **The Prediction Game** (page 142) and the **Behind the Screen Activity** (Example 6–5) are in effect estimation exercises that should lead to mastery of mentally adding one. See the *Teachers' Guidebook* (Baroody and Hank, 1989) for additional suggestions.

Appendix B

Suggested Developmental Sequence of K Skills and Concepts

Oral Counting	Numbering	Numerical Relationships
—	Enumeration of sets 6 to 10	—
—	Recognition of sets 4 to 6	Same number 6 to 10
—	Production of sets 6 to 10	—
—	—	Fine comparisons 6 to 10
—	—	Gross comparisons of less 1 to 10
Number before 2 to 10	—	—
Count by ones 20 to 29 and	Enumeration and production of	—
Number after 10 to 28	sets 11 to 20	
—	—	—
—	—	—
—	—	—
—	—	—
—	—	—
Count backwards from 10	—	—

Informal Arithmetic	Symbol Skills	Formal Representations
—	—	—
—	Recognition of 1-digit numerals	—
—	Reading 1-digit numerals	—
—	—	—
—	—	—
—	—	—
—	—	—
Count all: sets 1 to 5	—	—
Mentally add one more	—	—
Take away with objects	—	—
Mentally take away one	—	—
—	Copying 1-digit numerals	Cardinal value
—	Writing 1-digit numerals	—
—	—	—

Appendix C

Suggested Instructional Sequence of Grade 1 Skills and Concepts

Oral Counting	Numbering	Numerical Relationships	Informal Arithmetic
—	Finger patterns 6 to 10	—	—
—	—	Matching sets	—
—	—	—	—
—	—	—	—
—	—	—	—
—	—	—	Count all: sets more than 5
—	—	—	Count from one to add 2 to 5
—	—	—	—
—	—	—	Count on 2 to 5 from larger addend
—	—	—	—
—	—	—	Take away: 2 to 5
—	—	—	—
—	—	—	—
—	—	—	—
—	—	—	—
Count by tens to 100 and Decade after 10 to 90	—	—	—
Number before 11 to 29	—	—	—
Count by ones 30 to 100 and Number after 29 to 99	—	—	—
—	—	Gross comparisons 11 to 100	—
—	—	Fine comparisons of less 1 to 10	—
Count by fives to 100 and Count by twos to 20	—	Fine comparisons 11 to 100	—
—	—	Fine comparisons of less 11 to 100	—
—	—	—	Mentally add on 6 to 9 more
—	—	—	—
—	—	—	—
—	—	—	—

Symbol Skills	Arithmetic Concepts	Formal Representations	Number Combinations
—	—	—	—
—	—	—	—
Recognition of = & ≠	—	Equivalence and inequivalence relationships	—
Recognition of > & <	—	Magnitude relationships	—
—	—	Ordinal relationships	—
—	—	—	—
—	Same-sum-as and Commutativity of addition	—	—
Recognition of + sign	—	Symbolic addition	$n + 1$ and $1 + n$ $n + 0$ and $0 + n$
—	Union of sets and Part-part-whole	—	—
—	—	—	—
—	—	—	—
Recognition of − sign	—	Symbolic subtraction	$n - 1$, $n - 0$, and $n - n$
—	Addition-subtraction inverse	—	$n + 2$, $2 + n$, and small $n + n$
—	—	—	$n - 2$
—	Associativity of addition	—	—
—	—	—	—
—	—	—	—
—	—	—	—
—	—	—	—
—	—	—	—
—	—	—	—
—	—	—	—
—	—	—	—
—	—	—	—
—	—	—	—
—	—	—	—
—	—	—	—

(continued)

Appendix C

(Continued)

Multidigit Skills	Place Value	Base Ten	Mental Computation	Estimation
—	—	—	—	—
—	—	—	—	—
—	—	—	—	—
—	—	—	—	—
—	—	—	—	—
—	—	—	—	—
—	—	—	—	—
—	—	—	—	—
—	—	—	—	—
—	—	—	—	—
—	—	—	—	—
—	—	—	—	—
—	—	—	—	—
—	—	—	—	—
—	—	—	—	—
—	—	—	—	—
—	—	—	—	—
—	—	—	—	—
—	—	—	—	—
—	—	—	—	—
—	—	—	—	—
Reading and writing teen numerals	Place recognition: ones, tens, hundreds	Base 10 equivalents: ones for 10	$10 + n$ or $n + 10$	—
Reading and writing 2-digit numerals	Ones and tens notation	Base 10 equivalents: tens for 100	Teen − 10 and Decade + n	—
—	—	Smallest/largest 1- and 2-digit terms	Decade + 10 and Decade − 10	—
—	—	—	—	Front-end estimates: 2-digit terms

Note that key elements of the multidigit place-value base-ten training provide *concrete models* for written calculational procedures involving renaming.

Appendix D

Suggested Instructional Sequence of Grade 2 Skills and Concepts

Oral Counting	Informal Arithmetic	Arithmetic Concepts
Count odd numbers 1 to 19	—	—
Count backwards from 20	—	—
Count by tens 100 to 200 and Decade after 100 to 190	—	—
Number before 30 to 100 and Decade before 20 to 100	—	—
Count by ones 101 to 200 and Number after 100 to 199	—	—
—	Take away: 6 to 9	—
—	Take away: teens	—
—	—	Missing part
—	—	—
—	—	Additive-subtraction and Difference
—	—	—
—	Adding 2 to 5 like sets	—
—	—	—
—	—	—
—	—	—
—	—	—
—	—	—
—	—	—
—	—	—
—	—	—
—	—	—
—	—	—
—	—	—
—	—	—
—	—	—
—	—	—

(continued)

Appendix D

(Continued)

Formal Representations	Number Combinations	Multidigit Skills	Place Value
—	—	—	—
—	—	—	—
—	—	—	—
—	—	—	—
—	—	—	—
—	—	—	—
—	—	—	—
Addition-subtraction inverse	—	—	—
Missing addend	—	—	—
—	—	—	—
Other names for a number and Commutativity of addition	—	—	—
Associativity of addition	—	—	—
—	Small misc. addition	—	—
—	m − small $n = n$ and Difference of one	—	—
—	Large $n + n$ and Equals 10	—	—
—	Small misc. subtraction	—	—
—	$n + 9$ and $9 + n$	—	—
—	m − large $n = n$	—	—
—	—	Reading and writing 3-digit numerals	Place recognition: Thousands and hundreds notation
—	—	—	—
—	—	—	—
—	—	—	—
—	—	—	—
—	—	—	—
—	—	—	—
—	—	—	—
—	—	—	—
—	—	—	—

Base Ten	Mental Computation	Estimation	Written Calculation
—	—	—	—
—	—	—	—
—	—	—	—
—	—	—	—
—	—	—	—
—	—	—	—
—	—	—	—
—	—	—	—
—	—	—	—
—	—	—	—
—	—	—	—
—	—	—	—
—	—	—	—
—	—	—	—
—	—	—	—
—	—	—	—
—	—	—	—
—	—	—	—
—	—	—	—
—	—	—	—
Base 10 equivalents: hundreds for 1000	—	—	—
—	Decade + decade and Decade − decade	—	—
—	2-digit $n + 10$ and 2-digit $n - 10$	—	—
—	2-digit $n +$ decade and 2-digit $n -$ decade	—	—
—	Parallel addition and minus facts	—	—
—	$100 + n$ and $n + 100$	—	—
—	Hundreds + 100 and Hundreds + hundreds	—	—
—	—	Front-end estimates with 3-digit terms	—
—	—	—	2- and 3-digit addition with and without renaming
—	—	—	2- and 3-digit subtraction with and without renaming

Appendix E

Suggested Instructional Sequence of Grade 3 Skills and Concepts

Informal Arithmetic	Symbol Skills	Arithmetic Concepts
—	—	—
—	—	—
—	—	—
—	—	—
—	—	—
—	—	—
—	—	—
—	—	—
—	—	—
—	—	—
—	—	—
—	—	—
Adding more than 5 like sets	—	—
—	Recognition of x	—
—	—	Commutativity of multiplication
—	—	—
—	—	—
—	—	—

Formal Representations	Number Combinations	Multidigit Skills
—	Large misc. addition	—
—	$10 - n$	—
—	Teen $- 9$ and Large misc. subtraction	—
—	—	—
—	—	—
—	—	Reading and writing 4-digit numerals
—	—	—
—	—	—
—	—	—
—	—	—
—	—	—
Missing augend	—	—
—	—	—
Symbolic multiplication	—	—
—	$n \times 1$ and $1 \times n$ and $n \times 0$ and $0 \times n$	—
—	$n \times 2$ and $2 \times n$	—
—	$n \times 5$ and $5 \times n$	—
—	[Other small and large times]	—

(continued)

Appendix E

(Continued)

Place Value	Base Ten	Mental Computation	Estimation
—	—	—	—
—	—	—	—
—	—	—	—
—	Smallest/largest 3-digit term	—	—
—	Flexible enumeration: ones and tens	—	—
—	Smallest/largest 4-digit term	—	—
—	Flexible enumeration: ones, tens, and hundreds	—	—
Notation with renaming	—	—	—
—	—	3-digit n + 10	—
—	—	3-digit n + decade	—
—	—	—	Rounding with 2- and 3-digits
—	—	—	—
—	—	—	—
—	—	—	—
—	—	—	—
—	—	—	—
—	—	—	—
—	—	—	—

References

Allardice, B. (1977). The development of written representation for some mathematical concepts. *Journal of Children's Mathematical Behavior, 1,* 135–148.

Allardice, B. S. (1978, July). *A cognitive approach to children's mathematical learning: Theory and applications.* Paper presented at the American Association of School Administrators, Minneapolis.

Allardice, B. S., and Ginsburg, H. P. (1983). Children's learning problems in mathematics. In H. P. Ginsburg (Ed.), *The development of mathematics thinking.* New York: Academic Press, pp. 319–349.

Anderson, R. C. (1984). Some reflections on the acquisition of knowledge. *Educational Researcher, 13* (9), 5–10.

Ashcraft, M. H. (1982). The development of mental arithmetic: A chronometric approach. *Developmental Review, 2,* 213–236.

Ashlock, R. B. (1982). *Error patterns in computation.* Columbus, OH: Charles E. Merrill.

Ashlock, R. B., and Humphrey, J. H. (1976). *Teaching elementary school mathematics through motor learning.* Springfield, IL: Charles C. Thomas.

Baroody, A. J. (1984a). The case of Felicia: A young child's strategies for reducing memory demands during mental addition. *Cognition and Instruction, 1,* 109–116.

Baroody, A. J. (1984b). Children's difficulties in subtraction: Some causes and questions. *Journal for Research in Mathematics Education, 15* (3), 203–213.

Baroody, A. J. (1984c). More precisely defining and measuring the order-irrelevance principle. *Journal of Experimental Child Psychology, 38* (1), 33–41.

Baroody, A. J. (1985). Mastery of the basic number combinations: Internalization of relationships or facts? *Journal for Research in Mathematics Education, 16* (2), 83–98.

Baroody, A. J. (1986a). Basic counting principles used by mentally retarded children. *Journal for Research in Mathematics Education, 17* (5), 382–389.

Baroody, A. J. (1986b). Counting ability of moderately and mildly mentally handicapped children. *Education and Training of the Mentally Retarded, 21* (4), 289–300.

Baroody, A. J. (1987a). *Children's mathematical thinking: A developmental framework for preschool, primary, and special education teachers.* New York: Teachers College Press.

Baroody, A. J. (1987b). The development of counting strategies for single-digit addition. *Journal for Research in Mathematics Education, 18* (2), 141–157.

Baroody, A. J., and Gannon, K. E. (1984). The development of the commutativity principle and economical addition strategies. *Cognition and Instruction, 1* (13), 321–329.

Baroody, A. J., and Ginsburg, H. P. (1983). The effects of instruction on children's concept of "equals." *Elementary School Journal, 84,* 199–212.

Baroody, A. J., and Ginsburg, H. P. (1986). The relationship between initial meaningful and mechanical knowledge of arithmetic. In J. Hiebert (Ed.), *Conceptual and procedural knowledge: The case of mathematics.* Hillsdale, NJ: Lawrence Erlbaum Associates, pp. 75–112.

Baroody, A. J., Ginsburg, H. P., and Waxman, B. (1983). Children's use of mathematical structure. *Journal for Research in Mathematics Education, 14,* 156–168.

Baroody, A. J., and Hank, M. (1989). *Elementary mathematics activities: Teachers' guidebook.* Boston: Allyn and Bacon.

Baroody, A. J., and Price, J. (1983). The development of the number word sequence in the counting of three year olds. *Journal for Research in Mathematics Education, 14* (5), 361–368.

Bebout, H. C. (1986, April). *Children's symbolic representation of addition and subtraction verbal problems.* Paper presented at the annual meeting of the American Education Research Association, San Francisco.

Beckwith, M., and Restle, F. (1966). Process of enumeration. *Psychological Review, 73,* 437–444.

Behr, M. J., Erlwanger, S., and Nichols, E. (1980). How children view the equals sign. *Mathematics Teaching, 92,* 13–15.

Behr, M. J., Lesh, R., Post, T. R., and Silver, E. A. (1983). Rational number concepts. In R. Lesh and M. Landau (Eds.), *Acquisition of mathematics concepts and processes.* New York: Academic Press, pp. 91–126.

Bell, M. S. (1974). What does "everyman" really need from school mathematics? *Mathematics Teacher, 67,* 196–202.

Bell, M. S., Fuson, K. C., and Lesh, R. A. (1976). *Algebraic and arithmetic structures: A concrete approach for elementary school teachers.* New York: The Free Press.

Bernard, J. (1982). Creating problem-solving experiences with ordinary arithmetic processes. *Arithmetic Teacher, 30* (1), 52–55.

Bley, N. S., and Thornton, C. A. (1981). *Teaching mathematics to the learning disabled.* Rockville, MD: Aspen.

Briars, D. J., and Larkin, J. H. (1984). An integrated model of skills in solving elementary word problems. *Cognition and Instruction, 1,* 245–296.

Bright, G. W., Harvey, J. G., and Wheeler, M. M. (1985). *Learning and mathematics games (Journal for Research in Mathematics Education* Monograph Number 1). Reston, VA: National Council of Teachers of Mathematics.

Brown, J. S., and Burton, R. R. (1978). Diagnostic models for procedural bugs in basic mathematical skills. *Cognitive Science, 2,* 155–192.

Browne, C. E. (1906). The psychology of the simple arithmetical processes: A study of certain habits of attention and association. *American Journal of Psychology, 17,* 2–37.

Brownell, W. A. (1935). Psychological considerations in the learning and the teaching of mathematics. In D. W. Reeve (Ed.), *The teaching of arithmetic* (Tenth Yearbook, National Council of Teachers of Mathematics, pp. 1–31). New York: Bureau of Publications, Teachers College, Columbia University.

Brownell, W. A., and Chazal, C. (1935). The effects of premature drill in third-grade arithmetic. *Journal of Educational Research, 29,* 17–28.

Buckingham, B. R. (1927). Teaching addition and subtraction facts together or separately. *Educational Research Bulletin, 6,* 228–229, 240–242.

Buswell, G. T., and Judd, C. H. (1925). Summary of educational investigations relating to arithmetic. *Supplementary Educational Monographs,* No. 27. Chicago: University of Chicago Press.

Byers, V., and Herscovics, N. (1977). Understanding school mathematics. *Mathematics Teaching, 81.*

Carlow, C. D. (1986). Critical balances and payoffs of an estimation program. In H. L. Schoen and M. J. Zweng (Eds.), *Estimation and mental computation.* Reston, VA: National Council of Teachers of Mathematics, pp. 82–102.

Carpenter, T. P. (1985). Research on the role of structure in thinking. *Arithmetic Teacher, 32* (6), 58–59.

Carpenter, T. P. (1986). Conceptual knowledge as a foundation for procedural knowledge: Implications from research on the initial learning of arithmetic. In J. Hiebert (Ed.), *Conceptual procedural knowledge: The case of mathematics.* Hillsdale, NJ: Lawrence Erlbaum Associates, pp. 113–132.

Carpenter, T. P., and Bebout, H. C. (1985, April). *The representation of basic addition and subtraction word problems.* Paper presented at the annual meeting of the American Educational Research Association, Chicago.

Carpenter, T. P., Coburn, T. G., Reys, R. E., and Wilson, J. W. (1976). Notes from national assessment: Estimation. *Arithmetic Teacher, 23* (4), 297–302.

Carpenter, T. P., and Moser, J. M. (1982). The development of addition and subtraction problem-solving skills. In T. P. Carpenter, J. M. Moser, and T. A. Romberg (Eds.), *Addition and subtraction: A cognitive perspective.* Hillsdale, NJ: Lawrence Erlbaum Associates, pp. 9–24.

Carpenter, T. P., and Moser, J. M. (1983). The acquisition of addition and subtraction concepts. In R. Lesh and M. Landau (Eds.), *Acquisition of mathematics concepts and processes.* New York: Academic Press, pp. 7–44.

Carpenter, T. P., and Moser, J. M. (1984). The acquisition of addition and subtraction concepts in grades one through three. *Journal for Research in Mathematics Education, 15,* 179–202.

Carrison, D., and Werner, H. (1943). Principles and methods of teaching arithmetic to mentally retarded children. *American Journal of Mental Deficiency, 47,* 309–317.

Cobb, P. (1985). A reaction to three early number papers. *Journal for Research in Mathematics Education, 16,* 141–145.

Court, S. R. A. (1920). Numbers, time, and space in the first five years of a child's life. *Pedagogical Seminary, 27,* 71–89.

Crowley, M. L. (1987). The van Hiele model of the development of geometric thought. In M. M. Lindquist and A. P. Shulte (Eds.), *Learning and teaching geometry, K-12.* Reston, VA: National Council of Teachers of Mathematics, pp. 1–16.

Dana, M. E. (1987). Geometry—A square deal for elementary school. In M. M. Lindquist and A. P. Shulte (Eds.), *Learning and teaching geometry, K-12* (1987 Yearbook). Reston, VA: National Council of Teachers of Mathematics, pp. 113–125.

Davis, R. B. (1984). *Learning mathematics: The cognitive science approach to mathematics education.* Norwood, NJ: Ablex.

Davis, R. B. (1986). Conceptual and procedural knowledge in mathematics: A summary analysis. In J. Hiebert (Ed.), *Conceptual and procedural knowledge: The case of mathematics.* Hillsdale, NJ: Lawrence Erlbaum Associates, pp. 265–300.

DeGuire, L. J. (1987). Geometry: An avenue for teaching problem solving in grades K-9. In M. M. Lindquist and A. P. Shulte (Eds.), *Learning and teaching geometry, K-12* (1987 Yearbook). Reston, VA: National Council of Teachers of Mathematics, pp. 59–68.

Descoeudres, A. (1928). *The education of mentally defective children.* Boston: Heath.

Dienes, Z. P. (1960). *Building up mathematics.* New York: Hutchinson.

Driscoll, M. J. (1981). *Research within reach: Elementary school mathematics.* Reston, VA: National Council of Teachers of Mathematics.

Easley, J. A. (1983). Japanese approach to arithmetic. *For the Learning of Mathematics, 3* (3), 8–14.

Elkind, D. (1964). Discrimination, seriation, and numeration of size and dimensional difference in young children: Piagetian replication study VI. *Journal of Genetic Psychology, 104,* 275–296.

Engelhardt, J. M., Ashlock, R. B., and Wiebe, J. H. (1984). *Helping children understand and use numerals.* Boston: Allyn and Bacon.

Ernest, P. (1986). Games: A rationale for their use in the teaching of mathematics in school. *Mathematics in School, 15,* 2–5.

Fendel, D. M. (1987). *Understanding the structure of elementary school math.* Boston: Allyn and Bacon, pp. 5–9.

Flexer, R. J. (1986). The power of five: The step before the power of ten. *Arithmetic Teacher, 34* (3), 5–9.

Folsom, M. (1975). Operations on whole numbers. In J. N. Payne (Ed.), *Mathematics learning in early education.* Reston, VA: National Council of Teachers of Mathematics, pp. 161–190.

Fuson, K. C. (1984). More complexities in subtraction. *Journal of Research in Mathematics Education, 15,* 214–225.

Fuson, K. C. (1986). Roles of representation and verbalization in the teaching of multi-digit addition and subtraction. *European Journal of Psychology of Education, 1,* 35–36.

Fuson, K. C. (1987, April). *Teaching the general multi-digit addition and subtraction algorithms to first and second graders.* Paper presented at the biennial meetings of the Society for Research in Child Development, Baltimore.

Fuson, K. C. (1988). *Children's counting and concepts of number.* New York: Springer-Verlag.

Fuson, K. C., and Hall, J. W. (1983). The acquisition of early number word meanings: A conceptual analysis and review. In H. P. Ginsburg (Ed.), *The development of mathematical thinking.* New York: Academic Press, pp. 49–107.

Fuson, K. C., Richards, J., and Briars, D. J. (1982). The acquisition and elaboration of the number word sequence. In C. J. Brainerd (Ed.), *Children's logical and mathematical cognition.* New York: Springer-Verlag, pp. 33–92.

Garofalo, J., and Lester, Jr., F. K. (1985). Metacognition, cognitive monitoring, and mathematical performance. *Journal for Research in Mathematics Education, 16,* 163–176.

Gelman, R. (1972). The nature and development of early number concepts. In H. W. Reese (Ed.), *Advances in child development and behavior,* Vol. 7. New York: Academic Press, pp. 115–167.

Gelman, R. (1977). How young children reason about small numbers. In N. J. Castellan, D. B. Pisoni, and G. R. Potts (Eds.), *Cognitive theory,* Vol. 2. Hillsdale, NJ: Lawrence Erlbaum Associates, pp. 219–238.

Gelman, R. (1982). Basic numerical abilities. In R. J. Sternberg (Ed.), *Advances in the psychology of intelligence,* Vol. 1. Hillsdale, NJ: Lawrence Erlbaum Associates, pp. 181–205.

Gelman, R., and Gallistel, C. (1978). *Young children's understanding of number.* Cambridge: Harvard University Press.

Gelman, R., and Meck, E. (1986). The notion of principle: The case of counting. In J. Hiebert (Ed.), *Conceptual and procedural knowledge: The case of mathematics.* Hillsdale, NJ: Lawrence Erlbaum Associates, pp. 29–57.

Gibson, E. J., and Levin, H. (1975). *The psychology of reading.* Cambridge, MA: The M.I.T. Press.

Ginsburg, H. P. (1982). *Children's arithmetic.* Austin, TX: Pro-Ed.

Ginsburg, H. P., and Mathews, S. C. (1984). *Diagnostic test of arithmetic strategies.* Austin, TX: Pro-Ed.

Ginsburg, H. P., and Russell, R. L. (1981). Social class and racial influences on early mathematical thinking. *Monographs of the Society for Research in Child Development, 46,* 16 (Serial No. 193).

Goodnow, J., and Levine, R. A. (1973). "The grammar of action": Sequence and syntax in children's copy. *Cognitive Psychology, 4,* 82–98.

Groen, G. J., and Resnick, L. B. (1977) Can preschool children invent addition algorithms? *Journal of Educational Psychology, 69,* 645–652.

Hatano, G. (1980, April). *Mental regrouping strategy for addition: An alternative model to counting-on.* Paper presented at the National Council of Teachers of Mathematics Research Presession, Seattle.

Hebbeler, K. (1977). Young children's addition. *Journal of Children's Mathematical Behavior, 1,* 108–121.

Herron, D. J., Agbeki, E. K., Cattrell, L., and Sills, T. W. (1976). Concept formation as a function of instructional procedure. *Science Education, 60,* 375–388.

Hershkowitz, R., Bruckheimer, M., and Vinner, S. (1987). Activities with teachers based on cognitive research. In M. M. Lindquist and A. P. Shulte (Eds.), *Learning and teaching geometry, K-12* (1987 Yearbook). Reston, VA: National Council of Teachers of Mathematics, pp. 59–68.

Hiebert, J. (1984). Children's mathematics learning: The struggle to link form and understanding. *Elementary School Journal, 84,* 497–513.

Hiebert, J., and Lefevre, P. (1986). Conceptual and procedural knowledge in mathematics: An introductory analysis. In J. Hiebert (Ed.), *Conceptual and procedural knowledge: The case of mathematics.* Hillsdale, NJ: Lawrence Erlbaum Associates, pp. 1–27.

Holt, J. (1964). *How children fail.* New York: Delta.

Hope, J. A. (1986). Mental calculation: Anachronism or basic skill? In H. L. Schoen, and M. J. Zweng (Eds.), *Estimation and mental computation*. Reston, VA: National Council of Teachers of Mathematics, pp. 45–54.

Ilg, F., and Ames, L. B. (1951). Developmental trends in arithmetic. *The Journal of Genetic Psychology, 79*, 3–28.

Jerman, M. (1970). Some strategies for solving simple multiplication combinations. *Journal for Research in Mathematics Education, 1*, 95–128.

Kaput, J. J. (1979). Mathematics learning: Roots of epistemological status. In J. Lochhead and J. Clement (Eds.), *Cognitive process instruction*. Philadelphia: The Franklin Institute, pp. 289–304.

Kiernan, C. (1980). The interpretation of the equal sign: Symbol for equivalence relations vs. an operator symbol. In R. Karplus (Ed.), *Proceedings of the Fourth International Conference for the Psychology of Mathematics Education*. Berkeley, CA: International Group for the Psychology of Mathematics Education, pp. 163–169.

Kirk, U. (1981). Learning to copy letters: A cognitive rule-governed task. *Elementary School Journal, 81*, 29–33.

Klahr, D., and Wallace, J. G. (1973). The role of quantification operators in the development of conservation of quantity. *Cognitive Psychology, 4*, 301–327.

Knight, F. B., and Beherns, M. S. (1928). *The learning of the 100 addition combinations and the 100 subtraction combinations*. New York: Longmans, Green.

Kouba, V. (1986, April). *How young children solve multiplication and division word problems*. Paper presented at the National Council of Teachers of Mathematics research presession, Washington, D.C.

Lampert, M. (1986). Knowing, doing, and teaching multiplication. *Cognition and Instruction, 3*, 305–342.

Lankford, F. G. (1972). *Some computational strategies of seventh grade pupils*. Charlottesville, VA: University of Virginia. ERIC document.

Lawler, R. W. (1981). The progressive construction of mind. *Cognitive Science, 5*, 1–30.

Lawson, G., Baron, J., and Siegel, L. (1974). The role of number and length cues in children's quantitative judgments. *Child Development, 45*, 731–736.

Leutzinger, L. P., Rathmell, E. C., and Urbatsch, T. D. (1986). Development estimation skills in the primary grades. In H. L. Schoen and M. J. Zweng (Eds.), *Estimation and mental computation*. Reston, VA: National Council of Teachers of Mathematics, pp. 82–92.

Lindquist, M. M., and Shulte, A. P. (Eds.). (1987). *Learning and teaching geometry, K-12* (1987 Yearbook). Reston, VA: National Council of Teachers of Mathematics.

Lindvall, C. M., and Ibarra, C. G. (1979, April). *The relationship of mode of presentation and of school/community differences to the ability of kindergarten children to comprehend simple story problems*. Paper presented at the annual meeting of the American Educational Research Association, Boston.

Lunkenbein, D. (1985, April). *Cognitive structures underlying processes and conceptions in geometry*. Paper presented at the research presession of the annual meeting of the National Council of Teachers of Mathematics, San Antonio, TX.

Noddings, N. (1985, April). *How formal should school mathematics be?* Invited address presented at the annual meeting of the American Educational Research Association, Chicago.

Olander, H. T. (1931). Transfer of learning in simple addition and subtraction. *Elementary School Journal, 31*, 427–437.

Payne, J. N. (1986). Ideas. *Arithmetic Teacher, 34* (1), 26–32.

Payne, J. N., and Rathmell, E. C. (1975). Number and numeration. In J. N. Payne (Ed.), *Mathematics learning in early childhood.* Reston, VA: National Council of Teachers of Mathematics, pp. 125–160.

Peck, D. M., Jencks, S. M., and Connell, M. L. (in press). Improving instruction via brief interviews. *Arithmetic Teacher.*

Piaget, J. (1964). Development and learning. In R. E. Ripple and V. N. Rockcastle (Eds.), *Piaget rediscovered.* Ithaca, NY: Cornell University, pp. 7–20.

Piaget, J. (1965a). *The child's conception of number.* New York: Norton.

Piaget, J. (1965b). *The moral judgment of the child.* New York: The Free Press.

Post, T. R. (1981). Fractions: results and implications from national assessments. *Arithmetic Teacher, 31* (6), 14–17.

Post, T. R., Wachsmuth, I., Lesh, R., and Behr, M. J. (1985). Order and equivalence of rational numbers: A cognitive analysis. *Journal for Research in Mathematics Education, 16,* 18–36.

Quintero, A. H. (1985). Conceptual understanding of multiplication: Problems involving combination. *Arithmetic Teacher, 33* (3), 36–39.

Rathmell, E. C. (1978). Using thinking strategies to teach basic facts. In M. N. Suydam and R. E. Reys (Eds.), *Development computational skills.* Reston, VA: National Council of Teachers of Mathematics, pp. 13–50.

Resnick, L. B. (1982). Syntax and semantics in learning to subtract. In T. P. Carpenter, J. M. Moser, and T. A. Romberg (Eds.), *Addition and subtraction: A cognitive perspective.* Hillsdale, NJ: Lawrence Erlbaum Associates, pp. 136–155.

Resnick, L. B. (1983). A developmental theory of number understanding. In H. P. Ginsburg (Ed.), *The development of mathematical thinking.* New York: Academic Press, pp. 109–151.

Resnick, L. B., and Ford, W. W. (1981). *The psychology of mathematics for instruction.* Hillsdale, NJ: Lawrence Erlbaum Associates.

Resnick, L. B., and Omanson, S. F. (1987). Learning to understand arithmetic. In R. Glaser (Ed.), *Advances in instructional psychology,* Vol. 3. Hillsdale, NJ: Lawrence Erlbaum Associates, pp. 45–91.

Reyes, L. H. (1984). Affective variables and mathematics education. *Elementary School Journal, 84,* 558–581.

Reys, B. J. (1986). Teaching computational estimation: Concepts and strategies. In H. L. Schoen and M. J. Zweng (Eds.), *Estimation and mental computation.* Reston, VA: National Council of Teachers of Mathematics, pp. 16–30.

Reys, R. E. (1984). Mental computation and estimation: Past, present, and future. *Elementary School Journal, 84,* 544–557.

Riley, M. S., Greeno, J. G., and Heller, J. I. (1983). Development of children's problem-solving ability in arithmetic. In H. P. Ginsburg (Ed.), *The development of mathematical thinking.* New York: Academic Press, pp. 153–200.

Ross, S. (1986, April). *The development of children's place-value numeration concepts in grades two through five.* Paper presented at the annual meeting of the American Educational Research Association, San Francisco.

Schaeffer, B., Eggleston, V., and Scott, J. (1974). Number development in young children. *Cognitive Psychology, 6,* 357–379.

Schoen, H. L., and Zweng, M. J. (Eds.). (1986). *Estimation and mental computation.* Reston, VA: National Council of Teachers of Mathematics.

Schoenfeld, A. H. (1985). *Mathematical problem solving.* New York: Academic Press.

Siegler, R. S. (1987). Strategy choices in subtraction. In J. Sloboda and D. Rogers

(Eds.), *Cognitive process in mathematics*. Oxford University Press, pp. 81–106.

Siegler, R. S., and Shrager, J. (1984). Strategy choices in addition: How do children know what to do? In C. Sophian (Ed.), *Origins of cognitive skills*. Hillsdale, NJ: Lawrence Erlbaum Associates, pp. 229–293.

Silver, E. A. (1983). Probing young adults' thinking about rational numbers. *Focus on Learning Problems in Mathematics, 5,* 105–117.

Sinclair, H., and Sinclair, A. (1986). The relationship between initial meaningful of arithmetic. In J. Hiebert (Ed.), *Conceptual and procedural knowledge: The case of mathematics*. Hillsdale, NJ: Lawrence Erlbaum Associates, pp. 59–74.

Slavin, R. E. (1983). *Cooperative learning*. New York: Longman.

Slavin, R. E. (1987). Cooperative learning and individualized instruction. *Arithmetic Teacher, 35* (3), 14–16.

Starkey, P., and Gelman, R. (1982). The development of addition and subtraction abilities prior to formal schooling in arithmetic. In T. P. Carpenter, J. M. Moser, and T. A. Romberg (Eds.), *Addition and subtraction: A cognitive perspective*. Hillsdale, NJ: Lawrence Erlbaum Associates, pp. 99–116.

Steffe, L. P. (1987, April). *Principles of mathematical curricular design in early childhood teacher education*. Paper presented at the annual meeting of the American Educational Research Association, Washington, D.C.

Steffe, L. P., von Glasersfeld, E., Richards, J., and Cobb, P. (1983). *Children's counting types*. New York: Praeger.

Steinberg, R. M. (1985). Instruction on derived fact strategies in addition and subtraction. *Journal for Research in Mathematics Education, 16,* 337–355.

Stodolsky, S. S. (1985). Telling math: Origins of math aversion and anxiety. *Educational Psychologist, 20,* 125–133.

Struck, R. (1987). Those magical nines. *Arithmetic Teacher, 35* (4), 4–5.

Suydam, M., and Weaver, J. F. (1975). Research on mathematics learning. In J. N. Payne (Ed.), *Mathematics learning in early childhood* (37th Yearbook of the National Council of Teachers of Mathematics). Reston, VA: National Council of Teachers of Mathematics, pp. 43–67.

Svenson, O. (1975). An analyses of time required by children for simple addition. *Acta Psychologica, 35,* 289–302.

Svenson, O. (1985). Memory retrieval of answers of simple additions as reflected in response latencies. *Acta Psychologica, 59,* 285–304.

Swenson, E. J. (1949). Organization and generalization as factors in learning, transfer, and retroactive inhibition. *Learning theory in school situations* (University of Minnesota Studies in Education No. 2). Minneapolis: University of Minnesota Press.

Thiele, C. (1938). *The contribution of generalization to the learning of addition facts*. New York: Bureau of Publications, Teachers College, Columbia University.

Thompson, C. S., and Van de Walle, J. (1980). Transition boards: Moving from materials to symbols in addition. *Arithmetic Teacher, 28* (4), 4–8.

Thompson, C. S., and Van de Walle, J. (1984). Let's do it: The power of 10. *Arithmetic Teacher, 32* (7), 6–11.

Thornton, C. A. (1978). Emphasizing thinking strategies in basic fact instruction. *Journal for Research in Mathematics Education, 9,* 213–227.

Thornton, C. A., and Smith, P. J. (1988). Action research: Strategies for learning subtraction facts. *Arithmetic Teacher, 35* (8), 8–12.

Thornton, C. A., and Toohey, M. A. (1985). Basic math facts: Guidelines for teaching and learning. *Learning Disabilities Focus,* 10–14.

Trafton, P. R. (1978). Estimation and mental arithmetic: Important components of computation. In M. N. Suydam and R. E. Reys (Eds.), *Developing computational skills.* Reston, VA: National Council of Teachers of Mathematics, pp. 196–213.

Trafton, P. R. (1986). Teaching computational estimation: Establishing an estimation mind-set. In H. L. Schoen and M. J. Zweng (Eds.), *Estimation and mental computation.* Reston, VA: National Council of Teachers of Mathematics, pp. 16–30.

Traub, N. (1977). *Recipe for reading.* New York: Walker.

Trivett, J. (1980). The multiplication table: To be memorized or mastered? *For the Learning of Mathematics, 1* (1), 21–25.

Van Lehn, K. (1983). On the representation of procedures in repair theory. In H. P. Ginsburg (Ed.), *The development of mathematical thinking.* New York: Academic Press, pp. 197–252.

von Glasersfeld, E. (1982). Subitizing: The role of figural patterns in the development of numerical concepts. *Archives de Psychologie, 50,* 191–218.

Wagner, S., and Walters, J. (1982). A longitudinal analysis of early number concepts: From numbers to number. In G. Forman (Ed.), *Action and thought.* New York: Academic Press, pp. 137–161.

Weaver, F. (1973). The symmetric property of the equality relation and young children's ability to solve open addition and subtraction sentences. *Journal for Research in Mathematics Education, 4,* 45–46.

Weaver, J. F. (1982). Interpretations of number operations and symbolic representations of addition and subtraction. In T. P. Carpenter, J. M. Moser, and T. A. Romberg (Eds.), *Addition and subtraction: A cognitive perspective.* Hillsdale, NJ: Lawrence Erlbaum Associates, pp. 60–66.

Wertheimer, M. (1945). *Productive thinking.* New York: Harper & Row.

Wirtz, R. (1980). *New beginnings.* Monterey, CA: Curriculum Development Associates.

Woods, S. S., Resnick, L. B., and Groen, G. J. (1975). An experimental test of five process models for subtraction. *Journal of Educational Psychology, 67,* 17–21.

Wynroth, L. (1986). *Wynroth math program—The natural numbers sequence.* Ithaca, NY: Wynroth Math Program.

Zimiles, H. (1963). A note on Piaget's concept of conservation. *Child Development, 34,* 691–695.

Index of Games and Activities*

---

*Italics indicate pages on which a game or activity is described.

Index of Skills and Concepts*

---

*Italics indicate pages on which instruction on a skill or concept is described.